INTRODUCTION TO PLANNING PRACTICE

INTRODUCTION TO PLANNING PRACTICE

edited by
Philip Allmendinger
Alan Prior
and
Jeremy Raemaekers

JOHN WILEY & SONS, LTD

Chichester • New York • Weinheim • Brisbane • Singapore • Toronto

OTHER WILEY EDITORIAL OFFICES

John Wiley & Sons, Inc., 605 Third Avenue, New York, NY 10158-0012, USA

WILEY-VCH Verlag GmbH, Pappelallee 3, D-69469 Weinheim, Germany

Jacaranda Wiley Ltd, 33 Park Road, Milton, Queensland 4064, Australia

John Wiley & Sons (Asia) Pte Ltd, 2 Clementi Loop #02-01, Jin Xing Distripark, Singapore 129809

John Wiley & Sons (Canada) Ltd, 22 Worcester Road, Rexdale, Ontario M9W 1L1, Canada

LIBRARY OF CONGRESS CATALOGING-IN-PUBLICATION DATA

Introduction to planning practice / edited by Philip Allmendinger, Alan Prior,
and Jeremy Raemaekers.
   p. cm.
   A collection of 17 papers by various authors in the U.K.
   Includes bibliographical references and index.
   ISBN 0-471-98521-X. — ISBN 0-471-98522-8 (pbk.)
   1. City planning—Great Britain. I. Allmendinger, Philip, 1968– .
II. Prior, Alan, 1951– . III. Raemaekers, Jeremy.
   HT169.G7 I56 2000
   307.1'216'0941—dc21   99–040030
                                              CIP

BRITISH LIBRARY CATALOGUING IN PUBLICATION DATA

A catalogue record for this book is available from the British Library

ISBN 0-471-98521-X (hardback)
ISBN 0-471-98522-8 (paperback)

Typeset in 9/12pt Caslon 224 from authors' disks by Mayhew Typesetting, Rhayader, Powys
Printed and bound in Great Britain by Bookcraft (Bath) Ltd.

This book is printed on acid-free paper responsibly manufactured from sustainable forestry, in which at
least two trees are planted for each one used for paper production.

CONTENTS

CONTRIBUTORS

Philip Allmendinger, Department of Land Economy, University of Aberdeen

Claire Carr, Oscar Faber, Edinburgh

Chris Couch, School of the Built Environment, Liverpool John Moores University, Liverpool

Roy Darke, School of Planning, Oxford Brookes University

Iain Docherty, Department of Urban Studies, University of Glasgow

Julie Grail, Kingston upon Thames Borough Council

Daniel Groves, City of Edinburgh District Council

Cliff Hague, Department of Planning and Housing, Edinburgh College of Art/Heriot-Watt University

Marilyn Higgins, Department of Planning and Housing, Edinburgh College of Art/Heriot-Watt University

Andi Karski, Tibbalds, Monro

Gary Mappin, Mappin Planning and Development

Alan Prior, Department of Planning and Housing, Edinburgh College of Art/Heriot-Watt University

Matthew Quinn, Government Office for the South West

Jeremy Raemaekers, Department of Planning and Housing, Edinburgh College of Art/Heriot-Watt University

Madhu Satsangi, Department of Planning and Housing, Edinburgh College of Art/Heriot-Watt University

Tim Shaw, Department of Town and Country Planning, University of Newcastle

Preface

This book is an introduction to the practice of town planning. It is written for students on town planning and related courses, and for practitioners who want to locate their practice within the developing breadth of the activity of town planning. It is written by town planners in practice and academics with practice experience. Its purpose is to introduce students, and young professionals, to the range of town planning practice today. It is not intended to be exhaustive of that practice. No book on the topic could be, since planning practice today is characterised by a wide variety of circumstances and innovative approaches to developing, conserving and enhancing the physical environment.

As well as their practice experience, the editors worked together on an undergraduate planning course that included a sandwich year of professional practice. They were struck by the impact that working in practice – whether in a central government office, a local authority, a planning consultancy or a developer's office – had on students who had two or three years' learning in college. Typical responses were 'I now know why I did that module on politics in first year' or 'now I see the point of knowing about the Permitted Development Order'. Often they would come back with more questions about practice than answers. The world of practice can reinforce material introduced in the world of academe. The best of academe encourages reflection on the scope and detail of daily practice.

Practice does not necessarily make perfect, but it invariably reinforces knowledge gained in the lecture theatre and skills developed in the studio. It is only through the world of professional work that the planning student can appreciate, for example, the relevance of a professional code of conduct, the differences between the roles of the professional planner and the elected member, and the transferable skills that can only be developed through real-life interactions with professionals from other disciplines and the consumers of planning services. For practitioners, exploring other kinds of practice encourages reflection about their own practice.

Like the universe, the scope of knowledge and skills required of the town planner is ever expanding. Twenty years ago, a career in planning usually meant a career in local government, either in development control or development plans. These remain key areas of contemporary practice, and have been re-emphasised in the 1990s. But the world of practice is much more than control or plan making. There are increasing demands for planning knowledge and skills in the private sector. The employment opportunities for graduates have expanded beyond the limits of local government to embrace consultancies, developers, housing agencies and the like. Contributions in the following chapters reflect this change.

This book will therefore be of interest to the practitioner as well as the student. Given the sheer breadth of the world of work that now calls for the knowledge and skills provided on planning courses, it is all too easy for the practitioner to become specialised in a particular field, such as conservation, development control, town centre management, or transport planning. This book therefore provides a slice through the world of practice today, and will assist practitioners seeking to locate their own developing career interests in the wide agenda that characterises planning at the end of the 1990s.

As well as laying out the terrain of key areas of contemporary practice, the following chapters include many case studies of actual practice. Making connections between theory and practical examples is an important aptitude for undergraduate and postgraduate planning students, as well as a valuable source of information for the practitioner. If you want to know the story behind the 'Oxford Shark', or what the Warwickshire Structure Plan is trying to achieve, or the implications for planning of town centre management, then the following chapters are there to help.

This book should stimulate the reader to want to find out more. It is a gateway to the exciting and varied world of town planning practice in all its forms. It may not teach you 'how to do it' (that is what car workshop repair manuals do) but it should heighten your appreciation of practice in all its forms and widen your horizons of the exciting world of the professional town planner.

CHAPTER 1

WHAT IS PLANNING AND WHAT DO PLANNERS DO?

Cliff Hague

INTRODUCTION

This chapter poses two questions: 'What is planning?' and 'What do planners do?' It is divided into six sections. After this short introduction, the second section reviews the problems and opportunities posed by urban and rural development. It sets these in an international and historical context. Very different types of countries have some system for planning and managing development; so what common factors persuade different governments to plan the use and development of land? What are the problems and opportunities created by the spread of settlements and relocation of activities, and what do these tell us about the practice of planning? The third section looks at some of the concerns in the context of the European Union today, and shows how planning is taking on a European dimension.

The fourth section introduces the planning system as it currently exists in the UK. It gives a picture of the roles of central and local government, the main types of work planners do, and the powers they can operate. But planning practice does not only belong to professional planners. Politicians are involved, as are the public, pressure groups, developers, and many others. We call these diverse bodies 'stake-holders' because they have a stake that is a legitimate place in, and concern for the outputs of, the planning system. The section reviews these stakeholders and their perspectives on planning practice. It stresses that not everyone agrees about how places should be planned. Conflicts over attitudes and values permeate all aspects of planning practice, and require of planners a range of appropriate skills. Conflict is one reason why planning is so interesting and features so often in the newspapers.

In view of this, the fifth section concludes by suggesting that planning is a process of debate.

PROBLEMS AND OPPORTUNITIES IN URBAN AND RURAL DEVELOPMENT

The Ancient Greek, Hippodamus of Miletus, can lay claim to being the first town planner in Europe, as he was creating regular grid layouts as early as 450 BC, although there were carefully planned towns in other parts of the world long before then. These early Greeks contributed some seminal technical ideas which informed the planning of settlements, ideas about the orientation of buildings and streets, the need for supplies of pure water, and to avoid developing on marshy ground. The grid has proved a very robust form for town development, creating rectangular blocks for building, an orderly street pattern, and flexibility to handle slow or rapid development. The settlements built by the Romans also typically have a grid layout, and effective drainage and sewage disposal systems. Urban civilisations outside Europe also organised the streets, spaces and buildings in a deliberate manner, giving prominence to palaces and religious buildings, for example, and taking care over their orientation. The Mayas in Central America, the Incas in South America, the Chinese and the Japanese all planned important urban settlements over centuries, laying out road systems, defining building plots, and providing good locations for key facilities such as market places. The notion that a conscious geometry could make towns attractive and efficient was revived as part of the European Renaissance in the sixteenth century.

The onset of the industrial revolution challenged the idea that towns could be designed. For a century the burgeoning concentrations of people and factories astounded and frightened observers. Practical means had to be invented to make such places and densities manageable. Germany invented the town extension plan to give local councils legal power to achieve orderly suburbanisation. In different forms the idea was taken up in other countries, including America and Britain, where the Houses of Parliament passed the first British Act mentioning 'Town Planning' in 1909. There had already been attempts to grapple with the problems of the slums. For example, there were local 'Improvement Acts', such as the Edinburgh Improvement Act of 1867, which made it possible to acquire and clear the most degraded properties and rebuild areas with wider streets and better buildings. Another significant, practical solution to the squalor of the burgeoning industrial city was the Garden City, an idea elaborated by Ebenezer Howard in a famous book first published in 1898, *Tomorrow: A Peaceful Path to Real Reform* (Howard, 1898). By building a new settlement on cheap agricultural land, but connected to a transport network, it was possible to provide low density housing away from pollution but accessible to employment (see Chapter 9 for more on transport and land uses).

People are flocking to the towns and cities in many poorer countries today. Much of the new development is 'spontaneous', as people occupy vacant land and begin to build rudimentary dwellings. In such circumstances there is little value in trying to produce a very detailed plan – it would take too long and soon be out of date. Instead planners can produce a general strategy for the settlement, identifying areas where essential services such as water, sewers and electricity will be provided, and creating basic layouts of roads and building plots that will allow adequate space for circulation and access by emergency vehicles. In such situations the planner may be 'barefoot', working in shanty towns with local groups, and helping them to develop and manage their areas.

Meanwhile in the rich countries there has been an exodus from the urban areas to suburbia and beyond. Old smokestack industries have closed, leaving large tracts of land poisoned by pollutants. The car allows people to drive long distances to work, shops, cinemas or schools, or to seek out solitude by touring the countryside or the coast. It might appear that there is nothing in common between the shanty towns of Calcutta and the commuter belt of Cheshire or Copenhagen, but we are one world. Town planners have long argued that 'everything affects everything else', and today this is true at a global level. How we plan and live in the settlements in the rich Northern hemisphere matters globally. These settlements account for a high proportion of the world's consumption of resources, not least energy. They make a major contribution to global greenhouse gas emissions. They add to the threat of – but are also affected by – climatic change resulting from global warming. Planners have to be aware of this global dimension:

> The need for planning becomes ever more necessary in the light of the increased social, economic and environmental impacts of urbanization, growing consumption levels and renewed concerns for sustainable development since the adoption of Agenda 21 (United Nations Centre for Human Settlements, 1996, p. xxxi).

The urban challenge is global. The United Nations recognise this. They convened a summit for all the countries of the world in 1996 to consider what action governments need to take. Box 1 illustrates the principles set out in the Habitat Agenda, to which all the countries signed up. This is not a 'World Charter for Planning', and some of the concerns are beyond the boundaries of the work of planners (e.g. concerns for legal security of tenure, or provision of housing finance or 'education for all'). What it does show is that the goal of creating sustainable settlements matters everywhere, and that those involved in planning urban settlements in the twenty-first century need to engage with issues of equity, participation, and sustainability. In the spirit of 'think globally, act locally', read through the list in the box and try to think of how the Habitat Agenda could be put into practice in your own area. (See Chapter 2 for a discussion of sustainable development generally as a concept and how it can be pursued through the planning system.)

Box 1 *Some key commitments in the Habitat Agenda*

Adequate shelter for all
- Legal security of tenure and access to land for all people
- Access to safe drinking water and adequate sanitation
- Access to appropriate housing finance
- Implementing accessibility standards for disabled persons
- Increasing the supply of affordable housing

Sustainable Human Settlements
- An enabling environment for economic and social development and environmental protection that will attract investment

---

- Enhancing the potential of the informal and private sectors in job creation
- Promoting upgrading of informal settlements and urban slums as appropriate
- Improving access to work, goods and services through promoting efficient, quiet and environmentally sound transportation systems
- Eliminating as soon as possible the use of lead in petrol

Enablement and Participation
- Promoting democratic rule and the exercise of public authority in ways that ensure accountable, just and effective governance of towns and cities
- Decentralising authority and resources to the level where needs are most effectively addressed
- Ensuring the availability of education for all

Gender Equality
- Integrating gender perspectives into human settlement legislation, policies and programmes
- Strengthening policies and practices to promote the full and equal participation of women in human settlements planning and decision-making

An international report noted that:

> Underlying virtually all urban environmental problems is the issue of land use, from lack of affordable housing, to congestion and pollution from motor vehicles, to inner cities marred by abandoned buildings. Indeed, urban form and land use patterns within a city are critical determinants of environmental quality (The World Resources Institute *et al.*, 1996, p. 116).

Let us illustrate some of these issues. Across Europe and North America the trend is towards smaller households, as people live longer and more independently. Although national population totals may have plateaued out, the number of households is increasing, and so more houses are needed for the future. In addition older housing falls into disrepair and decay – a trend especially apparent in some of the deindustrialised urban areas where incomes are low, the environment poor, and the fear of crime haunts an ageing population. Those who can afford it want to live in the comfortable parts of town, or to settle in suburbs or move to a village in the countryside. This means that there will be intense competition for land and housing in attractive locations.

What should we do about it? We might decide to do nothing. Let the market decide – many economists will tell you that by relying on the market you meet consumer preferences most fully and efficiently. The result would almost certainly be the extensive *urbanisation of the countryside*, longer commuting and greater reliance on the car. It is a model that can be observed in affluent societies where land is plentiful, such as the US or Australia. But this 'solution' immediately highlights some of the important ideas that underpin planning practice. As new houses replace green fields they destroy forever the very asset that attracted their residents. Longer commuting means more demands on the earth's resources – and more pollution of the atmosphere. Air pollution is known to kill thousands of people prematurely each year and put others in hospitals, and in Britain, and other rich countries, motor vehicles are now a major cause of that pollution. Unfettered market forces overlook such effects. The sum of individual interests is not the same as the interest of humanity as a whole.

Developers usually find it cheaper and easier to build on green fields than to reuse so-called brownfield land abandoned by previous uses. If the land has been used for industry, for example, then it may be contaminated by poisonous metals; even the extent of the contamination may be unknown, for in the days before regulations existed industrialists did not have to account for their treatment of the environment (see Chapter 13 for more on contaminated land). Small, awkwardly shaped sites are difficult to develop, and often the old areas of cities are unfashionable, so developers may worry about whether they will be able to sell new houses in such neighbourhoods. Left to itself, the market will not take a risk in such areas. The challenge is to regenerate these places, to restore the confidence of residents and investors. Creative planning, combining vision with dialogue with local residents and developers, can begin to restore assets. Abandoned warehouses, for example, might be converted into flats; shopping parades might be given a facelift; the canal cleaned up and made an asset to be enjoyed instead of an eyesore.

However, the *regeneration* of such areas may also depend on restricting development elsewhere – removing the easy option of the greenfield site so as to make developers more willing to consider the brownfield alternative. This is one of the reasons why many countries have planners working for regional scale authorities. Journey to work patterns, and so housing markets, stretch over extensive areas. The development of a major shopping centre can have an impact on town centres many miles distant (for more on this topical matter, see especially Chapter 8 on retail, but also Chapter 2 on sustainable development, Chapter 9 on transport, and Chapter 10 on town centre management). It is not just local residents who use the countryside or the coast as a recreational resource, but city dwellers as well. Nobody wants the incinerator or sewage treatment plant in their area, but such facilities are essential and have to go somewhere. *Planning at a regional scale* is a way to manage such issues.

There are also opportunities and problems at a *local scale*. The character of an area is a delicate balance of sights and sounds (and sometimes smells!), buildings, spaces, trees, monuments, and activities. The *mix and relation of land uses* is important. Try to think about an area that you have enjoyed being in, and then ask yourself what made it enjoyable. Development can enhance the quality of an area or destroy it; it can make a place safer or more dangerous. Think about an existing football stadium, for example. For fans it is likely to be a place rich in memories, a shrine for their passion, a place where the incense of sausage rolls and meat pies is the prelude to the excitement of the game and the roar of the crowd. Any suggestion that the ground might be relocated would be sacrilege. However, people living in the area suffer the nuisance of the crowds, parked cars, etc. They might welcome relocation of the football and redevelopment of the site for other uses. And if the ground were to relocate, what might be a suitable site? The move of Ajax from a congested old inner area of Amsterdam to a more suburban location is a good example. The new arena is next to a business park, has plenty of land around it, and is adjacent to two metro stations, while on the other side of the elevated metro line there are housing areas from which fans can easily walk to the ground.

Good planning at a local scale involves spotting ways to balance economic viability, public safety, accessibility, and amenity. It is wrong to try to fossilise places – all areas need investment, and planners should always be trying to improve on what currently exists. On the other hand, not all development is good development, and maximising the profitability of a development is not the same as maximising the quality of the scheme. Again, a local environment is more than the sum of the individual buildings. It is the relations of buildings and activities to each other, to spaces, to the scale and grain of the area that gives us a sense of place, a feeling of identity, an appreciation of the character of an area. *Conservation* means more than just preserving historic buildings, it means managing reinvestment in a way that recycles those aspects of the historical legacy that are still assets. It is very difficult for individual developers by themselves, and working on separate plots, to deliver projects that enhance an area overall and reinforce each other. To fully realise the opportunities of the public realm – the spaces and place experience that are shared by all of us, including those who own or design individual buildings – we need plans and codes that see this bigger picture.

In summary, the way we develop places is enormously important. It impacts both on Spaceship Earth and on how we live our daily lives alongside our neighbours. Of course development takes place through the efforts of a host of different companies, agencies and individuals, but it is the integration of their efforts, through planning, that can fully realise the opportunities and gain long-term benefits to the public as a whole as well as to the short-term returns to the investors themselves. To do this effectively, planners have to understand the grammar of places, the inter-connectedness of ecology, the opportunities for investors, the policy and culture of institutions, and the framework of legislation.

THE EUROPEAN DIMENSION OF PLANNING

In Europe today economic activity, transport links, and environmental impacts extend even across the old national boundaries. For example, on a sunny weekend

Germans from the Ruhr drive to Holland for a day by the sea. Britain's acid rain is accused of destroying Scandinavian forests and lakes. Lille, once on the north-eastern periphery of France, is now the central hub on the fast railway linking London and Brussels via the Channel Tunnel. Governments within the European Union have recognised that the Single European Market means that regional scale planning now has a *European dimension*. At a meeting in 1994 the various governments agreed a set of principles to guide European thinking on urban and regional development. These are set out in Box 2.

Box 2 *The 'Leipzig Principles' agreed by the informal Council of Ministers in Leipzig in 1994*

- To encourage a more balanced and polycentric system of cities and a new urban and rural relationship. This implies discouraging the combined con-centration around some large centres and marginalisation of other areas.
- To encourage parity of access to infrastructure and knowledge – i.e. strengthening cohesion, and reducing locational disadvantages attributable to poor infrastructure or a low knowledge base.
- To encourage prudent management and development of the natural and cultural heritage – including the establishment of a European network of open spaces.

Building on these principles, a *European Spatial Development Perspective* has been produced which analyses trends in the European Union and the countries of Central and Eastern Europe (Meeting of Ministers responsible for spatial planning of the member states of the European Union, 1998). The Perspective, and EU programmes such as INTER-REG, seek to promote cross-border collaboration in the planning and management of territory. In addition, the EU produces *Directives* which must then be given legislative effect in each member state. There are many concerned with environmental matters, some of which affect the work of planners. A good example is the requirement to carry out an environmental impact assessment (EIA) when major development is proposed; in Britain the majority of such assessments are carried out through the planning system. Another example is a Directive which requires member states to declare sites to conserve wild birds and important habitats for fauna and flora, a process in which planners are consulted.

While the European dimension is of growing importance in the UK, town planning is predominantly a local activity, which is typically undertaken by local government operating within a code of legislation passed by national government (or by a state/province within federal countries like Germany, Australia, or the US). While there may be common pressures on settlements and the countryside in many different countries, the words used to describe the response, like the legislation, tend to be peculiar to each country, and to carry important nuances of difference in how the problems are conceived and tackled. Thus the British talk of 'town and country planning' reflecting the priority since the early decades of the twentieth century to maintain a separation between town and country, and to contain urban sprawl. The French distinguish between strategic level *aménagement du territoire*, a term hinting at political intervention to manage broad regional economic development, and town level *urbanisme*, which smacks more of urban design. In the Netherlands, the term is *Ruimtelijke Ordening*, the ordering of space, in a nation where land is scarce and threatened by water, and there are important traditions of major public sector engineering and infrastructure works. In contrast, the land-rich countries that were settled by European colonists have systems of land use zoning which seek to subdivide parcels of land for new development and to specify the kinds and intensities of uses that would be acceptable. These differences should not obscure the more basic point: development of settlements and the countryside is something that most countries now recognise to be an important issue, and one requiring skilled management through governments and/or some other form of institution, which operates for the benefit of the public rather than to make a profit.

The European Union has coined the phrase *spatial planning* to encompass some of the variety between different systems. It has now produced a Compendium (Commission of the European Communities, 1997), which describes and analyses the key features of the planning systems in each of the member states. There are also important networks now linking planners across Europe. The Association of European Schools of Planning has developed ideas about what knowledge and skills a planning education should impart, as has the European Council of Town Planners, which groups the professional institutes of planners in the different countries. There is also a European Town Planning Biennial, an exhibition and conference held every other year, to showcase the latest developments in practice. In addition many planners are now involved in other European networks dealing with topics such as sustainable cities or coastal management, while many planning schools are involved in the SOCRATES programme which supports student and staff exchanges between different European countries.

PLANNING IN THE UK

Box 3 shows the main roles of central and local government in delivering planning in Britain. Although the system operates mainly at the local government level, the role of central government is important in setting the overall framework of law and policy and is decisive when there are controversies about planning applications.

Box 3 *The roles of central and local government in planning*

Central government	Local government
• Legislation & Regulations	
• Policy Guidance	

• Powers to call in Development Plans	• Development Plans
	   – Structure Plans
	   – Local Plans
	   – Unitary Development Plans

• Powers to call in Applications and decide on Appeals	• Development Control
	   – Planning Applications
	   – Permissions and Conditions
	   – Enforcement

• Research & Monitoring	• Special controls
	   – Conservation Areas
	   – Listed Buildings
	   – Hazardous Industries

Planning practice is therefore rooted in a system of *law*, which sets boundaries, within which planners and those individuals, companies or agencies seeking to develop must act. Historically it has been the parliament at Westminster that has passed the legislation that forms the basis for the planning system, though there have been some significant differences in detail between the legislation for England and Wales, Scotland, and Northern Ireland. These may become more marked with the establishment of the parliament in Scotland and the assemblies in Wales and Northern Ireland – although, as outlined above, the European Union has been exerting a broadly harmonising influence, most notably through its use of Directives on environmental matters.

The 1947 Town and Country Planning Act was really the first UK legislation to provide the legal tools necessary for the practice of planning and the control of development. Before then planning was a largely voluntary activity, severely limited in its effectiveness by the costs in compensation that a local council would have to pay to a landowner if it refused planning consent to any development. Because there was (and still is) a vast difference in the value of land in agricultural use and the value of the same plot for use as housing, shops or offices, the compensation for loss of the right to develop land would have been very expensive for a council. The system of development plans and development control introduced in 1947 overcame this serious constraint, so that refusal of planning permission now does not automatically entitle a landowner to compensation. This nationalisation of the right to develop made it possible to protect historic environments or to use green belts to contain the spread of cities.

As well as creating the legislation, central government also provides *policy guidance* to planners and developers, setting out in official documents the national priorities that need to be followed (see Chapter 5). For example, the purposes of the planning system are defined in Planning Policy Guideline 1, emphasising the importance of sustainable development:

> The planning system regulates the development and use of land in the public interest. The system as a whole, and the preparation of development plans in particular, is the most effective way of reconciling the demand for development and the protection of the environment. Thus it has a key role to play in contributing to the Government's strategy for sustainable development by helping to provide for necessary development in locations which do not compromise the ability of future generations to meet their needs (Department of the Environment and The Welsh Office, 1992, para. 39).

National guidance must be taken into account when preparing plans and considering planning applications, and changes in national policy guidance can be very important to developers and planners. For example, in the late 1990s national policy moved against the development of out-of-town shopping centres, and with plans and decisions on planning applications expected to conform to this policy, it became much harder for developers to build out of town. Sharp-witted readers will sense some tension here. Is this guidance (i.e. a gentle steering) or a diktat (something that must be obeyed)? The strict answer is that it is somewhere between the two – the guidance cannot be ignored, but it is possible to argue for local exceptions if you can put forward convincing reasons.

The actual preparation of *development plans* is the responsibility of local government, except in Northern Ireland where the system has been centralised. As Chapter 3 explains in more detail, there are different types of development plan in different situations. In some cases there is a strategic plan, called the Structure Plan, backed by a more detailed Local Plan, but in the main urban areas in England there is just one plan, called a Unitary Development Plan, which covers both the overall strategy and local implementation. The various types of Development Plan are all *policy-based* plans. This means that rather than concentrating on mapping the intended use for every piece of land, they primarily set out in writing the *policies* to be applied when considering applications for planning permission. The aims and intentions of a plan should be clear, and the plan should also include *proposals*, i.e. actions which the authority preparing the plan intends to undertake itself, and *recommendations* to others about desirable actions that would help in the implementation of the plan.

Such features make the mechanics of the British planning system rather unusual, certainly when compared with systems in continental Europe. In most other countries the plan is very definitive and strict – development that conforms with what the plan for that site specifies can go ahead, and similarly other development that does not match what is in the plan will be refused, unless the plan is changed. In Britain, by contrast, the plan may not say anything about the particular piece of land which an applicant wants permission to develop; rather the proposal will be judged against policies. For example, one of the policies in a Local Plan is as follows:

> In all new housing developments, open space shall be provided principally as a single space in one accessible area in accordance with the standard of: 0.4 hectares for every 100 houses in large developments; 10% of the site area in small infill developments; to meet both recreational and amenity needs (Edinburgh District Council, 1990, South West Edinburgh Local Plan Written Statement, Policy E21).

Whatever type of plan it is, the essence of a plan is that it provides a vision of a desired and attainable future. Plans have to have a clear sense of purpose, of what it is that they are produced to achieve. That purpose will be reflected in the various policy statements within the plan, but also in a map or diagram communicating its main spatial aspects. Thus a typical plan for a small town might aim to retain and enhance the existing character and identity of the town, while accommodating growth. To these ends the plan might preserve an area of open space between the town and its nearest neighbour, while also having policies to protect the built heritage in an old village by making it a Conservation Area. It might also seek to regenerate the run-down town centre, and identify land for new housing and business park developments along the route of the railway, where it might be possible to create a new station to serve the growth of trips generated by the development.

The various parts of a plan should complement each other – the plan should be consistent. For example, a policy to 'protect the countryside by refusing all applications for new housing development there' is not likely to succeed if, at the same time, there is another policy saying 'new industrial development will be encouraged except in residential areas'. The inconsistency is that the policies would allow for industrial development in the countryside, while seeking to 'protect' it. It is particularly vital to remember that land use and transport are closely intertwined. Planning a new road will create new pressures for development, just as planning a business park or shopping centre will probably mean a need to increase the capacity of the transport links.

Plans also need to be clear about *implementation*. Who is to carry out the development envisaged in the plan? In the UK the majority of development is undertaken by the private sector. Even the provision of water and sewerage systems, vital to development of new areas, is now through private companies in England and Wales, or, in Scotland, public agencies that are operating by commercial criteria. There is thus no guarantee that private developers will want to do what the plan wants them to. The implication is that plans need to be realistic and appreciate the criteria that will shape investment decisions in the private sector. This is not to say that the plan should simply be sanctioning any and every development. Rather planning in a market economy demands sophisticated skills in understanding the way that developers, public sector and voluntary agencies operate, and then in steering the different players in a common direction to achieve the aims of the plan. Consultation is a way of making sure that the ideas in a plan are realistic, though a plan is not simply the passive residue of others' aspirations. Developers are not stupid; they will listen to the messages being sent out by a plan, and factor those messages into their own behaviour and decisions.

The plans are then the main basis for the operation of the system of *development control*, discussed in Chapter 4. Development control provides the real teeth that make plans bite, and is an activity in which many planners are employed, either as development control officers in local government, or as private planning consultants advising and representing clients seeking planning permissions.

Anyone wanting to carry out development must first get planning permission. This involves putting in an *planning application* and paying a fee. Development is defined in the legislation as 'the carrying out of building, engineering, mining, or other operations in, on, over or under land, or the making of any material change in the use of any buildings or other land'. In the vast majority of cases, permission is granted, but often with some conditions attached to protect the public interest. If the application is refused, the applicant may lodge an appeal, which will be dealt with by an official appointed by central government.

Finally, we should note that central government also commissions *research* as a basis to develop and disseminate good practice about planning. Of equal importance is that it monitors the performance of planning authorities and publishes the findings. We therefore have 'league tables' showing the percentage of planning applications decided within 8 weeks of being submitted, or the progress of local authorities in their plan-making. Such monitoring is not unique to planning – it is now widespread across British local government. Central government expects local government to achieve what it calls best value. This means questioning what is being done, why it is being done, and how efficiently it is being done.

The results of such endeavours are leading to dramatic changes in local government in general. In planning the trend is to separate the strategic policy-making aspects of work from the regulation and implementation aspects. Thus we are seeing important restructuring, with, for example, development control increasingly linked to other forms of local regulation, such as control of buildings, which covers matters like insulation standards and the safety of the construction. Similarly, strategic planning is increasingly being practised in an integrated way across activities that had traditionally been in separate departments within the local authority or even in separate authorities, such as education, housing, and social work. In 1999, for example, the Edinburgh Council produced what it called a Vision for the city, looking ahead and defining key strengths and priorities. Such cross-cutting planning has been called *community planning*. It seeks to involve ordinary people in identifying issues and opportunities. It is about making connections between the kind of policies in development plans and other services such as health and education.

The result is that while development plans and development control remain the legal basis of planning, the practice of planning can take on different forms and appear under different labels. For example, in many local authorities planning is closely linked with *economic development* (see Chapter 14). Land and premises are an important part of bringing jobs into an area, but they are not the whole story, and economic development work is also likely to involve initiatives to work with existing local businesses, identifying new needs and opportunities. There are also agencies outside local government that have important roles in local economic development work, for example the Training and Enterprise Councils in England, or their equivalents in Scotland, the Local Enterprise Companies.

Similarly, *environmental initiatives* are increasingly important as a means of achieving the sustainable development aims that are at the heart of the planning system today. Local Agenda 21 (see also Chapter 2) has encouraged local projects concerned with conserving and enhancing local environments. Often such initiatives involve voluntary groups, but the co-ordination and planning of the work benefits from the input of professional skills. Likewise, *regeneration part-nerships* are locally based bodies involved in intensive improvements of areas that have suffered serious decline (see Chapter 6). The partnerships typically involve people from the local council, local companies, and voluntary groups, as well as organisations concerned with housing or training and employment. Such bodies need to plan how to tackle the problems of the area, identify land that can be reused, or assets such as interesting buildings that can be retained and improved. They are involved in 'networking' to draw on a wide range of resources, and they also need to evaluate the results that they achieve. Environmental projects, regeneration, conservation of the cultural heritage, and economic development are the kinds of activities that often feature in *European projects*. Bidding for such projects, and then delivering them, is another area where planners are often working in a proactive way, spotting new opportunities and being innovative.

So the development plans and development control are the bedrock of planning practice, but not the whole story. Similarly, while many planners work in local government, not all of them are involved in processing planning applications or making new local plans. Many planners work as private consultants or directly for developers, advising clients or employers (e.g. house-building companies or the superstore chains) about planning policies and development opportunities. In summary, planning practice today takes many forms and is likely to continue to change and develop in the future.

THE STAKEHOLDERS

Box 4 shows who is involved in planning. We have already reviewed the role of some of them.

Box 4 *The stakeholders in planning*

European Union		

Central Government	Quangos	Local Government
Parliaments	Environment & Heritage	Planners
Civil Servants	Economic Development	Other Professions & Departments
	Housing	Councillors

National pressure groups	Landowners	Local voluntary organisations
	Developers	Individual members of the public

The day-to-day operation of the planning system is rooted in local government. People elect local councillors who together take the decisions about a whole array of matters affecting the area covered by the council, including decisions about planning. Although elected councillors have the final say on planning matters it would be unrealistic to imagine that they can do all the work themselves, and so the councillors are advised by their officials who are trained and qualified as planners. So as to ensure efficiency, in many councils the elected members have agreed to devolve decisions on most routine and uncontentious planning applications to these officials. This also helps the councillors to give more time and thought to the big developments or policies to be included in plans.

Of course there will be times when councillors may disagree with the recommendation from their officials. For example, a new development may bring in jobs but have (in the view of the planner) an unacceptable impact on the landscape. The planner will be able to rehearse the arguments from all points of view, but in the end the power to decide rests with the councillors. Similarly, the councillors may be lobbied by their constituents or other interested parties about plans or applications for planning permission, and then they have to decide which way to vote on the issue, knowing that if they alienate some of their constituents those people may vote against them at the next round of elections to the council. Of course in the UK and over most of the urban world councillors are usually elected on a party ticket, and that can be another source of pressure on them when they consider planning matters (ethical issues of this sort are discussed in Chapter 16). For example, it may be party policy to build a new road to open up land for an industrial estate, but the road may have a detrimental effect in the part of the city for which the individual councillor is elected. That said, planning policy is not normally politicised in local government, and conflicts are just as likely to be between different adjacent local authorities (e.g. over where a new retail centre should be) as between different parties within the same council.

In most countries today nearly all the new development is carried out by the private sector. However, there has also been an important growth in two forms of institutions which are rather blurred between the public and private sectors. These are called 'Quangos' and 'public–private partnerships'. Quango is an abbreviation for Quasi Autonomous Non-Governmental Organisation. Typically these bodies are spending money that comes from the public purse and so have to be economical, efficient, and effective in what they do; but they are not like private firms who depend on making profits. Quangos have powers and are set up by governments, but operate at arm's length from the actual politicians or civil service, and so are not subject to the kind of interference from elected politicians that would occur in a typical central or local government department. The idea is that a Quango can be given a clear brief and then left to get on with the job in an expert manner.

The carrying out of major development is the type of role that is well suited to a Quango, and examples are the Urban Development Corporations set up in England and Wales in the 1980s, or the New Town Development Corporations set up to build the new towns after the Second World War. As councils have become less involved in house-building so the role of new social housing provision has come increasingly to depend on housing Quangos – such as the Housing Corporation, which operates in England, or its equivalents in Scotland, Wales and Northern Ireland. As Chapter 7 describes, such agencies are important sources of finance for housing development. Similarly, there are important agencies whose primary concern is economic development and regeneration. English Partnerships originally developed industrial estates but is now likely to be a key institution in many regeneration projects. At a more local level there are Training and Enterprise Councils (England) and Local Enterprise Councils (Scotland) which combine training of the local labour force with land acquisition, development and subsidy. Again these are non-elected bodies, separate from local government, and while they do not produce structure plans or local plans they are likely to be important instigators of development and able to influence the implementation of plans that councils have produced.

Not all Quangos are primarily development bodies. There are important bodies concerned with conservation and nature protection. The Environment Agency (and Scottish Environmental Protection Agency) is a good example of how government has hived off the regulation of pollution hazards to a special purpose agency, rather than undertaking the work through a department within the civil service. English Heritage or Scottish Natural Heritage are other examples of institutions that provide expert views on aspects of conservation, as well as some funding support for projects, usually in partnership with other funders (see Chapter 12).

These types of bodies are likely to be consulted by planners where their expertise is relevant to a particular planning application, and may also have an input into the formulation of policies in plans.

Quangos are often key players in public–private partnerships. These are likely to be area based, and often aim to regenerate an area or to manage a town centre. The private sector brings investment which is then often topped up by money (in cash or in kind, such as land) from public bodies such as a Quango or a local council. Similarly, the private sector is likely to contribute expertise in market analysis and marketing while the public body provides a route through bureaucracies and a link to local schools, residents, etc.

The public get involved in planning in various ways. Planning, more than any other local government service, has a long record of informing and *consulting the public*. When a plan is being prepared information will be made available to local residents and their opinions will be sought. A copy of the draft of the plan will be available for inspection in the council offices and public libraries and there may be special public meetings or exhibitions too. Similarly, applications for planning permission are notified to neighbours of the site, while some are also advertised in the local newspapers, so that anyone can go along to the council and find out more about what is being proposed, and express a view upon it. They may then write a letter to the planners or perhaps telephone their local councillor.

People with shared concerns often group together to support each other and to have a stronger voice. For example, there are many local organisations concerned with the amenity of their area, often with a special interest in conserving its character and historical features. Other organisations may spring into being to oppose some controversial development such as a new road, and will have a narrower focus of concern and may disappear again when the issue has been resolved. There are also bodies with members all over the country, and perhaps abroad, with interests in environmental questions, for example Friends of the Earth or the Royal Society for the Protection of Birds. Such bodies are likely to seek to exert influence at the national level, but their local branches may also be consulted or may put forward their views on local planning matters.

There are some pressure groups and campaigning organisations at the national level that are centrally concerned with planning. The Town and Country Planning Association is a good example – it was founded to advance the ideas of garden cities and today is strongly committed to campaigning for sustainable development within the UK. Another body whose origins and interests fundamentally concern planning is the Council for the Protection of Rural England, which operates both nationally and locally to resist what it sees as inappropriate development in the countryside. These are all examples of pressure groups and they are a vital part of the democracy of planning.

Landowners and developers are also important stakeholders in the planning system. They have a right to have their planning applications handled fairly and efficiently, and if they are unhappy with the decision they receive on an application they have some rights of appeal (these are discussed more fully in Chapter 5). They are likely to hire the services of planners and other professional consultants to present their case. For example, a superstore company seeking to develop a new store will want to find a site where they are likely to be able both to acquire the land from a landowner and to get planning permission for their development. They will need to show how their store will impact on other shopping centres and will also have to be able to explain the level and kind of traffic that it would generate. Similarly, house-building firms employ trained planners to examine development plans and to find sites on which they will be able to build.

As well as acting individually and competitively landowners and developers also come together to form their own pressure groups to ensure that their interests as a whole are put across to government and other key decision-makers. The Country Landowners' Association, for example, is generally concerned about the damage that public access can do to rural land. The House Builders' Federation represents the big companies who build most of the new housing and brings its expert understanding of housing markets into the arguments about how much land is likely to be needed for new housing, and where.

As you can see, the planner is just one player in the system that produces development. The image of the planner as a colossus, able single-handedly to shape the future by designing a whole new city, has little basis in reality today, and that is no bad thing. That type of planning is only likely to work in a totalitarian society. It is no coincidence that such planning when practised in the past tended to favour designs that celebrated centralised power, with grand avenues focusing on vistas of palaces or triumphal arches (the capital cities of the former British empire and the former Soviet bloc are among the more recent examples).

Planners working in local government in particular now operate in situations where they have to listen to the public, consult with voluntary organisations, be sensitive to the views of elected members, work in teams with other professions, and persuade developers in both public and private sectors to bend their wishes to fit the plan (see Chapter 15). A lot of planning involves listening to what others have to say, really listening to pick up the clues and nuances, and to tease out the areas where negotiation and compromise might be possible, or to spot an opportunity to achieve some unanticipated spin-offs from another's ideas. Self-awareness is necessary, and an ability to understand the needs of very different groups within complex modern societies – for example, how do the elderly feel about an area, or what are the special needs of an ethnic minority group?

Planners also have to be good communicators, able to express their ideas clearly and concisely in writing and through graphic images; they have to be able to speak at a public meeting or handle telephone enquiries in a courteous and accurate manner. They have to be logical thinkers, able to justify their ideas under cross-examination by lawyers when controversial cases go to public inquiry, for example. The best planners are able to combine vision with practicality; they are sensitive to the qualities of places and to the needs of people.

They need a strong awareness of ethics and a commitment to creating a better quality of life for the benefit of others. The issue of ethics inevitably arises in a process in which competing interests are at stake and a regulatory body, such as a planning authority, can determine the outcome. This opens the way to potential abuse, particularly when the authority has an interest in the case itself. Commentators differ in their views of how fair the planning system is as a whole in a structural sense; but generally the system has maintained a high level of probity, despite some well publicised lapses (see Chapter 16).

PLANNING AS A PROCESS OF DEBATE

In such diversity, what is the common thread? Above all, planners do the '*joined up thinking*'. While an architect is concerned about the look and function of a building, the surveyor about land and property values, the traffic engineer about the design and details of a road, the planner sees places as something more than the sum of the parts, a view emphasised in Chapter 11. Buildings, land uses, and roads all have impacts on adjacent sites, and sometimes on places far away. The planner also looks to the future, weighing short-term and long-term costs and benefits. This is one reason why planners have embraced the idea of sustainable development, which emphasises an equitable and long-term approach to issues of development (see Chapter 2). Equity matters because another traditional concern of planners has been to balance the rights and interests of individuals with the needs of others (see Chapters 14 and 15). In practice this appears in many different ways, for example ensuring that a hot food take-away shop is not a nuisance to neighbours, or striving to achieve 'parity of access to infrastructure' at a European scale, so that whole regions are not excluded from the benefits of high-quality transport links. The fact that not everyone agrees about how to achieve concepts like 'balance' or 'parity' means that planning is fundamentally a process of debate with numerous voices contesting the arguments about priorities, who gets what, and whether development should be allowed or refused.

Planning is often controversial because it involves choices and uncertainty. Different people, groups, and even different planners will have different priorities and values. A shopkeeper may want to erect a metal grill over windows to protect the property from malicious damage, but the grill is likely to be unsightly and to detract from the appearance of the streetscape, creating a 'dead' frontage. It may be possible to find some other solution that satisfies all parties, but often in planning there will be winners and losers. Evaluation and choice of policy is central to planning, and means we must always be asking '*Who gains? Who loses?*' Often gains will become more evident in the future, though losses will be experienced more quickly. This complicates evaluation, as there is inevitably greater uncertainty the further we peer into the future. Planners do not know the future,

but they should be able to make educated guesses and to set out in a clear way the
likely options and consequences.

REFERENCES

Commission of the European Communities (1997) *Regional Development Studies: The EU
Compendium of Spatial Planning Systems and Policies*, Office of Official Publications of
the European Communities, Luxembourg.

Department of the Environment and The Welsh Office (1992) *General Policy and Principles*,
Planning Policy Guidance Note 1.

Edinburgh District Council (1990) South West Edinburgh Local Plan Written Statement.

Howard, E. (1898) *Tomorrow: A Peaceful Path to Real Reform*, Swann Sonnenschein,
London.

Meeting of Ministers responsible for spatial planning of the member states of the European
Union (1998) *European Spatial Development Perspective: Complete Draft*, Glasgow.

The World Resources Institute, The UN Environment Programme, The UN Development
Programme, and The World Bank (1996) *World Resources: A Guide to the Global
Environment – The Urban Environment*, Oxford University Press, Oxford.

United Nations Centre for Human Settlements (1996) *An Urbanizing World: Global Report
on Human Settlements 1996*, Oxford University Press for UNCHS, Oxford.

CHAPTER 2

PLANNING FOR SUSTAINABLE DEVELOPMENT

Jeremy Raemaekers

INTRODUCTION

The purpose of this chapter is to explore one of the most prominent 'cross-cutting' themes of current planning practice, namely sustainable development. Since much of planning policy today claims to pursue sustainable development, it is desirable that you should have an overall grasp of the subject, to enable you to look at topics from this angle as you explore them in the other chapters of the book.

In the second section of this chapter we explore the *idea* of sustainable development as it relates to the field of town and country planning. We start with a specific planning policy and work outwards from there to draw out the meaning of sustainable development, especially as it relates to planning, and the many conceptual issues that it raises.

The third section looks at the *practice* of planning for sustainable development in four spheres of practice: national planning policy, Development Plans, development control, and Local Agenda 21.

The fourth section closes the chapter by trying to *evaluate* how well planners are implementing sustainable development and by asking just what, if anything, it represents that planners were not doing before the term became current.

THE MEANING OF SUSTAINABLE DEVELOPMENT IN PLANNING

TWO DEFINITIONS OF SUSTAINABLE DEVELOPMENT

Before we consider the meaning of sustainable development in planning specifically, we need to look at general definitions of it. Box 1 presents and comments briefly on two well-publicised definitions. There is common ground between the two definitions, but they also differ considerably. In part, this is because they are concerned with different contexts. *Our Common Future* relates the development–environment question to the North–South question. It is concerned about the inequalities between the rich industrial nations and the poor less industrialised nations, and how this reinforces a vicious circle of poverty and environmental degradation in the poor ones. *This Common Inheritance* is concerned mainly with the physical environment of the UK, and the impacts on it of a modern industrial lifestyle. Such conceptual malleability makes it difficult for planners to pin down what they are trying to implement; in what follows we try to provide some signposts through the maze.

Box 1 *Defining sustainable development*

The best known definition of sustainable development is that of the Brundtland Commission report *Our Common Future*:

> Sustainable development is development that meets the needs of the present without compromising the ability of future generations to meet their own needs (World Commission on Environment and Development, 1987, p. 43).

The quote is almost always stopped at this point, leaving the reader with a good deal of interpreting to do. In fact, the report goes on to clarify what it means:

> It contains two key concepts:
> - the concept of 'needs', in particular the essential needs of the world's poor, to which overriding priority should be given; and
> - the idea of limitations imposed by the state of technology and social organization on the environment's ability to meet present and future needs.

We see at once three key features of the Brundtland concept. First, it is people-centred. The word environment does not appear until near the end. Second, it is about equity. Third, the focus is not on the ultimate limits which the environment imposes on how people can exploit resources – the so-called outer limits to growth – but on the limits which current human know-how and organisation impose on the environment's capacity to support us – the so-called inner limits to growth.

Now read this definition from the UK Government's *This Common Inheritance*:

> [Sustainable development] means living on the earth's income rather than eroding its capital. It means keeping the consumption of renewable natural resources within the limits of their replenishment. It means handing down to successive generations not only man-made wealth . . . but also natural wealth, such as clean and adequate water supplies, good arable land, a wealth of wildlife and ample forests (UK Government, 1990, p. 47).

This was the UK government's first attempt at a definition of sustainable development (since revised, Department of the Environment, Transport and the Regions, 1999a). How does it compare with the Brundtland definition? Both speak of future generations and of limits. But the UK definition is environment-centred rather than people-centred, it does not speak of poverty or needs, and it focuses by implication on the outer rather than the inner limits to growth.

Other definitions are purely ecological or purely economic. The endless variety reflects the paradox of the sustainable development idea: its appeal is so wide precisely because everybody can interpret it differently. It is on the surface so simple as to seem hardly to be a concept at all; yet when you look beneath the surface, it seems to raise most of the great choices of life. Small wonder that planners cry out for guidance on how to apply the concept, and that government's interpretation shifts over time.

THREE DIMENSIONS OF SUSTAINABLE DEVELOPMENT IN PLANNING

Planning is commonly conceived of as seeking to reconcile the three-fold demands of society, economy, and environment. A good place to start considering the meaning of sustainable development is therefore to examine a planning policy from these three dimensions.

Suppose that you are seated at your desk in the planning unit of Sometown Council. Before you lies a draft of the Council's Development Plan. Your boss wants you to appraise how well the Plan's policies promote sustainable development. You choose a policy at random:

The Council will resist major new out-of-town shopping developments in order to retain the town centre's vitality and viability and to reduce longer car trips by shoppers to places less well served by public transport.

This policy is in fact in line with national planning guidance issued by central government, which seeks to promote sustainable development. The argument that the policy favours sustainable development would run something like this:

Viable retailing helps other town-centre businesses like eating and entertainment outlets: if the shops in the town centre begin to fail, the rest of the town centre will also. The town's total retail trade might grow, but it would be at the expense of the vitality of the town centre as a place, which a ring of out-of-town malls can never supply. Even a famous town-centre shopping street like Edinburgh's Princes Street is considered to be under threat from the explosion of out-of-town malls in recent years, whose combined floor space is now greater than that of the centre (Cockburn Association, 1997).

Moreover, out-of-town malls may discriminate socially in favour of well-to-do car-owners, who can easily reach them and the lower prices they offer, which result from economies of scale and lower out-of-town rents. The less well-to-do, who do not have easy access to a car, must pay higher town-centre prices, and may even face a loss of shop variety in the town centre as a result of closures forced by competition from out of town.

The arguments above are essentially about the *social* sustainability of out-of-town malls. The policy can also be argued to favour *environmental* sustainability. An out-of-town mall fosters more and longer trips, particularly in private cars to which it caters with a vast car park, thus promoting more fuel use and more exhaust emissions. In Edinburgh, for example, 84% of the 80 000 shoppers per week at The Gyle out-of-town mall arrive by car, compared with only 20% of those shopping in Princes Street (Roger Tym and Partners, 1996). In addition, new malls are often built in green belts, supposedly reserved as landscape settings and visible boundaries for cities.

The loss of green belt land, and the amenity impacts of the extra traffic the mall generates both in construction and in operation are examples of local impacts. The exhaust emissions from the many thousands of shopping trips have both regional and global impacts. Regionally, they will contribute NOx (nitrogen oxides) to what becomes acid rain; globally, they will add to the CO_2 (carbon dioxide) emissions which are widely held to contribute to human-induced excess global warming, which in turn is predicted to affect climate regimes. Of course, a single shopping mall will have a minute effect at the global scale, but add together all the malls in all the countries and you begin to see the point. Hence the well-worn dictum 'think global, act local' – indeed, the concern about global warming is the specific justification of much local planning policy promoting sustainable development.

You might, of course, not agree with all this. You might argue that the policy is plainly resisting the general direction of consumer demand and is counter to economic efficiency, and is therefore *economically* unsustainable. What is more, there are doubts about the environmental sustainability of the policy, because some recent research suggests that the number of extra car trips generated by out-of-town centres, e.g. by diverting shoppers (most of whom would not have used a car) from town centres, is a lot lower than commonly supposed. For example, Edinburgh's Gyle mall is estimated to have diverted less than 5% of the city centre's share of shopping trips (Roger Tym and Partners, 1996). Worse still, some would argue that the out-of-town malls actually do a favour to those who are left to shop in town by forcing town prices down, and that the closures in town centres are fewer than supposed, calling into question even the social sustainability of the policy.

Evidently, deciding the course of action that most favours sustainable development is not going to be easy. We have seen in this example that what is sustainable in terms of one dimension may not be in another (see also below for an analogous case); also that we may simply not have enough information to know for sure whether a course of action will have the desired effect.

CONFLICT BETWEEN SUSTAINABLE DEVELOPMENT GOALS

We have already explored above in the case of the out-of-town shopping mall one type of conflict that may arise between different sustainable development goals, namely that between the economic, social, and environmental dimensions of development. Conflicts of interest may also exist *within* a dimension between sustainable development goals that appear equally respectable. Two examples of such conflicts within the environmental dimension, which we shall dub 'the wind farm dilemma' and 'the bypass dilemma', will illustrate the point.

The bypass dilemma continues the theme of traffic and towns from the previous section, and illustrates how conflict may arise between the different geographical scales of sustainable development. Suppose a fine historic city centre is suffering from traffic congestion, and suppose it is partly due to through traffic which has no wish to cross the city centre but has to do so because, historically, main roads have linked city centres. A common response is to build a bypass, with or without imposing restrictions in the city centre.

Traffic congestion may lead to severe local air pollution from vehicle fumes, with potentially damaging health effects (Department of the Environment *et al.*, 1997, chapters II.3–II.10). Indeed, it has prompted the government to introduce, through the Environment Act 1995, provisions for declaring local air quality management areas where the pollution exceeds new standards set nationally. Since any interpretation of sustainable development would surely rate the preservation of human health as a goal, on this ground alone the bypass would appear to be an environmentally sustainable action.

Unfortunately, it is now officially recognised that new trunk roads, including motorway standard bypasses like Edinburgh's, do not merely divert and speed up traffic flow, but actually generate new trips (see Chapter 9 on transport policy). The savings in congestion emissions brought by a motorway standard bypass are soon outweighed by the extra emissions from more vehicles running at high speeds. While these emissions may have little health impact because they are outside the city, they do add to both regional acidification and excess global warming. Thus a solution that is environmentally sustainable at one scale may not be at another. This does not undermine the value of the dictum 'think global, act local', but it does show that applying it does not automatically guide you to the right answer.

The wind farm dilemma raises the same global–local issue, but it also raises conflict between protection of *different kinds* of environmental good: sourcing energy from renewable resources and scenic heritage conservation. This dilemma has been the subject of heated debate in Britain in the mid-1990s (Coles and Taylor, 1993). Wind farms are not farms at all, but electricity generating stations composed of a number of wind turbines. The turbines are perched on the top of very tall masts and driven by huge propeller blades turned by the wind; hence they need to be sited in windy places like the coast or the uplands, and to be spread out so that the disruption of air flow by one does not affect the next. Groups like Friends of the Earth are enthusiastic about wind farms because they generate power from an endlessly renewable source, the wind, neither drawing down a finite stock of fuel nor emitting pollution – the perfect environmentally sustainable source of power.

Not everybody likes them, however. A vocal counter-lobby has grown up around the local impacts of wind farms, especially their scenic impact. Sites suitable for wind farms tend to be in parts of the countryside designated for their scenic beauty, including our national parks, which are also places where very large numbers of people come to enjoy that beauty. Personally, I find modern wind towers strikingly handsome, but they do transform the view.

An analogous problem arises with cleaning up the sulphur emissions of traditional coal-fired power stations, which are a prime contributor to acid rain. Nobody wants acid rain, but the equipment fitted to the smoke stacks to scrub the sulphur out of the emissions requires a lot of limestone. Limestone is bulky, so you are under pressure to quarry it close to the point of use to keep transport costs down. As it happens, given the location of our biggest power stations, the best sources of limestone are quarries in scenic uplands, including national parks. A wind farm may have a beauty of its own, and it is easily removed at the end of its life; but nobody would call a working quarry beautiful, and it changes the landscape forever.

Few would doubt that renewable energy generation and cleaning up sulphur emissions are moves towards sustainable development. But then, should preserving the best of our scenic heritage, designated for the nation as national parks, not also be a goal of sustainable development? Taking the argument to extremes, would you flourish in a world that was squeaky-clean in energy generation, but devoid of landscapes you cherish for their beauty and tradition?

WHAT DO WE SUSTAIN?

The more you come up against these sorts of dilemma in trying to implement sustainable development, the more you are forced to ask *what* it is we are trying to sustain. This approach is particularly relevant to development that would threaten an obvious natural asset such as a nature reserve, but is also applicable in a general way.

This approach thinks of the world in terms of the stocks and flows of resources we need to sustain a satisfactory quality of life. This 'capital stock' can be human – knowledge, skill and organisational capacity; man-made – the assets we make with that knowledge and skill; and natural. The mission of sustainable development then becomes the search for a development path that allows us to prosper, but also to pass on to the next generation undiminished or even increased capital stock. The idea is that you live off the interest generated by the capital, leaving the capital untouched, in the best tradition of accounting. If you go back to Box 1, you will see that the UK Government definition of sustainable development says just that. (For a classic early discussion of this approach, see Pearce *et al.*, 1989, chapters 1 and 2.)

At this point, however, we come to a parting of the ways between what have been called weak and strong sustainable development. *Weak sustainable development* views all forms of capital stock as interchangeable. Thus you can trade off the last of the world's supply of oil and gas so long as you substitute some equally valuable asset, which need not be of the same type, but offers a service of equivalent value. This in fact is pretty close to how the world does operate at the moment: we use up natural capital stock on the assumption that the technological advances we make in doing so allow to us to develop other assets that permit us to keep on growing economically.

Strong sustainable development believes we depend in the end on the world's natural assets, and that those are finite: the natural world has a limited supply of resources, and has a limited capacity to absorb our wastes before the life support systems on which we depend are damaged. If we damage them too badly, we shall ultimately undermine the very sources of our wealth, possibly even threaten our survival. Under this approach, it follows that not all natural capital is substitutable. Some of it is *critical natural capital*, which cannot be traded off at any price. Strong sustainable development requires that we identify and protect it.

In between this critical natural capital and the fully substitutable stuff there are natural assets of middling importance. Different specimens of the same type can be substituted one for another, so long as the sum of that type remains the same – the *constant natural assets* rule. An example would be allowing a nature reserve of only local value to be sacrificed to development so long as another of equal value were created as compensation. Extracting compensation from a developer for the damaging side-effects of development is in fact a long established planning principle, and in a planning context this would be just a particular case of it.

So runs the theory; but in practice how do we identify what assets fall into what class? This is a real conundrum at the heart of making the concept of sustainable development operational in planning. You could follow a purist line on strong sustainable development, arguing that only what is needed for maintaining human life support systems can be classed as critical natural capital. By this criterion, protection of the stratospheric ozone layer or sustaining fresh water supply would count, but our heritage of architectural styles or of treasured landscapes would not. But, as we argued above in the case of the wind farm dilemma, it would be a pretty poor sort of human existence which did not count any of its cultural heritage as critical. Yet, as Owens (1993) says:

> There is an irony in the application of these ideas to the planning system. Where the concept of critical natural capital is easiest to grasp, as in the case of limits on the concentration of pollutants or the clearly unsustainable use of living resources,

the role of land use planning has not always been accepted or even apparent. In contrast, where planning has a strong traditional role, and in particular in the protection of amenity, it is far more challenging to conceive of what is 'critical'.

Owens goes on to argue that we have to develop a theory of value to decide what is critical capital in these traditional areas of planning. We are still far from that. Meantime, planners do the best they can, for example by making use of the systems of valuing natural and cultural heritage which already exist. Thus Sites of Special Scientific Interest, National Parks, buildings listed for their architectural or historical importance, and so forth, are assumed to be critical.

This is however a stop-gap measure, and can lead to haphazard differences in the way we treat different assets. For example, the European Union's Habitats Directive requires the UK to identify sites of internationally important natural habitats, requiring us to demonstrate that we can and will protect them. Only overriding national interest or human health can justify action that would damage a listed site. No such international designations happen to exist for the scenic or cultural value of landscape. As a result, wildlife but not landscape is effectively treated as critical (see Chapter 12).

It is partly because of these frustrations that a recent report advocates abandoning the attempt to classify natural assets in this way. Instead, it suggests that we should go direct to the different services or functions which an asset performs, and ask to what extent each would be threatened by the proposed development, and what it would take to replace those that would be lost. We should treat each case individually, coming to a balanced judgement about what to do in each case (CAG Consultants and Land Use Consultants, 1997). Making such judgements is the stock-in-trade of development control, so that it presents no obstacle in itself. The real obstacle is that it may still be very difficult to establish the values of the functions performed by the threatened asset: it needs information, which means time and resources, which may not be available, and cause unwelcome delays, which cost money. The advantage of classifying, say, all Sites of Special Scientific Interest as critical natural capital, is precisely that you avoid such costs. There really is no easy answer.

SUSTAINABLE DEVELOPMENT AND THE PRESUMPTION IN FAVOUR OF DEVELOPMENT

Before we go on to look at how planning is actually trying to implement sustainable development, we should address a particular issue. In planning law, there had long been a presumption in favour of development: it should go ahead unless it can be shown that it would cause harm to interests of acknowledged importance.

The waters have now been muddied by introducing a presumption in favour of development which accords with the Development Plan (section 54A of the Town and Country Planning Act 1990). If an application accords with the Plan, it is likely to be approved unless there are strong material reasons for refusing it; and if it runs contrary to the Plan, then it is likely to be refused unless there are strong material reasons for approving it; always supposing that the Plan is up to date. Meanwhile, the general presumption in favour of development has not been abolished. This has created uncertainty about what is the bottom line (e.g. Tewdwr-Jones, 1994).

Further confusion has been created by changing the criterion of approval in the case of one specific type of development, namely open-cast coal mining. At the time of writing, the government recently issued a policy which demands that proposals for open-cast mining must show a *net benefit* to society – and in Scotland, a net benefit to the local community specifically. The reason is political pressure that has built up from resentment of successive open-cast mines in particular localities where the coal outcrops at the surface (see the first section in Chapter 13). We should take good note of this turn of events, because it has reversed the burden of proof from allowing development unless it can be shown to be unacceptably damaging, to refusing development unless it can be shown to yield a net benefit. This is pretty fundamental. Might it be applied to other types of development in the future, according to the political pressure of the moment?

The new policy on open-cast is close to the view of some that sustainable development should place the onus on the promoter of a development to demonstrate that it will not harm the environment – and therefore that the general presumption in favour of development means that the planning system is therefore not inherently pro-sustainable development.

The difference is fundamental in theory, but it must be recognised that in the vast majority of planning cases the distinction is likely to be a fine one in practice. The planning system subjects all proposals to environmental scrutiny, routinely asking whether the proposed development would harm the environment. Additionally, in 1988 a regime of formalised environmental impact assessment was added to this scrutiny (see below).

SUMMARY

We have seen that sustainable development is a proposition that looks simple on the surface, but becomes harder to pin down the deeper you dig. There are common themes: leaving the world in at least as good a condition as you found it, which means living off its interest rather than its capital; bearing in mind impacts at wider scales when making local decisions; a sense that quality of life depends on social, economic, and environmental actions being mutually supportive.

But beyond such broad notions it means different things to different people. To some it is people-centred, to others environment-centred. Always ask yourself, when you see the terms sustainable development or sustainability, what is the hidden adverb: is it environmentally, or economically, or socially, or all three? Sustainability, in particular, is often used as shorthand for environmental sustainability, with no consideration of distributional issues implied.

To some it means securing the best deal for the environment while carrying on much as before (weak sustainable development), while for others it means identifying what natural assets can and cannot be traded, and forbidding development that would harm the former (strong sustainable development).

To some the British planning regime's presumption in favour of development (notwithstanding its recent amendment to that which conforms with the Development Plan) is inherently at odds with sustainable development. To others, the scrutiny to which the regime subjects proposals is a major force for sustainable development.

Even within a consistent framework of sustainable development principles, it is often difficult to decide the best course of action, because there may be goal conflicts between dimensions (economic, social, and environmental), between kinds of goal within a dimension (e.g. health of the physical environment versus cultural heritage), and between global, regional, and local scales.

SUSTAINABLE DEVELOPMENT IN CURRENT PLANNING PRACTICE

We have explored the meaning of sustainable development and some of the problems in making the concept operational in the field of planning. We can now turn to look at the tools planners are using to try to implement the concept up and down the planning hierarchy, from national policy through plan-making to development control and development projects. We shall also look at how what planners are doing fits in with what other actors are doing in the pursuit of sustainable development.

NATIONAL PLANNING POLICY

National planning policy is conveyed through ministerial statements, government policy papers ('white papers'), and national planning guidance. It is the last which most closely guides planning decisions from day to day.

The government's first formal commitment to planning for sustainable development was made in its first ever comprehensive white paper on the environment, *This Common Inheritance* (UK Government, 1990). This policy statement appeared with remarkable speed following a famous 'conversion on the road to Damascus' speech by Prime Minister Margaret Thatcher to the Royal Society in the autumn of 1988, in which she espoused the cause of the environment. The white paper's definition of sustainable development was given above in Box 1. The paper under-took to overhaul national planning guidance better to reflect this philosophy, and this was duly done in a flurry of activity.

The key planning guidance note following *This Common Inheritance* was PPG12, *Development Plans and Regional Planning Guidance* (Department of the Environment, 1992; the note has since been revised: Department of the Environment, Transport and the Regions, 1999b). Although it fought shy of explicitly defining sustainable development, it argued that:

> The planning system, and the preparation of development plans in particular, can contribute to the objectives of ensuring that development and growth are sustainable. The sum total of decisions made in the planning field, as elsewhere, should not deny future generations the best of today's environment (para. 1.8).

Chapter 6 of the guidance note went into some depth about the range of environmental concerns that planning authorities should consider, including global warming and the consumption of non-renewable resources.

Sustainable development has since featured ever more prominently in planning guidance, often in the opening paragraph of guidance notes. This is in keeping with background policy, reflected in the publication in January 1994 of a set of four white papers collectively known as the *UK Sustainable Development Strategy* (UK Government, 1994a–d). Each was a response to one of the international agreements made at the United Nations Conference on Environment and Development at Rio de Janeiro, Brazil, in 1992 (see Box 2 for a comment on the international context). They effectively took over from *This Common Inheritance* as a policy platform on which to base specific planning guidance for sustainable development.

It would seem, then, that at least the appearance of commitment to sustainable development is firmly embedded in national policy; but how well is it backed by substance? We can briefly cast an eye over one or two key policy areas, i.e. transport, housing, and aggregates, the first two of which have been taken to the people by Ministers as arenas of public debate.

With regard to transport, we have already highlighted above the importance of curbing traffic growth as an important goal of sustainable development. We also implied that integrating transport and land use planning decisions can contribute to managing the growth of traffic.

The UK has not been a leader in strategic planning to manage traffic growth. For example, it does not have as systematic a policy for matching the transport demand and accessibility profiles of major land uses as do the Netherlands (Amundson, 1995). You have probably heard about celebrated cases of major roads proposals being pushed through against vigorous opposition at the loss of valuable natural sites (e.g. the M3 at Twyford Down and the Newbury bypass).

Nevertheless, there has been a major shift in national policy in the last few years. The *UK Sustainable Development Strategy* (UK Government, 1994a) admitted that unrestrained growth of traffic would lead to unacceptable consequences. In 1994, the Department of Transport was eventually forced to admit what everybody else had long appreciated, that new trunk roads create traffic, when it was told so by its own Standing Advisory Committee on Trunk Road Assessment. The traditional policy of 'predict and provide', which extrapolated current trends in traffic growth and then provided the roads to meet them, is now tempered by acceptance that demand must be managed, and the English trunk road programme has been scaled back. In 1997 a Road Traffic Reduction Act was passed requiring local authorities to set traffic reduction targets. In 1998 a white paper on integrated transport planning *A New Deal for Transport: Better for Everyone* (Department of the Environment, Transport and the Regions, 1998a) marked a leap forward. It heralds a shift to maintaining trunk roads rather than building new ones, and signals regional transport strategies that will be incorporated into regional planning guidance and in turn guide local transport strategies, which will eventually be statutory. Local authorities will be allowed to charge road users for congestion and for private off-road parking. National planning guidance on transport, PPG13 (Department of the Environment, Transport and the Regions, 1999c) has been revised accordingly.

Box 2 *The international policy context for sustainable development*

Some people dismiss the spread of references to sustainable development as tokenism and jumping on the bandwaggon. But we are in truth bound by agreements at the European and United Nations levels which leave us little choice but to follow this path:

- As a member of the European Union Britain is part of a single market, one of whose underpinnings is equality of environmental standards in order to create an even playing field in manufacturing competition. Much of British environmental law is shaped by the need to implement European Union directives. The Union has also recently acquired competence in the field of land use planning. A substantial slice of the public money spent on social and regional development in Britain is channelled through the European structural funds and matching national funds. Those European fund allocations are subject to environmental appraisal for compatibility with the Union's environmental policy *Towards Sustainability* (Commission of the European Communities, 1992).
- The 1992 United Nations Conference on Environment and Development (Earth Summit) was the largest gathering of heads of state the world has ever seen. Britain signed up there to *Agenda 21 for Sustainable Development*, to the biodiversity convention, and to the climate change convention (Grubb *et al.*, 1993). This last commits signatory nations to tackling the greenhouse gas emissions that increase global warming. Such action will

> strike at the very heart of our economic systems. Yet human-induced global warming is not even wholly proven, and its impacts can be only hazily predicted. That represents a stunning penetration of the idea of sustainable development to the very highest levels of power.

The housing debate has centred on the projected demand for new homes in England, currently put at 3.8 million between 1996 and 2016. This is an awesome statistic which, on current trends, would mean a lot more development in small settlements and the open countryside. The previous Tory government required that many of the homes should be built on brownfield (previously built-on) sites, rather than greenfield (undeveloped) sites; in 1995 they said 50% brownfield and in 1996 they said 60%. The present Labour government has, after some vacillation, retained the 60% target (Department of the Environment, Transport and the Regions, 1999d), also floating a possible tax on developing greenfield sites. Most controversially, it said that it would end the 'predict and provide' policy, replacing it with one of 'project, plan, monitor' which is more responsive to local issues that may arise.

Requiring a high proportion of new homes to be built on brownfield sites is claimed to be sustainable because it will reduce new land take, protect small rural settlements and the countryside, reduce travel, and revive our flagging cities – a whole flock of birds with one stone. On the face of it, the argument is compelling. Yet the sustainability of this policy has been questioned on grounds that illustrate the goal conflict between dimensions of sustainable development discussed in the first section (MacDonald, 1997). It has been estimated that 37%–44% of the projected new households will not be able to compete on the open market because they are too poor. Following the inexorable economic law of supply and demand, the scarcer the supply of greenfield land released for housing in desirable rural locations, the higher will be its price.

What then is to prevent the wealthy who can afford to buy their homes being the ones who corner the desirable rural greenfield sites, while the less well off are channelled into rented flats on less desirable urban brownfield sites, exacerbating the existing trend of social segregation? In other words, a spatial policy on its own may achieve *environmental* sustainability by reducing new land take, protecting the countryside, and reducing travel, but you need a parallel social policy on access to housing in order to secure *social* sustainability as well. And, argues MacDonald, the former is not worth much without the latter.

At the opposite end of the sustainable development spectrum from PPG12 and PPG13 lies the planning guidance on aggregate extraction (MPG6, Department of the Environment 1994b). This has been criticised for adopting a fundamentally demand-led rather than demand-management approach, and proposes to export the environmental problem of securing more supplies for the South East of England by creating superquarries in Scotland (see the first section in Chapter 13).

DEVELOPMENT PLANS

Two changes were made to the planning system in 1991 which bear directly on the contribution of Development Plans to sustainable development. First, the Planning and Compensation Act 1991 inserted section 54A in the Town and Country Planning Act 1990, that development control decisions should accord with the Development Plan unless material conditions indicate otherwise. This is known as the plan-led system. Previously, the Plan was just one material consideration among others, whereas now it has primacy.

Second, the Town and Country Planning (Development Plan) Regulations 1991 for the first time statutorily required authorities to have regard to environmental considerations in preparing their general policies and proposals in Structure Plans and Part 1 of Unitary Development Plans. PPG12 (Department of the Environment, 1992) elaborated this to something akin to a requirement that all Development Plans should be subject to environmental appraisal:

> Most policies and proposals in all types of plan will have environmental implications, which should be appraised as part of the plan preparation process (para. 5.52). The outcome of that appraisal should be set out in the explanatory memorandum or reasoned justification for the policies proposed to demonstrate that environmental concerns have been fully integrated into the plan-making process (para. 6.2).

Taken together, these two moves turn the Development Plan into a potentially powerful instrument of environmentally sustainable development. The Department of the Environment subsequently commissioned guidance on the environmental appraisal of Plans (Department of the Environment, 1993), and a growing number of planning authorities are undertaking them. The new PPG11 on regional planning also requires a sustainable development appraisal of the new-style Regional Planning Guidance notes (Department of the Environment, Transport and the Regions, 1999e). [*Note*: You may find the term strategic environmental appraisal or SEA applied to such appraisals. SEA in fact refers to the environment appraisal of any policy, plan or programme, not just statutory Development Plans; for a review of practice, see Therivel, 1996.]

Although each planning authority adopts its own method to suit its circumstances, there appear to be two types of approach. The first, following the Department of the Environment guidance, starts from an assessment of the current *state of the physical environment*, and attempts to quantify what effect the plan will have on this state. Fifteen environmental elements are grouped into global sustainability, natural resources, and local environmental quality. The second approach, piloted in Scotland and favoured there because it is simpler and quicker, starts from a set of environmental *sustainability aims*, and assesses the plan against those.

Both approaches set up matrices, with elements of the environment or sustainability aims along one axis, and plan policies along the other. Each policy is scored against each environment element or sustainability aim, according to whether it is judged that it will improve matters, make no difference, or be harmful. Generally, separate matrices will be set up for the overall plan strategy and each of its major subjects, such as housing or transport (see Figure 1).

Refinements can be added, such as matrices to check that policies in different parts of the plan do not contradict each other, or comparisons with other plans to check that policies have not been left out which would promote sustainable development. An important part of a Local Plan or Part 2 of a Unitary Development Plan is the identification of precise sites for housing. For this reason, Edinburgh City Council and Clackmannan Council included separate exercises using a dedicated set of criteria to identify the most environmentally friendly housing sites from all the possible ones.

When carried out for the first time, such an appraisal may be done at different stages in the plan-making cycle, depending on where in the cycle the council is. The aim thereafter is to incorporate appraisal as a regular part of the plan-making cycle. Kent County Council (1993) appraised its existing 1990 county Structure Plan, the 1992 consultation draft of the plan review, and finally the 1993 deposit version of the review, to be sure that overall environmental performance was improving as the review evolved. It did this by comparing the ratio of policies in each section of the plan judged to produce negative and positive effects on the environment.

You might object that the appraisal method itself is mechanistic, even crude – 'planning by numbers'. On the face of it this is so, but what really matters is the quality of the decision in each cell of a matrix about the effect of a policy on an environmental element or aim, and that is a judgement drawing on the experience and skill of the people making it. The appraisal method is just a way of making sure that those judgements are made, and of organising the results. Edinburgh City Council tried to ensure quality judgements by holding brainstorming sessions involving staff with different expertise, and then backing that up by asking local community representatives whether they agreed with the judgements[1].

DEVELOPMENT CONTROL

It was explained in the previous section that development control now operates within a plan-led system. It follows that the most effective way to contribute to more sustainable development through development control should be to ensure there is an up-to-date plan which has been subjected to environmental appraisal, and to screen development control decisions for their conformity with the plan.

Notwithstanding that, there are additional ways in which the development control process can be used to promote sustainable development. These are:

- environmental impact assessment
- design guidance and design briefs
- planning gain through legal planning agreements.

Policies / Criteria	Global sustainability						Natural Resources				Local Environmental Quality				
	1 Transport energy: Efficiency: trips	2 Transport energy: Efficiency: models	3 Built environment Energy: efficiency	4 Renewable energy potential	5 Rate of CO_2 'fixing'	6 Wildlife habitats	7 Air quality	8 Water conservation and quality	9 Land and soil quality	10 Minerals conservation	11 Landscape and open land	12 Urban environmental 'liveability'	13 Cultural heritage	14 Public access open space	15 Building quality
1 To provide a network for open space corridors	●	✓	●	●	✓	✓	✓	●	✓	●	✓?	✓	✓	✓	●
2 To concentrate residential development on an existing public transport corridor of the city	●	✓	✓	●	●	✓?	✗	●	●	●	✓?	✓	✓?	✗	✓
or															
3 To concentrate residential development on a new rural 'green' settlement (c. 800 pop).	✗	✗	✓	✓?	✓?	✓?	●	✓?	✗	✓?	✗	✓	✓?	✓	✗

Context: District-wide plan for a city of 150 000 and its hinterland
Illustrative properties: 1 For open space. For fuller explanation see Figure 5.5   2 & 3 Represent options for the location of housing

Suggested Impact Symbols

| ● No relationship or insignificant impact | ✗ Significant adverse impact | ✓? Likely, but unpredictable impact | ? Uncertainty of prediction or knowledge | ✓ Significant beneficial impact |

Figure 1 Policy impact matrix for environmental appraisal of Development Plans: worked example. Source: Reproduced with permission from Department of the Environment (1993, Figure 5.4)

Environmental impact assessment (often abbreviated to EIA) is the project-level equivalent of the environmental appraisal of Development Plans described above, and which it preceded in Britain by a number of years. It is a process of predicting the likely impacts on the environment of a proposal, assessing their significance, recommending measures to avoid or at least mitigate them, and proposing a programme to monitor the proposed development, should it go ahead, to check what its impact actually is by comparison with predictions and targets.

It was formalised in a European Community directive (85/337/EEC), interpreted into UK law by the Environmental Assessment Regulations 1988 (following which it was referred to in the UK as environmental assessment, rather than environmental impact assessment). The regulations identified certain types of project which must be subject to an assessment submitted by the developer to the planning authority along with the planning application, and identified other types of projects for which the planning authority *may* require an assessment if it thinks the impacts would be significant. The UK government resisted the introduction of formal assessment on the grounds that the UK discretionary planning system pre-empts the need for it, because each proposal is judged on its merits anyway, and because, as the government thought, too few assessments would be required to justify another layer of bureaucracy.

In the event, over 200 such assessments are now made annually under the planning acts. Their quality, the ability of planners to interpret them and assess their worth, and the details of the process, all continue to be criticised nearly a decade after the regulations came into force (David Tyldesley and Associates, 1996; Department of the Environment, 1996; Glasson *et al.*, 1997; Thompson *et al.*, 1997). Yet those same critics would acknowledge that environmental assessments have proved an important tool not only for screening the environmental acceptability of particular proposals, but also for raising the environmental awareness and ultimately knowledge of planners in development control.

A revised directive was issued in 1997 (97/11/EC) and was implemented in 1999. Amongst other things, this introduces thresholds below which certain types of development will *not* require assessment. There is an enormous literature on environmental impact assessment (e.g. Glasson *et al.*, 1994; Wood, 1995), and you can find more about it in the first section of Chapter 13 in the context of minerals planning.

Design guidance for developers is another potentially powerful tool for promoting sustainable built development. A wide ranging good practice guide to environmentally sustainable design of settlements is Barton *et al.* (1995). Design guidance produced by planning authorities, which is supplementary to but not included in the Development Plan, lacks statutory force, but can still be a material consideration in deciding an application (PPG12, Department of the Environment, 1992, paras. 3.18–3.19). Examples of 'green' design guidance are those of Stockport Metropolitan Council (1991) and the Sutton London Borough Council (undated). The latter asks whether proposals

- minimise loss of green space
- minimise loss of and damage to historic buildings and archaeological sites
- favour a high degree of local recycling of water and permeability of the ground
- green-up the site as much as possible
- consider the wider environmental implications of materials used
- improve energy efficiency of new buildings and encouraging use of renewable sources of energy
- minimise noise and pollution arising from new development
- encourage the recycling of materials and reduce the waste stream
- minimise the use of unsuitable chemicals and ensure proper handling of hazardous materials
- assist bicycling in the borough
- improve access and facilities for people with disabilities.

There is, however, a limit to how much planning authorities can require of developers. If a planning authority tries to insert in a Development Plan a policy that is perceived by developers as burdensome and that is not clearly supported in relevant legislation or in national planning guidance, then it will be objected to and have to be deleted. Likewise, if an authority seeks to impose upon an unwilling developer a condition attached to the planning permission which is not clearly supported by the Development Plan, then the developer can appeal against it and is likely to win. The authority could not, for example, expect to *impose* higher energy efficiency standards than are required by the building regulations. The planning authority may sometimes be able to secure what it wants through a legal planning agreement made with the developer and attached to the permission to develop. What can be gained by this route is however limited, e.g. some form of compensation elsewhere for environmental damage resulting from the development.

Where the local authority has control over the land, then it is in a much more powerful position and can write a design brief specifying what it wants. For example, a design brief can require a certain social mix in a residential development so as not to add to social segregation. It can require energy efficient architecture. It can also steer the transport behaviour of site users towards environmentally friendly modes, through control of parking spaces and provision of walking and cycling facilities and links to public transport. There are even examples of major site redevelopments in which occupiers are bound by legal planning agreement not to own cars; an example exists in Bremen, Germany, and it is intended for a site in central Edinburgh from which a large hospital is to be moved.

An example of what can be achieved under a green brief is Red Cottage in Calcot, Reading (Tobin and Bailey, 1995). Here a stylish, energy efficient development of 41 affordable homes for rent was built in a partnership between Reading and Newbury Councils, Toynbee Housing Association, and the Housing Corporation. Energy efficiency was achieved through site selection, lay-out and orientation to allow the architectural design to take advantage of passive solar gain (Figure 2).

Figure 2 *An energy-efficient house near Carrbridge, Northeast Scotland. Reproduced by permission of Marilyn Higgins*

These sorts of issues are addressed further within the wider role of planning in design in Chapter 12. If you are interested in 'green' architecture, the work of Brenda and Robert Vale is a good place to start (Vale and Vale, 1991a, b).

PLANNING, CORPORATE ENVIRONMENTAL MANAGEMENT AND LOCAL AGENDA 21

We have focused above on Development Plans and development control because these are the core statutory activities of planning authorities, and on national planning guidance because it guides these activities. Planning authorities are however involved in all sorts of other plan-making and project implementation work, often in partnership with other units of a local authority or with external organisations. They differ from most local authority services in having a broader overview of local life: they are not concerned with, say, cleansing or social services alone. Because of this, they often play an important role in making corporate policy across all functions of the authority.

This multi-faceted role is evident in the field of sustainable development, and the greening of Development Plans and development control described above is often just part of a web of such initiatives in the authority, in most of which the planners are likely to be involved.

In the mid-1980s a few local authorities began concerted efforts to raise their environmental performance across all their functions in a coordinated manner, and beyond that to promote better care of the environment by others in the communities they serve. The subsequent evolution of this movement has been so rapid that one seems to be in the next phase before the last has barely begun. One can define four phases.

Phase 1 saw the appearance of *environmental charters* and *environmental action programmes* in the late 1980s. Charters are general principles to guide action on environmental issues (e.g. 'This council recognises the threat of global warming and undertakes to promote the efficient use of energy'); action programmes identify practical actions to implement those principles. Phase 2 saw *environmental audits* and *state of the environment reports* added in the early 1990s. Audits are reviews of the environmental performance of the local authority's own operations and services. State of the environment reports seek to measure and assess the significance of the condition of the environment in the territory of the local authority. Phase 3, from 1993, added externally verified *environmental management systems*, formal documented systems of monitoring and improving the organisation's environmental performance (two systems are current: EMAS, the European Union Environmental Management and Audit System, and BS7750, an environmental version of the British Standards Institute quality assurance standard BS5750; Department of the Environment, 1995; these are themselves now being superseded by the international standard ISO 14001). The mid-1990s saw Phase 4, *Local Agenda 21*, which we discuss in more detail below.

Three features of this evolution merit mention. First, it has been driven by local rather than central government; indeed, local government has been pushing Whitehall to catch up. Second, the voluntary sector has also been an important driver, especially Friends of the Earth. In 1989 they bump-started environmental charters by drawing up a model, containing 193 useful actions which an authority could take to protect and improve the environment, and circulating it to all local authorities (Friends of the Earth, 1989). Third, you may already have spotted that it has largely been about the environment, that is, the physical and biological environment, rather than more broadly about sustainable development, embracing social and economic considerations.

The focus on the physical has widened to include the social and economic with the arrival of Local Agenda 21, though to what extent varies between authorities. Local Agenda 21 is the process of developing local policies for sustainable development and building partnerships between local authorities and other sectors to implement them (Local Government Management Board, 1994). It is a product of the 1992 Rio Earth Summit (see Box 2). The central document agreed at that summit, *Agenda 21*, required that most local authorities in each country should by 1996 have initiated the process of drawing up a *Local* Agenda 21 (United Nations, 1992, chapter 28).

The *goal* of Local Agenda 21 is to move towards sustainable development, therefore in terms of its content it is integrative, seeking to break down barriers between sectors in both public and private life. It is not a one-off event, but rather a continuing *process*. The nature of that process is crucial. It is founded on an ethic of including everyone as equally as possible to arrive at consensus on what to do. Hence it tries to get around the barriers that exclude so many people in practice from existing processes of local governance, including the Development Plan system. It tries to be bottom-up, inclusive, participative, and open to scrutiny. It is therefore radical, yet it is not subversive. While its very existence is an admission that established systems of local governance cannot of themselves deliver sustainable development, it is not at all political, and tries to supplement rather than supplant the Establishment. Indeed, this is inevitable, since it is driven by the local authorities.

How then do you set about identifying the issues, representing all sectors of society in debating them, and managing a process that arrives at consensus on action? This is a lot to ask! The local authority, as facilitator, must first put its own house in order, both to be effective and to be credible to others in the community. The initiative must have political backing in the authority – so it must include elected councillors as well as officers. The initiative must be owned by as many staff in the authority as possible – so the message must be actively spread and ordinary staff must feel they can affect outcomes. The initiative must be corporate – so the structure must cut across functions in order that it is not seen to be the province of only some units and others therefore feel they do not have to act.

Then structures and processes must be set up to reach out to the rest of the authority's community. A range of methods are practised, from traditional consultation on draft plans, public meetings, through fora bringing together representatives from different interests, round tables and focus groups, to 'visioning' (Parfitt, 1996), 'planning for real' exercises (Neighbourhood Initiatives Foundation, 1985) and getting people to produce 'parish maps' researching and depicting their view of their local world (Crouch and Hennessey, 1996). Finally, the processes internal and external to the authority must be linked to each other, and to a whole range of outputs, including of course town planning documents and decisions.

One useful tool for engaging the public and ensuring that the local authority is focusing on the issues that people think are important is the *sustainability indicator*. Most people are not familiar with the idea of sustainable development, which (as you will have discovered by now.) is difficult to pin down. Rather than trying to reach agreement on what sustainable development is, you can take a short cut and ask people to identify specific, measurable aspects of their living environment which to them indicate its health. Then you can try to put in place actions that will push the indicators up rather than down.

The example of one council, Fife, illustrates how the various threads of sustainable development activity in a local authority are bound together, and how they relate to the planning process (see Box 3). Fife is relatively forward-looking in

42
—

this field, but many other authorities are active (Lancashire County, Leicester City, and the London Borough of Sutton are well publicised examples). A survey in 1996 found that 90% of local authorities had made a commitment to Local Agenda 21. In 75%, respondents reckoned that sustainable development principles were now a major influence on land use planning. Over a third of authorities were working with their communities to develop sustainability indicators. Is it having an effect? Respondents considered that it is on the physical environment, but much less so on the socioeconomic environment, reflecting the extent of local control over different spheres of life (Tuxworth, 1996).

SUMMARY

Sustainable development has permeated national planning policy statements since 1990. This amounts to more than token references, with a wholesale overhaul of planning guidance to reflect the new thinking to a greater or lesser degree. A glance at two prominent arenas of debate as test cases, transport and housing, indicates both some progress and some problems. Transport policy has begun to exhibit a move away from a demand-led to a demand-management approach, despite high profile cases of trunk roads being built at the expense of valuable natural sites. The debate over where to put the millions of houses that will be demanded over the next 20 years, however, shows up a possible conflict of goals between minimising travel and preventing spatial segregation by wealth.

The at least partial orientation of new planning guidance towards sustainable development is echoed farther down the planning hierarchy in the application of environmental appraisal to Development Plans and of environmental impact assessment in development control, and the appearance of design guidance and briefs promoting environmentally friendly building.

Beyond statutory roles, the planning system is positively engaged in a range of regional and local level activities, which have evolved over the last decade from improving local authorities' environmental performance to a broader and more outward-looking quest for sustainable local development.

Box 3 *Fife Council's sustainable development activities*

Listed below are the council's sustainable development activities identifed by one of its planning staff (McGregor, 1996). As you go through the list, identify how they relate to the items described above:

- Fife's Charter for the Environment, first produced in 1991, and rolled forward through a series of annual action programmes.
- Partnership in EMAS: a European Union funded project launched in 1993 jointly with three local authorities in Scotland, Denmark and Ireland to develop application of the EMAS environmental management system.

- The Sustainable Development Policy, written by planners as a council corporate document in 1994: this was not tied to specific action plans, so was largely ignored by staff other than planners.
- The Sustainability Indicators Project 1995: piloted in three communities, and a stern reminder of some home truths about ordinary people being more interested in their quality of life than global warming, and public involvement depending on visible benefits to participants. Nineteen indicators were grouped under the headings of basic needs, such as rate of homelessness (worsening); community, such as nursery education (improving); quality of the environment, such as air quality (inconclusive); and use of resources, such as household waste (inconclusive).
- The Sustainable Fife Round Table: a standing forum bringing together different interests at the level of the whole authority territory, which first met in autumn 1996.
- Local Agenda 21 Framework set up by the new unitary council in 1996: the structure which binds together the internal and external processes (Figure 3).

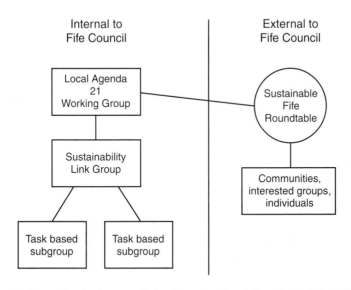

Figure 3 *Example of a framework for delivering Local Agenda 21: Fife, 1996. Because of the changing operating context of local government, the particulars of any such framework, including this one, are liable to change. Nevertheless, this serves as a generic example. Source: Fife Council, reproduced with permission*

CONCLUSIONS

HOW IS PLANNING PERFORMING?

Hall *et al.* (1993) look back at the performance of the British planning system since 1947 through the eyes of sustainable development. They judge it to have achieved the policy goals of the 1940s, particularly the demarcation of town from country and the protection of designated areas of natural heritage. But they judge it to have been far less successful in evolving to address the modern concerns of sustainable development. They argue that it has not been able to tackle the loss of natural heritage and loss of people from the land resulting from the modernisation of agriculture; that it has largely failed to fulfil its potential to mitigate pollution; and that it has not curbed the massive growth of motorised personal transport.

Hall *et al.* are however not condemning town and country planning. What they are pointing out is that its potential beyond the role to which it has been confined is not being fulfilled because of the failure to *integrate* policy *across* these sectors, each of which has been the territory of a separate governmental regime. Each may have been successful in its own terms, but has failed to take account of its effects on the others. Without such integration, they argue, you are most unlikely to produce sustainable development other than by chance.

But policy is now evolving fast and we can already see advances, even in the few years elapsed since Hall *et al.* wrote. The previous section has shown how 'sustainability thinking' is permeating the planning regime from top to bottom, and it has illustrated how planning is interacting with other regimes at the local level in seeking to promote sustainable development. Sustainability thinking is also a force for integration of policy at higher levels because it provides not only a common ethic but even specific common targets. For example, the government's programme for meeting the national target for curbing CO_2 emissions is to be met by mutually supportive actions of widely differing types in all sectors – transport, the home, business, and the public sector – with planning contributing at several points as facilitator or regulator (Department of the Environment, Transport and the Regions, 1999f).

BUT IS IT ANYTHING NEW?

I recall being interviewed for a very modest grant to research sustainable development activity in local authorities. Opposite me sat a venerable figure, universally held to be one of the finest and most effective planners this country has produced. As I explained the object of my proposal, his face showed pain, and he interjected: 'Then what on earth do you think we have been doing for the *last* fifty years?'

The answer to that question depends on your interpretation of sustainable development. If your interpretation stops at weak sustainable development, trying to negotiate the best deal for the environment in a world where everything is in principle tradeable, then you could convincingly argue that planning has always been about that. But if for you sustainable development must be strong to be anything at all, accepting a world in which there are ultimate limits to development set by the capacity of natural life support systems, then there really is a new planning game in town.

Merrett (1994) points to this difference between traditional planning thought and strong sustainability thinking by considering one of the icons of British planning thought: Ebenezer Howard's social city concept, put forward at the turn of the century. In several ways, Howard's ideas resonate closely with modern ones at the local and sub-regional scales. His scheme for a core city surrounded by satellite towns, interspersed with fields and linked by public transport corridors, is intended to equalise land values, to get people away from pollution, to bring them within reach of green spaces and close to the sources of the farm produce they consume, to reduce travel time and cost, even to recycle organic urban wastes as compost in the surrounding fields.

Yet Howard explicitly sees the abundance of nature as an inexhaustible asset, makes no reference to the conservation of nature, and none to the depletion of non-renewable resources such as land, fossil fuels, and minerals – issues that lie at the heart of today's sustainability discussions. He shows plenty of concern for social equity and for the quality of the *local* environment, but no *global* consciousness. As we saw at the start of this chapter, thinking global may indicate a different planning decision locally.

NOTE

1. Environmental appraisals are now being widened to sustainability appraisals including socio-economic aspects (Department of the Environment, Transport and the Regions 1998b, ch. 6; City of Edinburgh Council and Midlothian Council, 1999).

REFERENCES

Amundson, C.R. (1995) Right business, right place – simple as ABC? *Town and Country Planning*, **64**(1), 22–25.

Barton, H., Davis, G. and Guise, R. (1995) *Sustainable Settlements. A Guide For Planners, Designers And Developers*, University of the West of England and Local Government Management Board, Bristol and Luton.

CAG Consultants and Land Use Consultants (1997) *What Matters and Why. Environmental Capital: A New Approach. A Provisional Guide*, Report to the Countryside Commission, English Heritage, English Nature and the Environment Agency, Countryside Commission, Cheltenham.

City of Edinburgh Council and Midlothian Council (1999) Sustainability Appraisal of the South East Wedge Joint Development Study, Edinburgh.

46
___

Cockburn Association (1997) Retail development in Edinburgh and the Princes Street Gallery Proposal, *The Cockburn Association Newsletter*, **43**, 4–9.

Coles, R. and Taylor, J. (1993) Wind power and planning, *Land Use Policy*, **July**, 205–226.

Commission of the European Communities (1992) *Towards Sustainaiblity. A European Community Programme of Policy and Action in Relation the Environment and Sustainable Development* ('5th Action Programme'). COM(92) 23 Final – vol. 2, The Commission, Brussels.

Crouch, D. and Hennessey, N. (1996) Local knowledge, community maps and empowerment, *Ecos*, **16**(3/4), 39–43.

David Tyldesley and Associates (1996) *The Treatment of Nature Conservation in Environmental Assessment*, Royal Society for the Protection of Birds, Sandy, Bedfordshire.

Department of the Environment (1992) PPG12 *Development Plans and Regional Planning Guidance*, HMSO, London.

Department of the Environment (1993) *Environmental Appraisal of Development Plans. A Good Practice Guide*, HMSO, London.

Department of the Environment (1994a) PPG13, *Transport*, HMSO, London.

Department of the Environment (1994b) MPG6, *Aggregates*, HMSO, London.

Department of the Environment (1995) Circular 2/95, *The Voluntary Eco-management and Audit Scheme (EMAS) For Local Government*, HMSO, London.

Department of the Environment (1996) Changes in the Quality of Environmental Statements for Planning Projects.

Department of the Environment, Scottish Office and Welsh Office (1997) *The UK National Air Quality Strategy*, HMSO, London.

Department of the Environment, Transport and the Regions (1998a) *A New Deal for Transport: Better for Everyone*, HMSO, London.

Department of the Environment, Transport and the Regions (1998b) *Planning for Sustainable Development: Towards Better Practice*, HMSO, London.

Department of the Environment, Transport and the Regions (1999a) *A Better Quality of Life*, HMSO, London.

Department of the Environment, Transport and the Regions (1999b) PPG12 *Development Plans*, HMSO, London.

Department of the Environment, Transport and the Regions (1999c) PPG13 *(Revised) Transport*, HMSO, London.

Department of the Environment, Transport and the Regions (1999d) *Planning for the Communities of the Future*, HMSO, London.

Department of the Environment, Transport and the Regions (1999e) PPG11 *Regional Planning*, HMSO, London.

Department of the Environment, Transport and the Regions (1999f) *Tackling Climate Change*, HMSO, London.

Friends of the Earth (1989) *The Environmental Charter for Local Government*, FoE.

Glasson, J., Therivel, R. and Chadwick, A. (1994) *An Introduction to Environmental Impact Assessment*, University College London, London.

Glasson, J., Therivel, R., Weston, J., Wilson, E. and Frost, R. (1997) EIA – learning from experience: changes in the quality of environmental impact statements for UK planning projects, *Journal Environmental Planning and Management*, **40**(4), 451–464.

Grubb, M. *et al.* (1993) *The Earth Summit Agreements. A Guide and Assessment*, Royal Institute of International Affairs/Earthscan, London.

Hall, D., Hebbert, M. and Lusser, H. (1993) The planning background, in: Blowers, A. (ed.), *Planning for a Sustainable Environment. A Report by the Town and Country Planning Association*, Earthscan, London, pp. 19–29.

Kent County Council (1993) Methodology of strategic environmental appraisal of the third review of the Kent Structure Plan, Working Paper, The Council, Maidstone.

Local Government Management Board (1994) *Local Agenda 21 Principles and Processes. A Step by Step Guide*, The Board, Luton.

MacDonald, K. (1997) Where shall *who* live? *EG*, **3**(3), 9–10.

Merrett, S. (1994) New age of planning, *Town and Country Planning*, **June**, 164–165.

McGregor, D. (1996) The Fife experience with sustainability indicators and the incorporation of sustainability principles into Structure Plan preparation, Paper to seminar on The Role of Development Plans in Achieving Sustainable Development, Edinburgh College of Art/ Heriot-Watt University, 11 October 1996.

Neighbourhood Initiatives Foundation (1985) *Planning for Real*, The Foundation, Telford.

Owens, S. (1993) The good, the bad and the ugly: dilemmas in planning for sustainability, *Town Planning Review*, **64**(2), iii–vi.

Parfitt, A. (1996) What is this visioning business? *Ecos*, **17**(3/4), 36–41.

Pearce, D., Markandya, A. and Barbier, E. (1989) *Blueprint for a Green Economy*, Earthscan, London.

Roger Tym and Partners (1996) *The Gyle Impact Study*, Sottish Office, Edinburgh.

Stockport Metropolitan Council (1991) *The Green Development Guide: New Housing*, The Council, Stockport.

Sutton London Borough Council (undated) *Environmental Awareness and Building. A Checklist To Be Used With All Construction Work In The London Borough Of Sutton*, The Council, London.

Tewdwr-Jones, M. (1994) The Government's planning policy guidance, *Journal of Planning and Environment Law*, **February**, 106–116.

Therivel, R. (1996) *The Practice of Strategic Environmental Appraisal*, Earthscan, London.

Thompson, S., Treweek, J. and Thurling, D. (1997) The ecological component of environment impact assessment: a critical review of British environmental statements, *Journal of Environmental Planning and Management*, **40**(2), 157–171.

Tobin, L. and Bailey, N. (1995) *Red Cottage*, in: National Housing and Town Planning Council, *Energy Efficient Design*, The Council, London, p. 9.

Tuxworth, B. (1996) Local Agenda 21 progress in the UK, *EG*, **2**(5), 8–11.

UK Government (1990) *This Common Inheritance. Britain's Environmental Strategy*. Cm 1200, HMSO, London.

UK Government (1994a) *Sustainable Development: The UK Strategy*, Cm 2426, HMSO, London.

UK Government (1994b) *Climate change: The UK Programme*, Cm 2427, HMSO, London.

UK Government (1994c) *Biodiversity: The UK Action Plan*, Cm 2428, HMSO, London.

UK Government (1994d) *Sustainable Forestry: the UK Programme*, Cm 2429, HMSO, London.

United Nations (1992) *Agenda 21: An Agenda for Sustainable Development into the 21st Century and Beyond*, United Nations Association.

Vale, R. and Vale, B. (1991a) *Towards a Green Architecture. Six Practical Case Studies*, RIBA, London.

Vale, B. and Vale, R. (1991b) *Green Architecture. Design for a Sustainable Future*, Thames & Hudson, London.

Wood, C. (1995) *Environmental Impact Assessment: A Comparative Review*, Longman, Harlow.

World Commission on Environment and Development (1987) *Our Common Future*, Oxford University Press, Oxford.

CHAPTER 3

DEVELOPMENT PLANS

Alan Prior

INTRODUCTION

This chapter explores the role of development plans as a main component of the town and country planning system in the UK. It looks at their scope and purposes, and how these have changed since the first introduction of comprehensive plans 50 years ago. It considers how and why they have changed, looks at current practices, problems and issues. It illustrates practice through cases of plan preparation, public participation, and plan review, including tackling sustainable development. It concludes with an exploration of current issues, and how development plans might change in the near future.

PLANS AND PLANNING

The spatial land-use plan covering all or part of the territorial area of a local authority has been an integral part of the statutory town and country planning framework in Britain. The first powers to produce statutory plans were introduced incrementally during the inter-war period, but it was not until the passing of the first comprehensive Town and Country Planning Act in 1947 that it became a requirement on all local planning authorities to achieve comprehensive development plan coverage of their areas. The principal mechanisms for the delivery of the objectives of the planning system have therefore been, for the last 50 years or so, the development plan and development control. Although most people's experience with the planning system is through development control – either applying for or making representations about proposed development – control in accordance with a statutory plan has been, and continues to be, the basic tenet of the system.

Development Plans are intended to set out the main considerations on which planning applications are decided and to guide a range of other responsibilities of local government and other agencies. They are also intended to contain the local planning authority's policies and proposals for the development and use of land. While the Town and Country Planning Acts set out the statutory requirements on planning authorities for plan preparation, content and coverage, more detailed regulations specify, for example, minimum requirements for consultation and participation during the preparation of the plan. In drawing up development plans for their areas, local authorities are required by the Town and Country Planning

Acts and associated Regulations to take into account (Department of the Environment, 1992a):

- current national policies
- any regional or strategic guidance given by the Secretary of State
- resources likely to be available for the implementation of the plan
- social, economic and environmental considerations.

Within this national policy context, development plans have a wide variety of purposes, as Box 1 shows.

Box 1 *Major purposes of development plans*

- To indicate how the local planning authority envisages its geographical area developing in future, bearing in mind social, economic and environmental issues.
- To ensure that the provision of essential infrastructure (e.g. roads, sewers) is coordinated with land development.
- To ensure coordination and compatibility between plans at different spatial scales, and in adjoining districts.
- To coordinate the provision of major development (e.g. houses with shops and employment land).
- To provide a clear framework for development control decisions and guidance to those proposing development.
- To provide some certainty to those seeking planning permission and those seeking to maintain their local environment and amenity.
- To safeguard the cultural and natural heritage (e.g. green belts and conservation areas).
- To act as promotional documents indicating locations of development opportunities.
- To steer development onto land most suited to it.
- To provide vision and a sense of place for inhabitants and existing and potential investors.
- To devise policies at an appropriate level of detail.
- To implement national and regional planning policies.

Source: adapted from Thomas (1997).

Since the 1960s, debates in the UK around the value of plans and plan-making processes in planning have centred around different ideas about what form a plan should take. This depends on whether plans should concentrate on guiding future land-use change, spelling out in detail what the future form of a place should look like, the extent to which it should consider social and economic (as well as land use and environmental) matters, or whether it should have a strictly geographical or policy-specific focus. For example, should the statutory plan be:

- A two-dimensional representation of the preferred physical lay-out of a geographical area?
- A general, comprehensive policy plan for the guidance and control of development over a rolling time period (usually 5–15 years)?
- A blueprint for the ultimate end state following a period of rapid comprehensive development?
- A sector-based policy plan, such as for economic development, housing, waste management, mineral development or transport?
- A procedural tool used by government agencies as an element of programmes for intervening in the way land is used and developed?

SCOPE AND PURPOSES OF STATUTORY DEVELOPMENT PLANS IN THE UK

Development plans produced in the British context have distinctive characteristics. They can be regarded as *guidance frameworks* intended to *co-ordinate* and *regulate* the activities of a range of development agencies in the public and private sectors. They are not zoning plans of the kind found in the US. They are quasi-legal policy-based plans, not the full legally binding plans found in continental Europe, in countries like Germany. Although land may be allocated for specified preferred uses, landowners have no right to develop land without first obtaining planning permission. Since the first comprehensive Town and Country Planning Act in 1947, planning authorities have normally made planning decisions in accordance with the provisions of the plan, but are not bound to do so, since there are provisions for legitimising departures from plans.

British development plans are not general social and economic development plans either (though they are expected to base their land-use policies and proposals on a survey of the social and economic characteristics of their areas), nor are they principally mechanisms for co-ordinating the overall investment of public authorities. According to Healey (1983, pp. 45–46)

> development plans were thus to provide principles for translating such policy into spatial allocations and detailed development, co-ordinate the public sector development effort, and indicate the basis on which small scale private development would be regulated. In effect, the plan was both to provide a *rationale*, demonstrating that public sector decisions were not arbitrary, and *a tool* for efficient management.

In the British context, therefore, development plans are not *prescriptive*, in the sense that development that conforms to the plan is lawful, while development that does not conform is not (as in many other planning systems). They are *indicative*, in the sense that the plans do not confer development rights (i.e. planning permission) but each planning application is treated on its merits, in the context of what the plan says. British development plans also have *legal procedural* and *preparation* dimensions, as shown in Box 2.

Box 2 *Stages in plan-making*	
Procedural stages	Preparation in practice
• Declaration of intention to prepare a plan • Publication of consultative draft plan • Publication of finalised plan • Public Inquiry or other Hearing into objections • Proposed modifications to the plan • Adoption of the plan	• Surveys and studies of the plan area to identify issues • Analysis of issues and objectives and generation of alternative solutions • Selection of the preferred plan • Implementation • Continuous monitoring, followed by periodic review • Plan replacement

Plan-making has been generally regarded as a central component of the planning process, and a key means of devising and delivering planning policies for the improvement of the environment, the management of traffic, and the conservation of the natural beauty and amenity of the land (Town and Country Planning Act 1990). With concerns about environmental pollution and congestion in cities, and global warming, plans can be a means of setting out long-term strategies for providing more sustainable patterns of development. In terms of democratic processes, plans provide opportunities for people to have their say in decisions that affect their environments and access to opportunities such as decent housing, employment, social, health and educational facilities, transport, and their overall co-ordination. It is through plans that we can define, argue, and (hopefully) agree about our desired environments and patterns of land use in the future, and make orderly arrangements for getting there.

EVOLUTION OF DEVELOPMENT PLANS

The 1947 Town and Country Planning Act established comprehensive development planning for the UK. The Act defined a 'development plan' as a plan 'indicating the manner in which the local planning authority propose that land in their area should be used'. The plans that resulted were essentially detailed land allocation maps that provided the basis for the control of development. The original definition, as set out in the first draft of the Bill, was 'a plan indicating the general principles upon which development in (the) area will be promoted and controlled'. The emphasis in this definition is on general principles, rather than the precision of detailed land allocations, and on the promotion, as well as the control, of development.

Plans prepared under this Act consisted of a Report of Survey, a short summary of the main proposals (but with no reasoned argument or justification to support them) and detailed maps at various scales, indicating development proposals for a 20-year period, an intended pattern of land use, together with a programme of stages by which the plan would be realised over this period. The plans were approved by the responsible Minister (with or without changes) following a local Public Inquiry. Any significant departures from the approved plan similarly required Ministerial approval. In practice, these plans took years to prepare and approve, and were quickly out of date. They also took a very long time to review and update, and most were in effect not updated from their initial versions.

The requirement for determining and mapping land uses produced spurious detail and precision. Plans became bogged down in detail and procedure, and quickly out of tune with contemporary circumstances and development pressures. This system of development plans was replaced by the current system after a mid-1960s review by a Planning Advisory Group (PAG) appointed by the Minister of Housing and Local Government. The PAG Report, as it became known, concluded that development plans had 'acquired the appearance of certainty and stability which is misleading . . . it is impossible to forecast every land requirement over many years ahead' (Ministry of Housing and Local Government, 1965, p. 5). In particular, PAG concluded that it had proved extremely difficult to keep plans up to date, forward looking, and responsive to change. Accordingly, it proposed a radical reappraisal of the form and function of development plans and a redistribution of responsibility for them between central and local government. In PAG's vision, plans should be statements of policy rather than expressions of preferred detailed distributions of land use. PAG's proposed system of broad strategic (or 'structure') plans and local 'tactical' plans, is the basis of the present system, and was effectively implemented with the establishment of new planning authorities after local government reorganisation in the mid 1970s.

Healey (1983) suggests that the revised development plan system, as advocated by PAG and enacted in the 1968 (1969 in Scotland) Act, was an attempt to recover the capacity to link the guidance of land development to broader social and economic policy. The two-tier hierarchy of plans was aimed at achieving both more central direction over policy and more local discretion over detailed implementation of these policies. Structure Plans would require Ministerial approval, but not Local Plans, which could be approved by the local planning authority provided it conformed to the approved Structure Plan. Plans were to demonstrate clearly the rationale (or 'reasoned justification') for policies which it was expected would be implemented substantially by private sector developers.

During the 1980s the planning system in general came under review by a government suspicious of the benefits of planning's intervention in markets for land use and development. As part of this review, Structure Plans were initially proposed for abolition (Department of the Environment, 1984). Instead, the government abolished Structure Plans and Local Plans in the English metropolitan regions, as part of the dismantling of the regional tier of government in these areas, leaving borough councils in sole charge of the planning function. In their place, from 1986 the metropolitan borough councils were required to prepare Unitary Development Plans (UDPs), which would combine, in one plan, the strategic features of the Structure Plan, and the tactical features of the Local Plan. Outside metropolitan England, the two-tier system of structure plans and local plans remained in place (though as part of local government reorganisation in Wales, establishing unitary councils, these councils would also prepare UDPs) (see Box 3).

Box 3 *Purposes of current types of UK statutory development plans and who prepares them*

Structure Plans
- assist implementation of national and regional policy
- indicate policies and proposals concerning the scale and general location of new development
- provide a regional policy framework for accommodating development
- take account of current and emerging national issues
- provide a strategic framework for Local Plans and major planning applications
- are prepared by Shire Counties in England and Unitary Councils in Scotland.

Local Plans
- assist implementation of national and regional policy
- assist implementation of the Structure Plan
- set out detailed policies and specific proposals for the use of land
- provide a policy framework for development control
- provide guidance for public and private sector investment
- are prepared by Districts in England and Unitary Councils in Scotland.

Unitary Development Plans
- combine the purposes of Structure Plans in Part 1 (the framework of general policies and proposals) and Local Plans in Part 2 (detailed policies and proposals)
- include Minerals and waste policies
- are prepared by London Boroughs, Metropolitan Councils in England, and Unitary Councils in Wales.

STRUCTURE PLANS

The term 'structure plan' originated in the PAG report and reflects the essentially physical view of urban areas by its authors. Two types of strategic plan were identified: urban structure plans and county structure plans. Such plans were to 'emphasise the broad structure of the town and policies, objectives and standards, rather than in detailed and static land use allocation' (Ministry of Housing and Local Government, 1965, para. 2.5). The term 'structure plan' was transferred directly into the legislation. By 1970, when central government produced *Development Plans: A Manual on Form and Content* (Ministry of Housing and Local Government, 1970), 'structure' had come to mean

> the social, economic and physical systems of an area, so far as they are subject to planning control or influence. The structure is, in effect, the planning framework for an area and includes such matters as the distribution of the population, the activities and the relationships between them, the pattern of land use and development the activities give rise to, together with the network of activities and the systems of utility services (Ministry of Housing and Local Government, 1970, para. 3.6).

Figure 1 shows what the PAG Report intended the representation of a spatial strategy for a 'county structure plan' area to look like. It was intended to be diagrammatic, rather than site specific. Compare this with Figure 2, which shows the actual spatial strategy for the structure plan for the Edinburgh city region (Lothian Regional Council, 1985). The same approach was intended for wholly urban areas. The emphasis was on encouraging strategic thinking about the inter-relationships involved in producing a spatial development strategy, and to address the criticisms of the narrow and prescriptive focus in development plans produced under the 1947 Act.

Structure Plans cover large areas, usually the whole of a County in England, city region or extensive rural area in Scotland. They set out the broad land-use strategy for a 10–15 year period ahead. They provide the framework of strategic policy and direction for local planning and development control. They are prepared after widespread public consultation, and usually after a public hearing (Examination in Public). In Scotland, they are subject to the final approval, with or without modification, by the Secretary of State. There is now complete Structure Plan coverage of the whole of the UK.

LOCAL PLANS

Local Plans are concerned with the detailed distribution of land uses and specific policies to guide the day-to-day determination of planning applications. In this, they are intended to be a principal means of implementing the wider spatial

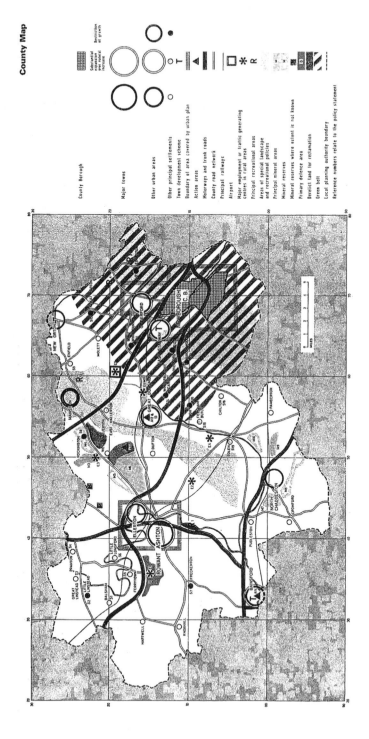

Figure 1 *A key diagram for a County Structure Plan, the new style of plans proposed in 'The Future of Development Plans', the report of the Planning Advisory Group, Ministry of Housing and Local Government 1965. Crown copyright is reproduced with the permission of the Controller of Her Majesty's Stationery Office*

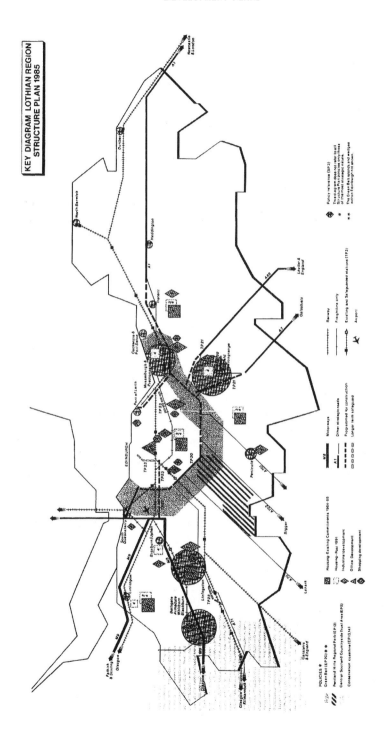

Figure 2   Key diagram, Lothian Structure Plan, written statement, Lothian Regional Council, 1985

development strategy as set out in the Structure Plan. Local Plans cover a period of 5–10 years ahead, are subject to widespread public consultation, and show what is proposed for individual sites and areas over the short/medium term. They are much more specific than Structure Plans, in that they should set out policies and proposals for specific sites or well-defined geographical areas. Figure 3 is an example of the Proposals Map for a statutory local plan. Compare this with the Structure Plan Key Diagram in Figure 2. Unlike in a Structure Plan Key Diagram, in a Local Plan Proposals Map it *should* be possible to identify individual sites and the boundaries of specific areas to which policies or proposals apply.

The preparation of Local Plans for all parts of the UK is now mandatory (since 1975 in Scotland and 1990 in England and Wales). These plans are District-wide in England (i.e. one Local Plan to cover a whole Council area) while in Scotland a Council area can be covered by one plan, or a set of interlocking plans for constituent parts of the Council's area.

UNITARY DEVELOPMENT PLANS

UDPs were introduced in English metropolitan areas from 1986. UDPs combine the functions of Structure Plans (Part 1 of the UDP) and Local Plans (Part 2 of the UDP) in one development plan for the whole of each London Borough, Metropolitan District in England, and Unitary Council in Wales. Figure 4 shows part of the key diagram for the UDP for the Metropolitan Borough of Sefton. Because they cover both the strategic aspects of Structure Plans, and the local aspects of Local Plans, UDPs contain both Key Diagrams and detailed Proposals Maps, and set out broad stratgic policies as well as site-specific policies and proposals. There are no UDPs in Scotland, which aims for national coverage of Structure and Local Plans. Although the PAG report assumed a nation-wide pattern of two-tier development plans (the broad Structure Plan and detailed Local Plans), reorganisations of local government areas and responsibilities since then have resulted in, to date, different approaches to development planning in Scotland, England and Wales and, within England, different approaches in the conurbations compared with the rural areas.

The 'development plan' of whatever type consists of a written statement, setting out the policies and proposals of the plan and their supporting documentation, and a Proposals Map (Local Plan) showing how these apply at a site or area level, or a Key Diagram (Structure Plan) showing diagrammatically the broad distribution of development (such as housing land allocations). Statutory minimum requirements for the content and preparation of plans are set out in Regulations produced by the government and approved by Parliament.

Since the patterns and types of plans vary across the UK, and since some plans are changed more quickly and frequently than others, the 'development plan' will comprise all the relevant plans for a particular area (e.g. the Structure Plan and

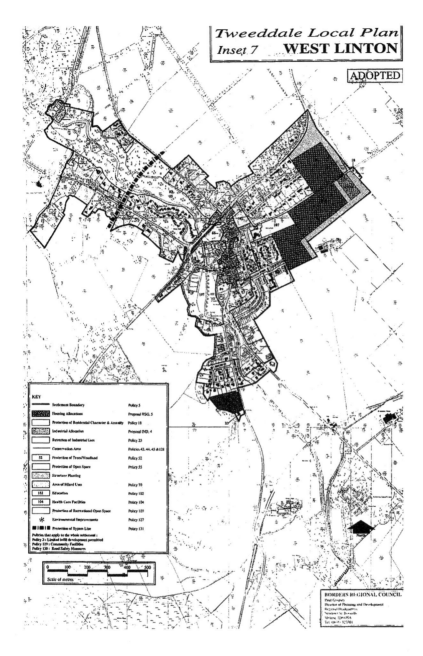

Figure 3 *A local plan proposal map, Tweeddale local plan, written statement, Planning Department, Borders Regional Council, 1996*

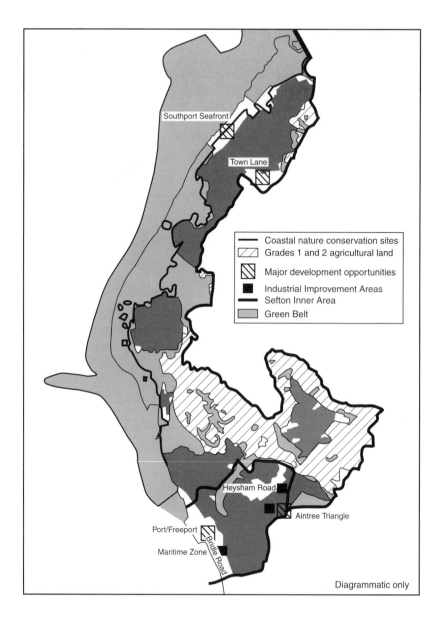

Figure 4 *Extract from the key diagram for the Sefton Metropolitan Unitary Development Plan, 'A Plan for Sefton', draft for deposit, Sefton Borough Council, 1991. Reproduced by permission of Sefton Metropolitan Borough Council*

Local Plan/District-wide Plan in Scotland and the Shire counties of England, the UDP for London Boroughs, Metropolitan Districts and Welsh Councils) and may consist of a number of documents. Sometimes 'old style' plans prepared under the 1947 Act may still be in force as the statutory development plan where they have not yet been replaced by a more up-to-date plan. Two of the enduring criticisms of development plans are that they take too long to prepare and, once approved, are rarely reviewed, if at all.

OTHER TYPES OF PLANS

The Acts allow for the preparation of plans which do not comprehensively cover all land uses, but instead concentrate on a particular use or uses where this is felt by planning authorities to need special attention. An example is the Loch Lomond (Subject) Local plan for recreation and conservation. Loch Lomond straddles a number of local authorities, and the land-use pressures are especially acute in relation to public access, recreation and tourism, in an area of outstanding landscape beauty. *Subject Plans* have also been prepared for Minerals. In general, such plans have been discouraged by central government in favour of comprehensive plans. An exception is the waste management plan.

Since the start of the 1990s, development plans have enjoyed heightened importance, firstly with the publication of the government's white paper *This Common Inheritance* (Department of the Environment, 1990), and then with the passing of the 1991 Planning and Compensation Act, which amended the Town and Country Planning Acts to give 'primacy' to the development plan in decisions on planning applications, planning appeals, and other matters. Previous government guidance in the 1980s gave the plan no special weight in relation to other factors influencing planning decisions. There is now more than ever an obligation on planning authorities to keep development plans up to date, and therefore under periodic review, altering or replacing them when necessary to keep them relevant to changing circumstances.

THE FORM AND CONTENT OF UK STATUTORY DEVELOPMENT PLANS

Development plans should contain the planning authority's proposals for the development and use of land in its area. In so doing, they must take account of:

- national or regional policy guidance
- current national policies
- resources likely to be available

- social, economic and environmental considerations
- policies and proposals in development plans for adjoining Council areas
- policies of government agencies, such as the Countryside Commission, Urban Development Corporations, English Heritage, Scottish Environment Protection Agency, Scottish Homes, Scottish Enterprise, the Welsh Development Agency.

Local Plans contain a mix of 'policies' and 'proposals' shown on a Proposals Map. Policies are statements of attitudes or intentions towards existing or prospective situations that require action. They are usually of two types:

- *Policies for land use*, relating solely to physical land-use development, including the management of traffic, the improvement of the environment, and the protection and conservation of the natural beauty and amenity of the land. They are usually limited to those policies that can be applied by the planning authority itself, or by other public bodies after full consultation and agreement.
- *Supporting policies*, which do not deal with physical land-use matters, but which the planning authority considers desirable to include in the plan because they contribute to the implementation of land-use aspects.

'Proposals' are intended actions of some significance to the plan area, by the planning authority or by other private or public bodies or individuals, which the planning authority is confident will be implemented within the period of the plan.

Local Plans deal with a broad range of policy issues and serve a number of functions, and there is sometimes a limit to how far the statutory documents can go in providing specific guidance or encouraging local investment and action. Detailed documents such as *development briefs*, *site planning briefs*, or *design guidance*, can provide a useful follow-up. These are generally known as 'supplementary planning guidance'. They can be effective in promoting specific opportunities for development or highlighting the standards expected for particular areas or types of development. But government guidance to planning authorities, and the Courts, stress that such supplementary guidance should derive from the policies and proposals in the plan, and not introduce new elements to the decision-making process. Figure 5 shows an extract from the Central Area Local Plan for Edinburgh, showing supplementary guidance for the redevelopment of part of the city centre (City of Edinburgh Council, 1997).

Stimulating development and identifying local opportunities for change are primary functions of plans in many areas, and supplementary guidance, perhaps in the form of brochures that highlight investment opportunities in land and buildings, can be a useful adjunct to the statutory documents. They are not themselves substitutes for the development plan, but they augment one of the main functions of the plan, and can be prepared and updated quickly.

Major Development Opportunity

LOTHIAN ROAD

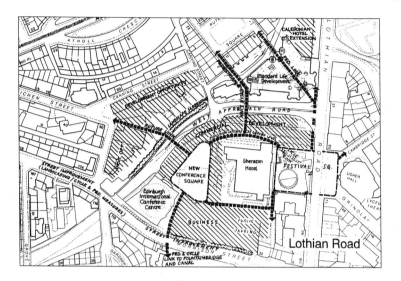

Lothian Road

Background

■ The major development opportunities at this location are based on the extensive area of former railway land acquired originally for possible road construction and partly utilised for this purpose (West Approach Road). There remains 4.9 hectares of land in this site. Redevelopment was initiated with construction of the hotel and a new public space (Festival Square). In 1989 the Council adopted a Master Plan prepared by consultants following a competition. This provided for a conference centre with seating capacity for 1200 people and further office accommodation amounting to 100,000 sq.m. developed around new traffic free spaces and pathways.

Development Principles

■ The significance of this area lies in the contribution it will make towards meeting the city's economic needs for modern office accommodation and expanding the business core towards Morrison Street and Haymarket. The new conference centre is a catalyst for that expansion. The guiding principles of development are as established in the 1989 Master Plan.

Figure 5 *Extract from Supplementary Development Guidance, Central Edinburgh Local Plan, written statement approved for public deposit, City of Edinburgh Council, 1994*

PLANS FOR LAND OR PLANS FOR PEOPLE?

A continuing feature of debates about the content of development plans, and therefore what is legitimate for them to address, is the extent to which plans are primarily about making arrangements for the use of *land*, or about providing access to quality environments for different groups of *people*. Many commentators have criticised both the statutory requirements, and the content and outlook of plans themselves, as neglecting the *people* aspects. In particular, as well as addressing *environmental* aspects, plans should explicitly address *equal opportunity* aspects. In other words, as well as being vehicles for bringing about a 'desired' pattern of development, plans should also be sensitive to the distributive consequences of land allocations, in the ways they improve or reduce opportunities for different groups in the population. These groups include ethnic minorities, women, children, disabled people, and older people. In this view, plans should not only be sensitive to the impacts of their policies and proposals on these groups, but they should ensure that they address the *needs* of such groups, through effective public participation.

In this view, part of the purpose of plans is to help address and overcome disadvantage within society and within the planning process itself (since these are groups who generally do not participate in the preparation of development plans, and therefore whose needs are not being articulated as policies and proposals are being decided). 'Planning for all the people rests on talking to the community and more importantly listening and understanding what it is like to view the world from a particular outlook' (Gilroy, 1993, p. 42).

For example, plans that favour the private car over public transport as the main means of connecting home, work, education, and leisure uses leave women (who are less likely to be car drivers), often responsible for young children or older relatives, without easy means of getting about. Poor design of the built environment and facilities restricts mobility for disabled people, for the elderly, and for parents with young children. Lack of thought about effectively communicating development plans in languages other than English effectively excludes from participating in the preparation of the plan ethnic minorities whose mother tongue is not English. Many of the problems faced by these groups are compounded by low incomes arising from discrimination in employment, access to benefits, and education. Many planners do not regard these as matters falling within their sphere of influence, but in making arrangements for the 'optimum' distribution of land uses, guiding development to preferred locations, and organising the transport links between them, land-use policies in plans can help or hinder access to opportunities for different groups in the population.

Different planning authorities have different perspectives on these matters and, where some take a broader, more people-centred view of the purposes of development plans, they have sometimes come into conflict with central government when attempting to adopt Local Plans or approve Structure Plans or UDPs where policies and proposals in plans are deemed to have gone beyond 'matters of land use'. Although PPG12 states that 'policies for non land-use matters should not be included' (Department of the Environment, 1992a, para. 5.6) it also states that, in justifying and explaining the plan, it is necessary to refer to economic, social, and other relevant considerations in the reasoned justification. So, while policies and proposals should be restricted to 'land use', it is not always straightforward to distinguish between purely land-use and purely non-land-use matters. The debate about the legitimate content and aspirations of plans goes to the heart of their purpose, which some regard as being hidebound by over-concentration on what they regard as peripheral matters of land use, rather than the broader social and economic considerations central to people's lives (see Box 4).

Box 4 *What should the statutory development plan cover? The case of the Bristol Local Plan*

The Bristol Local Plan covers the period 1989 to 2001. The Draft Local Plan was published in 1992 and the finalised (deposit) version in November 1993. A Public Local Inquiry into objections to the plan was held in 1995, and the modified plan published in 1997, with the intention to finally adopt it in 1998.

A key purpose of the plan is to address *equal opportunities*, by removing barriers which prevent many people from being able to take advantage of all the facilities of the city, from gaining access to their fair share of resources, and from achieving their full personal potential. These people are identified as including many elderly and people from black, ethnic and other minority communities, women, people with disabilities, and children. Another purpose of the plan is to address *quality of life* issues by adopting and implementing a long-term environmental strategy to ensure a cleaner, greener, healthier and safer city, both for present and future generations.

The plan also addresses issues of *economy and regeneration* by promoting the city centre and other key areas across the city, to encourage economic recovery and create a more prosperous and vibrant city, in partnership with private sector and community interests. Land use and physical environment are regarded as inseparable from wider social, economic and natural aspects.

Source: Bristol City Council (1993).

DEVELOPMENT PLANS AND DEVELOPMENT CONTROL

The British approach to land-use regulation is a discretionary one: decisions on particular development proposals are made 'on their merits' against the policy background of a generalised plan. The plan does not, of itself, imply that permission will be granted for particular developments, even if they appear to conform to the plan. Similarly, developments that appear to be in conflict with the plan are not automatically refused. As well as the general presumption in favour of the plan, enshrined in the 1991 Act, there is an equal presumption in government policy that favours development unless there is 'demonstrable harm to interests of acknowledged importance' (section 70 of the 1990 Act). All proposals for development must be considered by the planning authority in terms of the 'material considerations' relevant to any decision on the merits of the application.

Despite *the plan-led system* (section 54A of the Town and Country Planning Act 1990; section 25 of the Town and Country Planning (Scotland) Act 1997), this does not mean that the plan will always prevail in planning determinations. Planning applications may be for proposals for which the plan has no policies, and there will always be considerations material to a planning application other than the development plan alone (see Chapter 4 for a discussion of material considerations), and the weight to be given to them will be a matter for the judgement of the decision-maker in any particular case.

The provisions of section 54A/25 only come into play when regard is to be had to the development plan. It is first necessary to determine whether the provisions of the plan are material. So, the plan can influence development only when it has something to say about a particular development proposal. The provisions of the development plan have to be taken as the starting point, and are to be followed in the absence of any overriding material considerations. Recent court decisions have demonstrated that planning authorities would now be failing in their duty if they did not explicitly 'have regard' to the development plan in making any decisions under the Town and Country Planning Acts.

So, there is a degree of presumption in favour of the plan, but this can be overridden by material considerations, and the Courts have not been prepared to indicate how strong these other considerations have to be in order to override the plan (for a detailed discussion of the implications of section 54A, see Gatenby and Williams, in Tewdwr-Jones, 1996).

Development Plans and Sustainable Development

Since the publication of the government's environmental strategy in 1990 (Department of the Environment, 1990), development plans have been generally seen as having a key role in assisting the delivery of *sustainable patterns of development* by taking environmental considerations comprehensively and consistently into account through careful long-term planning. In this way:

• environmental protection and improvement can be plan-led
• social and economic requirements of the population can be met

- local, regional and global natural systems and resources can be protected
- individual planning decisions can be taken against an overall national, strategic and local framework that reflects environmental priorities.

In guiding the preferred pattern of development, plans can be a main instrument of providing for sustainable patterns of development, by consciously seeking to maximise the public transport linkages between areas of development, and between parts of urban areas, by encouraging patterns less dependent on the use of the private car for mobility, and by minimising the need to travel between home and work, and between home and other social activities (Box 5) (see also Chapter 2).

Box 5 *How development plans can assist sustainable forms of development*

- by encouraging development which makes full and effective use of land within existing urban areas;
- by guiding development to locations that are closely related to public transport networks, such as near an existing rail or bus station with spare capacity;
- by guiding new development types (such as offices and retailing) that attract trips to locations (such as town centres) which are capable of acting as nodes for public transport networks, discouraging car use, and enabling one journey to serve several purposes;
- by guiding new housing to locations where the need to use private cars for journeys to work, school and other facilities is minimised;
- by limiting town centre car parking (whether public or as part of other developments);
- by identifying land for appropriate interchange opportunities between major public transport networks (such as a bus station adjacent to a rail station);
- by providing positive encouragement of facilities to increase the attraction of walking and cycling.

Source: Department of the Environment (1992a).

PUBLIC PARTICIPATION IN DEVELOPMENT PLANS

No other public service is required by statute to consult the general public to the same extent as town and country planning on its plans and policies. It is not surprising that, given the nature of planning, and particularly its importance in relation to amenity and land values, public involvement in some form has long been a key feature of the planning system. Successive changes to the Town and Country Planning Acts since 1947 have given greater emphasis to involving the public in the process of preparing and approving development plans. As well as introducing Structure Plans and Local Plans, the 1968/9 Acts set in legislation the statutory requirement for public involvement in the production of development plans prior to their finalisation.

The basic statutory requirements for public involvement in development plans confer certain *rights* on the public and *obligations* on planning authorities. Planning authorities are required to consider views and objections from the public in the preparation of Structure Plans and Local Plans, and public representations must be taken into account by the Secretary of State or by the planning authority when these plans are formally approved or adopted. Publicity is required for any 'matters arising from a survey' as well as 'matters proposed to be included in the plan' (Town and Country Planning Acts 1990, 1997). In practice, these two requirements are generally regarded as being met in the production of a consultative draft plan, on which comments are invited before the local planning authority prepares its finalised plan. Once a plan is finalised, formal objections can be made, which may result in the need to hold a Public Inquiry (or 'Examination in Public' for a Structure Plan) before the plan can be adopted as the statutory plan.

Legislation does not prescribe precise techniques for public participation, although Regulations do require planning authorities to publish a report on the participation arrangements they have undertaken. The choice of techniques for involving the public is left to individual authorities to make in the light of their own special circumstances. The government issues Circulars and advice, and commissions and publishes research, to assist planning authorities in this choice. The Department of the Environment *Good Practice Guide* (Department of the Environment, 1992b) suggests that consultation demands commitment and investment of resources. Early phases demand widest involvement. 'Allowing people their say will build support for the plan' (p. 20).

Public involvement usually takes two forms: during the preparation stage, where planning authorities invite views on key issues or survey findings or, more commonly, on a draft version of the plan; and during the finalisation stage, where the planning authority prepares its finalised plan, and the general public and other interests have the opportunity to formally object to specific aspects of it, and thus cause a Public Inquiry or other local hearing to be held, before the plan can be approved. For Structure Plans in Scotland, the Secretary of State retains the power of approval, with or without making modifications to take account of objections or other matters he considers appropriate. In England and Wales, councils approve their own Structure Plans.

Figures 6 and 7 show the usual stages in the preparation of Structure Plans and Local Plans, respectively, including the key stages in plan preparation at which statute requires public involvement, by what means, and for how long. Just as the

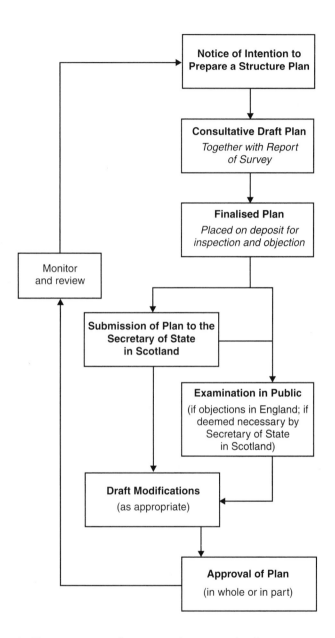

Figure 6 *The preparation of structure plans, procedural stages*

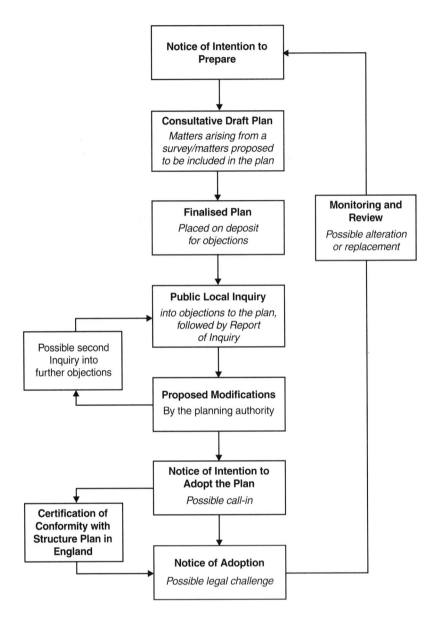

Figure 7 *The preparation of local plans, procedural stages*

Secretary of State for Scotland is not bound to heed objections to the Structure Plan, so planning authorities are not bound to take on board the recommendations arising from an Inquiry or Examination in Public. Similar stages apply to the preparation of UDPs.

At the time of the 1968/69 Act, the government established the Skeffington Committee 'to consider and report on the best methods, including publicity, of securing the participation of the public at the formative stage in the making of development plans for their area'. The resulting report *People and Planning* published in 1969 brought in a much wider definition of 'participation' in planning and distinguished between 'participation' as 'the act of sharing in the formulation of policies and proposals' and 'publicity' which was 'the making of information available to the public' (Ministry of Housing and Local Government, 1969).

Skeffington assumed that more effective public involvement in planning would reduce delays in plan-making through fewer objections, as the public came to better understand the rationale of plans and the basis of planning decisions. Skeffington's ideas have become enshrined as common practice. But there is concern that the procedural framework may be less able to cope with increased levels of such involvement, especially since the general effect of section 54A has been to heighten the importance of development plans at key stages in their preparation, most notably at consultative draft and deposit stages. This may tend to undermine both the efficacy of the process, and the efficiency with which decisions are reached.

It is important that the system is as effective and efficient as possible, and that it is sufficiently robust to meet the many expectations made of it, in terms of heightened community interest and environmental awareness. Today, therefore, there is expectation (both in statute and in good practice) that, in the preparation of development plans by local authorities, the public should:

- have access to the information that councillors and officers have used in preparing a plan
- be informed when work on a new plan or review of an existing plan is beginning, and be able to contribute to certain stages
- be able to comment on a draft plan before it is approved or adopted
- have the opportunity to object formally when a plan has been finalised, and have the right to be heard at a Structure Plan Examination in Public or a Local Plan Public Inquiry
- be provided with details of how and when they can make representations or objections
- expect that, whenever they make representations or objections, the planning authority will properly consider these and subsequently explain their decisions to those making representations or objections
- be able to challenge any decision by a planning authority or the Secretary of State by Judicial Review or complaint to the Ombudsman, as appropriate.

In the new 'plan-led system' following section 54A of the 1991 Act, Development Plans should be 'well prepared' in that they should:

- be properly justified to explain their intention
- provide clear guidance to the public and the developer
- set out any criteria necessary for their interpretation
- be readily monitored
- be relevant to prevailing and future prospects for development and conservation
- be expressed in simple and unambiguous terms.

A key issue in all of this is whether people are truly 'participating' in the making of development plans, or are merely being 'consulted' on the planning authority's (and others') ideas. There have been difficulties reconciling the rights of individuals, communities, amenity groups, and the development industry to comment on planning policies and proposals at various stages, with improvements in the speed of plan preparation, finalisation, approval/adoption and review. In practice, there is some confusion and ambiguity over the explicit function of participation:

- Is it the means whereby a better plan can be prepared, or purely an expression of local democratic involvement in the plan-making process?
- Does it facilitate consensus or raise awareness, potentially heightening scope for opposition or challenge?
- Does the move towards District-wide Plans and UDPs in England and Wales covering broader areas tend to make them lean towards quasi-strategic plans, with implications for local identity and meaningful public involvement?
- Is it an opportunity to devolve power and responsibility for town and country planning matters?
- Is it a means of empowering people to take more responsibility for plans that affect them?
- Is it a means of formal acknowledgement of the environmental rights of the public and the policy obligations of local planning authorities?

Government policy states that 'the planning system operates to secure the efficient and effective development and use of land in the public interest' (see, for example, Scottish Office Environment Department, 1994b, para. 3). Under the development plan system established in the 1947 Act, the public interest was assumed to coincide with the interest of the planning authority. Accordingly, beyond a legal right to object to the finalised plan, there were no formal or informal mechanisms for public involvement in its preparation. Since the 1960s, it has been understood that there are a number of different public interests, reflecting the different customers of the planning service, and their different and often competing needs. These include applicants for planning permission, developers, large and small businesses, government departments and agencies, statutory undertakers, neighbours, and the general public. This has been acknowledged in, firstly, changes to the Town and Country Planning Acts to require public involvement prior to the finalisation of a plan and, secondly, innovative attempts in some plan-making exercises to encourage public involvement such as preparation of the Warwickshire Structure Plan in video and world-wide web formats (see Box 6).

Box 6 *Content of Structure Plans*

Warwickshire Structure Plan 1996–2011 Written Statement

The Warwickshire Structure Plan 1996–2011 replaces the previous Warwickshire Structure Plan Alterations 1989–2001. The role of the Structure Plan is to provide clear strategic land-use guidance for Warwickshire over the next 15 years, steering the detailed planning policies and proposals that are decided in Local District Plans, prepared by the five Borough and District Councils. The overriding aim of the Structure Plan is to emphasise a pattern of development which:

- allows homes and jobs to be provided to meet the needs of the whole community, including overspill households from Birmingham and Coventry;
- promotes greater use of public transport, walking and cycling, to avoid restricting future generations of Warwickshire residents to a style of living which depends on the use of a car to get to work, school or shop;
- nurtures Warwickshire's legacy of distinctive towns and villages, countryside, environmental wealth and heritage which continue to make it an attractive place in which to live, work and visit;
- enables the economy to grow and change, diversifying in rural areas in ways appropriate to the location, bringing new industry to the towns where old ones have been in decline, and ensuring that disadvantaged communities share more fully in the County's prosperity;
- emphasises the benefits of town centres as places to live and work, as well as re-asserting their role as the main providers of shops, financial and professional services and places of entertainment;
- conserves resources of land and energy, including minerals and water, and makes maximum use of renewable energy resources.

Structure Plan targets include:

- accommodating housing overspill population from Birmingham and Coventry, amounting to about 18 400 new dwellings within the overall total of 31 100 new dwellings needed in Warwickshire over the period 1996–2011;

- providing up to 880 hectares of land for industrial development;
- balancing mineral extraction to meet national and regional as well as local needs for energy and building and construction, with environmental and transport constraints;
- promoting waste recycling to reduce waste imports as well as locally generated waste which has currently to go to landfill.

Local Plans should make provision for the phased release of land for

- the construction of about 31 100 new dwellings over the period 1996–2011;
- up to 880 hectares of industrial development.

Source: Warwickshire County Council (1997).

The Environment White Paper *This Common Inheritance* (Department of the Environment, 1990) declares that one of the government's objectives is

> to encourage greater public involvement in environmental matters. People, as individuals and in groups, have important contributions to make through consultation at key stages in development planning and in development control. Public information and opportunities to contribute are essential to the proper conduct of the planning service (Scottish Office Environment Department, 1994a, para. 12).

The government argues that development plans that meet the criteria for being well-prepared and up to date will provide a sound basis for public confidence in the planning system. There are now heightened concerns, following the increased emphasis given to development plans in the 1991 Planning and Compensation Act, about:

- implications for a plan-led decision-making system of the 'up-to-datedness' of plans, especially the speed of plan-making and the frequency of plan review;
- implications of 'well-preparedness' of plans, especially the approach to involving the public and key development agencies in the process of plan-making;
- the focus and relevance of plans to local problems and issues;
- the scope for streamlining plan consultation, with implications for the nature of the process and level of public involvement;
- the scope for further deregulation of the plan approval process.

Following generally poor levels of public involvement in the preparation of development plans (especially in structure planning), research into public attitudes to town and country planning (Department of the Environment, 1995) indicated that people generally do not recognise the various types of development plan or know who prepares them. Few recall having the opportunity to comment. Many developers and landowners do not believe that the system is simple, fair, speedy or responsive, but they do think that it improves the quality of development. There are concerns about the complexity of plans. The research found that more than 80% of planning authorities used some form of written material to inform households (either separate leaflets or inserts into commercial free newspapers, plan summaries, press releases, parish councils). More novel approaches included local radio, a touring bus with radio broadcasts and local personality, local television, video, summaries in large print or talking books, exhibitions in shopping centres, and 'Planning for Real' exercises. Benefits that could come from Planning for Real exercises are: dismantling of professional barriers; more corporate and holistic working by local authorities; a more meaningful way of involving people without the problems of traditional public meetings.

KEEPING PLANS RELEVANT AND UP TO DATE

Planning authorities are required by statute to keep their plans under review, and to alter in part or wholly replace them in the light of their implementation or changing circumstances. There is no specific requirement to replace a plan after a certain period of time, but government policy is that plans should normally be reviewed at no more than five yearly intervals (Department of the Environment, 1992a, para. 4.4). In addition, the older a plan becomes, the less primacy it will have as a material consideration in planning decisions, and the less credible it will be as a means of guiding development, environmental change, and protection.

Many parts of the UK still do not have up-to-date development plan coverage, plans are still taking too long to prepare, and there is limited updating of Local Plans in particular. A 1996 review of Local Plans and UDPs (Department of the Environment, 1996) indicated that plans are taking, on average, over 4 years to prepare, ranging from just over 2 years to more than 8 years (see Table 1). A review of District-wide plan performance commissioned by the Royal Town Planning Institute (RTPI) (1997) indicated that many plans are resulting in large numbers of objections, leading to lengthy Public Inquiries and ultimately delays in adopting plans. A similar story emerges in Scotland, where national coverage of Local Plans has been a statutory requirement since 1975, and where plan-making is more advanced, but where there is also a growing backlog of adopted Local Plans with no immediate prospects of review or replacement (see Table 2).

MONITORING AND REVIEW OF PLANS

The production, monitoring and updating of plans is central to the effective working of a system based on the primacy of development plans in planning determinations. The impact of section 54A will therefore depend on the coverage

Table 1   Extent of area-wide Local Plan and Unitary Development Plan adoption in England. Councils that have, or were expected to have, an adopted plan by 31 December 1996

Government office region	Number of councils with adopted plan	Total number of councils in region	Percent of councils with adopted plan
North East	5	24	21
North West	17	39	44
Merseyside	1	5	20
Yorkshire & the Humber	2	24	8
East Midlands	13	40	33
West Midlands	20	36	56
South West	12	47	26
Eastern	31	49	63
London	24	33	73
South East	32	69	46
England	**157**	**366**	**43**

Source: Department of the Environment (1996).

Table 2   Extent of adopted Local Plans in Scotland at December 1996

Year	1992	1993	1994	1995	1996
No. of adopted Local Plans	72	79	90	128	211
No. of adopted plans > 5 years old	23	29	33	60	89
% > 5 years old	32	37	37	47	42

Source: Scottish Office Development Department (1997).

of development plans and whether they are up to date. According to PPG12, an up-to-date, comprehensive, statutory Local Plan should reduce the resources devoted to planning appeals. The planning system should become simpler and more responsive, reducing costs for both the private sector and local authorities. At the same time, the system should make it easier for people to be involved in the planning process (Department of the Environment, 1992a).

A major reason for the review of a Local Plan will be the alteration of the Structure Plan. These should follow in a logical sequence. A balance needs to be struck between the need to keep plans up to date and having too frequent reviews. Partial reviews can confuse the user. Annual monitoring reports are useful and can be used as a basis for consultations with other authorities. Yet no plan, however up to date, can embody all considerations relevant to the decision-making process: 'However good it might be, the local plan is far from perfect and can never be comprehensively rational or long lasting . . . it is, however, always partial, transitory, and at best a guide' (Jones, 1996, p. 66). The basic principles of the process (according to Jones, 1996) are: make it simple; keep it local; involve the public; do it quickly. Plan monitoring and review seems to have been more systematic and frequent at the strategic planning level. In Scotland, complete Structure Plan coverage was achieved in 1989, and all Structure Plans have been reviewed and replaced at least once since then (see, for example, Box 7).

Box 7 *Keeping plans up to date: the Highland Structure Plan*

Highland Council covers the area north of the industrialised central belt of Scotland, including much of the Highlands and islands. It is populated by 200 000 people in an area covering one-third of Scotland. Highland Council was among the first in Scotland to achieve area-wide coverage of Structure Plans and Local Plans in the early 1980s, and has been in the forefront of keeping plans up to date through regular review and replacement.

- August 1985 – public Notice of Intention to Review the 1980 Highland Structure Plan
- September 1986 – internal draft replacement plan prepared
- June 1988 – draft plan approved by Council for publication
- January 1989 – publication of Consultative Draft (replacement) Structure Plan
- June 1989 – public representations on the Draft considered
- September 1989 – Council approve finalised plan
- January 1990 – finalised plan sent to Secretary of State for approval
- November 1990 – approval by Secretary of State
- August 1992 – Notice of Intention to prepare Alteration No. 1 to Structure Plan on 'Draft Indicative Forestry Strategy'
- June 1993 – Council approve finalised Draft Alteration
- November 1993 – Alteration submitted to Secretary of State for approval
- June 1994 – Secretary of State proposes modifications to finalised Draft
- June 1994 – Council agrees modifications
- September 1994 – Secretary of State approves Alteration
- June 1994 – Notice of Intention to Prepare Alteration No. 2 'Housing Land'
- February 1995 – consultation on proposed Alteration No. 2 (draft housing land audit)
- June 1996 – Forum on housing land issues

Source: Highland Council.

CONCLUSIONS

Development plans have been an integral part of the modern planning system since their establishment in the 1947 Act. They have a long history as a key tool of spatial planning practice. However, their form and content, and responsibilities for their preparation, have been subject to change over this period. The weight given to them in determining planning decisions has also changed as central government policy has fluctuated between favouring development and free enterprise on the one hand, and control and regulation on the other. A central concern in this has been to find the right balance in plans between *prescribing* the future pattern of development, *guiding* land use change, and being sufficiently *flexible* to adjust as circumstances for planning change.

In the 20 years following the 1947 Act, development plans effectively set a 20-year blueprint for development on the assumptions that major change would happen only in very specific circumstances (such as town centre redevelopment or slum clearance) while the countryside would largely be protected from development in order to maximise the area under food or forestry production, following wartime shortages. Such plans, once approved, were not easy to change quickly. In the 1960s, the more apparent pressures for change, especially in urban areas (but also in the countryside as a consequence of the growth of leisure pursuits and increased penetration from car-borne visitors), created a need for more flexible, indicative (rather than prescriptive) plans. The development plan was reincarnated as the two-tier Structure Plan/Local Plan to address changed circumstances for forward planning. They were introduced coincidentally with local government reform in the mid-1970s.

The two-tier development plan advocated by PAG was intended to be prepared by the same authority. It was local government reorganisation in the mid-1970s that split the functions of plan-making between Counties (Regions in Scotland) and Districts. The introduction of Unitary Development Plans (UDPs) for the English metropolitan areas in the mid-1980s, and the extension of unitary authorities through local government reform in the mid-1990s, could be said to have reverted to the PAG concept.

Plans now seek to guide development rather than provide a deterministic blueprint for a future pattern of development. In so doing there are trade-offs between certainty and flexibility, between indicative and prescriptive plans. The development plan is now of prime significance, as the 'main component' of the planning system (Department of the Environment, 1992a, para. 1.3). The government's aim is that plans should provide certainty for property owners, developers and local communities by giving clear signals as to what will and will not be acceptable development in given locations. Development plans provide an 'essential framework' for decisions and 'should convey a clear understanding of the public interest in the use of land and common expectations about the likely broad patterns of development' (Department of the Environment, 1992a, para. 1.1).

The radical changes proposed by PAG to the old style land use blueprints, the subsequent statutory basis for Structure Plans and Local Plans, and the plan-led basis of planning decisions re-established from 1991, were intended to make development plans simpler, more quickly prepared and updated, easier for people to participate in, and more responsive to changing circumstances for development. The heightened importance of the development plan reflected the government's desire to move away from the 1980s philosophy of market-driven or appeal-led planning. With the heightened status of development plans comes heightened awareness of their under-performance, in terms of up-to-date coverage of Local Plans and UDPs, and the time taken to prepare and update them. Once again there are calls for a 'robust spatial framework' which 'relates the local environment and infrastructure to the proposed pattern of development, providing firm land allocations for the most common forms of development' (RTPI, 1997).

Plan-making is part of the ongoing process of planning. Plans are means to ends; they are not ends in themselves. As such, they need to be implemented, monitored, kept under review, and changed when necessary. Changes in national or regional policy guidance from central government may have knock-on effects for policies in Structure Plans. Changes in the content of Structure Plans may have knock-on effects for the policies and proposals in Local Plans. Key implementation agencies, such as English Estates or Scottish Enterprise, may adjust their capital projects, which may mean proposals in Local Plans may slip, or be implemented earlier than anticipated. Similarly, developers such as major house-builders may not take up vacant sites for housing as quickly as anticipated, or alternatively sites for housing may be developed more quickly than forecast. All of this means that plans need to be seen as part of an ongoing *process* that requires constant management, rather than as once-and-for-all solutions to physical land use problems.

DEVELOPMENT PLANS: THE FUTURE?

Spring 1997 saw the election of a new government with a modernising agenda (Department for the Environment, Transport and the Regions, 1998a). It has promoted political devolution for the administrative parts of the UK, including the establishment of a Welsh Assembly, Regional Development Agencies for England, and a Scottish Parliament. It is also introducing new concepts of 'best value' in the delivery of local government services, which emphasise enhanced consultation with communities, and 'community planning' (Department for the Environment, Transport and the Regions, 1998b) which stresses the importance of local authority plans interlocking with the plans of other public agencies to deliver 'joined-up government'. All of this is likely to impact on how development plans are prepared in the future.

The establishment of a Scottish Parliament, with legislative and financial responsibility for the planning system in Scotland, has re-invigorated debates among planning professionals and academics north of the border about whether the system of structure planning and local planning requires a radical overhaul to meet new challenges, or whether the system is sound enough to require refinement. While the Parliament will have responsibility for national planning policy guidance, some commentators have suggested an early priority should be the replacement of discretionary guidance with an indicative or prescriptive national development plan. Some have also suggested that Structure Plans would then become redundant, and that all Scottish councils should be required to prepare UDPs on the English and Welsh model (Hayton, 1997). However the development plan develops in future, it is clear that it has never been a static concept, and will change again to meet new times.

REFERENCES

Bristol City Council (1993) *Bristol Local Plan: Written Statement*, the Council, Bristol.

Cameron Black, J. and Graham, D. (1996) Planning for progress in development, *Planning Week*, 25 April, 14–15.

City of Edinburgh Council (1997) *Central Area Local Plan: Written Statement*, the Council, Edinburgh.

Department for the Environment, Transport and the Regions (1998a) *Modern Local Government*, White Paper, HMSO, London.

Department for the Environment, Transport and the Regions (1998b) *Community Planning*, Consultation Paper, the Department, London.

Department of the Environment (1984) *The Future of Development Plans*, Consultation Paper, the Department, London.

Department of the Environment (1990) *This Common Inheritance: Britain's Environment Strategy*, Cm1200, HMSO.

Department of the Environment (1992a) *Development Plans and Regional Guidance*, Planning Policy Guidance Note 12, HMSO, London.

Department of the Environment (1992b) *Development Plans: A Good Practice Guide*, HMSO, London.

Department of the Environment (1995) *Attitudes to Town and Country Planning*, HMSO, London.

Department of the Environment (1996) *Preparation of District Wide Local Plans and UDPs*, Report of an internal review.

Gilroy, R. (1993) *Good Practices in Equal Opportunities*, Avebury Press, Aldershot.

Hayton, K. (1997) *W(h)ither Development Planning?* Monograph, University of Strathclyde, Department of Environmental Planning, the University, Glasgow.

Healey, P. (1983) *Local Plans in British Land Use Planning*, Pergamon, Oxford.

Jones, A. (1996) Local planning policy: the Newbury approach, in: Tewdwr-Jones, M. (ed.), *British Planning Policy in Transition*, UCL Press, London.

Lothian Regional Council (1985) *Lothian Structure Plan: Written Statement*, the Council, Edinburgh.

Ministry of Housing and Local Government (1965) *Report of the Planning Advisory Group*, HMSO, London.

Ministry of Housing and Local Government (1969) *People and Planning*, Report of the Skeffington Committee, HMSO, London.

Ministry of Housing and Local Government (1970) *Development Plans: A Manual on Form and Content*, HMSO, London.

Royal Town Planning Institute (RTPI) (1997) *Review of District Wide Local Plans*, Department of City and Regional Planning, University of Wales College of Cardiff, the Institute, London.

Scottish Office Development Department (1997) *Review of Development Planning in Scotland*, Interim Report for Consultation, Hillier Parker, School of Planning and Housing, Edinburgh College of Art/Heriot-Watt University, Dundas and Wilson, HMSO, Edinburgh.

Scottish Office Environment Department (1994a) *Review of the Town and Country Planning System in Scotland*, Scottish Office, Edinburgh.

Scottish Office Environment Department (1994b) National Planning Policy Guideline 1: *The Planning System*, Scottish Office, Edinburgh.

Sefton Metropolitan Borough Council (1991) *A Plan for Sefton*, Sefton Metropolitan Borough Unitary Development Plan: Written Statement, the Council, Liverpool.

Tewdwr-Jones, M. (1996) *British Planning Policy in Transition*, UCL Press, London.

Thomas, K. (1997) *Development Control: Principles and Practice*, UCL Press, London.

Warwickshire County Council (1997) *Warwickshire Structure Plan 1996–2011: Written Statement*, the Council.

CHAPTER 4

DEVELOPMENT CONTROL

Daniel Groves

INTRODUCTION

Development control is the *executive* arm of the planning process. It is the means whereby policies are implemented, specific land use proposals brought to fruition and unlawful development prevented. It enables a local authority to protect residential areas from inappropriate intrusions, reserve land for new industries, maintain a Green Belt, keep valuable buildings and trees and prevent ugly signs.

The key to understanding the process lies in the word 'development'. This is defined in statute as:

> the carrying out of building, engineering, mining or other operations in, on, over or under land, or the making of any material change in the use of any buildings or other land.

It does not therefore include planting hedges, or grubbing them out. It does not cover the growing of crops or turning a greengrocer's into a florist's. It does not cover renewing the paintwork inside a house. Much of the understanding of the meaning of development has been defined by statute and secondary legislation. For example, demolition is now considered to be development by virtue of recent Acts. Prior to that it was argued that it was not a building work and thus not development. Many other cases have been established by 'case law' – a testing in the Courts in the event of a dispute. For example, in a case called *Coleshill and District Investment Company Limited* v. *Minister of Housing and Local Government* it was held that rubble and soil screening blast walls surrounding explosives were part of the blast wall building and that their removal constituted 'building works' ([1969] 2 All ER 525).

THE PRIMARY LEGISLATION

The Town and Country Planning Acts, dating originally for development control purposes, from 1947 and updated regularly since that date, set out the framework for the development control process. It is important to note at the outset that the Acts do not contain any statutory requirement to apply for planning permission before development is commenced. This means that in such circumstances no offence has been committed and no fine or other penalty attaches to it.

The Acts empower the Secretary of State to make Orders (secondary legislation) to cover various matters relating to procedure, which will be looked at in more detail below. They do however contain some specific requirements which must be followed.

1. They allow for various forms of advertisement and publicity for planning applications (again as detailed in an Order) and specify very clearly that a planning authority *shall not entertain* any application for planning permission unless and until the necessary steps have been taken as required. This is not the same as determining the application, which may only occur after the expiry of the relevant time periods allowed to the public to examine the proposals and submit their comments or objections. This is a matter of whether a 'competent' application has been made.

2. In a similar vein, the Acts require that specific notice is given to the owner of the land to which the application relates, and any agricultural tenant who is farming the land. It is important to remember that you do not need to own land to make an application to develop it, nor do you need to own a building before seeking planning permission to use it for a different purpose. To require such would be to stifle the property market unnecessarily. It is equally important, however, to remember that any consent granted will 'attach' to the land or building, and not to the person who made the application. This can have far-reaching consequences for land values and property transactions.

3. As well as applying for planning permission, the Acts make provision for a range of other consents that may be obtained or necessary from a local authority for a variety of 'development' activities. These include:
   - applications for listed building consent (to alter or demolish a building of special architectural or historic interest);
   - conservation area consent (to carry out works in a Conservation Area where special rules apply);
   - advertisement consent (to erect hoardings, illuminated neon signs, shop signs);
   - certificate of lawful use (to gain approval for a pre-existing use).

4. The Acts then move on to the matter of determination (deciding) the planning application and direct that the local authority shall decide the application in accordance with the provisions of the Development Plan unless material considerations indicate otherwise. There is a wealth of case law surrounding what constitutes 'material considerations' and this will be looked at later. The Acts also require that the decision-making authority shall take into account any representations received by them on that application. This is not to say that they must be unduly swayed by public pressure, but they may not ignore it in the decision-making process. They must also take into account the results of any Environmental Impact Assessment of the likely environmental results of any proposal.

The authority may, by statute, grant planning permission, grant planning permission subject to conditions, or refuse planning permission. They may not, except in one particular circumstance, refuse to determine the application at all. The only circumstance where this may occur is when a very similar proposal on much the same site has been rejected on appeal to the Secretary of State within the past two years.

The consent may be granted subject to conditions. The statute says that these may be such as the authority 'think fit'. This wide-ranging power is then limited (in effect) by later sections that limit those conditions to those 'expedient for the purposes of or in connection with the development authorised by the permission'. The discretion of authorities is also limited to any land under the control of the applicant (e.g. it excludes the public highway running alongside his property) and to any land within their own jurisdiction (i.e. they may not require work to be carried out in another planning authority's area).

In the event that the conditions are not acceptable to the applicant, or the application is refused outright, there is by statute a right of appeal against the decision to the Secretary of State. The appeal process will be discussed in more detail later. At this stage there are two important points to grasp. One, that the applicant, and only the applicant, may appeal, and then only against refusal or conditions, i.e. those aggrieved possibly by a grant of consent have no right of appeal. Two, that the decision of the Secretary of State, who will look at the whole case and decide it anew, is final. There is a legal remedy in the Courts for those who believe an error of law has occurred – there is no appeal against the decision itself.

The consent granted has a limited life span, set out by statute, during which it can be taken up. In the majority of cases this is five years from the date of the consent but this may be shorter or (rarely) longer, as the planning authority may decide. It is important to remember at this stage that the five-year period is the time-span in which the development must be *begun*. It does not have to be finished and the consent cannot expire once work has begun to implement the consent. A substantial body of case law has arisen on what constitutes 'beginning'. For a new house, for example, if bricks have been laid, clearly work has begun. If foundations have been dug but not constructed, has work begun? Generally, yes. If trial pits have been dug to locate sewers and cables, has development commenced? Generally, no. Individual judgement, some flexibility and not a little common sense are required in the day-to-day workings of the system.

Finally, it is worth recording that the statutes allow the authority to vary permissions granted, before they have been fully taken up, to allow for minor ('non-material') changes that become necessary, expedient or desirable.

THE GENERAL PERMITTED DEVELOPMENT ORDERS

The definition of what constitutes development divides into two parts. The first of these is the carrying out of building, engineering and mining works. The second we shall examine later. Clearly, if all such works had to be the subject of an application for planning permission, the whole system, and the construction industry with it, would rapidly grind to a halt through sheer weight of paper.

To avoid this, Ministers are empowered under the Act, and have exercised that power over the years, to make Orders which set out certain forms of development for which permission is given by the Order, thus avoiding the need to apply to the local planning authority. Over time, the amount and variety of such 'permitted development', as it is known, has increased to meet changing circumstances.

As an example, let us look at the latest Order in Scotland, published in 1992. The principal classes of interest to most people concern development in and around their own homes and we will look first at this. The Order allows the enlargement, improvement or other alteration to a dwelling house, up to a certain size and height, with restrictions near roads and in Conservation Areas. So all internal works to a house are permitted development, as are new doors and windows, outside painting, putting up a garage or conservatory, flooring the loft and so on.

Furthermore, these residential classes allow for buildings and enclosures within the grounds or garden for uses 'incidental to the enjoyment of the dwelling house'. This covers the garden shed, the rabbit hutches and runs, bee hives, swimming pools, patios, barbecue pits – you can think of other examples from your own neighbourhood.

The classes continue to allow for an access to the road for a car and a hard surface to park it on, putting up satellite dishes, installing oil storage tanks, gates, walls, fences, all subject to various limitations as to size and location.

The classes then broaden out to cover temporary uses, caravan sites, agricultural buildings, land drainage, and forestry operations. Again these are hedged about with restrictions on size and other matters, and in some cases written notification has to be given to the planning authority. Much industrial development of existing works is permitted development and there are substantial permitted development rights given to local authorities. For example, Part 12 Class 33 (a) permits the carrying out of:

> works for the erection of dwelling houses, so long as those works conform to a local plan adopted under Section 12 of the Act.

Much of the work of 'statutory undertakers' (including lighthouses!), aviation authorities, mining and coal exploration, telecommunications and amusement parks) is also included in the Order. The Order also specifies what 'bad neighbours' are – we will look at them later (see below).

THE USE CLASSES ORDERS

Hand in hand with the General Development Order come the Use Classes Orders. Remember that the second part of our definition of development was 'the making of any material change in the use of land or buildings'. Obviously the big question is: 'What is material?' It would be impossible to provide a list of every conceivable circumstance and the interpretation is mainly entrusted to the skilled planner to determine. The test that will be used will be the impact or effect of the proposed change, and in this the planner is assisted by the Use Classes Orders.

They specify various uses of land and buildings (*not* an exhaustive list) and group together various uses so that change within the class is not development. The most commonly used is Class 1 which defines a shop. Surprisingly the group includes:

- a post office
- a travel agency
- a hairdresser
- a funeral undertaker
- a launderette
- a dry cleaner.

Of more critical importance is what is excluded from the 'shop' class and may not therefore be established in existing retail premises without getting planning permission. The two most obvious examples are a public house (which is in no class, being a *sui generis* use – a use on its own) and a restaurant of any description, which is given a class of its own.

In recognition of the changing nature of business office and light industrial use in the technologically driven world of today, the Orders set a standard Business Class which allows for office use, the research and development of products or processes, and any light industrial use to manufacture such products.

It is useful at this stage to understand what is meant by 'light industry' since it is a question that arises constantly in practice and the test is very straightforward. The Orders describe it as:

a use which can be carried on in any residential area without detriment to the amenity of that area by reason of noise, vibration, smell, fumes, smoke, soot, ash, dust or grit.

Note that the definition specifically relates to *residential* areas – any resistance therefore to the establishment of such uses in residential areas would have to be based on external factors, i.e. appearance and traffic generation, and not on the intrinsic unsuitability of the use.

The later Classes in the Order distinguish on the basis of the degree of care required between hostels/hotels and residential institutions. The final two Classes split non-residential institutions such as churches, libraries, museums and day nurseries from the commercial world of cinemas, casinos, skating rinks, disco-theques and bingo halls.

Remembering, then, that a change within a Class is not considered as con-stituting 'development', the situation is slightly complicated by provisions in the General Development Orders which grant permission for some changes from one Class to another. The first is the change from storage and distribution – the warehouse Class to the business Class. This may have some substantial implica-tions in land use terms in practice as warehouses on trading estates established in the 1950s and 1960s become offices in out-of-centre locations, paying less rentals and fewer overheads than town centre properties which quickly fall vacant.

The other change of note, which may be viewed as beneficial, is from the hot food take-away/restaurant, either to a professional office (bank, building society) or a shop selling goods by retail or anything else we listed above as being Class 1. The thinking behind this is simply that there is less likelihood of adverse effects and more strength to a shopping centre if a cafe becomes a post office or a green-grocer's. It must be emphasised therefore that the ruling does *not* apply the other way round, e.g. you cannot turn a bank into a restaurant without getting planning permission.

Let us look at an example:

The most usual use made of empty shops is as charity shops. Increasingly, moves are being made to turn them into dwellings because of their low purchase price and easy adaptation. Mainly, however, the pressure on shopping centres is for office/bank/estate agency type uses. These are described in the Use Classes Order as 'appropriate to provide in a shopping area, and provided principally to visiting members of the public'.

Mr Kalra bought a shop in High Road, Leyton, in 1992 in order to turn it into a solicitor's office, and applied for planning permission to that effect, identifying the proposal as Class A2 Use, described in the paragraph above. Permission was refused and an appeal against refusal dismissed on the grounds that this was a general Class B1 office.

Mr Kalra appealed to the High Court and then to the Court of Appeal [Kalra v. Secretary of State for the Environment and Waltham Forest LBC] [JPL 1986, p850].

The Court decided that it was not necessary to prove that a professional office such as this was appropriate to provide in a shopping area. The terms of the Use Classes Order made it clear that it was the 'other services', other that is than professional and financial, that need to demonstrate appro-priateness. As to use by visiting members of the public, the fact that Mr Kalra had an appointments system did not mean that he failed this test. After all, the judge said, hairdressers had them, and they are shops. The appeal was allowed.

The case is another demonstration of the need to maintain a discretionary approach in dealing even with secondary legislation.

Armed then with the General Development Order and the Use Classes Order, and with the definition of what constitutes 'development' firmly fixed in our minds, we are now in a position to advise any caller or letter-writer whether planning permission will have to be applied for, because they wish to spend their lottery win on improving their home.

THE GENERAL DEVELOPMENT PROCEDURE ORDERS

These Orders, regularly updated, are made by the Secretary of State and set out the nuts and bolts of procedures for planning applications. They are daunting documents at first glance, couched in very precise, if not complex, 'legal' language.

In practice, however, you will find that much of the material they contain, such as how to set out application forms, how to set out neighbour notification forms, notices to tenants and so forth, has already been implemented by your authority and you will need to familiarise yourself with the forms, not the regulations in the Order. Similarly, much of the procedural requirements will have been incorporated into Office Policy Notes or an Office Practice Manual. This you must read, learn and inwardly digest since procedural error can often have more serious consequences than a 'planning' mistake.

So what are the principal features of the Orders? Firstly, they contain a list of definitions which is often overlooked but can prove very useful. For example, it defines 'landscaping' as:

> the treatment of land (other than buildings) being a site or part of a site in respect of which an outline planning permission is granted, for the purpose of enhancing or protecting the amenities thereof and the area in which it is situated, and includes screening by fences, walls or other means, planting of trees, hedges, shrubs or grass, formation of banks, terraces or other earth works, layout of gardens or courts, and other amenity features (The Town and Country Planning (General Development Procedure) (Scotland) Order 1992, No. 224 (3.18)).

Note that this definition includes 'walls' and 'any other amenity features' – a very wide definition.

The Orders then go on to set out how an application for planning permission shall be made, how many copies of the plans, and which certificates and fees must accompany the application. The rules for outline applications are set out, as are the rules for notifying owners and tenants (and in Scotland the neighbours too!).

The Orders then go on to explain exactly what the authority must do, and by when, on receipt of an application, what to do if parts of it are missing, how and by when to ask for more information and time limits for determining the application. They set out who the 'statutory consultees' are, i.e. those bodies which the authority *must* consult. These are also wide ranging, e.g.:

the Theatres Trust where the development involves any land on which there is a theatre as defined in the Theatres Trust Act 1976.

They set out what to do with applications that affect listed buildings and in what circumstances planning authorities must refer applications to the Secretary of State. Most significantly in this section of the Order is set out the requirement that where a planning authority decide to grant permission subject to conditions or refuse an application, the decision notice shall:

state the reasons for the decision.

This is a crucial provision that sits at the very heart of the development control process and ensures that administrative action taken by a local authority is democratically accountable and not an arbitrary whim. This will lead, as we shall see later, to a practical need for the development control officer to focus on the issues relevant to planning and to base the whole of his or her recommendation on well-founded and clearly stated reasons, so that, if so required, these may be challenged on Appeal (of which more later).

One final matter on the procedural side of things before we move on to dealing with the paperwork: this is contained in one of the schedules to the Order and is termed 'Bad Neighbours'. This does not relate to the habits of the folk next door, but to a specific list of potential problem uses. If the authority receives an application for any of these, or indeed anything which they think might include one of these, they must advertise that the application has been submitted.

Briefly, the sorts of development involved include:

1. Public conveniences.
2. Waste disposal of all salts and mineral workings.
3. Slaughter houses.
4. Bingo halls, cinemas, hot food shops, licensed premises, gyms etc.
5. Cemeteries, crematoria, zoos and animal kennels.
6. Car and motor bike racing.
7. Buildings over 20 metres high.
8. The Catch-All category:
   - any buildings or uses that will affect residential property by reason of fumes, noise, vibration, smoke, light or discharge of substances;
   - anything that alters the character of an area of 'established amenity';
   - anything that brings crowds into a generally quiet area;

- anything creating activity or noise between 8 pm and 8 am;
- anything that introduces significant change.

The rule therefore would appear to be – if in doubt, advertise!

ENVIRONMENTAL IMPACT ASSESSMENT

You will recall that the Planning Acts contain provisions for the Secretary of State to make Regulations on this topic – among others! This is to enable planning authorities to comply with European Law, specifically the European Community Directive No. 85/337. This has recently been revised by Directive 97/11/EC, but Regulations are still under discussion.

The current Regulations set out two Schedules of types of development. Those appearing in Schedule One must, if a planning application is made, be accompanied by an Environmental Statement which sets out the predicted impacts on human beings, flora, fauna, soil, water, air, climate, landscape, material assets and the cultural heritage. Furthermore, the Statement must include a description of the measures proposed to avoid, reduce or remedy any significant adverse environmental impacts that are identified. It should also include an outline of the alternatives – *if any* – and the reasons for the choice.

The new Directive, in Article 5(3), requires environmental statements to include an outline of the main alternatives, adds a number of developments to the mandatory list, and most importantly, includes a requirement that the planning authority, if they grant consent for any development supported by an Environmental Statement, should publish the decision – *and the reasons for it*. For the first time then, in planning history, authorities are to be asked to give *reasons* for granting consent. This is a very radical departure.

The Regulations also set out a large number of different types of development, ranging from agricultural works, extractive industries and metal processes to food processing, oil and gas pipeline and installations and knackers yards for which a Statement *may* be required, depending upon the size, scale and location of the proposal. These categories too are added to and expanded upon in the new Directive.

Once such an application has been received, there are several changes to the standard procedures which must be followed.

First and foremost the authority have twice as long to deal with the application and come to a decision than for 'ordinary' applications. (Thus it allows 16 weeks in England and Wales, four months in Scotland.) There is a specific list of bodies who must be consulted on every such application, and in practice this means sending them copies of all the reports and papers. There are specific rules about advertising the proposal for public response and an obligation on the applicant to provide a Non-Technical Summary of the Environmental Statement to assist the general public in their consideration of the issues.

Finally of course you must note that any such Statement is a 'material consideration' and must therefore be taken into account by the authority in coming to a decision.

MATERIAL CONSIDERATIONS

Let us review where we are. The proposal has been looked at and it does constitute development and it is not permitted development, so an application has been made in the proper form and the planning officer has ensured that all the necessary procedures have been followed. The application must now be considered in the light of the Development Plan and any other *material considerations*.

There has been a wealth of cases to clarify what this means. The best starting point is *Stringer* v. *Minister of Housing and Local Government* ([1971] 1 All E R 65). In this famous case, the judge said:

> In principle, any consideration which relates to the use and development of land is capable of being a planning consideration.

The most common consideration is 'amenity'. This word, which covers a multitude of sins, relates to the effect of a proposal on its surroundings. These effects may vary. The physical height or proximity to boundaries may be such that it would look out of place, detract from the quality, beauty or scale of its surroundings, and be generally not welcomed. This 'material consideration' is particularly used in Conservation Areas, in established residential suburbs and near listed buildings and open spaces. Unfortunately it is often used as a blanket objection by people seeking to have the application refused for other, non-material reasons.

What does this mean? Clearly the procedure requires that all letters of representation written to the planning authority about an application have to be taken into account, but they frequently contain arguments against a development which have been established by the Courts as not 'material considerations'.

The first and most crucial of these 'non-matters' is the effect on property values. The planning authority cannot take into account that the building (say) of new houses for sale will have a detrimental effect on the value and saleability of older properties already in the area. Nor can they take account of the potential loss of trade to two existing hot food take-aways from the establishment of a third in the same street. Planning does not exist to regulate the market or protect private property rights.

On the other hand, it has been held to be a material consideration where the planning authority is concerned about the effect of new development, particularly retail, and most particularly out-of-town hypermarkets, on the viability of existing shopping centres. This, it must be stressed, is a recognition of the social need for shopping centres conveniently accessible to the non-car-owning population. In recent years it has taken on added momentum in a bid to reduce or at least contain traffic levels and the unrestricted use of the private car. At the time of writing, much government policy and thinking is being directed towards this issue.

So what else is not material? The other great plea put forward to resist new development is that 'it will spoil the view from my windows'. There is no right to a view, so there is no mechanism to protect it for individuals. Furthermore, it is a highly subjective subject where opinions can be very personal. One person's view of distant hills may be marred by wind turbines, another might feel it introduces a feature of interest into a bleak landscape. The planting of trees around a sewage treatment plant may screen it from view, but may also block views from bedroom windows that look over and beyond.

However, things are never as simple as they seem. If the view is a public one from a particular vantage point or well-known stopping place, for example, it may well be that a new development that intrudes into that view could be resisted as being detrimental to the amenity (that word again!) of the surrounding area. To be intrusive it would have to be (probably) very high, or very ugly, or very unnecessary (of which more later) or very big or incapable of screening.

Let us look at an example with a view:

Liberton Brae allotments extend about one and a half acres and are located on the roadside of one of the main traffic routes into Edinburgh about three miles from the City Centre. They slope away from the road and offer a wonderful view of the palace grounds of Holyrood. Over the years a large number of applications have been made to the City Council to develop housing on the site but they have been beset with problems. The earliest, in 1986, was for 48 houses and was refused because the scale, form and height would prejudice the panoramic view of the City skyline obtained at this site.

In 1989, 27 dwellings were refused because of increased traffic generation, a hazardous access and the loss of that wonderful view. In 1991, 24 flats in two blocks with a gap in between to allow the view to be seen was refused because of the traffic, the access and the monotonous design out of keeping with the locality. An appeal went to the Secretary of State, who dismissed the traffic argument as about a 1% increase on current levels, thought the access could be sorted out, but agreed that what was needed was a design that provided 'a well-mannered response to the characteristics of the site and its surroundings'.

A fresh application for eight detached dwellings was submitted in 1993, but eventually withdrawn because of objections from the Highways Department that the access does not meet, and cannot meet, current visibility standards. Years of intermittent negotiation and discussion with developers followed and in 1996 an application for 12 houses was submitted, with an access that satisfied the Highways authority and a layout of detached houses that followed the curve of the road and the housing opposite that satisfied the Planning Department. A quarter of the number of houses and 11 years of meetings and negotiations, but you will notice that the argument about the view disappears over the years in favour of the real argument which was about houses fitting in to their surroundings.

The next most popular argument advanced as a 'material consideration' is precedent. The argument runs that if this is allowed, then others will follow and the whole character of the area will change. There has been some hesitation by planning authorities in accepting this argument, given the requirement to treat each and every application on its own merits. However, the case of *Collis Radio Limited* v. *Secretary of State for the Environment* (1975 29 P & C R 390) has established that a planning authority may refuse permission for a development which, though unobjectionable in itself, would make it difficult to resist other similar uses which could result in an undesirable proliferation.

Turning from the private interest considerations to the more public, the most widely used is traffic generation and the consequent danger to road safety, noise and disturbance, smells and detriment to the quality of life. This is indeed a material consideration but one where the planning authority should tread warily. If a particular site is designated in a Local Plan for a specified purpose – a hospital perhaps, or a new shopping centre – then it would ill-become an authority to refuse consent because of the traffic it would cause. On the other hand, expansion of existing businesses and uses (quarrying springs to mind) may legitimately be resisted if the effect of such expansion would increase road traffic to such an extent that the detriment to the community and area outweighed the benefits of economic growth and expansion.

Similarly, where the result of the development is the likelihood of interference with the already established activities of others, this too is a material considera-tion. It may operate to prevent or restrict the establishment of new housing near existing industrial undertakings that generate noise and traffic. In the *Stringer* case we quoted above, Cooke J said that the likelihood of interference with the Jodrell Bank telescope was a material consideration. It can also be argued that a proposal should be resisted where it would deprive a neighbouring owner of the opportunity to make a beneficial use of his land, through overshadowing for example, or by taking up all the spare capacity for new traffic on the existing road network. This can be very difficult to prove.

Other 'public' considerations include the effect on public services (can the local schools cope with the likely increase in the number of children from a new housing scheme?), conflict with public proposals for the same or adjoining land, the sterilisation (by building over) of valuable mineral deposits, and the desirability of retaining the existing shops, even where there is doubt about their economic viability. Thus a planning authority will often seek to resist the loss of shops in shopping centres to building society, bookmaker, cafe, and other 'non-shopping' uses, in the interests of keeping local facilities. All too often such resistance merely generates charity shops. A planning authority will similarly seek to resist the loss of residential accommodation to other uses, especially offices, in a bid to maintain resident populations.

Finally, a word about need. The lack of 'need', however perceived, for any development is not a material consideration. If the applicant thinks another pub will be profitable, it is no part of the authority's remit to suggest that enough pubs exist to serve the local public. On the other hand, 'need' as expressed by personal circumstances may be taken into account where considerable hardship might otherwise result, but usually only on a fine balance of 'for and against' views.

Clearly, then, the definition of material considerations is not a precise science. The best guideline to what is 'material' is to ask: Does it matter – to someone/anyone other than a single private individual? If it does, it is probably material.

PLANNING AGREEMENTS/PLANNING GAIN

This is a relatively new and growing field of planning law which is entwined with statutory development control. The basis of it is the statutory provision that:

> A planning authority may enter into an agreement with any person interested in land in their area . . . for the purpose of restricting or regulating the development or use of land, either permanently or during such period as may be prescribed by the agreement.

The purpose behind it is to get something done, or prevent something happening, which cannot be handled by a condition attached to the consent. The circumstances can be very varied, covering road works, other land owned by the applicant, and offers of many kinds from developers to provide facilities for public use. The scope for abuse and confusion is obviously very wide in such cases but a recent decision by the House of Lords has introduced a degree of certainty into the process by laying down certain ground rules.

The case of *Tesco v. Secretary of State for the Environment* [1995] JPL 581 established that:

(a) an agreement must serve a planning purpose;
(b) an agreement must not be unreasonable;
(c) there must be a link or relationship with the planning application.

It should be clear from this that planning permission cannot be bought and sold – i.e. that an offer from a developer to provide some facility or benefit that is not directly related to the proposal cannot make an unacceptable proposal into an acceptable one. Circulars issued both in England and Scotland offer guidance on the policy and principles of such agreement; and they are regularly updated as more case-law further refines this subject.

PROFESSIONALISM

A word about professionalism in the practice of development control is in order. The development control officer has an enormous responsibility entrusted to him or her and it is essential to the credibility of the profession that this trust is honoured. The effect of the grant of consent can be to convert worthless land or buildings into highly valuable assets. It can equally wipe substantial sums off the values of other properties, as well as changing the circumstances and surroundings of many people.

The keynote consideration for the planner is fairness. In the first place fairness to the applicant to ensure that he has been given the proper pre-application advice, that his/her application is processed quickly, that extra information is asked for in good time, the right procedures for advertisement or referral are carried out and the final report to Committee is unbiased, accurate and comprehensive, as well as comprehensible.

Fairness too must typify the planning officer's dealing with neighbours, objectors and other representators. Their views must be properly considered and acknowledged, changes during the process which might affect them or what they have said must be made known to them. Procedures that have been established by the authority must be followed – people will expect all cases to be treated alike, and practices that encourage good and accurate record-keeping must be adopted.

The planning officer should be fair to himself/herself. In any cases where an applicant or agent is a personal friend (or enemy!), in cases where the officer lives nearby and may be a affected (adversely or beneficially), in cases where the applicant or his agent have attempted improper pressure to have the matter determined in a particular way, or in a particular timescale, the planning officer must pass the matter, usually to a more senior officer, but certainly to someone for whose final recommendation he or she has no responsibility or control.

Finally, the planning officer must be fair to the Planning Committee. The decision-makers are entitled to all the information – good or bad – about an application before coming to a decision. This means that any procedural difficulties, errors or omissions must be detailed and remedial steps taken explained, all objections must be clearly and fully stated, the policies of the authority must be set out as they apply, and a reasoned justification offered for the final recommendation.

The consequences of unfairness are serious. Unfairness to the applicant will usually be manifest either in unreasonable delay or in refusal on wholly inadequate grounds. In these circumstances the applicant's appeal to the Secretary of State will usually include an expenses claim against the authority.

Unfairness to objectors may result in Court action to have a decision of the authority reversed where they can show that their objections were not considered. Other than Court action the more likely alternative is reference to the Local Government Commissioner for Maladministration (the Ombudsman) whose concern is primarily not with what was done (in planning terms), but in *how* it was done, and whether injustice has resulted. And remember, the Ombudsman is not looking for malicious intent, deliberate falsehoods or lined pockets – organisational sloppiness and unnecessary delay is quite enough to bring a conclusion of fault against the authority.

The Use of Conditions

The 'material considerations' that were taken into account when examining and evaluating a proposal may result in a decision to grant planning permission, but only subject to certain conditions. You will recall that earlier we saw how the Act gave planning authorities the power to impose conditions and how this power has been subsequently modified.

> The objectives of planning however are best served when that power is exercised in such a way that conditions are clearly seen to be fair, reasonable, and practicable (SOD Circular 18/1986).

There are six tests for conditions which are generally accepted, as a result of Court decisions and government advice. Conditions should only be imposed where they are:

- necessary
- relevant to planning
- relevant to the development to be permitted
- enforceable
- precise
- reasonable in all other respects.

Let us look at each of these criteria in turn.

Necessity – the test for necessity is to ask whether any action would be taken to enforce the condition if it were not complied with. If it would, then the condition can pass the test. For example:

> The premises shall be insulated for the escape of noise so that sound levels of any kind above 30 dB are not audible in any nearby residential property.

Clearly if the night club operator ignored this requirement, then the planning authority would seek to enforce it.

On the other hand 'the exterior of the extension shall be painted white to match the existing dwelling' as a condition on a proposal which already includes white painted external walls is probably unnecessary.

At its strictest interpretation, the question that must be answered is: 'Would planning permission have to be refused if this condition were not imposed?' The notion that it does no harm to impose the condition will not do.

Relevant to planning – any condition must relate to the objectives of planning and not attempt to cover either social issues, or matters properly dealt with by other legislation. This can lead to troubled waters. For instance, where a developer has specified in an application that 30% of the dwellings will be single-person homes and consent has been granted because such provision accords with housing policy and *not* conditioned, how is the planning officer to react to a proposal to redesign the 30% by amalgamating the units into a much lesser number of large family homes? Similarly, where the authority granting consent for a night club is also the licensing authority, can they impose a condition on the planning consent requiring closure at 2 am when all the existing night clubs have licenses that allow them to operate until 4 am? The answer is yes, they can, provided that the reason for the 2 am closure is planning-related, e.g. nearby houses, and not public-order-related, which is the justification for the 4 am closure of all the others.

Relevance to the development – any condition imposed must relate to the development. Thus a condition that required the applicant to rebuild a front boundary wall in natural stone when the application was for a conservatory to the rear is not relevant. A condition requiring a factory owner to plant trees to screen his existing works does not relate to his proposal to extend a car park at another site owned by him. On the other hand, a condition that required the use of natural stone in the building of an extension for a day nursery would be relevant if the house were listed or in a Conservation Area. The 'development' here is a wider issue than the establishment of a day nursery.

Enforceable – this will sometimes regrettably turn on the authority's resources to carry out enforcement procedures, but it should not. A condition requiring that the number of children in our day nursery above be limited to 20 is enforceable, but what about a condition that restricted the use of the back garden to no more than five children at any one time? This may be unenforceable. A condition imposed on the owner of a property that restricts the rights he may otherwise enjoy as 'permitted development' is enforceable but discouraged by government advice. A condition that requires an applicant to do something other than that for which he has consent may well be unenforceable. If Mr A applies to build a house with a tiled roof, a condition may be imposed requiring red tiles. If, however, Mr A has specified that he plans to roof with green tiles, a condition cannot require red tiles instead. Under no circumstances should a condition be imposed requiring the development to be carried out in accordance with the submitted plans. Failure to do this simply results in unauthorised development for which no consent has been given.

Precise – it must be clearly understandable to the applicant what it is he is required to do in order to meet the condition and therefore a degree of precision is necessary. Some examples of imprecise conditions might be:

1. 'The premises shall be operated in a quiet and orderly manner.'
2. 'The development shall be constructed in a workmanlike way, using proper materials.'
3. 'The use of the rear garden shall be appropriate for a residential area at all times.'
4. 'Materials stored on site must not be detrimental to the amenity (that awful word again) of the area.'
5. 'The premises shall close at a reasonable time.'

And finally, your conditions must be reasonable in all other respects. They must not therefore expect the developer to gift land or money to the local authority for purposes unrelated to the application. They must not require that the works, or any part of them, are carried out to the satisfaction of a third party (who might *never* be satisfied!). They must not expect the developer to get agreement for an access over someone else's land. And what is even more important to remember is that an unreasonable condition does not become a reasonable one because the developer has suggested it or agreed to it. The consent that is granted relates to the *land*, not to the applicant, it runs *with* the land, and if a condition is unreasonable it may be struck out by the Courts in the future.

Frequently time controls are put on consents to limit their lifespans. These controls do not operate to vary the five-year rule for implementation, but to put an end date on the use, so that the matter may be reviewed at that time. This is most usually done where either the structure is temporary (sheds and prefabricated buildings) or the use is temporary – seasonal or interim use of the land or buildings pending redevelopment (car boot sales in old industrial premises are a favourite). However, there are circumstances where there is a measure of uncertainty on the part of the planning authority of the precise impact of the proposal, and in these circumstances it is reasonable to limit the development to a trial period so that this can be assessed. Where this occurs a very precise framing of conditions is necessary, since the development (our extension to house a day nursery) will have begun when the works are commenced, and not when the first children arrive. Thus a one-year consent in the first instance may have all but expired before there is any real evidence of the effect of this nursery on the neighbourhood.

Permissions that limit the occupation of premises to particular categories of people are discouraged – consent runs with the land. Personal permissions are therefore also to be avoided wherever possible. Conditions that restrict the freedom of an applicant to exercise his legal rights should be avoided as probably unenforceable. 'The granny flat shall only be occupied by a member of the applicant's family and shall not be sold, let or disposed of as a separate unit' is a fairly common condition which lays a minefield of dangers to the planning authority in almost every word.

Here is an example of what can go wrong:

In early 1972 a stockbroker from London approached a rural English County Council and told them he was giving up city life to become a farmer. To this end, he had agreed to buy a farm, but the farmer was not willing to sell him the old farm house where he lived with his family. Could he get planning permission for a new farm house? Naturally, said the planning authority, and granted consent for the new farm house, situated next to the old one on the roadside, subject to the following condition: 'The occupation of the dwelling shall be limited to a person employed or last employed, wholly or mainly locally in agriculture or the dependants of any such person.'

Clear enough? Certainly. However, our stockbroker, having built the house, sold the land back to the farmer and moved into the olde worlde farm house, giving the farmer in exchange a brand new luxury home. Life was so comfortable for the farmer in his new home that he decided to retire from farming and stay on in the house (last employed in agriculture). And so of course he sold the farm – without the farm house.

Less than a year later, another would-be farmer then approaches the County Council and says he's bought a farm with no farm house and can he have planning permission for one? What could the authority do? Nothing, except to grant consent again for another dwelling, restrict it in the same terms, and hope that the new farmer didn't decide to retire. So three farm houses ended up in a row in the countryside where previously only one traditional old dwelling had stood.

THE DECISION-MAKING PROCESS

Responsibility for taking decisions on planning applications rests primarily with the elected members of the Planning Committee. In many cases they will delegate authority to reach a decision on minor matters to the most senior official in the Planning Department. Such cases will usually include applications for house extensions, satellite dishes, minor works to commercial premises and other matters to which there has been little or no objection from the public. For the remainder, however, the Committee will require a report. At intervals, sometimes as frequently as weekly, in other areas once in four weeks, the Committee Members will meet to consider reports, ask questions of the planning officer and take decisions.

In order to take decisions, information that is clear, accurate and comprehensive will be required. There are varied formats for the presentation of such reports, but they will generally follow this sequence:

The Site: Bear in mind that many of the Councillors will not know the site and will not be familiar with its surroundings. The description should therefore accurately state the size, the condition, the whereabouts, the current use and any significant features. To do this properly it is essential that the site is visited by the planning officer at least once and preferably twice – once when the application arrives, and again just before the report is written. Bear in mind too that the site may well be within the area of a Councillor on the Committee – any inaccuracy or omission in your report will be spotted immediately. A general description of the surrounding area should also be included, as should any special controls which apply to the area – listed building, Conservation Area, Tree Preservation Order – to name but a few.

The History: The members of the Committee will probably not wish you to rehearse everything that has ever happened on the site – you probably won't know it, and you probably won't be able to find it out. What is being looked for here is any significant history that may have a bearing on the current application. This can vary enormously. Some examples are:

1. 'The site lies on the line of the Mediaeval Town Walls.'
2. 'The land was used for coal mining in the nineteenth century.'
3. 'The site forms part of a former Gas Works site.'
4. 'The site is formed from domestic refuse tipping in the 1920s.'
5. 'The buildings have been used for the assaying of gold and silver.'
6. 'The public house was granted consent in 1955.'
7. 'The use has persisted for many years and no complaints have been received.'

All these points, and many more like them, help to build up a picture of the site in the Committee's mind, so that a clearer and better decision can be made.

The Proposal: Do not rely on the brief and often misleading description offered by the applicant. 'Formation of a community focal point with licence' is an application for a public house. Tell the Committee it's a public house, tell them how big it is, and how many people it could accommodate, tell them how late the Licensing Committee would allow it to open.

It may be that the proposal, far from being briefly described, is accompanied by a supporting statement. This can range from a one-page summary of the company's operating procedures to a full Environmental Statement with Appendices and Maps and Diagrams. Do not attempt to recite the whole story to the Committee in your report. Here you must seek to select the main points, the main headings, the main likely environmental impacts and set them out. Make sure, however, that all the members had access to all the documents well in advance.

The Consultations: A full and faithful account of the response from your statutory consultees (the people/bodies/organisations that you *must* consult on particular application as required by the General Development *Procedure* Orders – remember?) should be provided. Having said this, do not overwhelm your members with a great deal of technical material of which you may have little understanding and they rather less. Make quite sure that you understand the main concerns, or the main requirements of your consultees and that you can explain them, or incorporate them into conditions attached to a consent. It is not of course necessary to explain to your Committee why you have consulted particular bodies – this is part of your job and you are expected to know how to do it.

The Representations: These are the responses from the public. First of all remember that not every letter is an objection – in many cases support from local people will be forthcoming for development which provides local employment, improves shopping provision or cleans up local eyesores. The key to reporting representations to your Committee is again thoroughness. It is not your task (at this stage) to set out what is relevant to planning objectives and what is not. To do so is to invite disaster. The aggrieved objector whose letter has been ignored may well seek redress through the Courts, who will set the decision aside, even where the grounds of objection were not well founded in planning. In summary, then, if the objector said it, you tell the Committee. The only exception to this rule is the letter that descends into vulgar abuse, racist remarks or rambling incoherence. In such circumstances the planning officer must use discretion and judgement in the manner in which the letter's content is reported. But make sure the Councillors have access to all the letters to read too.

Policy: It cannot be assumed by the planning officer that his/her Committee knows their own policies. They will generally be aware of the general 'thrust' of policy – discouraging new housing in the open countryside, protecting Green Belts, retaining shops in shopping centres and so forth, but the detailed 'chapter and verse' and the exceptions to those policies will require to be explained to them, in so far as they affect the proposal in question. Do not therefore write out huge chunks of the Local Plan which have nothing to do with the application, but select and present the relevant policies in clear and unambiguous language so that members know their own yardstick for decisions. You may also be required by the practice of your particular authority to cite examples of decisions taken by them in conformity with these policies in the recent past.

Assessment: This is your chance to practice your profession. Decisions are rarely clear cut, not requiring any input of judgement or the weighing of alternatives. If this were so, a computer could generate decisions. Here you are being asked to discuss the strengths and weaknesses of the proposal, evaluate those against the Local Plan and the views of consultees, consider the public response and how this may affect the acceptability of the proposal, and present a recommendation to your Committee based on your overall evaluation.

Members may ask questions, request further information, seek changes, decide to visit the site themselves and in the end ignore your advice and (say) refuse consent. This is their lawful right and duty, and the reason they were elected as decision-makers. It is crucial not to lose sight of this since their decision, whatever it is, does not affect the quality or value of your advice. You have been asked for advice, not on a casual basis, but as an informed and qualified professional. If your Committee choose to ignore that advice, or to give different weight to opposing views than you have given, it is entirely proper for them to do so. You have not lost anything.

The Right of Appeal

Because it is fundamental to any democracy that artibrary action by a public authority does not go unchallenged, the Acts provide a right of appeal against a refusal of planning permission or the imposition of conditions on a grant of consent. This right is defined in the Act as clearly limited to the applicant. There are two points to underline here. One is that the appeal procedure is only available to the applicant and only against refusal (or failure to determine, which comes to the same thing) or conditions. Thus it is not available to aggrieved objectors who see a consent granted against their wishes, or granted subject to conditions that do not meet their concerns. Nor is it available to a subsequent purchaser of a site who wishes to revive a proposal turned down to the previous owner.

The Procedure Orders then take over and set out the details of the how and when of an appeal. The most important requirement contained in the Order is that the applicant is required to 'state the grounds on which the appeal is made'. It is not sufficient therefore to cite disappointment and grievance at the authority's decision – the grounds of appeal, which may vary from a simple list of bullet points to a full statement prepared by planning consultants, are the key to the subsequent proceedings.

It is open to the applicant to request that his/her appeal is heard at a Public Inquiry. This is increasingly rare these days as they can prove very time-consuming and costly exercises for all concerned, and will almost certainly delay a final decision to a much later date than the alternative.

This alternative is known as Written Submissions. On deciding to appeal the applicant completes a form from the Secretary of State and submits his/her written argument to the relevant body charged with the business of determining appeals. This is the Planning Inspectorate in England and Wales, the Reporters Unit in Scotland. On receipt of an appeal, the relevant body will check that it is a competent appeal (i.e. that it has been made within six months of the date of refusal/decision and is by the proper person), and will advise the local authority of its receipt. The local authority should also have been sent a copy of the relevant papers.

The Inspectorate will then ask the planning authority to complete another form within 28 days in which the authority are asked to agree to the appeal method proposed, identify the consultees referred to during processing of the application, list the number of objectors, certify that all the proper advertisement procedures were observed, and name a local newspaper in which the appeal will be advertised.

The authority then has a further period in which to submit its 'Observations on the Grounds of Appeal'. These are sent to the Inspectorate and copied to the person appealing ('the appellant' as they are now called). The appellant may then submit comment on the local authority's Observations and the local authority may make further observations on these comments. In this way the appellant has two opportunities to put his case, i.e. grounds of appeal and comments, and the authority similarly has two opportunities, i.e. observations and further observations.

A date will then be set for a site inspection by the Inspector/Reporter. This will be attended by the appellant; the local authority planning officer and objectors are also invited to attend. The purpose of the site inspection is to enable the Inspector to determine the facts of the case for himself; only factual matters relating to the site may be drawn to his attention. It must not degenerate into a kangaroo court or a lobbying exercise and Inspectors/Reporters are always very careful to ensure this. Obviously, more leeway is permitted to objectors than to the principal parties and it is often difficult to distinguish where fact ends and merits begin. Thus if an objector points out how busy the road serving the development is, this is a matter of fact. If he/she points out how dangerous all this traffic is to children trying to cross the road to the park, have they strayed into the merits?

Finally, a decision letter will be issued, usually on the basis of authority delegated to the Inquiry official from the Secretary of State. That decision may allow or dismiss the appeal, or reverse or vary any part of the decision of the planning authority, whether the appeal relates to that part or not. Thus an appeal against conditions restricting the hours of operation of a night-club can result in a decision that varies the hours but imposes new conditions on the point of access, to prevent noise breakout for example.

The key to understanding all this is the provision that the Secretary of State 'may deal with the application as if it had been made to him in the first instance'. He is not bound by anything which the planning authority may have done or agreed or imposed or required.

Furthermore, the decision of the Secretary of State is final.

There does exist the opportunity for a challenge at law to the Secretary of State but not on the planning merits of the case with which we are primarily concerned.

Sometimes, the Secretary of State gets involved in some very odd cases indeed:

Bill Heine lives in a terraced house in the Oxford suburb of Headington. In 1986 he came up with the idea of an 18 ft shark in fibre glass appearing to plunge head first into the roof of his home. He called it a public sculpture 'Untitled 1986'. The planning authority was less than delighted, saying that the giant fish detracted from the harmonious appearance of the terrace, was out of place in the locality and that in consequence its deleterious impact on visual amenity amounted to demonstrable harm sufficient to justify its removal.

Mr Heine refused to remove his shark and a six-year battle ensued. Eventually the matter got to the stage of an appeal to the Secretary of State – and Mr Heine won. The Secretary of State said:

> It is not in dispute that the shark is not in harmony with its surroundings, but it is not intended to be in harmony with them. One must look at the relationship of the shark to the house, as well as to the terrace and wider surroundings. Even though the shark is large, prominent and out of character with both the appeal buildings and its surroundings, it is not gravely detrimental to visual amenity in this particular location.

He agreed with his Inspector who had said he could not believe that the purpose of planning control is to enforce a boring and mediocre uniformity on the environment. Any system of control, he said, must make space for the dynamic, the unexpected and the downright quirky.

Mr Heine was delighted. 'It's not every day that you get the Secretary of State saying "congratulations, keep your shark".'

OTHER CONTROLS

In this section we will look at some of the other powers exercised by a planning authority as part of the development control function. These powers divide into two groups – the supplementary powers available in the 'normal' development control world and the special controls available under associated legislation.

SUPPLEMENTARY POWERS

Completion Notice   In cases where the planning authority are of the opinion that a development, which has been started, will not be completed 'within a reasonable period' they may serve a completion notice which effectively says that the planning permission will expire after a certain date if the development has not been completed. There are two points you should remember (apart from the extreme rarity of such notices). The first is that the applicant must be allowed a minimum of one year to complete the work. The second is that the notice must be confirmed by the Secretary of State.

Variation of Existing Consent   Where a development is approved, and during the preparation of more detailed site drawings some problem comes to light, the applicant will frequently ask for the consent to be varied, and this the authority may do, provided that it is not a material variation. You will recall 'material considerations' and 'material changes of use'. Here we have 'material' again. Most authorities have developed their own code of practice in determining what is and is not 'material'. As a good working guide, you are again advised to ask the question 'Does it matter?'. If it does, then the variation is probably material and would need a fresh application. Try these examples – there are no answers!

1. A builder has consent for 100 detached houses but now wishes to build 98 detached and two semi-detached.
2. Consent for a retail park includes one unit for a restaurant. The developer now wishes to use the restaurant as another shop unit.
3. An extension to an old building was to be roofed in matching slate but cost means the builder would prefer to use grey tiles.
4. A retail warehouse site was to be edged with timber fencing but the railway alongside is insisting on a two metre high chain link fence.
5. Because sewer crossing the site is not as deep as originally thought, land will have to be mounded up by one metre and a house built on top of the mound.
6. Consent has been given for a garage to the left of the house and a conservatory to the right, but owner would now like them the other way around.

Modification and Revocation and Discontinuance This is a curious power allowing the planning authority 'if it appears to them expedient to do so' to modify or revoke a consent which they have granted. This modification or revocation can be done with or without the consent of the owner and occupier of the affected property. Where he/she does not consent, the Secretary of State must confirm the Order. Similarly the authority may by Order seek the discontinuance of an existing use. However, in order to avoid the arbitrary exercise of authority, once the consent has been implemented, or the use taken up, it cannot be modified or revoked, even with the applicant's consent. So, for example, a limit on the number of restaurants in one street might mean that a new application should be refused. An offer by the applicant to allow the authority to revoke his existing consent for his existing restaurant in the basement of the same premises would have no effect – the use has been taken up and cannot be revoked.

Regulating the Development or Use of Land Special agreements may be entered into – these have been looked at in the section 'Planning Agreements/Planning Gain'.

Trees An order may be made by a planning authority if it is 'expedient in the interests of amenity' to make provision for the preservation of trees or woodlands in their district:

● these orders generally prohibit the cutting down, topping, lopping, uprooting, wilful damage or wilful destruction of trees without the consent of the planning authority.

Consent is usually granted subject to conditions requiring replanting, but may be refused where trees are healthy and replanting is not an option. It is of interest to remember that unlike ignoring planning permission, cutting down a tree subject to a Tree Preservation Order (TPO) is an offence and may attract a hefty fine. Incidentally, all the trees in a Conservation Area are 'deemed' to be covered by a TPO.

Advertisements The statutes give the Secretary of State the power to make regulations about advertisement display where it is in the interests of amenity or public safety. Those Regulations effectively set out the classes or types of advertisement that are deemed to have consent and for which therefore it is not necessary to make an application.

There are six principal classes of deemed consent. The first is the functional advertisements of local authorities and transport undertakers for the purposes of carrying out their duties. You will see that this is necessary if you consider that among other things the authority must, in some cases, advertise by notice on land which is the subject of a planning application. To require the authority to get consent to put up such an advertisement would be nonsense. Similar thinking will relate to road signs, bus stops and footpath signs.

The second class, which is restricted in the size of the notice, is termed miscellaneous and includes 'brass plates', church notice boards and pub signs. The third covers temporary notices such as For Sale, Livestock Auction Here, Wimpey Homes, Church Fete – Sunday, and so on. The fourth covers notices on business premises that offer information about the business, the owner's name and so on; the fifth covers advertisements within buildings; and the sixth covers illuminated signs that do the same job as Class 4.

Clearly, then, what is controlled by application to the planning authority is the big advertisement hoardings in public places, illuminated signs outside buildings which promote the product sold, and advertisement panels attached directly to buildings. It is also worth noting at this stage that there are considerable powers available to an authority to control unauthorised advertisements.

SPECIAL CONTROLS

Listed Building Consent

In every local authority area there will be a number of buildings, ranging from a few hundred to many thousands, that have been 'listed' by the Secretary of State as being of Special Architectural or Historic Interest. If anyone wishes to carry out any works to a listed building, whether for their alteration, extension or demolition, they must get permission from the local planning authority.

But what are 'works'? Look at this case:

———

R v. The Secretary of State for Wales ex parte Kennedy JPL. August 1996, p. 645.

Leighton Hall, a mansion in Welshpool, Powys, contained three bronze chandeliers and a huge chiming clock which was located in the entrance tower. All four items were removed and the local authority served notices requiring their restoration to the building. They did so on the basis that listed building consent is required for the removal of any article within a listed building which constitutes a 'fixture'.

The person on whom the notice was served appealed to the Secretary of State for Wales, on the grounds that these items were 'mobile pieces of furniture'. The Secretary of State dismissed that appeal and the matter went before the High Court.

In this judgment the Court referred to the case of *Berkley* v. *Poulett and others*, and ruled that the test in Berkley should apply. The question of whether an article was or was not 'a fixture' fell to be determined by applying a dual test:

(a) the degree to which the article in question could properly be said to be annexed to the building;

(b) the purpose for which it was put there.

In this case the Court found that these items were fixtures, particularly because of their historical association with Lieghton Hall. The case also indicated that some degree of 'annexation' is necessary – in other words, a fireplace is clearly annexed to a listed building, where a chaise-longue is not. The purpose and relationship to the building are all-important and in applying the *Berkley* test it is essentially a matter of fact and degree.

Similar procedural requirements apply as they do for planning permission but with two notable exceptions.

The first is that anyone who fails to apply for listed building consent and then carries out any works, commits an offence, which may lead to a fine or imprisonment or both. This is in sharp contrast to the planning permission situation where no offence is created by statute for unauthorised development. It is incidentally a defence to a charge of this offence to prove that the works were urgently necessary for health, safety or the preservation of the building and the local authority were told all about it in writing as soon as possible.

The second major difference is that the authority, if they intend to grant consent, must inform the Secretary of State and give him an opportunity to review the decision and if he so wishes, 'call-in' the application for his own decision. It should not be thought that there are *two* decisions here – the planning authority, in the shape of their Planning Committee, will resolve that consent should be granted, provided the Secretary of State has no objections. If he has none, it is the planning authority who then grant the consent.

Similar rules apply in relation to conditions, reasons, modifications and revocations as they do to planning applications. The appeal procedure is also similar. Finally, you should be aware that ecclesiastical buildings currently in use as such do not require listed building consent – but this exception does not include the vicarage!

Conservation Area Consent

Where a planning authority have designated a Conservation Area in part of their district, special rules apply to demolition. In ordinary circumstances, most demolition is 'permitted development'. This is not so in Conservation Areas. Anyone wishing to carry out any demolition works (subject to some tiny exceptions) must apply for Conservation Area Consent before doing so. Failure to apply and the carrying out of unauthorised development is an offence, like doing things to a listed building. The procedures to be followed, and the checks and balances imposed, are broadly similar to those for listed buildings and planning applications. Again the Secretary of State requires to be notified if the authority intends to allow demolition in a Conservation Area.

Hazardous Substances Consent

This is a relative newcomer to the clutch of powers of planning authorities. Regulations control what constitutes a hazardous substance and how much may be stored without consent. Any amount over that and an application must be made to the planning authority. Again, certain consultations (notably with the Health and Safety Executive) must be carried out, and conditions may be attached to any grant of consent. There is the customary right of appeal against those conditions or outright refusal. The main difference to note here is that an offence is only committed when the quantity of hazardous substances stored exceeds that for which consent has been granted. Interestingly, the Health and Safety Executive have a supervisory jurisdiction over the whole process, and if the planning authority have unwittingly 'authorised' something which is in breach of regulations under other legislation, they can advise the authority that the consent is void, and the authority must revoke it.

CONCLUSION

Development control is a complex mechanism of processes designed to ensure that land use is controlled in the public interest. It is therefore heavily influenced by those matters of greatest concern to the general public. These include the prevention of pollution, the preservation of Green Belts and open spaces, the preservation of fine old buildings and 'attractive' areas, maintaining the peace and quiet of residential areas, keeping businesses and commerce alive and flourishing, and improving road safety.

All these very legitimate concerns have to be balanced against the freedom of an individual or company to pursue their own interests on their own land with their own property, the need to maintain a diversified and competitive economy, and the rights of individuals to be protected from arbitrary and unaccountable decision-making by public authorities.

This necessarily results in a fine mesh of detailed provisions in statute and by the interpretation of the Courts so that a proper balance is maintained. The Development Control planner is the fulcrum of that balance.

CHAPTER 5

CENTRAL GOVERNMENT PLANNING POLICY

Matthew J. Quinn

INTRODUCTION

This chapter explores the role of central government policy in the operation of the planning system in the UK, summarising the status of national guidance and the differing formats across the UK. It sets the changing function of guidance in the context of the commitment to ensure more sustainable development and points up the considerable changes being introduced by the 1997 Labour administration.

The second part of the chapter discusses the way in which guidance is prepared and debates criticism of its content and operation. It concludes that the system is robust enough to meet present and future challenges, provided it can be seen as making an effective and timely contribution to achieving our economic, environmental and social goals.

WHY CENTRAL POLICY?

Not every country has a national planning system and national guidance. In many countries, planning is seen as an almost exclusively local concern, albeit one that may have wider consequences. This has long not been the case in the UK, where concerns about local development led to national policy intervention even ahead of the 1948 Planning Act which set down the present national legal framework. This national role continues to develop but at its heart intervention and policy have aimed:

- to prevent development considered inappropriate at the national level (typified by Green Belt policy against urban sprawl and the protection afforded to nationally important nature and heritage sites);
- to ensure that nationally important needs are met (most clearly shown in the areas of national forecasting of housing and transport); and
- to promote consistency and quality in practice and decisions.

This broadly reflects the often-cited role of planning as providing the right thing in the right place at the right time.

OVERSEAS CONTRASTS

The benefits of a national approach can be illustrated by the problems faced by countries that have no national system.

In the US, for example, it has proved extremely difficult to prevent low density sprawl, despite the environmental, transport and social impacts it can have. There is generally nothing to stop individual local authorities granting permission in order to benefit their own tax base at the expense of neighbours. Concerned States have been forced to adopt State growth management legislation to seek to contain these pressures and promote more compact and hence sustainable forms of development. The Federal level has almost no levers over urban form, despite its importance for national and international concerns such as energy demand. Similarly, in Australia, the Federal level can generally only become involved where internationally designated sites are affected.

A LOCAL SYSTEM

The bedrock of the land-use planning system in the UK is the statutory responsibility placed on local authorities for drawing up development plans for their area and for making planning decisions through the refusal or granting in full or subject to conditions of planning permission for development. These are set out principally in the Town and Country Planning Act 1990 (for England and Wales (as amended)) and the Town and Country Planning (Scotland) Act 1997. Only in the special circumstances of Northern Ireland is local planning vested in national government (The Planning (Northern Ireland) Order 1991). The text of this chapter focuses principally on the approach taken in England, Scotland and Wales. In Northern Ireland, the system has been centrally controlled since 1972, when planning powers were removed from local government. In other respects it operates in close parallel to the English system although it has not been brought up to date with the statutory changes of the last years.

There are powers for the relevant Secretary of State to take individual planning decisions, to decide appeals against local authority decisions, to direct changes to plans, and even to make plans in part or in their entirety, but these are very rarely exercised. Over 95% of individual planning decisions are taken by local authorities.

The existence of central guidance does not change the fact that the essence of the system lies at the local level and in the locally prepared development plans. It is for local planning authorities to determine how best their areas should be developed in the light of national guidance and local concerns, following public consultation. While there are inevitable tensions between national demands and local concerns, this remains a genuinely locally based system. That it has remained so stems in no small part from its ability to reflect the concerns of the different interested parties, including central government, effectively.

NATIONAL GUIDANCE AND THE PLANNING SYSTEM

National planning policy for the UK has been delivered in a number of forms over the years but, for England, the bulk of guidance to local authorities is now found in the Planning Policy Guidance note series (the PPGs). PPGs were introduced in 1987 to provide a concise and readily accessible source of guidance to replace the various government circulars which until then had been the main vehicle for advice. Circulars are still used but are generally confined to more technical or administrative issues. There is a separate series of minerals planning guidance (MPGs).

For Scotland, National Planning Policy Guidelines (NPPGs) (Box 1) are the main policy documents, supported where appropriate by a locational framework. Circulars also provide statements of policy, containing guidance on policy implementation through legislation or procedural change. Planning Advice Notes provide advice on good practice.

In Wales, guidance has been brought together into a single PPG (Wales): Planning Policy, which has a single main note: Planning Guidance (Wales), an overall planning policy document which has superseded most of existing PPG guidance for Wales. It is supplemented by a series of Technical Advice Notes (Wales) or 'TANs' which give more detailed information on particular subjects. A separate series is in preparation for minerals planning guidance.

Box 1

Current National Planning Policy Guidelines (NPPGs) in Scotland. These differ from those in England and Wales in detail and titles though their general thrust is similar.

NPPG 1 *The Planning System*
NPPG 2 *Business and Industry*
NPPG 3 *Land for Housing*
NPPG 4 *Land for Mineral Working*
NPPG 5 *Archaeology and Planning*
NPPG 6 *Renewable Energy*
NPPG 7 *Planning and Flooding*
NPPG 8 *Town Centres and Retailing*
NPPG 9 *The Provision of Roadside Facilities on Motorways and Other Trunk Roads in Scotland*
NPPG 10 *Planning and Waste Management*
NPPG 11 *Sport, Physical Recreation and Open Space*
NPPG 12 *Skiing Developments*
NPPG 13 *Coastal Planning*

NPPG 14 *Natural Heritage*
NPPG 15 *Rural Development*
NPPG 16 *Opencast Coal and Related Minerals*
NPPG 17 *Transport and Planning*
NPPG 18 *Planning and the Historic Environment*

In Northern Ireland, the Planning Service, a Next Steps Agency of the Northern Ireland Office, prepares Planning Policy Statements (PPSs) which do or will cover a similar range of topics to PPGs in England. These are gradually replacing other forms of advice such as an existing Rural Planning Strategy. There are also a series of Development Control Advice Notes on specific types of development or technical issues.

National government also issues regional and strategic guidance to guide development in specific areas after advice from the relevant local authorities. In England these take the form of Regional Planning Guidance, plus strategic guidance for larger metropolitan areas. A regional strategic framework has been prepared by Northern Ireland's Planning Service. The area of regional/strategic planning is most directly affected by current changes to the governmental system in the UK.

National guidance has been supported by nationally drawn up projections of future housing, minerals and transport demands in its role in ensuring that future needs are met. Nationally important road infrastructure has also been planned and developed directly by national government. The role of these projections and the methods of planning for nationally important infrastructure are areas where the 1997 Labour administration is developing new approaches.

To support the role of avoiding development where it would cause national harm, there are processes for national designation of sites or areas, often in other legislation, to afford them particular protection. The most important are the international wildlife sites, Sites of Special Scientific Interest and Areas of Outstanding Natural Beauty.

THE FORMAL STATUS OF GUIDANCE

GUIDANCE AND PLANS

National, regional and strategic guidance must by law be taken into account by local planning authorities when they are preparing their development plans which set out the policies for development over the coming years in their areas.

The development plan in England, Wales and Scotland generally consists of the structure plan prepared at county level (region in Scotland); and the local plan – which must be in general conformity with the structure plan – at the district level. In metropolitan authorities in England – and since 1996 for the 25 local planning authorities in Wales – a two part unitary development plan covers both strategic and local issues.

Since changes to the primary legislation in England and Wales introduced by the Planning and Compensation Act in 1991, and in Scotland by the 1997 Act, development plans are now the primary consideration in determining applications for planning permission. Decisions must now accord with the plan unless there are overriding reasons to the contrary. This has been dubbed the 'plan-led system'. In this way, the plan is the main determinant of decisions. Because national guidance is a major influence on plans, it thus has a major indirect effect on individual decisions (see Box 2, also Chapter 5).

Box 2 *Plan preparation*

Consultation

The start of the development plans process remains some form of consultation process on the proposals being put forward by the local planning authority. The basis on which consultation is undertaken remains for the authority to decide, but PPG12 emphasises that, with a two-stage deposit process, there is no need for consultation to be undertaken on the basis of a full draft plan. However they decide to undertake consultation, local authorities need to consider any representations made during the consultation process, and the regulation which requires the preparation of a statement outlining who has been consulted, the steps taken to publicise the plan proposals and the opportunities given to make representations will remain. There is no list of pre-deposit statutory consultees. It is for local authorities to decide whom they need to consult on particular issues relating to the plan in the period before deposit. Such decisions depend on the nature of the plan proposals – whether they comprise a minor alteration to an existing plan or a full replacement plan will clearly be one factor to be taken into consideration in reaching a decision on the level of consultation needed in particular circumstances.

Statement of Conformity

The need for a statement of whether a local plan is in conformity with the structure plan is required by the 1990 Act and must be sought before the plan is put on deposit.

Deposit of Plan

When plans are placed on deposit local authorities advertise where copies can be inspected.

Objections and Representations

The period for objections and representations on the plan at initial deposit is six weeks. Objections and representations need to be made at this stage as the opportunity for objections and representations at the revised (i.e. second) deposit stage will be limited.

After the end of the initial deposit period local authorities should make available details of objections that have been received in respect of the proposals deposited. This may take the form of a simple schedule of those objections received, with details of where further information about the objections can be viewed. This not only allows objectors to see whether there are others objecting to similar matters (thereby allowing objectors to consider whether to join together in any subsequent discussions with the local authority), but also allows people the opportunity to see details of objections and any alternative sites proposed by objectors. Local authorities may decide to invite representations on objections made, for example on those which propose alternative sites.

Handling of Objections and Negotiations with Objectors

The period between the two deposit periods allows local authorities to discuss objections with objectors and to consider whether there are changes that can be made to the plan proposals which will satisfy either fully, or at least in part, their concerns.

Where the local authority is prepared to make changes to the plan which fully resolves one or more objections, then those objections should be formally withdrawn by the objector when the revised proposals are deposited. If the local authority decides not to make changes, then the objections made will automatically transfer to the revised deposit stage and will be considered by the Inspector as part of the inquiry process (either heard at the inquiry or dealt with through written representations). However, there will also be situations where the local authority agree to make changes to the plan which only partially meet the objector's concerns.

Revised Deposit

When the local authority have considered all the objections made at the initial deposit and their response to them, they then prepare a revised plan and proposals map for deposit. The revised plan proposals should clearly identify the changes that the local authority have made, and a new, updated proposals map must also be produced for deposit. This revised deposit stage is needed in all cases except for those rare circumstances where no objections were made at the initial deposit, or in those cases where the local authority decide to propose no changes to the plan following their consideration of objections arising from the initial deposited proposals.

There is a need for adequate publicity of changes made to the plan. This is essential in order that people content with the plan proposals at initial I deposit (but who did not register a formal representation in support of the proposals) I are aware that changes have been made to which they now may wish to object.

Scope of Objections at Revised Deposit

The period for registering duly made objections at the revised deposit stage is six weeks. Objections at this stage can only be made to changes made to the plan by the local authority. New objections cannot be made on those parts of the plan proposals that have not been changed, nor can objections be made on the basis of omissions to the proposals. Those objections should have been made at the initial deposit stage.

Further Changes to the Plan

The local authority is required to consider objections made to the plan at the revised deposit stage and will want to consider their response to them. Normally, this would be expected to be undertaken as part of the public inquiry process. However, there may be occasions where the local authority wishes to respond to one or more objections with proposals for further pre-inquiry changes to the plan.

The Public Inquiry

During the inquiry, the Inspector will consider (either written representations or oral evidence):

- objections made to the initial deposit plan which have not been withdrawn (i.e. because no changes were made to the plan were made at revised deposit);
- outstanding issues of objection that were only partially resolved between first and second deposit (these will have been identified by the objector and the local authority);
- objections arising from changes made by the local authority at the revised deposit stage;
- supporting representations (unless the Inspector decides otherwise, these will normally only be considered as written representations).

In all cases, it is important to recognise that the inquiry will only be considering objections and representations in light of the revised plan proposals deposited at the second deposit stage. The initial deposited plan proposals have no locus once the inquiry is reached, and will not be considered by the Inspector at the inquiry. However, the local planning authority will be asked in their evidence to the inquiry to explain the changes made to the plan at revised deposit and the reasons for those changes. This should help the Inspector in making his or her recommendations, e.g. in not recommending an alternative site or proposal that had previously been rejected by the local planning authority because of the strength of objection at the initial deposit stage.

Inspector's Report

Local planning authorities must make the report of the Inspector available within eight weeks of its receipt. This will mean copies of the report being made available for inspection at the locations where the plan was deposited.

In order to assist procedures post-inquiry, the Inspector's report will contain an executive summary of all the recommendations made in the report.

Post-Inquiry Procedures

Having considered the Inspector's report and recommendations, the local authority is required to place on deposit their decision on each of the recommendations in the Inspector's report. Where the local authority choose not to accept a recommendation, they must provide clear and cogent reasons for not doing so. An objection can still be made to a decision not to accept an Inspector's recommendation.

Advertising Modifications

The local authority will also need to decide whether there is a need for advertising modifications to the plan. There may still be a need for modifications if, for example:

1. the local authority decide to accept an Inspector's recommendation which would involve a site or policy which had not been included in the revised deposit version of the plan proposals – an example would be if the local authority accepted an Inspector's recommendation which upheld an objection which proposed a new site-specific allocation;
2. there are pre-inquiry changes to the plan proposed by the local authority which are upheld by the Inspector's recommendations – even if these are subject to a process of advertisement and are open to objection, there will still be a need for a formal modifications process;
3. the local authority propose (for whatever reason) to make further changes to the plan after the inquiry – perhaps to take on board new information.

Where modifications to the plan are advertised post-inquiry, there will remain a statutory six week period for making objections to those proposed modifications.

Need for Modifications Injury

The decision as to whether new issues are raised by objections to modifications that justify a further public inquiry is for a local authority to decide in the light of the objections made.

Adoption of Plan

If the local planning authority decide to accept all of the recommendations in the Inspector's report and they do not need to put forward any modifications to the proposals to meet those recommendations, the local authority may issue a notice of their intention to adopt the plan. Where they do not accept one or more of the recommendations and/or modifications are needed to the plan, there will be an advertised six-week deposit period for objections to the modifications and the statement of reasons provided by the local authority for not accepting the Inspector's recommendations. Once that period is over and the local authority have satisfied themselves that there are no issues which require either further modifications or a further inquiry, the notice of intention to adopt the plan can be issued.

Through the Regional Offices of Government in England, and the work of the former Welsh and Scottish Offices (now the National Assembly for Wales and the Scottish Executive), national government has the opportunity to comment on plans in preparation to ensure that they are consistent with national policy or that any divergence is clearly justified. Comments will also be made on the quality of plans, both on their clarity and the extent to which they appear to address sustainably the needs of the area. Where necessary, central government will make formal objections to policies, and ultimately it can direct modification to a plan before it can finally be adopted. This 'oversight' role has been increasingly actively pursued since the introduction of the new legislation.

Objections to local plans or unitary development plans will be considered at a local inquiry by an independent inspector whose task is to report to the local planning authority on the plan. For the more strategic county structure plan, which until recently had to be approved formally by the relevant Secretary of State in England and Wales (and is still subject to approval in Scotland), an independent panel will consider views on the plan in an examination in public and offer advice to the authority.

GUIDANCE AND INDIVIDUAL DECISIONS

National guidance has no statutory role in individual decisions beyond its influence on the development plan but it has developed a strong role in case law. The Courts have held that the government's statements of planning policy are material considerations which must be taken into account, where relevant, in decisions on planning applications.

In addition to this backing in common law, the existence of a right of appeal for an aggrieved applicant against the decision of a local planning authority helps to ensure a degree of consistency and conformity with both local plan policy and national guidance. Planning inspectors in appeals will take decisions based on the provisions of the local development plan, informed by relevant national guidance and other material considerations raised by the parties to the appeal.

There is also a legal requirement for notification to the Secretary of State of proposed local decisions which do not accord with the adopted development plan and for certain categories of major development such as retailing. This provides national government with the opportunity to take the decision away from the local planning authority (to 'call it in'). The Secretary of State must then take the decision in the same statutory context against the plan and national policy framework (or in Scotland and Wales the relevant devolved administration).

Together these legal checks should ensure that the national guidance is properly taken into account in the production of development plans and in individual decisions (see Box 3).

Box 3 *Involvement of the Secretary of State in the plan process*

There are four main circumstances where the Secretary of State may become involved in the development plan process:

1. *Consultation*: Although there are no longer statutory consultees for local plans and UDPs, the Secretary of State remains a statutory consultee for structure plans. Government Offices for the Regions (who undertake the statutory responsibilities of the Secretary of State in respect of development plans) should however be consulted at an early stage of the plan-making process, whatever the type of plan. Ongoing dialogue with the Government Office may prevent the need for more formal interventions to be made later in the plan process.
2. *At deposit stage*. The Government Office may register objections on behalf of the Secretary of State to the deposited plan at either deposit or revised deposit stages.
3. *Direction to modify*. The 1990 Act gives the Secretary of State the power to issue a direction to a local authority to modify their plan in a specified manner before adoption. The Act also gives the Secretary of State powers to direct that a plan shall be altered or replaced.
4. *Call-in of plan*. Where a plan or part of a plan's proposals are called-in for the Secretary of State's own determination.

Government Offices on behalf of the Secretary of State scrutinise plans, alterations to plans, and replacement plans to identify whether they are consistent with national and regional guidance and whether there are conflicts with the guidance which do not appear to be justified by local circumstances. The Secretary of State's powers to direct modifications to the plan or to call-in all, or part, of a plan for his own determination is used sparingly and as a last resort.

THE CURRENT POLICY DIRECTION – SUSTAINABLE DEVELOPMENT

The national commitment to sustainable development has progressively shifted the nature of national guidance over recent years. In particular, pursuing sustainable development means that spatial patterns and scale of development, which might otherwise be a local, almost aesthetic, concern, have become a subject of national guidance. This is reflected in recent guidance on location of development, especially in PPG6 *Town Centres* and PPG13 *Transport*.

THIS COMMON INHERITANCE

The broad recent sustainable development emphasis in UK Government planning policy traces its origins to the Environment White Paper, *This Common Inheritance* (HM Government, 1990). *This Common Inheritance* was the UK's first comprehensive environmental policy statement. It committed the government to pursue the principles of sustainable development as set out by the Brundtland Commission for the United Nations.

The 1990 strategy set out a key role for land-use planning to contribute to sustainable development objectives. The planning system recurs throughout the strategy as a tool for implementing sustainable development. This role was restated in the UK's Sustainable Development Strategy (HM Government, 1994) and, although the 1994 strategy is now under review, remains a main plank of national policy.

SUSTAINABLE DEVELOPMENT

Sustainable development is a much abused term, but at its heart, sustainable development is about:

- conserving natural resources;
- enabling development and economic growth to take place in ways that preserve or enhance the environment and are socially inclusive; and
- maintaining quality and opportunity for future generations.

These objectives demand the effective and positive management of change, promoting economic development but in the context of seeking a better environment and a more inclusive society.

The planning system embraces all these aims. It has been concerned since its inception with judging environmental, social and economic issues when making individual decisions. It has also always been concerned with looking to the future

122
———

and making long-term strategic decisions about the release of land for development. Most important of all, perhaps, it has done all of these in the context of a descending hierarchy of strategic objectives set by the different tiers of government.

The environmental slogan 'think globally, act locally' might seem made for the UK planning system, yet the system is widely perceived as not yet meeting that role. It is seen to have concentrated too much in recent years on the minutiae at the expense of the wider picture; become too technical and remote from other areas of policy work; and continued to engage in short-term tradeoffs or 'balance' rather than long-term sustainability. There has also been concern that national projections in transport and housing have driven too much of local decision-making.

REVIEWING NATIONAL POLICY

The 1997 Labour administration identified a number of weaknesses in the current approach to planning:

- too much emphasis on predicting demands and providing for them, which seemed at odds with sustainable development principles;
- inconsistent approaches to planning for national infrastructure, especially concern that major national needs took too long to resolve through the inquiry system;
- delay in adopting plans undermining the plan-led approach;
- a lack of distinctiveness and coherence of implementation at the regional level.

CURRENT DEVELOPMENTS

The government has initiated a programme of democratic and governmental renewal that has major implications for the planning system. In particular, it poses the planning system the challenge of playing its full part in 'joined up government' seeing it as part of a coherent set of strategies and delivery mechanisms.

AN END TO 'PREDICT AND PROVIDE'

Ministers have reflected concern about the role of national projections in driving development by announcing new approaches to both housing and transport which they have heralded as the end of 'predict and provide'.

The approach to housing is set out in the White Paper *Planning for the Communities of the Future* (Department of the Environment, Transport and the Regions, 1998c). Under these proposals, national projections will continue to be made but the emphasis will shift to a more plan-led approach looking at the wider implications of meeting demand where it is likely to arise. There will then be much greater emphasis on monitoring the impacts of the policy decisions locally and being ready to respond to any problems. This has been termed 'project, plan, monitor'.

Transport policy is set out in the integrated transport White Papers, *A New Deal for Transport: Better for Everyone* (Department of the Environment, Transport and Regions, 1998a) and *A New Deal for Trunk Roads in England* (Department of Environment, Transport and Regions, 1998b). These place the emphasis on managing demand for travel against goals of traffic reduction. Road building is viewed as a last resort after other options have been pursued. All schemes are now assessed against an objectives matrix including environmental and social impacts. This changes the balance of the assessment process compared with the traditional cost–benefit approach (COBA) generated from the time savings to motorists and accident reductions. National forecasts will continue to be made but primarily to inform management. The policy looks to locally set targets for reducing traffic growth and leaves open the possibility of an eventual national target. There is a strong emphasis in the policy on the role of the planning system in ensuring that spatial patterns support traffic reduction. In particular, the document promises a stronger PPG13 *Transport* with more guidance on parking controls and better links between new 'local transport plans' and local development planning.

MODERNISING PLANNING

Ministers continue to be concerned about the comparative cumbersomeness of the planning system and have trailed a number of proposals aimed at greater speed and flexibility. These are set out in a series of papers under the title *Modernising Planning* (Department of the Environment, Transport and the Regions, 1998d). One of the major proposals is for a more policy- or parliamentary-based approach to very major planning decisions such as airports to avoid long-drawn-out local public inquiries. This would be a significant change to the present approach and would more clearly distinguish between national and local concerns than does the current approach. A national airports policy is promised in the integrated transport White Paper.

There are also proposals for speeding up plan-making to overcome legitimate concerns over the effectiveness of a plan-led system where the plan seems rarely to be in place much before the end of the plan period. Positive action in this area may well be essential for the continued health of a plan-led approach.

GOVERNANCE

The administration has pursued a radical agenda for governmental reform to devolve. In Scotland, the Parliament is responsible for its national planning policy and primary legislation, while in Wales, the Assembly has responsibility for all secondary planning legislation, guidance and oversight of local implementation.

For England, guidance on regional planning has shifted the onus on preparing Regional Planning Guidance from central government to the regional local authority conferences which currently serve simply to advise government. Under this approach, the local authority planning conferences will prepare draft guidance and submit it to an examination in public before central government issue final guidance in the light of the report on the public examination. There is a leading role for regional planning in determining housing supply and transport priorities as a key part of the shift from 'predict and provide'.

Devolution throws the spotlight on what is legitimately a national concern, what is purely regional and what is purely local. The art will be to set a clear context for planning at each more-local level, continuing to ensure consistency of objectives on the big issues while enabling appropriate local responses to meeting them. This has already been signalled by Ministerial statements on housing projections in England in 'Planning for the Communities of the Future' which has stressed the importance of regional solutions within a national framework of objectives. The practical resolution of tensions on issues such as housing at the regional level will be an interesting test for the new approach over the next years.

In addition to devolution of power to Scotland, Wales and the regions, the government is taking a new approach to local government which is likely to affect the delivery of planning locally. *Modern Local Government: In Touch With the People* (Department of the Environment, Transport and the Regions, 1998f) advocated new forms of local participation; more strategic cross-service working and funding by authorities, bringing individual objectives more closely into a coherent whole; and new political structures, including mayors and cabinets. Improved local participation and cross-service strategies can only strengthen the role of planning and its links to the delivery of objectives.

In the wider context, the Member States of the European Union have concluded agreement on the European Spatial Development Perspective. This seeks to set out the differing issues across the Union and to reconcile potentially conflicting economic, social and environmental objectives. The perspective may well form an important element in future European funding programmes and provide a clearer link at the European level between planning and funding to deliver plans. One of the most promising elements is a recognition that different areas will need to prioritise different types of economic development to meet sustainable development objectives.

FORMULATING GUIDANCE

This section looks at the process of preparing national guidance. The original batch of Planning Policy Guidance notes were issued in 1987 as a synopsis of the advice previously contained in government circulars. Subsequent revisions have been subject to an extensive consultative process.

A typical planning policy guidance note now goes through six public stages taking perhaps two to three years from research to final version:

- research, establishing the need for new guidance or the success of existing guidance judged against the criterion of sustainable development;
- consultation, seeking views on a draft revision to the guidance and issued usually alongside the research;
- revision and publication of the guidance in the light of consultation;
- dissemination of the revised approach using seminars and conferences;
- a good practice guide, promoting consistency and best practice for local authorities; and
- further research and monitoring, to see how the policies are being applied and to test their impacts.

In addition to this public work, guidance must also be agreed by the interested Government Departments before it can be issued for consultation or in final form. It thus reflects the collective view of government, although generally it will only be under the signature of one or two Secretaries of State.

RESEARCH

Examples of research work which may inform future guidance include:

- parking and accessibility
- brownfield development
- sustainable development appraisal for regional planning.

Best Practice Guidance offers additional help in translating wider objectives into specific action without prescribing solutions. Much of the sustainable development work is supported by such guidance. It includes:

- PPG13, *A guide to better practice*
- *Waste Management Planning – Principles and Practice*

The new forms of guidance were intended to be clear, concise and readily available. They have since been charged with setting a clear framework for promoting sustainable development in the UK. This is a tall order and it is hardly surprising if there are criticisms. Chief among these are:

- lack of clarity in the expression of objectives;
- setting out conflicting objectives without resolving them;
- leaving unresolved conflicts and inconsistencies;
- too long and a mix of policy and discussion;
- inconsistent coverage of topics;
- over-frequent revisions;
- lacking a clear relationship to other government programmes; and
- subject to amendment through Ministerial statements.

Clarity

One aim of new guidance is to be clear and accessible. Clarity avoids unnecessary debate and allows all parties to be sure of their ground. It thus reduces uncertainty and potential costs. A fudged or ambiguous statement is likely to lead to the opposite. Developers will generally say that they dislike uncertainty more than they dislike clear advice even if that advice means they have to rethink their approach. In practice, however, developers may seek to steel a march over rivals by exploiting the wording of policy to improve their case.

Under very close examination, not all guidance seems as clearly expressed as decision-makers might sometimes wish. Guidance notes are policy statements with all the subtlety and balance that that entails but they are often examined at public inquiry with forensic zeal as if they were some form of contract. This is an examination that they often cannot stand.

The fault for the apparent uncertainty of guidance may lie less with the notes themselves than with the advocate's desire to look at the detailed expression of policy rather than its intent (or indeed at the intent rather than the wording), but it does suggest that those who draft guidance may have to pay more attention than has sometimes been the case in the past to the way in which a text may be exploited.

Lack of clarity should not be confused with the proper expression of complex and multiple objectives. It is the nature of planning for there always to be competing priorities and it is right that guidance should set these out.

Conflict

When there are a wide range of conflicting objectives to address, some would like to see the guidance setting out how to achieve that synergy.

Outside Wales, each note covers a separate topic and the balance between potentially conflicting objectives is left to the interpretation of those making decisions. This seems perfectly proper. If national guidance were to set out a hierarchy of the importance of different issues, then there would be very little left for the system to undertake. Of course, each case or area will require a different solution to resolving conflicting objectives depending on the local circumstances. Other than those actions required by law, the system is essentially discretionary, shades of grey rather than black and white. In the context of sustainable development – finding answers that address multiple objectives – answers can only be developed locally against agreed criteria and goals.

Guidance notes have been revised over a number of years. This inevitably means that the exact wording or policy emphasis may not be entirely consistent. While more might be done to relate guidance and to ensure they are as up to date and consistent as possible, policy development and the need to keep advice fresh inevitably means that there will be some differences.

Length and expression of policy

It is not always easy to pick out key policy points from guidance or determine the weight to be attached to them. There is little point in having policy if it is unclear. In recent PPGs, an attempt has been made to draw attention to the key objectives of the guidance and distinguish new policy emphasis by setting out the key aims on the opening page and making greater use of bullet points.

PPGs in England are also perceived as becoming longer and a little more discursive. There may be a number of reasons for this:

- new policies can require more explanation than the continuation of existing policies;
- improved consultation leads to more points needing to be addressed;
- sustainable development is a more complex subject to convey than the previous objectives;
- the creation of the PPG series leads to expectations of comprehensive coverage of issues.

In principle, guidance could simply set out overall aims on a page or two and leave the rest to local planning authorities. There is some attraction to this 'bullet point' approach but it is unlikely that it could stand alone. In Wales, such an approach has resulted in the need for subsidiary guidance (the TANs) to ensure consistency and effective implementation. Indeed, the TANs are very similar in content to the later pages of the respective PPGs. There is also the risk of giving too much weight to the fewer words offered. One of the shortest circulars ever issued was circular 14/85, which in a side and a half stressed the presumption in favour of development and the importance of economic growth and then suggested that little weight should be given to an out-of-date development plan. Rightly or wrongly, that circular, which preceded the legislation introducing the plan-led system by some six years, was widely viewed as the cause of a substantial increase in the number of planning appeals and in the overturning of local decisions.

Coverage

Many people would like to see guidance on their topic. PPGs, NPGs and PG(W) are understandably seen as the premier league of advice, with circulars at best struggling for promotion.

Already some of the material in guidance is less about policy than practice. This may not make it any less useful. Indeed, in areas which the average local planning authority comes across rarely, it is an important aid to quality and consistency of procedure and decision-making, but it does beg questions about the proper role and means of dissemination of national advice. This is reflected in the differing approaches across the UK systems – with the Welsh and English guidance at opposite extremes in distinguishing between overarching principles and technical implementation.

Moving Target

The planning system has always produced its moving targets. Because it is based on a hierarchy of policy, there is always the danger that one part of the system is more advanced than another, with local plans prepared ahead of revised structure plans and national policy rarely coming out at the right time for everybody. This has been exacerbated by the near simultaneous commitment to revising the national policy guidance and to local planning authorities in England being asked to prepare local plans with a view to them being in place by the end of 1996.

Change is disruptive for everyone in a system. While revisions will be needed, the emphasis on sustainable development (which commands all-party support) should ensure a higher degree of continuity than has sometimes been the case in the past, provided that overall objectives can be translated into a coherent approach locally.

Relation to Other Programmes

Planning can only set the framework for development and help to facilitate it. Other measures may be necessary to deliver the objectives. Since the move to the plan-led system, greater emphasis has been placed on bringing other activities together with planning objectives. There should be no inconsistency between government programmes and the plan-led system because all the programmes must work within the local planning framework. If the framework is effective, then it should help to channel activity and support into those areas that will help to see it implemented.

This is true across a range of activities:

- Local authority transport programmes should flow from their development plan policies.
- Economic and housing strategies should also be consistent with plans and so funding in these areas should support plan aims.

- Regeneration Agencies such as English Partnerships are charged with working within the development plan framework.

Achieving consistency in these areas is primarily the task of the local authorities responsible for developing the different strategies and bids. These will generally be the same authority that prepares the local plan.

The new administration has focused on effective targeting and co-ordination of action at both national and local government level under the banner of 'Better Government'. This should strengthen the links across areas of work and ensure clearer common purpose. Proposals for regional governance alongside new Regional Development Agencies provide an opportunity for a coherent approach to setting and achieving regional priorities.

Other Policy Statements

Ministerial announcements have long served as a means of updating or clarifying published guidance. Although it can make policy less accessible, it is an essential tool to provide for rapid response to emerging issues. Such statements will generally be incorporated into published guidance at an early opportunity to ensure that they are widely known. Likewise, new national policies set out in White Papers may also need to be taken into account, but will typically be reflected in early revisions to guidance.

EFFECTIVENESS OF GUIDANCE

In 1994 the then Department of the Environment decided to commission research to assess how successful the PPGs were in meeting their objectives. Land Use Consultants carried out the research in three main stages:

- an initial questionnaire to all local planning authorities seeking their views on PPGs in general and the value of each PPG in particular;
- detailed interviews with practitioners, including central Government Departments;
- detailed interviews with selected authorities plus a seminar with elected members.

The main general findings were:

- a surprisingly high degree of support for the effectiveness and clarity of the PPG series among planning officers, with some 60% rating them very highly on those counts;

- a fairly predictable variation in the use made of the different PPGs, mainly depending on their date of issue and the likelihood of encountering the topic;
- a lack of penetration by the PPGs beyond the planning professionals, with few elected members having read one and fewer still members of the public; and
- a feeling among professionals that more could be done to meet the objectives of sustainable development, though a recognition that a useful start had been made.

The broad picture then was one of encouraging success in achieving consistency and quality for the planning professionals, a reasonable start on the sustainable development objectives but less success, perhaps inevitably, in one of the original 1987 objectives of the PPG series – making them accessible to the general public.

Conclusion

The planning system's survival in much the same basic form as that in which it was created in the 1940s owes much to its inherent flexibility and the wide respect which it has commanded. That flexibility and respect in turn rest in the structured role given to each participant in the system – central, regional and local government, the local inhabitant and the developer. Resolving the potentially conflicting interests of these different groups within the same system is both the constant challenge and the greatest strength of planning in the UK. With the plan-led system, the goal of sustainable development and the government's emphasis on coherence of strategies, the planning system has started a new and very healthy era but there are issues to tackle to realise the potential. Continued delay in the system will undermine the plan-led approach and breed dissatisfaction and the regional planning conferences will need to be strengthened to take on the role of arbiters on housing and transport priorities. More strikingly, there seems to be a reluctance to embrace sustainable development wholeheartedly as evidenced by a continued tendency to tradeoff and in local pressures for out-of-centre or road-based development.

The planning system cannot and will not deliver everything, but we all have the right to expect it to deliver as much as it can to make life a little better for us all now and in the future. That is the abiding challenge and attraction.

References

Department of the Environment, Transport and the Regions (1998a) *A New Deal for Transport: Better for Everyone*. White Paper on the Future of Transport, HMSO, London.
Department of the Environment, Transport and the Regions (1998b) *A New Deal for Trunk Roads in England*, HMSO, London.

Department of the Environment, Transport and the Regions (1998c) *Planning for Communities of the Future*, HMSO, London.

Department of the Environment, Transport and the Regions (1998d) *Modernising Planning – Improving Arrangements for the Delivery of Local Plans and Unitary Development Plans*, HMSO, London.

Department of the Environment, Transport and the Regions (1998e) *The Future of Regional Planning Guidance*, HMSO, London.

Department of the Environment, Transport and the Regions (1998f) *Modern Local Government – In Touch with the People*, HMSO, London.

HM Government (1990) *This Common Inheritance*, HMSO, London.

HM Government (1994) *Sustainable Development – The UK Strategy*, HMSO, London.

CHAPTER 6

URBAN RENEWAL AND GRANTS

Chris Couch

INTRODUCTION

This chapter is about urban restructuring and regeneration. It is concerned with two interlinked problems: housing renewal and the inner urban areas. On the one hand we are concerned with the problems of dealing with obsolete buildings, especially housing. Here we consider the development of policy from the days of slum clearance, through housing improvement to modern holistic approaches to area regeneration and estate renewal. On the other hand, and difficult to disentangle from the first issue, is the question of the economic decline and social change that has affected urban areas, especially in the inner cities, over the last 30 years. Here we consider the nature of the problem and the evolution of the state's response from the experimentation and investigative studies of the early 1970s, through the property-led responses of the Thatcher era, to the present integrated approaches encouraged by the Single Regeneration Budget.

Town planners and local planning departments play a number of important roles in the urban renewal process. Firstly, there is the traditional statutory planning role: development plans provide the strategic context within which local renewal projects are devised and through the development control process planners influence changes in the use of redeveloped land or buildings, their physical form and design. Secondly, many planning departments have today established teams of planners, variously known as implementation, project or regeneration sections, whose job is to adopt a positive or pro-active approach to an area: *to get things done*; not just through the use of statutory powers but by working with local people on problems that they have identified, by negotiating with other agencies, by persuading developers to invest and by seeking matching funds from different sources. Experience has suggested that planners are very good at these tasks. Thirdly, most modern renewal work, be it in Renewal Areas, City Challenge or Single Regeneration Budget projects, is carried out by multi-disciplinary teams rather than a single department or agency. Planners are invariably key figures in these teams as their ability to take an overview of local needs and their skills in policy formulation are seen as vital to successful area regeneration.

The chapter begins with some discussion of urban restructuring before proceeding to look first at the evolution of housing renewal policies and then at urban policy.

URBAN RESTRUCTURING

URBAN RESTRUCTURING AND STATE INTERVENTION

The form and structure of urban areas are constantly evolving. The patterns of development, the use and value of each building, the nature and distribution of population and economic activity are always changing in response to economic, social and physical forces. Whether an urban area is expanding or contracting there will be a process of internal restructuring than needs to be planned just as much as any suburban development or new town needs planning. Indeed this process of urban restructuring is becoming ever more important to the planning profession: particularly in the mature developed economies of Britain and other western European countries.

There are a number of reasons for this. Firstly all urban areas are gradually getting larger and older. As they get larger there is more existing infrastructure, more buildings and more open space to be maintained, repaired and renewed; the amount of land devoted to urban uses in England and Wales increased from 4.5% in 1947 to 6.5% in 1969 and to 7.3% in 1980. As they get older the need to spend on repairs and renewal will grow. Many British city centres and inner city areas were developed over 150 years ago and the renovation and replacement of the Victorian infrastructure of water supply, sewage disposal and other streetworks has strained the budgets of many cities in recent years. The proportion of construction output devoted to repair and maintenance (including renovation and conversion) has increased steadily in recent years.

The second reason is that state intervention in urban restructuring has become necessary in order to avert unwanted social or environmental costs of change. In spite of the growing necessity for urban renewal it is often very difficult for the market to accomplish the renewal process in an acceptable manner. Take two examples. The Victorians built many office buildings on very small sites within city centres often building right up to adjoining buildings and up to the pavement line. These offices were usually bespoke designs for owner-occupying firms. Today many of the buildings are regarded as obsolete in terms of their size, internal arrangements and facilities and need major refurbishment or replacing. The economics of modern office building drives developers, frequently building speculatively for rent, towards large rectangular buildings with space around the building for servicing, parking and landscaping. Many of the small Victorian office blocks cannot be redeveloped in this way without being assembled with others into a larger economically viable plot of land. This process invariably needs public sector support to make it happen in a reasonable period of time. Even if the preference is for the currently more acceptable policy of refurbishment it is likely that the cost of modernisation is so great that it exceeds the rent that can be achieved, except in prime locations, and requires subsidy if it is to be brought about.

The other example is from housing. The typical inner city street in England or Wales is the Victorian terrace (the tenements of Scottish cities present different economic problems). For many years up to the early 1970s public policy was to demolish this obsolete property and to replace it with new council housing. This process of demolition and rebuilding could not have occurred on such a scale without public intervention. The 'footprint' of the Victorian terraced house and backyard (typically 3.5 metres × 8 metres) provides too small an area of land on which to build a new house. Again adjoining plots had to be assembled to create viable parcels of building land. Often the number of replacement dwellings was only about half the original number of dwellings. This meant that further dwellings had to be provided elsewhere to accommodate the 'overspill' population. None of this could have been done without state intervention and planning. Today the conventional treatment for obsolete housing has become refurbishment and renovation rather than demolition, but even here little can be achieved without subsidy. This obsolete property is likely to be amongst the cheapest available within any urban area and occupied by those on the lowest incomes. If the market conditions in the area are such that the cost of renovation can be recovered through increased rents or selling prices beyond the means of the existing occupiers, then they will be forced out by economic pressures and a new more affluent population will move in: a process of gentrification will take place. To avoid rent rises and gentrification, subsidies are necessary. In other cases market conditions may make it impossible to increase rents or selling prices making it impossible for the market to renovate the property at all without the benefit of public subsidy.

Another policy aim that first emerged in the 1930s but has become a very powerful force in recent years has been the desire to contain urban areas and to protect the surrounding countryside from encroaching urbanisation. One consequence of this policy is that a proportion of development that might have sought a suburban or ex-urban location is forced back into the existing urban area either as building refurbishment or the redevelopment of existing urban land. Recent governments have had an ambivalent attitude to urban containment, encouraging strong protection through the use of Green Belts and similar policy mechanisms whilst at the same time allowing the development of out of town retailing and office parks at numerous locations. Nevertheless, there has recently been some significant success in controlling the location of housing development with the proportion of housing completions in England occurring within existing urban areas increasing from 38% in 1985 to 49% in 1993 (DoE Land Use Change Statistics).

The Economic Life of a Building

At the heart of understanding the urban renewal processes lies the idea of the economic life of a building and the timing and nature of the decision to refurbish, convert, replace or abandon it. For this is how urban renewal happens: individual

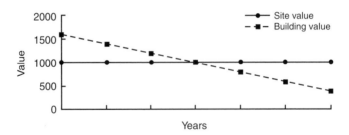

Market pressures will encourage redevelopment when the value of the building falls below the value of the cleared site.

Figure 1 *The economic life of a building. Source:* after Goodall (1972, p. 209)

consumers, firms or the state make these decisions and initiate some kind of urban renewal process, i.e. some modification to the existing urban structure.

The economic life of a building can be considered as the period of time over which the capital value of the building exceeds the capital value of the cleared site. Making development decisions in the market involves handling a large number of variables, some of which are very difficult to estimate. Valuers may have to make assumptions about the permitted replacement use and its density. They are concerned with the anticipated rent that can be achieved for the building and with estimating maintenance costs, repair intervals, management and energy costs many years hence. They have to estimate the demolition and site preparation costs (relatively simple in a housing area, problematic in an industrial zone). They have to decide on an appropriate discount rate with which to bring all future costs and earnings back to a current value and they have to make assumptions about the rate of inflation in each of these costs and earnings (none of which may necessarily inflate at the same rate). This decision-making process may be simple and straightforward for a local speculative builder replacing a Victorian villa with a new block of flats; or, for a major insurance company with millions of pounds worth of property assets it may be a highly sophisticated process using computer models to test a large number of possible decisions against a wide range of variables in order to select the preferred course of action. The economic life of a building is shown graphically in Figure 1.

The lifespan of the building is determined by the economic imperatives of the market or by state intervention; outside of this context there is no definable 'physical' lifespan of a building. That is to say it is not possible to make such a statement as 'typical British houses have a physical lifespan of 80 years', for it simply is not true. Thus in Britain it is possible to see dwellings up to 400 years old still providing perfectly adequate accommodation, or churches up to 1000 years old still fulfilling their original function. Equally there are new buildings in the London Docklands that have been demolished to make way for more intensive developments even before they have been occupied, and there are many thousands of local authority flats built in the 1960s that have already reached the end of their economic life and are being demolished. Thus the timespan in Figure 1 may be months or hundreds of years.

Following the argument of Harvey (1981), when a building is new it is generally the case that its income will be high in relation to its operating costs. (Note that in rented property the rent is the income; in owner-occupied property the income is the notional rent an owner pays to himself or could receive from renting out the building.) As time passes there will be a tendency for the real income to fall as the building becomes obsolete in relation to modern needs and patterns of building use or if other more appropriate buildings are being supplied elsewhere in the market; operating costs will rise in relation to income as the building ages and maintenance costs increase; refurbishment may be necessary, voids may become longer and more frequent. Eventually, operating costs exceed income. At this point the current use may cease. (In the case of housing the latter years of low income and high operating costs are likely to have led to slum conditions.) The building may then be turned over to another more profitable use, perhaps after modification or conversion, or it may be demolished and replaced if the returns on the redeveloped site exceed the costs of demolition and reconstruction. If none of these possibilities is financially viable, then the building may be abandoned and left vacant. In these circumstances nobody will have any reason to invest money in the premises and dereliction will tend to follow.

Thus, using this model of the economic life of the building it has been possible to offer some basic explanation for the way building occupancy and use changes over time, the creation of slums, building vacancy, abandonment and dereliction. These are all circumstances that have been seen to justify state intervention in urban renewal to facilitate a process of urban regeneration (Couch, 1990, ch. 3).

INNER URBAN AREAS

For many of Britain's inner urban areas these problems have been exacerbated by a long period of economic restructuring, population change, social deprivation and fiscal problems: the inner city problem. These areas find themselves in a spiral of decline from which it has been difficult to break free without substantial subsidy and inward investment from central government.

Throughout the twentieth century and particularly since the 1960s many inner urban areas have seen their industrial base decline. Structural changes in demand led to the closure of older manufacturing plants and changes in access requirements or the increasing use of technologies that are more land-extensive have encouraged decentralisation to suburban and rural locations. This loss of employment forced inner city populations to migrate in search of work or face the consequences of unemployment or early retirement. Typically it has been the

Figure 2 Short-life and long-life buildings. a) 18thC housing still in its original use. b) 20 year old flats in Liverpool being demolished.

Table 1 *Socio-economic conditions in selected urban areas*

	Liverpool	Inner London	Manchester	Bristol
Population				
1971	610 113	3 031 935	543 859	426 657
1981	510 300	2 496 800	449 200	388 000
1991	449 560	2 343 133	400 254	372 088
In 1991:				
Males, 16–64 in FT employment	47.3%	52.7%	48.7%	60.8%
Households with no car	56.9%	53.9%	56.6%	34.2%
Dwellings with exclusive use of bath/shower, inside WC and central heating	51.4%	77.9%	76.1%	79.4%
Single-parent households	7.0%	6.4%	8.6%	4.7%

Source: Census of Population, 1991, County Monitors.

young, mobile and better qualified workers who have migrated, leaving behind a residual population in which older people, lower income groups and the less skilled are disproportionately prevalent. This in turn has led to above-average needs for social support, health and welfare services. The lower aggregate income of these areas reduces spending power: the provision of shopping and other commercial services declines. There are fewer local employment opportunities. Social stress, poverty and frustration may lead to increased levels of crime and vandalism. It becomes a less attractive place in which to live and property values fall relative to other areas. Housing investment declines, less is spent on housing maintenance and repair and there is little incentive to refurbish or replace obsolete properties. Fewer businesses and falling property values mean that the tax base of the local authority will deteriorate: less will be gathered in from business rates and from the council tax. The local authority cannot meet the increased demand for social and other services without central government subsidy. Subsidy tends to bring with it increased external control of local affairs. Table 1 provides an illustration of socio-economic conditions in some selected urban areas. All these areas have experienced population losses but the greatest falls have been in Liverpool and Manchester, i.e. in the two conurbations worst affected by industrial change and relative economic decline. In affluent Bristol the decline has been more modest.

The low levels of male employment in Liverpool and Manchester are indicative of the decline in traditional industries in those areas whilst the buoyancy of Bristol's industrial base shows in the very high proportion of males in employment. Car ownership is a useful proxy measure for wealth and it can be seen that ownership is lowest in Liverpool and Manchester, higher in inner London, in spite of its excellent public transport network, and highest in Bristol. The quality of the housing stock can also be related to the level of economic prosperity with Bristol again in the best position and Liverpool lagging significantly behind the others. And as an example of the social issues that can arise out of this spiral of deprivation, the proportion of single-parent households is over 80% higher in Manchester than in Bristol. We discuss policy responses to problems of inner urban areas later in the chapter.

State intervention in housing renewal began in the nineteenth century in response to concerns about public health and sanitation but the issue of urban deprivation and inner city decay did not become a matter for public policy until the late 1960s. Despite some overlaps, housing renewal and inner city policies continued to evolve separately through the 1970s and 1980s and it is only in the most recent past, with the establishment of Renewal Areas and the Single Regeneration Budget, that a more holistic and comprehensive approach can be seen to be emerging. For this reason we will now discuss the evolution of policy as two separate strands: first housing renewal and then urban policy.

THE EVOLUTION OF HOUSING RENEWAL POLICIES

FROM SLUM CLEARANCE TO HOUSING RENOVATION

There were vigorous attacks on the obsolete housing stock through the 1930s and again from the mid-1950s. The approach was invariably to clear away the slums and replace them with new housing at the same location at a lower density and to complement this with overspill developments to accommodate those who could not be rehoused locally. The role of town planners in this process was threefold: to find sufficient land for overspill (either as local authority estates, town expansion schemes or new towns); to plan these overspill developments; and to plan the redevelopment of the former slum areas. Thus their role was essentially confined to physical planning with very little regard to social and economic issues.

The end of the 1960s marked a turning point in housing renewal as policy began to shift away from these large-scale slum clearance programmes towards housing renovation and area improvement. There were a number of factors leading to this change.

1. Until the 1960s, as a broad generalisation, clearance programmes had dealt with early or mid Victorian housing of very poor quality. After this time many cities were beginning to include better quality housing from the late Victorian period within clearance areas. Such moves proved controversial as it was argued by professionals and residents that these dwellings were often structurally sound and with some renovation could provide satisfactory housing. Newer dwellings and those in owner-occupation were also becoming more expensive to demolish as higher levels of compensation were paid to building owners. A number of official studies such as the *Deeplish Study* (Ministry of

Housing and Local Government, 1966) and academic works (e.g. Needleman, 1965) demonstrated the feasibility and economic benefits of renovation.

2. A growing conservation movement was becoming active on a number of fronts awakening public opinion to the problems of limited energy resources, the destruction of increasingly vulnerable natural habitats and landscape, and the importance of civic and cultural heritage including the built form and townscape of urban areas. With this last concern came an appreciation that even the Victorian city, which until then had been generally assumed to have almost no features worth keeping, should be more sensitively conserved.

3. The clearance programme itself had disappointed many people. What had been heralded as a new beginning for cities was now subject to much criticism. Firstly, the way many local authorities dealt with the inhabitants of clearance areas was often regarded as high handed and insensitive. Programmes were large, with big cities perhaps rehousing as many as 10 households each day using staff who were often inadequately trained in the social aspects of rehousing. Secondly, for some there was disillusionment with the nature and quality of replacement dwellings: high-rise flats, remote locations, excessive fuel bills and poor construction seemed an inadequate substitute for the insanitary but convenient and low-cost homes that many had left behind.

4. There was also a growing feeling that many of the areas earmarked for clearance housed long-standing, close-knit communities that should be protected. Whilst the sociological evidence, both then and subsequently, suggested that this was a gross simplification, it was a sufficiently powerful argument to influence opinion at the time.

5. A further social trend that was influential in the strategic thinking of big cities was that of population decline. By the early 1970s it was clear that most British cities were losing population (see Table 1). This caused councils to think hard about clearance and especially the inevitable associated overspill and loss of population to neighbouring authorities. In this climate an alternative area improvement policy that would retain population, rateable values and rate support grant became an attractive proposition (Couch, 1990, ch. 2).

Although grants for housing renovation had been available for many years the government signalled a major change of policy in favour of area improvements with the Housing Act 1969. With this Act the government introduced 'General Improvement Areas' (GIAs), within which housing renovation was encouraged. Owners of dwellings could receive grants of 50% of the cost of approved renovation works; local authorities were obliged to consult residents about improvement proposals and were given an allowance of £100 per dwelling to spend on environmental works (landscaping, car parking, streetworks, etc.). Town planners, either working in planning departments or seconded to housing departments, often played an important role in the consultation process and in planning these environmental improvements.

Nevertheless, the new policy was not without its problems. Only a limited number of GIAs were designated. Few grants had been taken up within the private rented sector or within the poorer inner city areas. The Housing Act 1974 brought a further strengthening of the area improvement policy. A key change was the introduction of 'Housing Action Areas' (HAAs). This was an attempt to focus attention and spending on those areas where the need for housing renovation was greatest. Local authorities could designate pockets of housing and social stress as HAAs within which a five-year 'crash programme' of housing renovations would be instigated using grants of up to 75% of the cost of approved work (rising to 90% in cases of hardship). It took some time for local authorities to gear themselves up to the intensive and subtle management that these programmes required and the level of renovations initially fell but gradually through the late 1970s and for most of the 1980s the policy produced an impressive flow of improving housing conditions within many urban areas.

Towards the end of the 1980s there was growing concern with housing renewal policy on two fronts, it was suggested: (i) that the policy had become too skewed towards renovation and that there was a need to resuscitate a clearance programme to deal with the worst problems; and (ii) that whilst much attention was being devoted to the physical renovation of dwellings not enough attention was being paid to the socio-economic problems of the degraded neighbourhoods in which these dwellings often existed.

RENEWAL AREAS

Under the Local Government and Housing Act 1989, HAAs and GIAs were abolished and replaced by the new and broader concept of Renewal Areas. These were intended to be larger and to incorporate a more comprehensive, holistic approach to area regeneration:

> The intention behind the new provisions is to focus attention on the use of a broader area strategy which may include environmental and socio-economic regeneration. The aim should be to secure a reduction in the number of unfit houses, whether by repair or demolition, as part of such a strategy. . . . This presupposes a more flexible approach in assessing the various renewal options. The Secretary of State considers that it is no longer appropriate to give automatic preference to renovation (Department of the Environment, 1990, p. 5).

In theory this was to be achieved by bringing a range of social, economic and environmental considerations into the decision-making process and through the co-ordination of a number of private and public sector actions into an integrated programme of area renewal. It was originally anticipated that Renewal Areas would range in size from 300 to 3000 dwellings and achieve their targets through a 10-year investment programme. At least 75% of the properties within the designated area were to be in private ownership and be unfit or qualify for grants under the terms of the Act. One of the main intentions of Renewal Areas was to develop the role of the local authority as 'facilitator', working with other 'stakeholders' to formulate and implement policy. Nevertheless designation of a Renewal Area gives the local authority additional powers to compulsorily acquire land and buildings. Designation also allows the local authority to spend up to £1000 per dwelling on environmental works and the provision of community facilities within the area, half of which is subsidised by central government.

At the same time as changing the framework for area-based initiatives, the government introduced a new housing fitness standard and a new regime for the subsidy of private sector housing renovation works in England and Wales under which applicants for grants would be subject to a test of resources: a 'means test'.

In order to assess the suitability of an area for Renewal Area status and to determine the most appropriate strategy for action, local authorities are expected to carry out a 'neighbourhood renewal assessment' (NRA). The NRA moves through a process of area identification, team selection, setting aims and objectives, boundary definition, option generation, appraisal and selection, to the formulation of a renewal strategy and implementation programme. As such, the NRA process will be recognised as having many of the features of the 'rational planning process' discussed elsewhere in this book. Stakeholder involvement was to be an important feature of Renewal Areas: that is to say, local authorities were expected to involve local residents, employers, property owners and others with a 'stake' in the area in the NRA decision-making process.

Reflecting this broader concern for socio-economic regeneration almost all renewal areas are implemented through multi-professional teams which include town planners as key members. The town planners tend to be particularly active in the NRA stage whilst other professionals such as housing officers and surveyors contribute more to the subsequent implementation stages.

Preparing a typical NRA might involve planners in a range of tasks. A house condition survey would be undertaken. This might include a quick external assessment of all properties with a detailed internal survey of 10% of dwellings, undertaken by public health officers or surveyors, in order to gauge the quality of the housing stock and the amount of work needed. A survey of the local physical environment would identify vacant and derelict properties, townscape features, environmental hazards and eyesores. Traffic and transport surveys would be undertaken. Economic surveys would be used to determine employment and training needs and together with social surveys would establish the structure of the local population and its needs. Consultations would be undertaken with local residents, employers and others to determine their perceptions, concerns and priorities for action. Stakeholder participation in the policy-making process (for example through the co-option of local people onto the renewal area team or through 'planning for real' exercises) would help to improve the responsiveness and relevance of policies and proposals to local community needs.

Thus Renewal Areas are not simply about housing renovation. From the outset the DoE made it clear that the policy should also be concerned with environmental and socio-economic regeneration. The evidence from the early Renewal Areas, with over 40% of capital expenditure going on non-housing investment, would suggest that the change of policy has seen some measure of success. For this reason Renewal Areas may be considered an advance on GIAs and HAAs, obliging local authorities to develop a clear regeneration strategy, providing a framework for inter-departmental and inter-agency working and a justification for the co-ordination of housing and non-housing investment (Couch and Gill, 1993, p. 37).

One common criticism of Renewal Areas has been that designation does not bring with it automatic access to any significant additional central government funding to support implementation. Until 1993 local authorities frequently used Urban Programme funding to subsidise initiatives. Since then, some have managed to incorporate Renewal Areas into bids under the Single Regeneration Budget Challenge Fund (Box 1) but others have had to rely on their own resources. However, recent research for the DETR has noted that:

> The most successful Renewal Areas are not those where the most public money was spent, but those where the best partnerships were forged (DETR, 1997, p. 106).

Box 1 *The Rock Ferry Renewal Area, an example of integrated action*

Rock Ferry is an area of mainly Victorian working class housing within the Metropolitan Borough of Wirral in Merseyside. Wirral MBC had produced an informal renewal strategy in the mid-1980s to which the Department of the Environment had responded providing additional funds for housing improvement.

In 1991, two adjoining Renewal Areas were declared: Rock Ferry East (455 dwellings) and Rock Ferry West (860 dwellings), although some work had begun a year or two earlier. The Renewal Areas were jointly run by an integrated multi-professional team seconded from various local authority departments – notably housing and town planning – and worked from a dedicated project office within the designated area.

The main achievements have been the simultaneous implementation of a number of environmental improvements together with important social initiatives. The local authority spent considerable sums improving the appearance of the main streets, removing eyesores including derelict and unfit property, rebuilding boundary walls and landscaping adjoining open spaces. The effect was a dramatic impact on the image of the area: it *looked* as if something was being done.

The local shopping centre had long since lost its function as a small district centre and was grossly over-provided with shopping floorspace, mainly of poor quality. As part of the renewal project many of the shop premises were removed whilst the remainder benefited from shop front improvements, the provision of off-street car parking and incidental landscaping.

Contiguous with the Renewal Area a small council estate built in the early 1960s was subject to an Estate Action programme that removed five blocks of flats and remodelled the remainder by downtopping to provide houses; also provided were new security measures, landscaping and a childrens play area to a design agreed with the local community.

The local industrial estate was declared an Industrial Improvement Area and was subject to an Industry Watch crime prevention initiative. A 'multi-skills training workshop' was also built with Urban Programme funding.

The southern half of the area has benefited from considerable private sector housing renovation activity and the conversion of a number of larger premises into flats. Two housing associations have built 60 new dwellings on cleared sites. These adjoin the Rock Park conservation area: a run down collection of Victorian middle class villas which the council is seeking to revitalise.

In addition to investments in the physical environment the renewal area has also been the location for spending from the Home Office 'Safer Cities' programme on security and crime prevention, a community care scheme, a careers project and various training schemes.

In total some £25m has been invested in the area including £17m from the public sector, around £4.0m from the private sector and £4.0m from housing associations.

One issue to arise from this example is the question of sustaining long-term commitment to an area. By the mid-1990s, after Urban Programme funding had been lost, the local authority found it difficult to sustain the momentum of regeneration. With other nearby communities demanding attention and the prospect of high profile developments elsewhere in the Borough, political interest waned, the area project office that had been the focus for stakeholder involvement was closed down and staff redeployed.

ESTATE ACTION

An emerging problem during the late 1970s was that of the so-called 'hard to let' council housing estates: estates that because of their obsolescence, poor design or bad reputation found themselves in a downward spiral of rising vacancy rates, declining environmental standards often exacerbated by poor management and maintenance, endemic vandalism and crime. Thus estates that had been part of the solution to the slum clearance problem in the 1950s and 1960s had now become part of the housing problem.

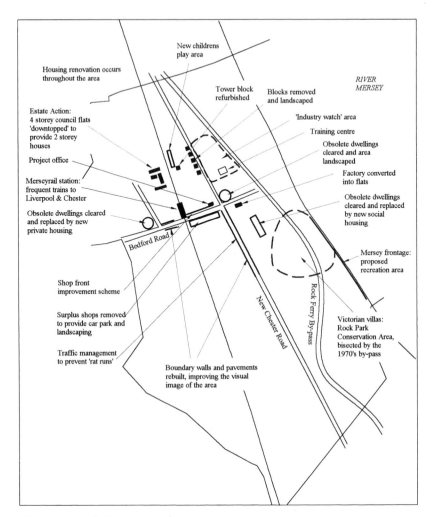

Figure 3a *Rock Ferry renewal area*

In 1979 government concern about these blighted estates had risen to the point where the DoE initiated the 'Priority Estates Project' to investigate and test ways of improving council estate management and maintenance. After an initial experimental phase the Urban Housing Renewal Unit was established in order to provide a mainstream route for the channelling of government funds and the dissemination of 'good practice'. In 1987 the programme was renamed 'Estate Action' and was responsible for an annual budget of some £140m (1988/89) for the renovation of council dwellings, enhancement of security, 'clean-up' campaigns, improved levels of maintenance and repair and supporting local business initiatives. In addition successful schemes were also expected to develop:

Figure 3b *Rock Ferry renewal area (Clockwise from top) (a) Shop front improvements; (b) Traffic calming – a cheap but effective barrier to through traffic; (c) Improving the image – new boundary walls and pavements; (d) Integrating crime reduction with area improvements; (e) Estate Action – maisonette blocks converted into houses with former public open space now incorporated within private gardens; (f) Estate Action – a refurbished tower block with a new entrance and entry phone system, renovated interior and double glazing to all flats*

- new ways of running estates to provide tenants with greater control over the management of their homes;
- measures to diversify tenure through partnership with the private sector and housing associations;
- housing improvements linked to the provision of enterprise, training and employment opportunities for residents (Department of the Environment, 1991, p. 3).

Thus, local authorities could bid for funding from the Estate Action programme in addition to their normal housing allocation. In addition to understanding the nature of the problems facing the estate, bids had to demonstrate how the local authority would:

- renovate the dwellings and improve the environment of the estate;
- improve security and reduce crime;
- improve housing management;
- involve tenants in both the regeneration and housing management processes;
- diversify tenure;
- lever in private investment;
- promote local economic development, job creation and training.

Estate Action is said to have provided a holistic approach to problem estates, encouraged innovation, targeted resources and increased confidence in the area. On the other hand, critics have pointed to the fact that it was merely a redistribution of funds from the housing investment programme and did not provide additional resources and that the annual cycle of funding created difficulties for local authorities' forward planning.

Nevertheless many Estate Action projects have been highly successful, especially in terms of improvements to the dwellings and the local physical environment. Housing management, frequently decentralised and incorporating some element of tenant participation, has become more sensitive to local needs. Schemes to 'design out crime' have often had some successes in reducing crime, or at least moving it elsewhere. Tenure has frequently been diversified through the sale of council homes to sitting tenants; the transfer of entire blocks or groups of houses to housing associations or other landlords; and the replacement of cleared council stock, such as obsolete multi-storey flats, with private or housing association developments. The private investment that has been levered in has tended to take the form of housing investment, renovation or replacement of local shopping facilities and occasional small-scale industrial developments.

This injection of capital investment has produced some impressive physical improvements in the estates that have benefited from Estate Action. However, in many areas there remain questions about sustaining adequate revenue spending on regular maintenance and repairs in the long term. Furthermore, most of the other social and economic problems faced by the population of these estates remain untouched: low income and unemployment, low educational attainment and poor health are still endemic in many inner city and peripheral council estates.

Today Estate Action funding has been absorbed within the Single Regeneration Budget and has been replaced by the 'Estate Renewal Challenge Fund'. Under these new arrangements local authorities may bid for funds to support estate improvements in preparation for transfer of the estate out of local authority control to another landlord.

Housing Action Trusts

Housing Action Trusts (HATs) were established under the Housing Act 1988 with powers to acquire housing stock from council ownership, to refurbish, redevelop, manage and, after treatment, to dispose of the properties to alternative, preferably private landlords. The government's original proposal was to go over the heads of local councils and designate a number of HATs in some of the country's worst problem estates. The argument was that these local authorities were 'incompetent' and opposed to government's aim of diversifying housing tenure and that direct intervention by central government would be welcomed by tenants (Karn, 1993, p. 75). HATs were proposed in six local authorities but the government had misunderstood the attitudes and desires of residents and in each case tenant opposition brought about by their fear of tenure changes and rent rises prevented designation. By 1990 it seemed as if the concept had been stillborn. However, later that year, two areas, Waltham Forest and Hull, had negotiated a revised approach to HATs whereby tenants and the local authority obtained considerable control over the running of the trust together with guarantees about rent levels and the return of housing to local authority ownership after treatment (Karn, 1993, pp. 74–90).

Subsequently four other local authorities have negotiated the designation of HATs on favourable and locally acceptable terms. The type of estate being treated varies considerably. For example, the North Hull HAT comprises an inter-war cottage estate whereas the Waltham Forest HAT contains high-density, system-built, multi-storey dwellings from the 1960s and 1970s, whilst the Liverpool HAT is not an estate at all but comprises the majority of the city's tower blocks. In no sense can the policy as implemented be seen as the concerted attack on the worst council housing estates that was originally intended and it now seems unlikely that further HATs will be designated.

New Deal for Communities

In 1998 the Government launched the 'New Deal for Communities'. This new programme will provide a funding contribution towards the intensive regeneration of some of the poorest neighbourhoods in the country. It is intended that the programme will support regeneration schemes that tackle poor job prospects, high levels of crime, educational underachievement and poor health. Partnerships of relevant agencies, local people and other stakeholders will be brought together to work on integrated programmes of investment and change. The emphasis is on flexibility and innovation and empowering local communities to find solutions that best meet their needs. As such the New Deal for Communities can be seen as a direct descendent and development from the social-economic elements of Renewal Areas and Estate Action schemes and the local innovation encouraged by City Challenge and the Single Regeneration Budget Challenge Fund (see below).

Housing Regeneration in Scotland

The large cities of Scotland have long had severe urban housing problems. The White Paper *New Life for Urban Scotland* (1988) stated the government's views on the regeneration of peripheral council estates. Subsequently 'Urban Partnerships' were established on peripheral estates in Dundee, Edinburgh, Glasgow and Paisley. The partners included the Scottish Office and Scottish Homes, the local authority, the local enterprise company (LEC – see below) and the local community. Urban Partnerships were intended to renovate housing and diversify tenure as well as tackling other local social, economic and environmental problems. A complementary policy 'Smaller Urban Renewal Initiatives' (SURIs) was designed to achieve similar objectives on smaller estates outside the big cities. In 1995, following a review of policy, the government proposed to encourage district-wide partnerships in areas of significant multiple deprivation.

URBAN POLICY

Parallel with the evolution of housing renewal policy we can see the separate emergence of policies concerned with broader issues of urban deprivation, especially in the inner urban areas. This strand of state intervention is usually known as urban policy. We now trace its development through the post-war period to the present day.

EARLY POLICY DEVELOPMENT

After the Second World War most British cities experienced a prolonged period of urban expansion, central area investment and slum replacement building programmes. It really seemed as if the quality of life in towns and cities was improving for all. However, by the late 1960s concerns were growing about inner city housing conditions, racial tension and falling populations. Social unrest in Notting Hill, London, and other inner cities prompted the Labour government in 1968 to establish an 'urban programme'. Initially administered by the Home Office, local authorities and community organisations could apply for 'urban aid': capital and revenue funding to support social and community development projects. These were to be small-scale projects that would fill gaps in local community provision and, it was thought, ameliorate social conditions. In the same year the Ministry of Education established an experimental series of 'educational priority areas' in inner city areas where educational attainment was perceived to be low. It was thought that by improving educational standards the 'cycle of deprivation' could be broken and young inner city residents would have a more prosperous economic future than their parents. This was a short lived scheme but it illustrates another aspect of thinking at that time.

In 1969 the Home Office launched a major initiative: the Community Development Project (CDP). What started as a series of isolated local action–research projects designed to improve value for money in the urban programme lasted nearly 10 years and gradually turned into a major social research movement. In their analysis of the problems of poor urban areas these research teams went well beyond the then current conventional wisdom of 'culture of poverty' or 'cycle of deprivation' explanations to produce a series of strongly argued reports that clearly located the causes of deprivation in fundamental changes in the economic structure of urban areas and in the imperatives of the capitalist economic system (Loney, 1983).

In 1972 the new Conservative government, through its Secretary of State for the Environment, Peter Walker, decided to sponsor its own studies and appointed consultants for three major 'Inner Area Studies' (IAS) in Liverpool, Lambeth and Birmingham, to examine the general nature of inner city problems and to recommend policies. Their reports began to appear in draft form from 1975 with final reports being published in 1977 (Department of the Environment, 1977a, b, c). Also, under the 1968 Town and Country Planning Act, Structure Plans were being prepared for the new metropolitan Counties. One requirement of this plan preparation process was the investigation of social and economic problems within the Structure Plan areas. Each of these metropolitan areas contained severely deprived inner cities which became a focus for planners' attention. While Structure Plans were essentially land use planning mechanisms with little power to tackle social and economic issues, many of their accompanying survey reports contained a wealth of socio-economic analysis which tended to reinforce the conclusions of the CDP and IAS as to the fundamental economic nature of the inner city problem.

It was left to the returning Labour government to respond to this wealth of evidence and analysis. In a famous speech in Manchester on 17 September 1976 Peter Shore, the new Secretary of State for the Environment, acknowledged the nature and growing severity of the inner city problem:

> All our major cities have lost population over the last decade and a half. Since 1961 the inner area of the Manchester conurbation has lost 20 per cent of its population and that of Liverpool 40 per cent. What is more worrying is the unbalanced nature of the migration . . . leaving the inner areas with a disproportionate share of unskilled and semi-skilled workers, of unemployment, of one-parent families, of concentrations of immigrant communities and overcrowded and inadequate housing. Though there has been a growth of office jobs in the centres of most of these cities this has not compensated for the extremely rapid decline in manufacturing industry in the inner urban areas. Manufacturing employment in Manchester declined by 20 per cent and Liverpool by 19 per cent between 1966 and 1971 (Peter Shore, 1976).

The subsequent policy changes included adjusting the 'needs' element of the rate support grant to give increased assistance to inner city local authorities; the new and expanded towns programme was cut back so as to reduce out-migration from the cities and the 1978 Inner Urban Areas Act placed inner city policy in the mainstream of government concern. Under this change of policy the Urban Programme was relaunched with increased funds and transferred from the Home Office to the Department of the Environment. A series of 'partnerships' were established under which central and local government agencies would work together to manage a co-ordinated programme of investment in all the most deprived inner cities in England: Birmingham, Hackney and Islington, Lambeth, Liverpool, London Docklands, Manchester and Salford, Newcastle and Gateshead . A second tier of 15 less severely affected 'programme' authorities (mainly less deprived metropolitan boroughs such as Sheffield or Wolverhampton) and a third tier of 19 other designated areas (a mixture of metropolitan boroughs and free-standing towns such as Blackburn, Doncaster or Newport) were also designated. Later this list was extended to include a total of 57 authorities eligible to bid for Urban Programme support.

The Act also permitted local authorities to designate Industrial and Commercial Improvement Areas (IIAs/CIAs) within which they could provide limited financial support to local firms for environmental and building works. A review of IIAs/CIAs in 1986 found that the measures pursued had increased business confidence in the area but had had little impact on overall investment so the effect on employment was minimal. The main impacts were found to be in improvements to the visual appearance of areas and small-scale physical changes such as site clearances and access improvements (JURUE, 1986).

Even before the 1979 election questions were being raised about the effectiveness of these partnerships in times of recession and public expenditure cuts and the relevance of this managerialist approach (i.e. changing government organisational and service delivery arrangements) to problems that many had analysed as requiring more fundamental economic solutions. But the arrival of the new Conservative government with its tough supply-side economic policies, its distrust of Labour-controlled local authorities and its different priorities, changed much of the emphasis of inner city policy.

POLICY DEVELOPMENT UNDER THE CONSERVATIVES

In 1980 under the Local Government, Planning and Land Act, the government obtained powers to establish Urban Development Corporations (UDCs): an application of the new town development corporation organisational model to the urban regeneration situation. This Act was the first in a series of measures through the 1980s that increasingly marginalised the role of local government in the regeneration process. This culminated in the 'Action for Cities' programme launched in 1988 in which the role of local authorities was accorded no more than a passing mention.

Initially two UDCs were created: the London Docklands Development Corporation and the Merseyside Development Corporation. These agencies were given very clear tasks in relation to the removal of physical dereliction, bringing land back into beneficial use and facilitating property development (Box 2). UDCs had power to acquire, manage and dispose of land, to carry out reclamation works and to provide roads and other infrastructure. They were also, controversially, given substantial powers over development control, effectively making them the planning authority for the designated area. UDCs were managed by a Board appointed by the Secretary of State. Although such boards usually included some local representatives this was seen by many as a poor substitute for local democratic control. Countering such criticism the government argued that the scale of investment needed and the nature of the property investment process required a single-minded and speedy style of decision-making that could not have been achieved within local authority structures. Neither job creation nor the provision of social housing or amenities to meet local needs were seen as primary objectives at that time. This property-led approach to urban regeneration was later extended in 1987 and 1988 as further UDCs were established in the West Midlands, Trafford Park, Central Manchester, Tyne and Wear, Cardiff Bay, Leeds, Bristol, Sheffield and Teesside. Commenting on this approach Atkinson and Moon suggest that:

> So long as UDCs prioritise property-led development, they will inevitably focus primarily on narrow physical regeneration strategies revolving around flagship schemes, they will not contain mechanisms for ensuring that local people benefit, and their appropriateness will be questionable (Atkinson and Moon, 1994, p. 153).

Box 2 *Central Manchester Development Corporation (Figure 4)*

Central Manchester Development Corporation (CMDC) was designated in 1988 and included 187 hectares of mainly mixed industrial and commercial land and property in an arc around the southern edge of Manchester city centre.

During its eight-year life the CMDC sought to regenerate the area by encouraging and subsidising private development and carrying out environmental improvements. In 1988 CMDC was faced with an area containing many derelict and vacant industrial and commercial buildings, obsolete textile warehouses and office premises. The nature of the regeneration that followed reflected the character and location of the district, the established policies of Manchester City Council and the nature of the property market during that period.

The designated area covered parts of the city centre fringe including the Castlefield historic area, the G-Mex exhibition centre and the main Piccadilly railway station. This location enabled the development corporation to encourage investment in cultural and tourist developments such as the new Bridgewater Hall concert hall and expansion of the Museum of Science and Industry in Castlefield. These have been complemented by the growth of many restaurants, bars and clubs as part of an attempt, in collaboration with the city council,

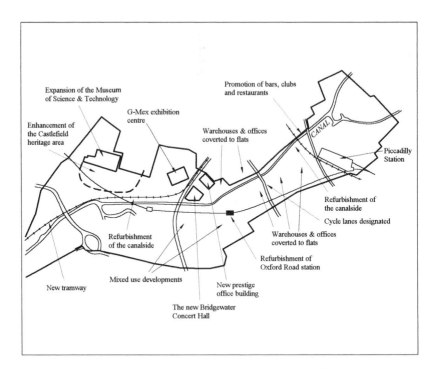

Figure 4a   *Central Manchester Development Corporation*

to expand leisure activity and extend the use of the city centre beyond the traditional working day.

Modern patterns of industrial development meant that little of the former industrial land was suitable for re-use by the manufacturing sector. Also, for much of the development period the property market was in recession and the demand for the building or occupation of office premises was well below the capacity of the area. As far back as 1984 the Manchester City Centre Local Plan had proposed more housing developments within the city centre and by the time of CMDC's designation a number of schemes had already been realised. This combination of circumstances led CMDC to support the creation of over 2000 new homes in the city centre during its lifespan. The effect was to increase the city centre population from less than 250 in 1988 to over 4000 by 1995 – a significant achievement. Mixed use developments have been a feature of the area. On the environmental side considerable effort has been put into turning the derelict Ashton and Rochdale canals into attractive recreation facilities, which included incidental landscaping, public art, improvements to street lighting and paving on key routes.

Figure 4b *Central Manchester Development Corporation (Clockwise from top)
(a) Much needed green space in the heart of the city; (b) The city no longer turns its
back on the canal, water is becoming a part of the townscape; (c) A new shop with
flat, surrounded by other new apartments; (d) New offices and canalside bar
adjoining the Bridgewater Concert Hall; (e) Chepstow House, former offices
converted to flats and fully occupied*

Another arm of economic regeneration policy that also focused on ways to
reduce developers' costs was the idea of Enterprise Zones announced in the 1980
budget. Within designated zones occupiers and developers benefited from certain
tax concessions and a relaxed planning regime. An evaluation of the experiment
for the DoE found that the zones had successfully stimulated the development of

derelict and vacant sites, attracted firms into the premises provided and increased employment opportunities. However:

> The cost effectiveness of the experiment could be improved by reducing the amount of 'dead-weight' on both capital allowances and rate relief, which could be differentiated across zones and between economic sectors or even 'tapered' downwards through time (PA Cambridge Economic Consultants, 1987, p. 88).

The early 1980s also saw the government attempt to limit local government spending and local rate increases, partly for macroeconomic reasons and partly in a belief that high inner city rates were deterring regeneration. In 1981 localised inner city riots in several cities, including Liverpool (Toxteth), London (Brixton) and Bristol (St Pauls) temporarily shook the confidence of the government and led to a high profile response which included Michael Heseltine, then Secretary of State for the Environment, for a short period being styled the 'Minister for Merseyside' and the setting up of the Merseyside Task Force, a local inter-ministerial team, to co-ordinate central government activity in the area; a Financial Institutions Group (FIG) was established to explore the scope for getting more private sector investment into the inner cities. One major outcome of the FIG was the Urban Development Grant (see below). Encouraging private investment became a major plank of subsequent urban policy development. One result of this was a change in the nature of 'partnership' from being a central–local government relationship to being a public–private relationship through the remainder of the 1980s. There was also a burgeoning of profit-seeking development companies keen to exploit this new found investment market. The consequences for the inner cities were an increase in ad hoc, sometimes uncoordinated and unplanned property development activities, and a number of significant improvements in the local physical environment, but frequently with scant regard for the social and employment needs of the indigenous local community.

The Urban Development Grant (UDG), based on the US Urban Development Action Grant, was launched in 1982 with the aim of promoting economic and physical regeneration in run-down urban areas by encouraging private investment that would not otherwise take place. The purpose of the UDG was to bridge the gap between the cost of a development and its value on completion. The notion was that in some inner city areas private developers were deterred by higher costs of development, for example the cost of clearing existing derelict buildings or dealing with contaminated land, and by the low selling price or rental value of completed buildings compared with projects in other more prosperous areas. Assistance could be in the form of grants or loans for any size of project. Applications had to be made through local authorities. The Urban Regeneration Grant was launched in 1987 to complement the UDG by enabling the private sector to redevelop larger sites or refurbish larger groups of buildings without the need for local authority involvement. Both types of grant were absorbed into the new City Grant under the government's 'Action for Cities' programme in 1988.

A number of other regeneration initiatives emerged through the 1980s. The main ones are listed and briefly described below, they include Garden Festivals, City Action Teams, Task Forces and the Safer Cities programme. Based upon a German concept, Garden Festivals were used as a mechanism for reclaiming derelict land, boosting tourism and improving the image of an area for private investment: the first International Garden Festival took place in Liverpool in 1984 with other national Garden Festivals following at Stoke on Trent (1986), Glasgow (1988), Gateshead (1990) and Ebbw Vale (1992). In spite of their direct benefits in land reclamation and the short-term impacts on tourism they are thought to have had limited long-term benefits and the programme has now ceased (Robson *et al.*, 1994, p. 124). City Action Teams (CATs) (1985–1993) were a government attempt to bring together civil servants from the Departments of Environment, Employment and Trade and Industry in an attempt to better co-ordinate the delivery of public spending programmes and to encourage local partnerships in selected inner city areas. CATs had small budgets and only a limited impact on the renewal process; they were absorbed into the new Regional Offices of Government in 1993. Task Forces (not to be confused with the Merseyside Task Force above) were launched by the Department for Trade and Industry in 1986. They were short life government agencies targeted at small selected inner city areas and intended to co-ordinate the work of local agencies and to build up the local capacity for self-sustaining economic regeneration. Located in a number of inner urban areas, their total expenditure rose from under £0.5m in 1986/87 to around £2.0m in 1990/91 (Robson *et al.*, 1994, p. 79). Safer Cities was a Home Office initiative announced as part of the Action for Cities programme in 1988 whereby the government would work with local agencies and communities in selected inner city areas, offering expert advice and some financial support for measures to reduce crime and the fear of crime.

CITY CHALLENGE

By the end of the 1980s it had become clear that substantial inefficiencies had crept into the government's urban regeneration spending programmes. The views of many were well expressed by the Audit Commission who suggested:

> The most critical need is for the three major actors in urban regeneration – central government, local government and the private sector – to pull together. This does not always happen now. There are important sources of friction, particularly in the relationship between central and local government . . .

> • local authorities believe that their role is undervalued by central government. They see themselves as increasingly marginalised.

- government (financial) support programmes are seen as a patchwork quilt of complexity and idiosyncrasy. They baffle local authorities and business alike.
- The rules of the game seem over-complex and sometimes capricious. They encourage compartmentalised policy approaches rather than a coherent strategy.
- key organisational structures have fallen into disrepair. Some partnership schemes do in practice operate (Audit Commission, 1989, p. 1).

This is a remarkably damning view to emanate from one of the government's own agencies. Clearly things had to change.

On returning in 1990 to be Secretary of State for the Environment for the second time Michael Heseltine announced a remarkable new initiative: City Challenge. Fifteen of the urban programme authorities were invited to submit bids for £37.5m of programmed spending over a five-year period. Each bid was to comprise a clearly expressed vision or aim developed into a practical strategy and programme for investment over a five-year period. Bids were to be prepared by the local authorities in collaboration with other local business and community partners and clear mechanisms for programme implementation had to be set out.

City Challenge was startling for its recognition of the key role that could be played by local authorities in facilitating developments; in its overtly competitive character; the encouragement of local partnerships; and the clarity of thinking required in the bid itself. For its competitive element, the wasted effort this involved and the way funds were allocated on the basis of local ability to design and sell a programme rather than local need, City Challenge was roundly criticised. On the other hand, the obligation on local agencies to clearly articulate their aims and objectives and to translate these into policy, a costed programme and implementation strategy were seen as positive benefits (De Groot, 1992).

Single Regeneration Budget

In further recognition of the need for change, on its return after the 1993 election the government decided to bring to England some of the benefits of regional co-ordination in government activity that were so apparent in the workings of the Scottish and Welsh Offices. The regional offices of the Departments of Environment, Employment, Trade and Industry, and Transport were amalgamated into new Regional Offices of Government (ROG). At the same time it was announced that there would be a 'Single Regeneration Budget' to bring the large number of regeneration programmes that had developed over the years into one single, better co-ordinated, focused and flexible spending stream.

The Single Regeneration Budget replaced more than 20 previous programmes including:

- Department of the Environment – Estate Action, Housing Action Trusts, City Challenge, the Urban Programme, the Urban Regeneration Agency (known as English Partnerships and including Derelict Land Grant and City Grant), Urban Development Corporations, Inner City Task Forces and City Action Teams.
- Department of Employment – Programme Development Fund, Education Business Partnerships, Teacher Placement Service, Inner City Compacts, the Business Start-up Scheme, Local Initiative Fund and TEC Challenge.
- Home Office – Safer Cities, Section 11 Grants (part), Ethnic Minority Grants, Ethnic Minority Business Initiative.
- Department of Trade and Industry – Regional Enterprise Grants, English Estates (absorbed into English Partnerships).
- Department for Education – Grants for Education Support and Training (part).

Source: Department of the Environment, Government in Partnership Factsheet No. 2, 1993.

The purpose of the Single Regeneration Budget was to support regeneration and development that meets objectives similar to those of many of the pre-existing programmes, namely economic development, job creation, improving environmental and housing conditions, tackling crime and other social issues including exclusion and racial equality. Community participation and the levering in of private sector and European resources were seen as particularly important elements of the regeneration process (see Table 2).

As shown in Table 2, a proportion of the Single Regeneration Budget is nationally 'top-sliced' to fund English Partnerships as well as the remaining Urban Development Corporations and City Challenge initiatives until their closure (neither programme being seen as relevant to the new flexible locally driven style of regeneration). A further element is allocated, with some discretion to the Regional Offices of Government, to fund Housing Action Trusts and the remaining Estate Action projects. The remainder is offered as a 'Challenge Fund' for which local agencies may bid. It will be noted that within a budget that is declining in total through the late 1990s, the proportion available through the Challenge Fund has increased from 10.1% of total SRB funds in 1995/6 to a planned figure of over 61.3% in 1999/2000. Bidding for Challenge Fund support is competitive with central government determining the choice of projects it wishes to support. Within the broad parameters of urban regeneration the government's priorities for the allocation of funds vary slightly from year to year. For instance, round four (1998/99) had a more explicit emphasis on tackling multiple deprivation than earlier rounds. Nevertheless the general principles remain constant.

According to the government:

> The Challenge Fund is a catalyst for local regeneration. It complements or attracts other resources – private, public or voluntary. It helps improve local areas and

Table 2 The Single Regeneration Budget (£ million)

	1991/2 outturn	1992/3 outturn	1993/4 outturn	1994/5 outturn	1995/6 outturn	1996/7 outturn	1997/8 planned	1998/9 planned	1999/2000 planned
UDCs	508.6	430.6	343.1	258.0	217.9	193.8	168.0	69.3	15.0
DLR	93.2	84.4	28.1	29.1	37.1	20.7	33.9	55.0	20.0
EP	99.1	153.3	164.9	191.7	211.1	229.6	209.6	209.0	208.7
HATs	10.1	26.5	78.1	92.0	92.5	87.7	88.7	88.6	88.4
Challenge Fund	–	–	–	–	136.4	264.9	481.6	568.8	625.5
Estate Action	267.5	348.0	357.4	372.6	315.9	256.7	169.9	98.2	61.5
City Challenge	–	72.6	240.0	233.6	226.8	230.1	143.0	7.0	–
Other SRB*	481.4	469.4	426.1	281.3	117.9	65.5	21.2	2.1	1.0
Total SRB	1459.8	1584.7	1637.7	1458.2	1355.5	1348.9	1315.5	1098.0	1020.1

* Prior to 1995/6 the Other SRB line includes all other programmes subsequently absorbed into the SRB.
UDC – Urban Development Corporation
DLR – Docklands Light Railway
EP – English Partnerships
HATs – Housing Action Trusts

Source: Figure 4.a, Department of the Environment *Annual Report* Cmnd 3607, HMSO, London, 1997.

enhance the quality of life of local people by tackling need, stimulating wealth creation and enhancing competitiveness. The activities it supports are intended to make a real and sustainable impact. It encourages partners to come together in a joint approach to meet local needs and priorities (Department of the Environment, *SRB Bidding Guidance*, 1993, p. 1).

Bids may be thematic, contributing to an external strategy, or local, focusing on small area regeneration or development. Many types of bid may be, and indeed have been, supported including funding for elements of Renewal Areas, the refurbishment of run-down council estates, town centre schemes, the redevelopment of large multi-faceted sites, employment creation or training projects. Generally bids are for areas or themes that cater for less than 25 000 population.

Bids must be made by a partnership of all those with a significant stake in the proposal. This allows local authorities to take the lead in facilitating development but specifically prohibits them from going it alone without the agreement of other stakeholders. However, it is not necessary for bids to include a local authority and a number of successful bids have been led by Training and Enterprise Councils, Higher Education Institutions and the Voluntary Sector. Local SRB funded project teams are frequently multi-professional and, depending upon the nature of the project, draw on the skills of town planners, architects, surveyors, economic development officers and community development specialists. Like the Renewal Areas and City Challenge programmes before them, many such teams are led by planners because of the policy overview and formulation skills that are their stock in trade.

The bid for funding support should include the following elements:

- a vision statement (in recent years the government has been increasingly keen on getting local regeneration agencies to think much more carefully about what they are really trying to achieve, in order to focus, co-ordinate and prioritise expenditure);
- an assessment of the problems and opportunities of the area (this would involve planners in establishing baseline conditions so that progress could thereafter be monitored);
- an explanation of the relevant development plans and other strategic policies to which the bid will contribute (again, the government are looking for co-ordinated strategies at the local level rather than *ad hoc* proposals);
- detailed and costed plans for the first year's spending and outline plans for subsequent years (enabling feasibility and value for money to be assessed);
- the targets and objectives to be achieved year on year (this enables performance to be monitored and evaluated);
- the organisational structure to be established to deliver the regeneration proposals (it is essential to know the powers and duties of each of the partners in the implementation process);

- an 'exit strategy', indicating how the process of regeneration might continue after SRB funding ceases (Department of the Environment, *SRB Bidding Guidance*, 1993, p. 16).

There are annual rounds of bidding and proposals are assessed against selected criteria: meeting the government's strategic objectives as well as fitting within local strategies; being well targeted; the leverage ratio (the amount of private investment generated by each pound of public subsidy); value for money; deliverability; innovation; and the sustainability of the project or programme beyond the life of SRB funding. Thus central government has a very large measure of control over the nature and location of public support for regeneration projects. To be considered bids must include a clear statement of aims and objectives; an analysis of the problems to be tackled; an explanation of the wider planning context (such as the Unitary Development Plan); costings; budgets; an implementation programme; an explanation of the organisational structure that will deliver the regeneration; and a statement of anticipated outputs.

As with City Challenge this structure forces local agencies to think very clearly about their mission and priorities. It also claims to allow regeneration spending to reflect local priorities, to offer flexible funding for projects of different character and time spans, and provides a sound framework for monitoring project outputs.

However, emerging criticisms of the SRB Challenge Fund are that many of the projects are still too small to overcome structural economic problems; that the real power still lies with central government and that its decision-making is inconsistent and opaque; that the competitive bidding process results in much wasted effort and no funding for many worthy schemes; that at local level the bidding is dominated by local authorities and TECs with the voluntary sector and others only playing a subordinate role; and that the bidding process favours large projects to the detriment of many of the smaller but locally useful projects, such as those that might benefit ethnic minority communities, that would have found financial support under the previous urban programme funding regime. Whilst SRB sought to increase flexibility and encourage co-ordination and partnership between local agencies

> . . . structural problems in the way the SRB Challenge Fund was established are undermining this process. Real flexibility means the SRB needs to become more transparent, the output-related funding regime needs to be relaxed and the problems caused by the brevity of the application process addressed (Ward, 1997, p. 80).

(See also Nevin *et al.*, 1977, for a full discussion of the outcomes of the first and second rounds of SRB Challenge Fund bidding.)

In Box 3 we see an example of the typical objectives, structure and funding arrangements for an inner city area-based SRB supported project (see also Figure 5).

Box 3 *The North Liverpool Partnership. A regeneration project supported by the Single Regeneration Budget*

The Partnership includes three districts within Liverpool's inner city: Breckfield, a predominantly residential area of private 'by-law' terraces and council housing; Everton, dominated by multi-storey council flats built to replace slums cleared in the 1950s and 1960s; and Vauxhall, a mixed industrial and residential area adjoining the former north docks.

In this run-down area of social deprivation and depressed environment a North Liverpool Partnership was established between the local authority, other public agencies, local businesses and the local community to bid for SRB support. In the event £21.9m was awarded for a six-year programme to: 'create, through effective partnership and the utilisation of the full potential of the whole community, a thriving area whose population enjoy good quality employment, education, health, housing and environment'.

The tone and style of this vision statement is typical of many regeneration programmes but the emphasis on community involvement and social objectives is interesting. The grant is large by SRB standards but rather less than the £37.5m awarded to five-year programmes for similar areas under the previous City Challenge initiative.

According to the Partnership's strategy document the problems of the area are manifold. Educational attainment and aspirations are low, truancy and exclusions are commonplace; youth and long-term unemployment are endemic. There is seen to be a need for very personalised forms of basic skills training. Small local firms need better access to sources of capital, business contacts and marketing in order to expand. Much of the housing stock is of poor quality. There are 15 former council owned tower blocks, many in a poor state of repair, all now taken over by the Liverpool Housing Action Trust. Fear of crime is a major issue. Everton Park, a large open area created by the City Council on former housing land, has lacked the investment to make it a useful amenity and yet, with its stunning views over the Mersey and North Wales, it has considerable potential for recreational development.

It is proposed to translate the strategic vision into action through a series of programmes referred to as 'routes'. Routes for People develops objectives, policies and projects for education and training, provision for young people, employment initiatives, housing renovation and management, the delivery of healthcare, public transport and other quality of life issues. Routes for Business are targeted at the expansion of indigenous local businesses, the development of new businesses and attracting inward investment. Routes to Partnership seeks to develop better working relationships and co-ordination between the multiplicity of agencies and stakeholders within the area.

The Partnership is managed by a steering group comprising representatives of local residents (6 members), local businesses (6 members), the public sector

(6 members), 4 ward councillors and a Chair appointed by the City Council. The work of the Partnership is carried out by an Executive Team including a Manager, Community Co-ordinator, two Community Development Workers and a number of other officers.

Through the six-year strategy it is intended that the £21.9m SRB funding will complement other public sector funds including £36m from the Liverpool HAT, £16m through the Housing Corporation, £12m European Union funding, £2.9m from the City Council, and £2.5m from English Partnerships. It is estimated that this investment will lever in some £43m of private/non-public sector funding. It is hoped that the total investment in the area over the six years will be in the order of £138m.

It can be clearly seen that the strategy is intended to be a comprehensive and holistic attack on the problems of the area and as such it represents a continuation and development of the approach to regeneration that emerged in the thinking behind Renewal Areas (1989) and City Challenge (1991). The co-ordination of spending programmes by public sector agencies is a key strategy. This reflects the lessons learned from the government-sponsored Task Forces and City Action Teams of the 1980s and the approach signalled by government in establishing their Regional Offices of Government. The levering in of private investment has been seen as an important measure of urban regeneration achievement since the early days of the urban development corporations.

ENGLISH PARTNERSHIPS

English Partnerships (EP) was established by the Conservative government in 1993 in fulfilment of a pre-election promise to set up an urban regeneration agency in England in answer to calls for greater co-ordination of regeneration spending and in order to complement the perceived successes of the Welsh Development Agency and the Scottish Development Agency (now Scottish Enterprise) in bringing about substantial economic regeneration in their respective regions.

English Partnerships brought together three strands of regeneration activity: English Estates, the government agency for building and managing advance factories and industrial estates; the Derelict Land Grant, the subsidy paid to landowners to bring back into use 'land so damaged by industrial or other development that it is incapable of beneficial use without treatment'; and the City Grant, the project-specific subsidy designed to bridge the gap between the high development costs and low returns from socially or economically desirable developments in marginal areas. It was already acknowledged that there was some overlap in the functions of the Derelict Land Grant and the City Grant.

The objectives of EP were to promote the regeneration of areas of need through the reclamation, development or redevelopment of land and buildings, and to

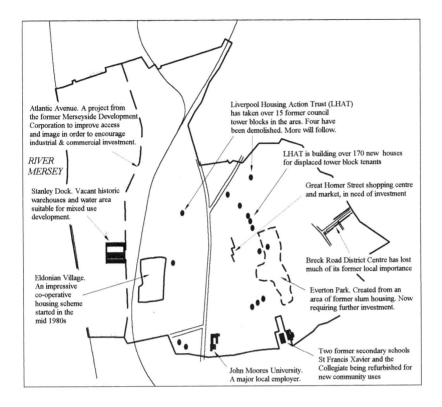

Atlantic Avenue. A project from the former Merseyside Development Corporation to improve access and image in order to encourage industrial & commercial investment.

RIVER MERSEY

Stanley Dock. Vacant historic warehouses and water area suitable for mixed use development.

Eldonian Village. An impressive co-operative housing scheme started in the mid 1980s

Liverpool Housing Action Trust (LHAT) has taken over 15 former council tower blocks in the ares. Four have been demolished. More will follow.

LHAT is building over 170 new houses for displaced tower block tenants

Great Homer Street shopping centre and market, in need of investment

Breck Road District Centre has lost much of its former local importance

Everton Park. Created from an area of former slum housing. Now requiring further investment.

John Moores University. A major local employer.

Two former secondary schools St Francis Xavier and the Collegiate being refurbished for new community uses

Figure 5a *North Liverpool Partnership problems and opportunities*

create economic growth, employment opportunities and environmental improvements in areas of most need throughout England.

The agency was able to operate in a wide range of locations including: European Objective 1 and 2 areas (see below – European Funding); coalfield closure areas; city challenge areas; inner city areas; other assisted areas; and areas subject to SRB support. It had power to offer financial assistance in support of development activity; to promote and enter into joint ventures with others; to acquire and manage property; together with a range of necessary ancillary powers such as rights to enter and survey land and to make highway connections. In appraising projects for financial assistance consideration was given to the strategic (planning) context, scale and practicality of the proposal as well as the degree of risk and, most importantly, the question of value for money.

Obtaining funding support from EP was a little different from bidding to the SRB Challenge Fund. Whereas the SRB may support a variety of economic, social or environmental regeneration projects, EP was essentially concerned with bringing land and property into beneficial use. One of the key phrases in understanding the

Figure 5b *North Liverpool Partnership (Clockwise from top) (a) Shaw Street – the derelict former Collegiate School, ripe for refurbishment and re-use; (b) Shaw Street – renovating listed but obsolete housing to provide new flats; (c) new houses under construction on the site of former multi-storey council flats (the site adjoins Everton Part); (d) Liverpool Housing Action Trust has taken over responsibility for all the remaining tower blocks in the area*

work of EP is that much of its work was done through providing 'gap funding' to support development proposals. The idea was that EP would bridge the gap between the development costs (land reclamation, construction costs, etc.) and the value of the completed development, where the development was not commercially viable (i.e. it makes a loss) but would be economically beneficial to the local community. Thus in determining whether to provide gap funding and in deciding how much to provide, EP was much concerned with estimating costs and values. Whilst the process included a contribution from planners, for EP also claimed a concern to see good design, the main skills involved were those of the estate manager and the economist. EP required applicants to provide information on the intended after-use of the land or buildings; the benefits to the community (e.g. hectares of land reclaimed or de-contaminated; net additional jobs; net additional dwellings; net additional commercial floorspace); estimated costs (value of the site before the project, reclamation and/or de-contamination costs, construction costs, other costs); and the estimated value of the completed project. From this information, which was carefully checked, EP could calculate the precise amount of gap funding needed to make the project viable.

English Partnerships was allocated £180.8m from the SRB in 1994/95, rising to over £220m in 1996/97. This money has been used in a variety of ways. For example, in Teeside, EP worked with ICI to establish a joint venture company to develop the Belasis Hall technology park; ICI made available 60 hectares of land for development and EP invested £10m, which led to occupation by 78 companies employing over 1300 people. In Nottinghamshire, the County Council and EP jointly embarked on a £4m reclamation of the 30 hectare former Shireoaks Colliery site to provide land for 50 dwellings together with industrial and commercial floorspace and a landscape area alongside the Chesterfield Canal. In Knowsley, Merseyside, EP spent £2.4m on purchasing and preparing a site to accommodate inward investment by the QVC mail order company bringing several hundred new jobs to the area. And at a much smaller scale, working with the community in Sheffield EP invested £15 000 to support provision of a creche and nursery at the Workstation, a local training and employment support facility.

Despite its many successes, emerging criticisms of EP are that its actions were too strongly influenced by this orientation towards property development. It is said by some to have been too cautious and wary of risk in supporting regeneration projects; there was an emphasis on supporting larger and fewer rather than smaller and more projects; and a concern to achieve profit-making end uses that might tend to encourage inappropriate development in some places.

REGIONAL DEVELOPMENT AGENCIES

In 1999 the Government established Regional Development Agencies in each of the English regions. The intention is to improve competitiveness through co-ordinated regional economic development and regeneration. These Regional Development Agencies have taken over responsibility for administering the Single Regeneration Budget and the work of the regional offices (the main operational functions) of English Partnerships. At the same time a small central core of English Partnerships was merged with the former Commission for the New Towns as a residual, mainly property managing, body.

ECONOMIC REGENERATION IN SCOTLAND

The Scottish Development Agency (SDA) was established in the mid-1970s to promote indigenous economic growth and inward investment. Unlike the situation in England at that time this agency was not bound to work within the confines of narrowly designated areas. It could take a broad geographic view of needs and opportunities and as an agency of the Scottish Office it was argued to be more in touch with local circumstances than the equivalent English ministry. It played a significant part in the Glasgow Eastern Area Renewal Project (GEAR). In 1988 the SDA was merged with the Training Agency in Scotland to form Scottish Enterprise with a mission to bring about economic regeneration and urban renewal. Much of its work is carried out through Local Enterprise Companies (LECs). These have powers to assist small firms, help companies with marketing, training and invest-ment problems, provide youth and adult training, reclaim land and undertake local environmental improvement projects. As such they combine many of the powers of English Partnerships and the Training and Enterprise Councils in England.

Thus the experience of urban renewal in Scotland has been very different from England, indeed:

> . . . the ability of the Scottish Office to focus a number of different initiatives on particular areas and the role of the SDA would appear to have created a more effective means to ameliorate the problems of inner cities and peripheral public-sector housing estates (McCrone, 1991). Additionally, the ongoing experience of the Glasgow Eastern Area Renewal Project may have helped establish a better working relationship between the Scottish Office and local government (Atkinson and Moon, 1994, p. 158).

REGENERATION IN WALES

Responsibility for urban regeneration in Wales lies with the Welsh Office, mainly working through the Welsh Development Agency, the Land Authority for Wales and area-specific projects such as the Cardiff Bay Development Corporation and the Programme for the Valleys.

The Welsh Development Agency has powers to acquire and reclaim land and to undertake environmental improvement works. The Land Authority for Wales may also assemble and make land available for development in economically difficult areas. Since 1994 Urban Investment Grants have been available to subsidise the private development of derelict urban sites.

The Cardiff Bay Development Corporation is Wales' only UDC, with ambitious plans to build a barrage across the harbour to create a freshwater lake and to regenerate the former docklands for business, tourism and housing.

The Programme for the Valleys began in 1988 and ran until 1998. In this area of severe economic decline and restructuring the programme is intended to encour-age sustainable economic growth, improve local services, housing and strengthen tourism and cultural activities. By 1995 it was claimed that 800 hectares of land had been reclaimed, 7000 homes had been improved and £700m private investment secured. The 1992 Ebbw Vale Garden Festival was also part of the programme (Central Office of Information, 1995, p. 66).

European Funding

There are two main sources of European Union funding to support urban renewal and regeneration. The European Regional Development Fund (ERDF) is available to support infrastructure projects, industrial developments and environmental improvements. The European Social Fund to intended to support vocational training, guidance and other measures to create employment. Subsidies from each fund are available on a match-funding basis, i.e. bidders must provide a proportion, typically half, of the investment themselves and the ERDF or ESF will provide the remainder. European Union funding including ERDF and ESF is only provided in support of certain EU objectives. There are six objectives, the two that most impact on urban renewal are:

- Objective 1 – Promoting development and structural adjustment of regions lagging behind. The criterion for qualification is that the per capita Gross Domestic Product of the region must be less than 75% of the EU average. Within Great Britain only Merseyside and the Highland and Islands of Scotland are designated Objective 1 regions.
- Objective 2 – Converting regions seriously affected by industrial decline. The objective is to support industrial restructuring in regions that have suffered major industrial decline, typically the former heavy industrial areas. A number of parts of Northern England and Scotland are designated Objective 2 areas.

ERDF is available to support projects within areas covered by a 'single programming document', a regional regeneration strategy produced by the local authorities and other agencies to meet the desire of the European Union to ensure that ERDF funds projects that form part of a wider regeneration strategy. Funds can be used to support capital (e.g. transport facilities, environmental improvements, industrial sites and factory units) or revenue projects (e.g. business development and support for small and medium sized firms, tourism promotion, research and development initiatives) (ERDF Guidance Notes, 1996). One of the key limitations on the use of ERDF funds is that applicants have to provide matched funding, typically 50%, from other sources. Thus, ironically, the more depressed the local economy the more difficult can be the task of finding matching funding support, especially from private investors, and the more difficult it can be to access ERDF.

CONCLUSIONS

During the 1970s and 1980s housing renewal policy evolved along two parallel tracks. To deal with obsolete private housing renovation grants combined with GIAs and HAAs were successful in treating more than five million dwellings over a 20-year period. And over the last 14 years, Estate Action and Housing Action Trusts have removed or renovated much of the worst of our public sector housing estates. Evolving as a separate stream of government spending, policies for the regeneration of inner urban areas (urban policy) developed from early experimentation through the central–local partnership approach of the late 1970s Labour government and the variety of initiatives employed by the Thatcher government to encourage and facilitate private investment until, by 1993, more than 20 different central government funding sources existed.

In recent years there have been moves to achieve a much more *integrated* and *focused* approach to regeneration. The first steps were taken in 1989 with the introduction of Renewal Areas. This policy obliged local authorities to consider not only housing but also the environmental and socio-economic aspects of area regeneration. This was the beginning of the *integration of housing renewal with local economic and social and environmental initiatives* and at the same time encouraged multi-professional team-working within local authorities. The introduction of Renewal Areas also required local councils to *work with other local stakeholders* to develop clearly articulated *strategies* and programmes based upon a mutual understanding of the problems and agreed *aims* for the area.

In 1991 the City Challenge programme, with its emphasis on inter-authority *competition*, reinforced this notion of *working with other local partners*, establishing clear *aims* and developing well worked out *strategies* for achieving these aims. City Challenge encouraged the notion of the local authority as a *facilitator* rather than the main undertaker of urban regeneration.

In 1993 the introduction of the Single Regeneration Budget and the establishment of the Regional Offices of Government in England reinforced many of these changes in policy. *Competition* between authorities was still seen by government to have a number of merits, especially in forcing up the quality of local thinking. Local authorities were still seen as *facilitators*, working with other partners in establishing area regeneration *aims, strategies and programmes* which could be carefully and systematically *monitored and reviewed*. The SRB, with its flexible approach, brought about the possibility of *integration* between public and private housing renewal and the further *integration* of housing renewal with other aspects of local environmental, social and economic regeneration.

Nevertheless, despite this recent progress, there remain some concerns with current urban renewal policy. Much of this can be encompassed within the debate around the necessity to achieve sustainable development in order to protect our resources and environment for future generations. One of the main contributions to sustainability that can be made by town planners is through the development of more compact cities and it is here that urban renewal and regeneration has a key role to play in maximising efficiency in the use of urban land and buildings and in creating the circumstances that will encourage developers to want to invest in, and people to want to live in, all parts of the urban landscape. It could be argued that whilst current policy is heading in the right direction there is still insufficient subsidy going into urban renewal and regeneration and that too much of that subsidy is tied to achieving easily measured short-term outputs rather than considering the long-term needs of the area. It is this thinking that has permitted the development of car-based shopping facilities on derelict sites or permitted suburban residential densities in the redevelopment of valuable inner city housing sites on the basis that any development is better than none and that developers might be frightened off by too harsh controls. Whilst there is some merit in these arguments, more thought has to be given to the long-term needs of an area and the long-term consequences of these decisions for sustainable development.

What is needed is for even more emphasis to be given to the provision of a *long-term holistic strategy* within which renewal and regeneration can take place; in other words, what is needed is more emphasis on town planning.

REFERENCES

Atkinson, R. and Moon, G. (1994) *Urban Policy in Britain: the City, the State and the Market*, Macmillan, London.

Audit Commission (1989) *Urban Regeneration and Economic Development: The Local Government Dimension*, HMSO, London.

Central Office of Information (1995) *Aspects of Britain: Urban Regeneration*, HMSO, London.

Couch, C. (1990) *Urban Renewal: Theory and Practice*, Macmillan, London.

Couch, C. and Gill, N. (1993) *Renewal Areas: A Review of Progress*, Working Paper 119, School for Advanced Urban Studies, University of Bristol.

De Groot, L. (1992) City Challenge: competing in the urban regeneration game, *Local Economy*, **7**, 196–209.

Department of the Environment (1977a) *Unequal City: Final Report of the Birmingham Inner Area Study*, HMSO, London.

Department of the Environment (1977b) *Inner London: Policies for Dispersal and Balance: Final Report of the Lambeth Inner Area Study*, HMSO, London.

Department of the Environment (1977c) *Change or Decay: Final Report of the Liverpool Inner Areas Study*, HMSO, London.

Department of the Environment (1990) *Circular 6/90 Area Renewal, Unfitness, Slum Clearance and Enforcement Action*, HMSO, London.

Department of the Environment (1991) *Estate Action Annual Report for 1990/91* Department of the Environment, London.

Department of the Environment, Transport & the Regions (1997) *Neighbourhood Renewal Assessment and Renewal Areas*, SO, London.

Goodall, B. (1972) *The Economics of Urban Areas*, Pergamon, Oxford.

Harvey, J. (1981) *The Economics of Real Property*, Macmillan, London.

172

JURUE (1986) *Inner Cities Research Programme: An Evaluation of Industrial and Commercial Improvement Areas*, HMSO, London.

Karn, V. (1993) Remodelling a HAT: the implementation of the Housing Action Trust legislation 1987–92, in: Malpass, P. and Means, R., *Implementing Housing Policy*, Open University Press, Milton Keynes.

Loney, M. (1983) *Community Against Government: The British Community Development Programme 1968–1978: A Study of Government Incompetence*, Heinemann, London.

McCrone, G. (1991) Urban renewal: the Scottish experience, *Urban Studies*, **28**, 919–938.

Ministry of Housing and Local Government (1966) *The Deeplish Study – Improvement Possibilities in a District of Rochdale*, HMSO, London.

Needleman, L. (1965) *The Economics of Housing*, Staples Press, London.

Nevin, B., Loftman, P. and Beazley, M. (1997) Cities in crisis – is growth the answer: an analysis of the outcome of the first and second rounds of the 'Single Regeneration Budget Challenge Fund', *Town Planning Review*, **68**(2), 145–164.

PA Cambridge Economic Consultants (1987) *Inner Cities Research Programme: An Evaluation of the Enterprise Zone Experiment*, HMSO, London.

Robson, B., Bradford, M.B., Deas, I., Hall, E., Harrison, E., Parkinson, M., Evans, R., Garside, P. and Harding, A. (1994) *Assessing the Impact of Urban Policy*, HMSO, London.

Ward, K. (1997) The Single Regeneration Budget and the issue of local flexibility, *Regional Studies*, **31**(1), 78–81.

CHAPTER 7

HOUSING

Madhu Satsangi

INTRODUCTION

In 1982, David Donnison and Claire Ungerson wrote that '. . . the boundaries which once distinguished public housing management from urban planning, from the regeneration of local economies and from community development are breaking down' (Donnison and Ungerson, 1982, p. 288). Nowhere is this more evident than in the concept of partnership – applied in our towns, cities and countryside – as a *sine qua non* of development and redevelopment. To the impartial outsider it may seem self-evident that professional people working on enhancing citizens' quality of life, of choice and of environment, and of adapting to social and economic change should work together. Yet, often to individual and public frustration, partnership is still bedevilled by boundaries, by different agendas – organisational, political and professional. This chapter aims to make a modest contribution to washing away these barriers by seeking to demonstrate to the reflective planner that housing policy and practice has no elusive mystique or dynamic anymore than does planning policy or practice. Rather both planning and housing, and more importantly the citizens they serve, can benefit from sharing approaches, lessons and professional knowledge.

The chapter is organised as follows. The next section discusses housing policy goals and how they relate to planning policy goals. The following section takes an historical perspective, looking at reasons for the professions having developed close ties even as they developed distinctiveness. Then we look at how the worlds of practice are coming together, at how housing professionals need planning professionals and vice versa. The final section offers some predictions for future policy and practice.

HOUSING POLICY GOALS AND THE PLANNING OF HOUSING

The broad goal of the housing policies of advanced industrial economies is often phrased along the lines of being 'to ensure that all citizens have access to a decent home at a price that they can afford'. In Britain, government has declared an objective:

> To offer everyone the opportunity of a decent home and so promote social cohesion, well-being and self-dependence (Treasury, 1998, p.13).

What this encompasses is a concern with citizens' quality of life, and a recognition that a fairly priced, decent standard of housing is an important aspect of that. Currently, the notion of decency that is built into the concern is one that takes into account the physical quality of dwellings and the quality of the environment in which they are situated. It also implies meeting – at least partly – citizens' aspirations for their housing, so that people have at least some degree of contentment with their homes.

The context for policy is that Britain's population is heavily urbanised, and its housing consumption increasingly privatised. But British society is strongly polarised. Evidence from the recent national house condition surveys shows that about four households in five currently live in cities, large and medium-sized towns (Department of the Environment, Transport and the Regions, 1998; Scottish Homes, 1997a). Urban change is a product of economic and social change, with Britain's cities having grown and declined on successive waves of industrialisation and de-industrialisation. And increasing *per capita* wealth has brought about increasing demand for suburban living. The challenges that these changes have wrought for housing policy and planning policy have been how to cope with changing demands for city living and semi-urban living. For the 12 million or so inhabitants of rural Britain, there have been two main sets of challenges: for some areas, coping with growth pressure, and for the others coping with out-migration. Finally, as we explore below, both housing policy and planning policy had their origins in concern about the living standards of poorer members of society. And that social concern is no less relevant today. One simple, yet persuasive, characterisation of modern Britain is Will Hutton's 'thirty–thirty–forty society' (Hutton, 1996), with the working population's households divided into:

- Thirty per cent being *disadvantaged* – including families of the unemployed and those able to secure only part-time work – with '. . . their children poorly fed, their families under stress and without access to amenities . . .' (*op. cit.*, p. 106).
- Thirty per cent being *marginalised* and *insecure* – its people working '. . . in jobs that are insecure, poorly protected and carry few benefits' (*ibid.*).
- Forty per cent being *privileged*, their market power having increased notably over the past two decades (*op. cit.*, p. 108).

Planning policies have at their core a notion of the need to balance protecting the natural environment with catering for the demands of economic growth and increasing social aspirations. As with housing policy, this core notion is clearly related to improving citizens' life quality, and it further recognises that an important part of the way in which we use the land and other resources available to us is the legacy that we leave for future generations.

From the most basic principles, then, housing and planning policies are closely bound to one another. We can see further bonds when we look at the means by which governments have sought to meet their housing policy objectives. The essence of housing problems is that, relative to people's incomes, housing is expensive. This means that, without some form of intervention or aid, people would consume less housing, or housing of a poorer quality (fewer housing services) than society considers desirable. Governments have therefore intervened

- to affect the quantity and quality of housing supplied, and
- to support people's ability to purchase housing.

Even the most cursory examination of the current shape and history of housing policy in Britain reveals significant differentiation according to the set of legal rights and responsibilities of the consumer – *tenure*. The two most important distinctions that need to be made are between home ownership and renting, and between renting from a commercial or private sector landlord and renting from a state or voluntary sector landlord. In the following section, we discuss their significance in terms of effects upon the supply of and demand for housing, but it is important to bear some points about scale in mind.

The first point to make is that the different countries of the UK have different shares of their housing stocks in the different tenures. Home-ownership does dominate, but local authority landlordism is directly relevant to fewer than one house in five in England and Wales yet to one in four in Northern Ireland and three in ten in Scotland (Table 1(a)). The second point is that home-ownership has grown in scale over the past 25 years or so, but municipal landlordism has declined (Table 1(b)).

THE SUPPLY OF HOUSING

For much of this century in Britain, governments of different political persuasions have used producer, or 'bricks-and-mortar', subsidies to affect the supply of housing. Most notably, local authorities have been empowered and subsidised to build and improve low-cost housing. (Low cost because it is specifically designed to be offered at rents below market-clearing levels.) And voluntary organisations – housing associations and co-operatives – have also received generous levels of public funding for new provision and for the repair of older private housing. Their provision also has, until very recently, been priced well below market rents. Finally, home-owners and landlords have been assisted in the repair and improvement of their properties with grants provided through local authorities.

The scale of the public investments is significant in a number of different ways. First, the amount of money spent on housing programmes currently accounts for around £300 billion of public expenditure (though there have been some important

Table 1 *Housing Tenure in the UK*

(a) Across the UK, 1996

Country	Owner-occupation	Private renting	Housing association/ co-operative	Local authority[1]	Total number of houses (000s)
England	68	11	5	16	20 699
Scotland	60	7	5	28	2267
Wales	71	9	4	16	1250
Northern Ireland	70	4	3	23	586
United Kingdom	67	10	5	17	24 802

Notes: Figures represent percentages of total occupied dwelling stock, save final column.
[1] Including Scottish Homes' stock (Scotland) and Northern Ireland Housing Executive stock (Northern Ireland).

Source: Wilcox (1999, Tables 17a, 17b, 17c, 17d).

(b) Great Britain over the past three decades

Year	Owner-occupation	Private renting	Housing association/ co-operative	Local authority[1]	Total number of houses (000s)
1971	51	19		31	18 999
1981	56	11	2	30	21 085
1991	66	10	3	21	23 130
1997	67	11	5	17	24 216

Note: Figures represent percentages of total occupied dwelling stock, save final column
[1] Including New Town stock, and Scottish Homes' stock (Scotland).

Source: Wilcox (1999, Tables 17c, 17d).

changes in the ways that the money has been spent over the past two decades). Second, at any one time, publicly sponsored housing programmes have accounted for an important share of the total volume of construction work underway. Recently, this has been of the order of 10% of output by value, with housing investment clearly having an important impact on employment. Third, the total number of new houses produced (at its heyday about 300 000 per annum across Britain) and the number of poor quality older houses improved means that the shape of neighbourhoods in the big cities and in towns and villages has been fundamentally altered by publicly led development. Indeed, were it not for public housing investments, it is doubtful whether the periphery of many cities (altered by large estates), or inner urban areas (altered by comprehensive redevelopment, and smaller-scale renewal programmes) would bear much resemblance to what we see today. So, as a planned land use, public housing makes a major impact upon local communities, and local economies.

PAYING FOR HOUSING

The demand for housing reflects people's ability to pay for different quantities and qualities of housing, and their willingness to buy it. Supply-side measures have been accompanied in Britain by a range of demand-side, or 'personal', housing subsidies. The most obvious of these is Housing Benefit, created in 1982 from the post-war rent and rate rebate system. At its most generous, tenants of a private, council or housing association landlord can have all of their housing costs met by the State. Home-owners, or those in the process of buying their own home, also have their housing costs reduced. There is some debate amongst economists about what the correct measure of owner-occupied housing subsidy is. But the one that is most commonly talked about is mortgage interest tax relief. Although this subsidy is now far less generous than it used to be, it can still make a significant difference to the budgets of many households – particularly those on lower incomes, or those buying cheaper housing. The demand for home-ownership was also heightened in a very targeted way in the 1980 Housing Act and Tenants' Rights Etc. (Scotland) Act that gave council tenants the right to buy their house at a discounted price, the amount of discount increasing with the tenant's length of council tenure. (For further discussion of all of these issues, see Gibb *et al.*, 1999.)

Together, it is apparent that the supply and demand subsidies significantly affect the sort of housing available and how much people pay for it. Private home-ownership accounts for the housing of the majority of the population of the UK, though there are significant country–country variations, and within the countries, areas vary in the relative share of socially rented and owned housing. It is also worth noting that the lesser degree of subsidisation of private landlordism, along-side waves of regulation and deregulation, have now more or less reduced that once majority form of housing into a residual tenure. (This is discussed further by Crook and Kemp, 1996.)

In order to meet, or attempt to meet, the goals of housing policy, there are then a number of public and semi-public organisations whose actions impinge upon the operation of land and housing markets. Table 2 brings out the key private and voluntary sector agents involved in mediating housing demand and supplying housing, and Table 3 identifies the principal statutory agencies involved in housing planning and supply.

Although not explicitly housing policy measures, there is a further series of influences on the quality and availability of housing. Land-use planning is the first and most obvious of these. Structure and local plans have an objective of meeting the needs of the whole community of the area for which they are designated. In housing, this means setting aside sufficient land for new housing development, making provision for affordable housing and planning for renewal of the physical fabric. We look at these issues in more detail in later sections. Spatial economic development policy also can have a considerable impact on local economic fortune, on local incomes and thus on housing affordability. Health and social

Table 2 *Private and voluntary sector agents in the housing market*

Housing Demand		Housing Supply	
Agent	Role	Agent	Role
Consumer	Purchaser of housing of different quantity and quality	Individual vendor	Seller of housing of different quantity and quality
Building Surveyors	Advise consumer	Private developer	Assembles land, building materials, services, labour into new housing developments/ redevelopment
Lawyers/Solicitors/ Estate Agents	Advise and act on behalf of consumer	Building Surveyors	Advise vendor
Banks and building societies	Provide finance for home-ownership	Lawyers/Solicitors/ Estate Agents	Advise and act on behalf of vendor/ developer/landlord
Residents'/tenants' groups	Coalesce consumer interests, usually around housing quality issues	Banks and building societies	Capital source for private developer and housing associations
Citizens' Advice Bureaux	Act as advocates of individual owner's/ tenant's rights	Private landlord	Leases houses to consumers, no public subsidy
Pressure groups – e.g. Shelter, Campaign for Homeless and Roofless, Scottish Council for Single Homeless	Act as advocates of individual rights, and of needs of homeless	Housing association/ co-operative	Develops and leases houses to consumers, with capital and revenue subsidy

welfare policy have significant influence as the level of welfare benefits affects how much expenditure poorer households can afford and the implementation of Care in the Community policies determines the housing demands of vulnerable people such as the frail elderly and mentally infirm.

PLANNING AND HOUSING – A SHARED HISTORY

In the introductory section above, we saw that housing and planning policies share, in broad terms at least, a common set of objectives. The argument that we pursue in this section is that this fact has clear historical causes.

Table 3 Statutory agents and institutions in housing supply

Agent	Role
Local authority	Strategic housing and planning authorities, develop and manage rented housing with capital and revenue subsidy
H.M. Treasury, Northern Ireland Finance Department	Macroeconomic policy formulation, tax and subsidy determination
Department of Social Security	Determines housing and welfare benefit rates
Department of Environment, Transport and the Regions	In England, the central government department responsible for housing and planning policy formation and implementation
Housing Corporation	In England, a non-departmental public body which provides capital and revenue subsidy to housing associations, and monitors their financial and managerial performance.
Scottish Parliament	For Scotland, decentralised political structure with housing, planning and environmental powers.
Scottish Homes	Similar to England's Housing Corporation, together with stronger strategic powers and a residual landlord function.
Welsh Office	Decentralised central government administration for Wales, including housing, planning and environmental responsibilities.
Northern Ireland Office	Decentralised central government administration for Northern Ireland, including housing, planning and environmental responsibilities.
Northern Ireland Housing Executive	Non-departmental public body in Northern Ireland, with landlord and strategic policy responsibilities

In the first place, both planning and housing have their roots in nineteenth-century social reform. Both follow Chadwick's 1842 *Report on the Sanitary Condition of the Labouring Population*, and subsequent public health legislation in recognising that disease, poverty, bad housing and a poor environment are clearly linked. For many Victorians, the idea that government should intervene in order to improve living conditions was anathema, equally so whether that intervention was ostensibly aimed at land use or at house condition.

But planning and housing grew on a countervailing philosophy, one that encompassed philanthropy and a degree of paternalism. Robert Owen's New Lanark, Joseph Rowntree's model village at Port Sunlight, George Cadbury's Bournville and Titus Salt's Saltaire are amongst the most well-known examples of the products of nineteenth-century enlightened entrepreneurialism. The significance of these schemes is:

- that they established a principle of employers, or those with power, acting to improve the material and moral well-being of their work people; and
- that they involved not simply the development of housing alone, but the planning of whole communities (Burnett, 1986).

Paternalism, and a concern for the moral health of poor tenants, was implicit in the work of these schemes' contemporary, Octavia Hill. Whilst her initial job remit was over the physical improvement of houses, she put forward the view that that should be coupled with the moral improvement of the tenants of those houses. Hill's work gained widespread attention, and was a significant influence in the development of housing management as a profession (Franklin and Clapham, 1997). That relationship is still crucially important today, for it helps to explain the orientation of a significant amount of public housing practice towards social care.

Late nineteenth-century housing and planning legislation did, step-by-step, pragmatically extend the possibilities of local action, principally on the grounds of public health or 'nuisance'. Intervention was, however, purely discretionary, mandatory action having to wait until the end of the First World War, and Addison's Housing, Town Planning etc. Act of 1919. There remains dispute as to whether the provisions of the Act symbolise a 'bulwark against Bolshevism' or 'homes fit for heroes'. In establishing a duty of local authorities to use state (i.e. taxpayers') money to build low-cost rented housing, however, the Act was to be of profound importance for the rest of the century. With the principle of mandatory state action established, and with the early results being positively viewed, the foundations were laid for the scope of action to be extended.

This happened in dramatic fashion after the Second World War. The expansion of public education, the creation of the National Health Service, the expansion of the scope and depth of welfare benefits were all symptomatic of a major shift in politics, favouring direct State provision. Again, reformers were influential too, notably Ebenezer Howard, who, in *Garden Cities of Tomorrow*, had advocated that housing should be planned as part of a general system of planning land use and protecting the countryside. The prevailing post-war philosophy engendered modern town planning and shaped change in Britain's housing system irreversibly (or so it appeared for the next 30 years). For town planning, the creation of the development plan system, on the back of the Barlow, Scott and Uthwatt reports, marked government signalling its responsibility for Britain's use of her land. The implementation of the system required the expanded development of town planning as a profession, adding to the expertise of surveyors and architects. Howard's ideas found their expression in the New Towns, where government took responsibility for trying to create socially balanced communities, planning for housing, social facilities and jobs.

For housing, the impetus for change came with the realisation that the extent of war damage was but one cause of a major mismatch between the number of households around and the number of homes available. Throughout the 1950s and 1960s, housing policy was aimed at correcting the homes deficit, with political parties making electioneering capital out of promises to build more houses than their rivals (Bramley, 1997). The physical consequence of this was the creation of large council housing estates, inner-city in many of England's cities, on the periphery of Scotland's cities. Public provision was made for 'general needs', rather than targeting those facing the worst housing conditions, which helps explain why in 1965 the newly formed Institute of Housing eschewed a welfare orientation for housing management (Franklin and Clapham, 1997). All the evidence points to the residents of the new estates welcoming their being allocated new housing, with modern fittings and in a fresh green environment, having escaped from dense, crowded, inner-city flats. Only two decades or so later, those same state-planned homes and estates had become the locus of many of Britain's worst social problems of unemployment, crime, poor health and poor educational attainment. And it is clear that the focus on demolishing (or comprehensively redeveloping) the slums, quickly providing new houses, had allowed homes to be created in areas with minimal social facilities, and limited provision of shops. For many people, though it was paved with good intentions, the road has led to hell.

From the mid-1970s, both housing policy and land-use planning have been subject to retrenchment and redirection. The causes of this are fairly clear-cut. On the expenditure side, Britain's Conservative governments of the 1980s followed Labour's start of reducing housing capital expenditure significantly as part of a drive to attempt to reduce general public spending. And the need to build substantial numbers of low-cost homes, if it had not disappeared, was clearly far less pressing than it had been (Whitehead, 1997, notes that the 1971 Census pointed to a surplus of 700 000 dwellings over households across Britain). The evidence generally suggested that a focus on the quantity of houses needed was rather less appropriate than a focus on the quality of homes. It could also be used to justify a focus on the way in which housing was consumed, as greater proportions of households in Britain were able and willing to buy their own homes rather than rent from a council or other landlord.

Governments of the 1980s also had a philosophy that promoted private enterprise and was suspicious of major State intervention, no matter how benevolently intended. For town planning, 'rolling back the State' involved the abandonment of the local authority as the lead figure in the organisation of land use and its reconfiguration as a partner to private capital. The clearest housing sector consequence of the philosophy was the encouragement to council tenants to take up the Right to Buy, and a series of mechanisms – principally around the theme of urban regeneration – to bring private funding into state housing.

Now, and looking to the future, the agenda that faces both planning and housing is a similar one, of dealing with division, social exclusion and sustainability. We return to this theme after looking at some of the inter-dependence between current housing and planning practice.

Current Housing and Planning Practice – Common Themes, Shared Expertise?

In the previous section, we saw that planning and housing policies owe their broad shape to a common set of philosophies, albeit that the two professions have developed distinct identities. An unfortunate implication of this is that housing and planning education and training are far more often separate than shared. Although the context which informs their development – of social, economic and political change – is obviously the same. In this section, we look at some examples of where housing and planning most closely interact.

Planning for New Housing Development

The land-use planning system and the housing planning system both have concerns with future as well as current needs. They are both concerned with how the housing market works, and the results of its operation, but from two slightly different perspectives. The main focus of action for the land-use planning system is how the housing market interacts with the land market. Structure plans thus have a concern with meeting the housing needs of the whole community, principally by ensuring that sufficient land is put aside to develop new houses, private or public, for any anticipated increase in household numbers over the 10-year planning horizon. The housing planning system is concerned with how the housing market generates needs that are unlikely to be met solely through private actions. Thus, the Housing Investment Programme (HIP) (in England, in Scotland, its equivalent is the Housing Plan, and in Wales the Housing Strategy and Operational Programme (HSOP)) provides a local authority's estimates of anticipated social housing requirements over a three-year planning horizon. The plan's purpose is to support bids for capital allocations to provide new housing or improve older stock.

Whilst the time horizons of the plans differ, as to a certain extent do the practical objectives, there should clearly be a close relationship between the frameworks of assessment, and so a reasonably straightforward way in which structure plan estimates should be reconcilable with HIP/Housing Plan/HSOP estimates. Structure plan estimates are carried out for larger areas than the district council base of HIPs/Housing Plans/HSOPs, but they are in most cases amalgamations of the districts. (In England, metropolitan authorities prepare Unitary Development Plans and HIPs for the same geographic areas.) And the proportion of the population in need of social housing should be derivable in some way from expected population changes at the district level given reasonable predictions on likely changes in income distributions, house prices and private sector rents.

At present, however, the methods that are used to derive the estimates do not generally permit ready reconciliation. Structure plan forecasts of housing land requirements are generally demographically driven – that is, a projection of past trends in household formation rates is used to determine the excess of 'demand' over 'supply' (in reality the sum of existing and projected new households minus the current housing stock). This is then multiplied by housing density to yield a broad land allocation target. Structure planning authorities should also engage with housebuilders over the estimates of land required and over local land avail- ability. The Scottish guidance on the provision of land suggests that provision be made whenever it is practicable and reasonable (Hague, 1997).

Housing plan forecasting, and specifically social housing needs estimation, also rely upon an extrapolation of past trends. In England and Wales, housing needs surveys have been used by many authorities to determine future requirements. Their aim is to estimate need arising from newly forming households, need arising from existing households likely to want to move house and unable to avoid private sector housing, and the needs of homeless households. Implicitly, the principle of the analysis is two-fold: that past behaviour yields a reasonable basis for looking at future change, and that it is possible to make a reasonable degree of judgement on future needs by reconciling people's housing aspirations with their likely resource constraints. (A fuller discussion of the approach of English authorities is given by Bramley *et al.*, 1999.) In Scotland, a common methodology has been to look at the waiting list for council housing, assess flows onto and off it, and then estimate the size of the future population in need of social housing, using the Registrar General's estimates of change in household numbers at the district level. Again, the principle is that current outcomes, which are clearly the result of behaviour in the past, can be used as a reliable source of predicting future patterns.

There has been some criticism of both of these approaches, bearing in mind that prediction can only ever be broad judgement rather than exact science. At a practical level, a common view expressed by housebuilders is that structure plan estimates can significantly understate the need for land allocation, and that land allocations bear little relationship to the places that people actually want to live. Maclennan (1986) has extended this point into an argument that structure plan forecasting methods are not sufficiently sensitive to the realities of how local housing markets work, bearing in mind that the forecasts take no account of price, choice, or the ability of people to pay. This is clearly a significant shortcoming in a context in which most people choose what housing to buy where on the basis of their purchasing power. And housing plan forecasts might similarly be seen to be over-reliant on extrapolation of past trends (Bramley and Watkins, 1995).

The argument over where land is allocated is one that is central to the rationale of the planning system – balancing land-use demands with environmental protec- tion. It often turns on the relative merits of using greenfield and brownfield sites. That debate has been heightened by evidence that Britain is likely to have many more households even though the overall population size is fairly stable. The predictions suggest that around another 4.5 million homes will be needed by 2016 (with the majority in England (House of Commons Environment Committee, 1996)). The claim of many housebuilders, often supported by survey evidence, is that, given a choice, housebuyers, or potential buyers prefer to live in unspoilt environments, with as much green space/gardens as they can afford. Catering to this demand would imply bringing greater amounts of agricultural/park land into urban use. The powerful counter-argument is that there are many sites of suitable land available in towns and cities, sites which have been cleared of their previous industrial/commercial use and which have retained their infrastructure provision. Given sufficient thought into the design of new housing on them, would it not be more economically efficient, and environmentally sustainable to re-use these brown sites? Developers argue, and there is evidence in their support, that the re-use of former industrial sites is expensive, as it involves getting rid of contamination. They tend not to build housing for sale on previously contaminated land, as the stigma attached makes it difficult to sell the houses. If housing is developed, it is likely to be socially rented housing, with the consequent outcome of environmentally sensitive planning clearly being iniquitous (see Syms, 1997). Finally, a frequent claim is that often sensitive design is sacrificed in the search for greater economy, so that what appears as effective town planning is effectively no more than town cramming.

Whilst the methodologies might appear to generate irreconcilable estimates, there is some chance that future practices may be more closely related. There are two grounds for saying this. In England, housing and planning departments and sections have been encouraged to share approaches to, and working upon, housing needs assessments. In Scotland, the Secretary of State is encouraging planning authorities' assessments of housing land requirements to be tailored to the 'particular circumstances of their area' (cited in Hague, 1997). And local authorities' assessments of housing need could be related to estimating future household numbers, and their likely flows into different tenures based upon some local economic forecasting and taking into account Care in the Community plan forecasts of their clients' housing demands. The methodology for this (PIEDA, 1997; Scottish Homes, 1998a) is one that would offer scope for using the combined expertise of strategic planners in both housing and planning authorities.

In England and Wales, and to a lesser extent in Scotland, the provision of affordable housing has been secured from land allocations for private housebuilding through the use of planning agreements (Barlow *et al.*, 1994; Gallent, 1997; Joseph Rowntree Foundation, 1994). By this means, local authorities have negotiated new social housing provision from private developers rather than built it directly themselves. Commentators have pointed out that the potential for using planning powers to meet housing need is, however, quite limited. Fundamentally, it is viable only when the development value of the land (known as the residual land value) is positive, and the planning authority therefore has some bargaining power (Bramley *et al.*, 1995). It would fail to clear this hurdle in many local housing markets, fragile and otherwise, during periods of modest growth, let alone during slump. But it has significance in a less-directly practical way. Recognition that using the land-planning system to secure social housing provision is legitimate marks an advance on a position that sees meeting aggregate housing numbers targets as the overriding concern. (And it therefore marks a way in which the statutory land-planning framework is becoming more closely related to the HIP/Housing Plan system.) More importantly, it marks a significant advance from an interpretation of town planning having legitimacy in respect solely of physical land use, to one dealing with the arguably more widely relevant issues of the social characteristics of that land use.

URBAN REGENERATION

One of the clearest ways in which planners and housing practitioners have come together is in urban regeneration (see Chapter 7). First applied to older private housing neighbourhoods, then to post-war council housing areas, the physical improvement of houses and their landscapes has provided a major focus of activity of government policy and spending, levering in private investment alongside. There have been parallel moves to attempt to revitalise town and city centres for commercial, retail and civic land uses. The two professions have also worked together to cope with the legacy of industrial change, reclaiming abandoned factory and warehouse sites for new residential and commercial use.

Physical improvement is clearly only a component of tackling what in the 1960s was called poverty, in the 1970s and 1980s multiple deprivation, and now 'social exclusion'. And what is seen as the legitimate focus of housing and planning practice has moved alongside policy change. A narrow policy focus on physical condition is commensurate with a narrow professional focus on building condition and its improvement. But, to tackle above-average crime rates, poor self-esteem, relatively low health status, relatively poor educational attainment and, crucially, relatively poor employment positions and prospects – all symptoms of urban decay – evidently requires the co-ordinated actions of a series of actors and their programmes. The ways in which urban policy funds are now directed – notably via the New Deal for Communities and Scotland's Social Inclusion Partnerships – clearly recognises this, and emphasises partnership between different practitioners. In these arenas, housing and planning policies and professional practices have vital roles to play. The two case studies presented in Boxes 1 and 2 help to demonstrate these points.

CONCLUSIONS – POLICY CHALLENGES IN THE NEW MILLENIUM

This chapter has reviewed why housing and planning policy and practice have grown closely together, through a shared social history. The argument that we have presented is that, fundamentally, land-use planning and housing policies share common objectives of improving citizens' quality of life. They derive their

Box 1 *Scottish Homes' Regional Plan for Glasgow and North Clyde*

Background: Scottish Homes is the government's national housing agency. A non-departmental public body, it funds and regulates Scotland's voluntary housing sector, and, according to an investment framework agreed with central government, targets investment, enabling and policy activities. Alongside national headquarters, Scottish Homes has five regional directorates, each of which works alongside councils, housing associations and co-operatives, local enterprise agencies, health boards and local communities. One set of officers, based in Glasgow, is active over an area including Glasgow and rural Argyll. They work to a framework of action set by the Regional Plan, the current one running from 1998 to 2001.

Objectives: The plan has four broad objectives:

- urban regeneration – to create successful housing neighbourhoods
- rural development – to support the development of rural communities
- particular housing needs – to enable people to live in the community as independently as possible
- contributing to the reduction of homelessness

Implementation: Dovetailing with Scottish Homes' National Strategy (Scottish Homes, 1997b), the plan recognises that strategic partnerships are fundamental to the achievement of the agency's objectives. Examples of partnership cited are the Glasgow Alliance, the Bute Partnership and Dunbartonshire 2000. Consider one example: the Glasgow Alliance. Relaunched in 1998, following a change in political administration in May, 1997, the Alliance brings together Glasgow City Council, Greater Glasgow Health Board, Glasgow Development Agency (the Local Enterprise Company) and Scottish Homes to co-ordinate policies and funding priorities. It also has significant support from central government to develop a '. . . comprehensive, city-wide strategy for Glasgow . . . setting a context for the regeneration of particular areas by developing a vision for the future role of the city as a whole' (Dewar, 1998).

Source: Scottish Homes (1998b).

legitimacies in the same way as any other social policies. We have also seen that the two professions do draw on distinct fields of expertise in order to achieve their goals. But what of the future? What are the challenges that face the policy fields?

The central point is that policy on both land-use planning and intervention in the housing market will need to be responsive to Britain's changing place in the European and world economy, that planning for housing provision will need to

---

Box 2 *Mixed use regeneration*

Background: The Urban Villages Forum was established in 1992, bringing public and private organisations together to facilitate integration of land uses in urban regeneration. It promotes the idea that people's model communities generally involve services and amenities being provided close to homes, a contrast to the tendency of many developments of the recent past

Objectives: To identify small scale urban developments where a mix of uses can be created, or taken further.

Implementation: The government initiative 'Making Mixed Use Happen' (1997) set aside a fund of £50m over four years to a link between the Forum and English Partnerships (a development agency). Funds are to be used to pump-prime development, by covering the costs of land reclamation, or putting in key infrastructure, and meeting a gap between development market value and cost. To date, three types of scheme have been identified, with work being directed at creating a planning and development framework and an investment framework:

- large brownfield development sites, such as the former Royal Ordnance site in Chorley, Lancashire;
- the redevelopment of decaying parts of city centres, such as Birmingham's Jewellery Centre;
- large council housing estates, such as Sheffield's Manor Estate

Source: Dugdill (1998).

---

better reflect changing employment demands, and individuals' demands for improved leisure, amenities and access to the countryside. This is not to say that these are new issues, but that we need to continue to bear them in mind in thinking about the purpose of the policy processes that we have, and that we review and update.

Beyond this are two further vital agendas. The first recalls Hutton's 'thirty–thirty–forty' society and calls on us to recognise that for 40% of Britain's citizens, a generally advancing society and economy have not yielded relief from poor housing, from fear of crime, from unemployment or insecure employment, nor brought access to the good and continually better material possessions that the rest of us enjoy. The evidence available is that cumulative disadvantage, both urban and rural, persists, despite rafts of social, economic and physical improvement policies. The cost of disadvantage – in division, exclusion and resentment – is one that should force us to think of the distributive consequences of our policies and practice. The calls for redistributive action are not always heard and heeded to the same degree as the undoubted need for government to ensure improved material well-being for the majority.

The second agenda is that development and redevelopment activities, planning and housing policies and practice demand resources from the natural environment and demand that the land, atmosphere and water absorb and render safe the unwanted by-products of our actions. We are aware of the adverse environmental consequences of our industries, and, partly through Agenda 21, are taking some redressive measures. But the environmental consequences of land use – implying, for example, more car use or housing design decisions; not using, for example, thermally-efficient materials or heating and lighting systems – are not always sufficiently high in the hierarchy of criteria used in decision-making. It is incumbent upon housing and planning professionals to make sure that these consequences are recognised and reflected in the way that we choose to adapt to social and economic change (see Chapters 2 and 16).

ACKNOWLEDGEMENTS

I am grateful to the editors and to Glen Bramley and David Donnison for their helpful comments.

REFERENCES

Barlow, J., Cocks, R. and Parker, M. (1994) *Planning for Affordable Housing*, Department of the Environment, London.

Bramley, G. (1997) Housing policy: a case of terminal decline?, *Policy and Politics*, **25**(4), 381–402.

Bramley, G., Bartlett, W. and Lambert, C. (1995) *Planning, the Market and Private Housebuilding*, UCL Press, London.

Bramley, G., Pawson, H., Satsangi, M. and Third, H. (1999) *Local Housing Assessment: A Review of Current Practice and the Need for Guidance*, Working Paper No. 73, School of Planning and Housing, Edinburgh College of Art/Heriot-Watt University.

Bramley, G. and Watkins, C. (1995) *Circular Projections: Household Growth, Housing Development and the Household Projections*, Council for the Protection of Rural England, London.

Burnett, J. (1986) *A Social History of Housing*, University Press, London.

Crook, A.D.H. and Kemp, P. (1996) The revival of private rented housing in Britain, *Housing Studies*, **11**(1), 51–68.

Department of the Environment, Transport and the Regions (1998) *English House Condition Survey, 1996*, HMSO, London.

Dewar, Rt. Hon. D., speech to Urban World Conference, Glasgow, May 1998, Scottish Office Press Release No. 1030/98.

Donnison, D. and Ungerson, C. (1982) *Housing Policy*, Penguin, Harmondsworth.

Dugdill, G. (1998) Foundations laid for more mixed use, *Urban Environment Today*, Issue 38, 10–11.

Forrest, R. and Williams, P. (1997) Future directions?, chapter 12 in Williams, P. (ed.), *Directions in Housing Policy: Towards Sustainable Housing Policies for the UK*, Paul Chapman, London.

Franklin, B. and Clapham, D. (1997) The social construction of housing management, *Housing Studies*, **12**(1), 7–26.

Gallent, N. (1997) Planning for affordable rural housing in England and Wales, *Housing Studies*, **12**(1), 127–137.

Gibb, K., Munro, M. and Satsangi, M. (1999) *Housing Finance in the UK*, 2nd edn, Macmillan, Basingstoke.

Hague, C. (1997) Planning for Scotland's new households, *Town and Country Planning*, March, 83.

House of Commons Environment Committee (1996) *Housing Need, 2nd Report, Session 1995–96*, volumes 1 and 2, HMSO, London.

Hutton, W. (1996) *The State We're In*, Vintage, London.

Joseph Rowntree Foundation (1994) *Inquiry into Planning for Housing*, Joseph Rowntree Foundation, York.

Maclennan, D. (1986) *The Demand for Housing: Economic Perspectives and Planning Practice*, Scottish Office, Edinburgh.

PIEDA (1997) *Assessing Housing Need*, mimeo.

Scottish Homes (1997a) *Scottish House Condition Survey, 1996*, Scottish Homes, Edinburgh.

Scottish Homes (1997b) *Scotland's Housing Into the 21st Century: Strategy, 1997–2000*, Scottish Homes, Edinburgh.

Scottish Homes (1998a) *Best Practice Guide to Local Housing Systems Analysis*, Scottish Homes, Edinburgh.

Scottish Homes (1998b) *Glasgow and North Clyde Regional Plan, 1998–2001*, Scottish Homes, Glasgow.

Syms, P. (1997) *The Redevelopment of Contaminated Land for Housing Use*, Joseph Rowntree Foundation, York.

Treasury, H.M. (1998) *Comprehensive Spending Review: Aims and Objectives*, HM Treasury, London.

Whitehead, C.M.E. (1997) Changing needs, changing incentives: trends in the UK housing system, chapter 2 in Williams, P. (ed.), *Directions in Housing Policy: Towards Sustainable Housing Policies for the UK*, Paul Chapman, London.

Wilcox, S. (1999) *Housing Finance Review, 1999–2000*, Joseph Rowntree Foundation/Chartered Institute of Housing/Council of Mortgage Lenders, York.

Chapter 8

Retail Development

Gary Mappin and Philip Allmendinger

Introduction

Planning for new and changing forms of retail facility is one of the most contentious issues in UK town planning practice. This situation culminated in the mid-1990s with a highly publicised struggle between town centres and out-of-town retail development. The debate on this issue presented town centres as victims of rapacious out-of-town developments that were draining the life out of them. But out-of-town developments were only meeting a consumer demand for easily accessible one-stop shopping. Is the current policy, which seeks to prohibit such development, actually limiting consumer choice? Or are out-of-town developments providing a form of retailing that discriminates against those without access to a car?

While attention has focused on this 'in-town and out-of-town' debate other issues in retail planning have been eclipsed. Town centre management (covered in Chapter 10), living over the shop initiatives, the growth of financial services and their threat to retail units, hot food take-aways, factory shopping, retail warehouse parks and, more recently, the growth of leisure developments such as cinemas, all impinge on the retail debate. Again, like the in-town/out-of-town debate there are a complex mixture of factors that both lead to such developments occurring and being supported by the public and why we should be wary of the market being allowed to dictate the pattern of retail provision. Those working in planning practice today are faced with a number of key questions that require continuing consideration, even if there are no simple solutions. These include the following:

- What will be the future demand for new retail development in terms of size, format and location?
- Where should the balance lie between out-of-town development and protecting town centres?
- Does the development control planner possess the necessary skills and knowledge to process planning applications in the wider public interest?
- How should local planning authorities go about determining proposals for new out-of-centre retail developments?
- How can town centres be revitalised?

Because of its high profile nature and the lack of space to fully explore other aspects of retail planning, this chapter will mainly focus on out-of-town retail development. This is not as narrow a perspective as it first appears since it touches upon many of the trends that have affected other aspects of retailing in a period of massive change. The increased access to private cars and the more relaxed approach to development taken from the late 1970s through to the early 1990s has seen an unprecedented change in UK retailing. In addition to significant structural economic developments, the pattern of retail provision has changed from a focus on traditional high streets and town centres, to a network of different retail formats which now include high street retailing, free-standing food superstores, retail parks and district and regional shopping centres.

This period of immense upheaval has led to both an increase in choice and competition, which in theory has benefited the consumer. However, there is also a concern that there has been a detrimental affect on the health and continuing viability of our traditional town and city centres. Furthermore, the strong emphasis on access to new forms of retailing by the private car has raised concerns in relation to both equity and, more critically, environmental sustainability.

Through a review of key background information, this chapter looks in particular at the significant changes in UK retailing experienced over the past 20 years, and reviews the way in which a statutory planning system has both reacted to and planned for the continuing development of the retail sector.

HISTORICAL REVIEW

A recent Department of Trade and Industry (DTI) study on retailing summarised its key features:

- The retail sector is one of the UK's top service sector industries with a £157 billion turnover and employing about 2.2 million people.
- It has gone through major structural changes over the last 15 years. The total number of retail businesses declined by 50 000 between 1984 and 1994 and now stands at around 290 000 units.
- Competition between retailers is strong in the UK, but some UK firms have been slow to look at opportunities for expansion overseas. There are no UK retailers in the top 15 retailing groups in the world.
- The sector is a major innovator and a driver of innovation in much of UK industry. New technology could have a major impact and offers enormous opportunities. The recent introduction of electronic data exchange, laser scanning and loyalty cards have all required new and expensive investment and provide new opportunities for greater competitiveness (DTI, 1998, p. 48).

These key features are comparatively new phenomena since up until the 1970s retailing in the UK was very much based on a traditional picture of both habits and facilities. The focus was still very much on the traditional marketplace, i.e. the high street, which was the location for food, non-food and related retailing activity. There was some evidence of retailing taking place from out-of-centre units, e.g. DIY stores on industrial estates, but this was limited overall.

The food retailers were in the vanguard of the move to larger units, which were seen as having significant benefits in terms of economies of scale. The inclusion of a wide range of food retail products, in particular under one roof, encouraged a single destination for food shopping. This made obvious commercial sense, and was the beginning of the onslaught on the traditional high street bakers, butchers, greengrocers, etc. Against a lack of central or local policy concerning such shifts the major retailers found it straightforward to relocate. Over time, the large food retailers built up a network of large stores, which were more frequently being located in out-of-centre suburban locations.

At the same time, there was development in the non-food sector, with the first wave of retail warehouse developments. The DIY operators were the pioneers in this sector, but furniture and carpet retailers were not slow to pick up on the obvious advantages of cheap large premises, not subject to the same property costs as the traditional high street, and affording an opportunity to display large amounts of stock in a showroom format.

Over time, the food superstore and retail warehouse sectors have expanded at a phenomenal rate. Retail parks are now a common feature of any local retail hierarchy, ostensibly selling a range of bulky goods, requiring large showroom areas. A network of district, sub-regional and regional centres has also sprung up, mainly in response to the burgeoning levels of increased consumer expenditure on non-food goods prevalent in the late 1980s. The planning system was significantly more disposed towards this type of development, and the proposals were advanced on the basis that existing high streets could not accommodate the significant amounts of new floorspace justified by the increases in retail expenditure.

During this time the fundamental changes in the requirements of retailers inspired property development interests to challenge the planning system with a constant stream of new out-of-centre proposals. This led to the creation of a particular sector of the planning system which included four key players, e.g. the retail industry/property development sector, central government, the local authorities and third parties. Through a normally high profile, high value process of planning via public inquiry, the new developments have slowly become an intrinsic part of UK shopping life.

Until the mid-1980s these shifts were largely retailer-led. However, growing concern with the impact on town centre retailers led to a number of changes, including a more cautionary approach. The real impetus for a less retailer-led approach came in 1990 with the publication of the Environment White Paper *This Common Inheritance* (UK Government, 1990) which committed the Government to review all planning policy guidance to meet the commitments made at the Rio Earth Summit. Of critical importance as far as retail planning was concerned was the Government's commitment to reduce the need to travel and this in turn was influential upon the deliberations of the House of Commons Environment Committee and its report entitled *Shopping Centres and their Futures* (House of Commons Environment Committee, 1994). Both the redrafting of PPG6 *Town Centres and Retail Development* (Department of the Environment, 1993) and PPG13 *Transport* (Department of Transport, 1994) were heavily influenced by the sentiments of *This Common Inheritance, Shopping Centres and their Futures* and the growing appreciation of the need to restrain further out-of-town growth. One of the headline conclusions of the report was the severe criticism of the retailer-led approach throughout the 1980s, though the Committee did acknowledge changes had been made to reverse this in the 1990s. It also gave strong support to the newly introduced sequential test (see below) for new retail developments, to the promotion of existing town centres as well as restrictions on new development out of town, strong support for town centre management and improvement in public transport. Following the Committee's recommendations came the Department of the Environment report *Vital and Viable Town Centres: Meeting the Challenge* (Department of the Environment, 1994) which explored ways of measuring impact and assessing the vitality and viability of centres in the face of the threat from out-of-town. The report came down heavily in favour of town centre management and was largely responsible for the legitimisation of the concept. But the latter part of the report had a great deal of influence on the emerging methodology for assessing the health of any centre and the impact any new out-of-centre proposal might have upon it. This support for the town centre was inevitable given the growing public reaction demanding that 'something be done' about the decline of centres while the same public were willing to continue to fraternise the main cause of this decline. The upshot of this has been further revisions of central government on guidance. In England Planning Policy Guidance Note (PPG) 6 was revised in 1996 and in Scotland, National Planning Guidelines dated 1978 and 1986 have now been replaced by the 1998 National Planning Policy Guideline (NPPG) 8, Town Centres and Retailing. These later changes introduced a more stringent set of guidelines, with a clearer focus on a sequential approach to development, i.e. that there should be a preference in the first instance for town centres, followed only then by edge-of-centre sites and out-of-centre schemes where these are well served by public transport (see later in the chapter for a more detailed exploration of this). However, at the local level it is unclear what impact this national policy guidance has had (see Box 1).

Box 1 *The impact of PPG 6 on greenfield expansion plans*

The evidence on whether or not the new restrictions on out-of-centre retail developments are being inhibited by the change in government policy is unclear. Immediately after the revision of PPG 6 there was evidence to suggest that it had directly influenced the future decisions of major retailers and forced them to begin to look at redevelopments of existing stores and shift back in-town. A spokesperson for Tesco admitted in 1995 that 'We are responding to the current planning trends because if a potential site does not meet with current guidance it will not get permission', while nearly half of Sainsbury's stores in 1996 were on in-town locations. However, by 1998 a report by Hillier Parker suggested the opposite and that town centre development was very 'sluggish'. 'There is as yet little sign that the Government's clampdown on out-of-town shopping centres is stimulating growth in town centres', the report concludes. Planning permission for more than 2 million square metres of new town-centre retail development existed in 1998 and was waiting to be developed. Although the amount of out-of-town land for which permission exists is around one-sixth of its 1990 level, there is still 0.49 million square metres of extant permissions. Part of the problem in assessing the impact of the new controls on out-of-town retail development is because of issues such as the property recession and the state of the economy generally.

This gives a broad overview of the shift in government thinking throughout the 1980s and into the 1990s. What we shall address now is the implications of this advice for local planning authorities and others in determining applications for new retail development. However, before we do that it is necessary to spell out in more detail what the current policy position is.

THE CURRENT POLICY FRAMEWORK

Current national planning policy in retail matters is contained in PPG6 (Department of the Environment, 1996) and NPPG8 (Scottish Office, 1998). It is the Scottish guidance that is more up to date on this issue and though there are some small differences between the two sets of guidances, on the whole they take a very similar line. It is perhaps worth mentioning here some important distinctions between different kinds of non-town centre retail development and different locations since these issues have become increasingly important as government policy has got more sophisticated. Thomas (1997, p. 123) gives a summary:

> Superstores and hypermarkets normally sell food and are 2500m^2 and over in floor area; they are different from regional out-of-town shopping centres, which are over 50,000m^2 and from retail warehouses, which are normally over 1000m^2 in floor area and sell only bulky durable goods. Readers should also be aware of locational terms: town centre, off-centre (i.e. edge of the built up area) and out-of-town (i.e. in the countryside).

(See also the glossary of terms at the end of the chapter.)

The Government's overall approach is summarised in Box 2.

Box 2 *General principles guiding retail development: NPPG8*

The government is committed to protecting and enhancing the vitality and viability of town centres. They offer a range, quality and convenience of services and activities that are attractive not only to the local population and visitors but also to investors. Despite recent pressures, they retain many natural advantages for shopping, leisure and employment. Shops in particular make an important contribution to their character. Town centres have a key role in contributing to the quality of life in urban areas and provide an important focus in rural areas, allowing both urban and rural communities to benefit from competition between retailers and types of retailing. Sustaining their vitality and viability depends on continuing investment in new schemes and refurbishments and a positive and a proactive approach by planning authorities, in partnership with other public sector agencies and the private sector, in the identification and development of suitable sites. Furthermore, a range of uses other than shopping should be encouraged to locate within the town centre, including commercial leisure developments.

For major developments, and certainly before the introduction of the sequential approach (see below), the consideration of impact on traditional shopping centres has been the key consideration. This has normally required the production of what is known as a Retail Impact Assessment. This is a supporting analysis of the likely effects a new retail proposal will have on its identified catchment area. A number of key quantitative economic indicators are examined, with conclusions reached on the likely effects a new proposal will have on existing retail floorspace, normally in the form of assumed trade diversion levels.

Retail impact assessment is not a science. It is a technically based exercise, which inevitably involves making assumptions on the likely future effects of new development. Acknowledged sources, industry standards, and other accepted statistical methods help refine the process, but it is still seen by many as an unproven mechanism. This is not helped by a complete dearth of research into the past implementation effects of new development, which would be essential in order to test earlier assumptions.

Another characteristic of the development control process has been the adjudication by public inquiry, either by way of appeals following refusals, or where government has called in major planning applications. This has often resulted in very high profile public inquiries, reflecting the level of controversy surrounding, particularly, out-of-town retail development. Highly paid QCs and inquiry teams have led to long-running appeals, often running into months rather than weeks, and often involving significant third-party representation including members of the public. This approach had been a broadly successful route for the retail industry, but on the evidence of more recent appeal statistics, it suggests that this may becoming less so.

ASSESSING NEW OUT-OF-CENTRE DEVELOPMENTS

To avoid drawn out planning inquiries and to provide some consistency in approach the government have issued advice on how proposals for new out-of-centre retail developments should be assessed. Of prime importance in the plan-led system (see Chapters 4 and 5) is whether any new proposal is in accordance with the development plan. If the plan has allocated new land for retail development because of a particular local need, then it will be relatively straightforward to determine whether a proposal meets those requirements. However, where the plan does not identify any sites either because it is not considered necessary for an area or because the plan is out of date (e.g. has not been renewed or has been superceded by more recent advice or events) or when a developer simply puts in a proposal, then government advice is that any application should be judged against the criteria in Box 3.

Box 3 *Assessing new development – NPPG8*

Where a proposed development is not consistent with the development plan, it is for the developer to demonstrate why an exception to policy should be made. Such proposals should be rigorously assessed by the planning authority against the policies set out in this NPPG and should be refused if all the following considerations cannot be met. The proposed development should:

- satisfy the sequential approach;
- not affect adversely, either on its own or in association with other built or approved developments, the plan strategy in support of the town centre, taking account of progress being made on its implementation, including through public and private investment;
- be capable of co-existing with the town centre without individually or cumulatively undermining its vitality and viability, if necessary supported by planning conditions limiting, for example, floorspace or the range of goods sold or the level of car parking; and should not lead to changes to the quality, attractiveness and character of the town centre, affecting the range and types of shops and services that the town centre would be able to provide, or undermine leisure, entertainment and the evening economy;

- tackle deficiencies in qualitative or quantitative terms which cannot be met in or at the edge of the town centre;
- not run counter to the Government's integrated transport policy. Locations for major growth and travel generating uses, including retail and commercial leisure developments, should be easily and safely accessible by a choice of means of transport providing a network of walking, cycle and public transport routes, which link with the forecast catchment population, in addition to the car. Consideration should be given to whether the development would have an effect on travel patterns, car use and air pollution ;
- be, or able to be made, easily accessible by existing regular, frequent and convenient public transport services. Such services should be available from the time of opening of the development and, where possible, improved over its life. Planning agreements may be used to secure such accessibility in appropriate circumstances;
- address at the developer's expense the consequences to the trunk and local road networks of the generated and redistributed traffic resulting from the development proposal. In certain circumstances the impact may not be restricted to junctions and road lengths adjacent to the development;
- result in a high standard of design, ensuring the built form, scale, materials and colour contribute positively to the overall environmental quality and attractiveness of the urban area, and should not, for example, result in sporadic and isolated development, especially along major road corridors;
- not threaten or conflict with other important policy objectives, e.g. green belt, urban regeneration, the loss of good quality industrial or business sites; or where priority is being given to the reuse of vacant or derelict land, the development should, in all other respects, provide an appropriate location for the proposed development;
- not affect adversely local amenity; and:
- not lead to other significant environmental effects

These criteria are also applicable to expansions of existing retail centres which may have a similar impact to a completely new development.

We have mentioned the phrase 'sequential test' throughout this chapter and Box 3 places it at the top of its list of criteria in determining any retail proposal. The sequential test is now a cornerstone of retail policy. In essence, it creates a presumption in favour of any new retail development being located within a town centre, and only if a developer can demonstrate that such a centre is unsuitable through lack of space or access, for example, can alternative non-centre sites be considered. Box 4 sets out the interpretation of the sequential approach.

Box 4 *The sequential approach to retail assessment – NPPG8*

Planning authorities and developers should adopt a sequential approach to selecting sites for new retail, commercial leisure developments and other key town centre uses. First preference should be for town centre sites, where sites or buildings suitable for conversion are available, followed by edge-of-centre sites, and only then by out-of-centre sites in locations that are, or can be made, easily accessible by a choice of means of transport. The sequential approach should apply to all food and comparison shopping as well as other attractions and facilities usually found in town centres, unless guidance in this NPPG or the development plan provides for a particular exception.

In support of town centres as the first choice, the government recognises that the application of the sequential approach requires flexibility and realism from developers and retailers as well as planning authorities. In preparing their proposals developers and retailers should have regard to the format, design, scale of the development, and the amount of car parking in relation to the circumstances of the particular town centre. In addition they should also address the need to identify and assemble sites which can meet not only their requirements, but in a manner sympathetic to the town setting. As part of such an approach, they should consider the scope for accommodating the proposed development in a different built form, and where appropriate adjusting or sub-dividing large proposals, in order that their scale might offer a better fit with existing development in the town centre. The scope for converting existing vacant and under-used premises in the town centre should be addressed as part of this approach. Consideration should also be given to whether the range of goods to be sold, including, say, bulky, electrical and fashion goods, could be retailed from a town centre or edge-of-centre site, in some cases in a different manner.

Planning authorities should also be responsive to the needs of retailers and other town centre businesses. In consultation with the private sector, they should assist in identifying sites in the town centre which could be suitable and viable, for example in terms of size and siting for the proposed use, and are likely to become available in a reasonable time, for example within the plan period or 5 years, where the plan period is short or silent on the matter. There may also be sites in town centres which are currently subject to constraint. The planning authority should indicate whether, how and when the constraints could be resolved, for example by assisting in land assembly.

The sequential approach, like the plan-led approach generally (see Chapter 4), places utmost emphasis on the development plan and requires others to provide evidence to overrule it. Even where a developer can justify an out-of-town proposal the sequential test still requires other criteria to be met including that any site be

Table 1 *Planning gain related to superstore development in Plymouth*

Developer	Planning gain
Sainsbury	• Provision of alternative employment land • Park and ride schemes • Crèche facilities • 'Per cent for art' contribution • Tourist information centre • Highway works associated with the development itself
Tesco	• Crèche facilities • Facilities for the disabled • Nature conservation areas • 'Per cent for art' contribution • Highway works
Plymouth and South Devon Cooperative Society	• Provision of three areas of public space • Community buildings

Source: *Planning*, 19th February 1993.

easily accessible by a means of transport other than the car. This includes walking, cycling and public transport, with the latter effectively ruling out certain less accessible by-pass sites. To help developers and local authorities the guidance also introduces the need for flexibility, which is a deliberately loose term that seeks to encourage a more pro-development interpretation of government advice and local policy. For example, if a local authority has a set standard on parking require-ments or design requirements for a part of the town, then these should be sub-ordinated to the need to encourage the development to take place.

Another key characteristic of many major retail applications is the provision of significant levels of planning gain. Box 3 mentions that the developer should be expected to pay for any road improvements necessary and any requirements to make the development more accessible by public transport. This usually means the retailer providing a free or subsidised bus service to the shop. These require-ments are commonly referred to as planning gain (see Chapter 5). Planning gain is not uncontroversial and while the two examples above are generally accepted to be part and parcel of any new out-of-town proposal there are plenty of grey areas.

Since it is up to developers to demonstrate the benefits of their proposal this has led to some abuse of planning gain when the benefits offered have been beyond what would be regarded as necessary. Table 1 sets out the gains offered by three developers for a site in Plymouth that clearly go beyond the examples given in Box 3. There has been recent up-to-date guidance from both the Department of the Environment, Transport and the Regions (DETR) and the Scottish Office in this regard, which states that planning gain should be solely related to the development in question, although it is ultimately for the Courts to set parameters on how this is to be interpreted.

Other criteria in Box 3 are that of vitality and viability which, along with the sequential test, is another cornerstone of retail policy.

THE IMPORTANCE OF VITALITY AND VIABILITY

Central to assessments of any new out-of-town proposal, the preparation of retail policies for a development plan and the maintenance and enhancement of town centres are the concepts of vitality and viability. Roughly, vitality refers to how lively a town is and viability to the extent to which it can maintain current levels of investment and attract new development. Assessment of vitality and viability is essential if the strengths and weaknesses of a town are to be analysed systematically and compared over time and with other centres. The government's commitment to the vitality and viability of town centres has featured in past versions of both PPG6 and NPPG8 though the actual methods of assessing whether a proposal affects the vitality and viability of an existing centre are not clear cut. There are a variety of different approaches that local authorities, developers and consultants employ and PPG 6 sets out of number of indicators of vitality and viability.

INVESTMENT YIELDS

Yield is a measure of investment return on property that relates rental return to capital purchase. The greater the rental growth forecast the lower the yield the investor will accept as the investment is more secure. Less secure investments in, for example, less profitable locations will typically have a higher yield to make up for the greater risk the investor is making. At a crude level, low yields indicate good economic performance and prospects and high yields indicate the opposite. Information on yields is generally kept by large surveying firms such as Donaldsons and Hillier Parker as well as the Valuation Office of the Inland Revenue, though there is little agreement between the different sources. This is not the only problematic issue to do with the use of yields as an indicator of vitality and viability. Generally, there is a difference in yields between larger and smaller towns thereby making it difficult to compare towns of different sizes and they also tend to reflect developers' rather than retailers' interest in an area.

PEDESTRIAN FLOWS

Moving on from financial indicators of vitality and viability is a more physical determinant that seeks to measure the number of people in an area or pass a point in a number of different locations within a town. This can then be compared with another town or over time to get an idea of the relative vitality of a centre and its change over time. It is not difficult to envisage why such an indicator needs to be used with caution because factors such as weather conditions, seasonal variations and even one-off events can distort figures.

Shop Vacancy Rates

Obviously, if a centre has many shop vacancies then it is not going to be considered to have a healthy vitality or viability. The degree of vacancy tends to vary between primary and secondary retail areas (i.e. the main shopping area and a less used area behind the high street, for example) and can lead to pressure for changes of use from retail to non-retail uses including hot food take-aways. Many local authorities seek to resist such changes through the use of restrictive policies in primary areas that set a proportion of retail to non-retail uses. One result of this is the growth of charity shops in prime retail areas as owners rent out their units for some return rather let their units remain empty. While the number of empty shop units on a primary shopping frontage can be a good indicator of vitality and viability the question of what is a primary shopping frontage is a more problematic issue. There is no agreed method of defining primary shopping frontage though commercial rental values are sometimes used. However, this simply shifts the issue to determining what rental level is primary. The final decision is usually a subjective judgement rather than one based on objective criteria.

The Diversity of Uses in a Centre

The Department of the Environment Research Report *Vital and Viable Town Centres: Meeting the Challenge* (Department of the Environment, 1994) considers that a vital and viable town centre will include a variety of uses including retail, services, culture, entertainment, business and residential. The idea behind this assertion is to create a critical mass of uses that perpetuates the use of the centre outside of normal working hours as well as having spin-off benefits such as natural surveillance through increased number of people being present at different hours. How this mixture of uses is changing over time is also an important factor to consider in assessing vitality and viability. However, the reasons for any change may be complex and potentially unrelated to vitality and viability. A further issue arises when one attempts to measure the *amount* of space dedicated to particular uses, which requires accurate and up-to-date information.

Retailer Representation and Profile

As a general rule certain retail outlets will only be present in an area if they can meet turnovers that local or one off shops would be less likely to meet. Marks &

Spencer, for example, is usually a good indicator of a centre that has a high turnover and would therefore be healthy. However, this is not a perfect measure as some towns, including many tourist-based centres such as Bath, have a much higher order of services than towns of equivalent size, thus making comparison difficult.

Retailer Demand and Rental Value

This gives an indication of the relative position of locations or streets within a centre and the desire of retailers to move to an area. This measure can be assessed over time through the use of data that chart the changing mixture of retailer representation in a centre. However, a more easily accessible source is a quali-tative survey of existing traders within a town and of other stores that may wish to move to a centre. This needs to be handled with care for two reasons. First, existing retailers are usually wary of providing sensitive commercial information on trading conditions. Second, those retailers wishing to move to an area are likely to be looking at a variety of sites rather than simply one, thereby increasing the climate of interest generally.

Physical Structure Including Accessibility

The physical attractiveness of a centre does not only relate to whether it has attractive buildings in which to shop (though this is an aspect of it) but also to other factors such as the range of facilities it has (a good mixture of shops and facilities such as cafes, clothes, food as well as financial services) and accessibility either by public transport or car. Car parking charges are an important issue as well as numbers of car parking spaces since two adjacent towns can have radically different charging regimes. Measuring issues such as accessibility is, understand-ably, difficult and ultimately as much a matter of public perception as physical accessibility.

It should be clear from the above that the measurement of vitality and viability is both a central aspect of government policy and fraught with difficulties. However, there have been alternatives that have sought to measure vitality and viability that build upon some of the problems with the existing approach.

Proposals to Overcome Some Problems with Vitality and Viability

As we mentioned earlier in the chapter, it is widely accepted that proposals for new retail centres take into account the impact upon existing centres. It is equally accepted that any attempt to measure vitality and viability is difficult and highly dependent upon the assumptions that underpin it. We briefly highlighted some of the problems with the indicators that the government recommends, but it is worth developing this further and examining a possible alternative measure of vitality and viability.

Although PPG6 and NPPG8 mention a number of factors in measuring vitality and viability, they place particular emphasis on commercial yield and pedestrian flow. Yield is basically about risk. An investor will judge the risk involved in investing in a particular area and whether the return on the investment is worth that risk. The assumption behind using yield as an indicator of vitality and viability is that it demonstrates confidence in the long-term profitability of a town. Consequently, if there is an average low yield on a centre then the conclusion the government draws is that the centre has the confidence of the market and must be healthy. However, this assumption ignores some other important aspects of an investor's decision-making. The yield may also be a reflection of the availability of current alternative sites as well as other factors such as interest rates. All of these factors are variable and as it is currently measured, yield cannot account for the reasons *why* an investor would want to invest in an area. This also assumes that the actual information on yield is easily accessible. In areas where there have been very few transactions for a number of years information is likely to be scarce. Even where transactions have recently taken place there are a number of other factors that could influence the decision to invest, including increasing a presence in an area, the need to spend funds before the end of the financial year or the low profitability of other investment options. Thus yields need to be treated with care in the assessment of vitality and viability.

Pedestrian flow is another problematic area of assessing the health of a centre. Again, there is a simplistic assumption behind its use that pedestrian flow equals retail trade. Although there is undoubtedly a correlation between the two, it is not a perfect one and will vary depending on the centre and other factors, such as the range of facilities and the purpose of pedestrian flow. For example, the route between a commuter station and a commercial area may have a high pedestrian flow but the purpose of that flow is not primarily shopping although some shops will undoubtedly benefit from it. But it is also not clear how information on pedestrian flow *per se* can help in the assessment of impact for a new shopping development. Change in pedestrian flow over a specified time needs to be related to purpose rather than simply a presence – i.e. why somebody is there rather than simply counting them as there. There are also issues to do with collecting data over a period of time which needs to account for other changes that may have affected pedestrian flow, such as a recession or even the weather.

In response to these issues, Healey and Baker (1995) have developed an alternative approach to those in PPG 6 and NPPG 8. This alternative approach is based on a combination of quantitative and qualitative measures similar to those outlined in government guidance but is adaptable to centres of different sizes. The factors Healey and Baker use include:

- The function of the centre
- Vacancy levels and retailer requirements
- Impact assessments.

THE FUNCTION OF THE CENTRE

Government guidance does not give adequate weight to the differences in centre size and how different centres fulfil different functions in the retail hierarchy. Different centres in the retail hierarchy will have different factors that affect their vitality and viability. The position in the retail hierarchy and a number of local factors that impact on the function of the centre will determine the indicators used in measuring vitality and viability and the weight to be given to them. Healey and Baker identify two main sources of information that are likely to be of use in determining the function of the centre. Goad Trader Plans are available from small market towns upwards and include information on the uses and occupants of retail units. Comparing plans over a number of years provides an analysis of change in retailer representation which gives an important indication of the place of the centre in the retail hierarchy and its vitality and viability. In Addition To Goad Trader Plans, household surveys of shopper habits can identify shopping catchment areas, frequency of visits and other data to help place a centre.

VACANCY LEVELS AND RETAILER REQUIREMENTS

This more or less follows the approach outlined earlier in the chapter, but Healey and Baker introduce some modifications. Their preference is for vacancy to be expressed as a percentage of retail floorspace within a defined primacy frontage, or percent of frontage, rather than simply empty units. They also want a qualitative element introduced that explains why certain units have been empty for a time and whether there are retail demands that are not being met within the centre, such as the units being too small.

IMPACT ASSESSMENTS

The preferred approach to impact assessments is for a broad brush method that was based on a common approach adopted by government. This would mean that local authorities and retailers would agree on the method and indicators to any assessment and avoid the syndrome of 'arguing past' each other by comparing different methods and sets of data.

The Healey and Baker report makes some good points, especially regarding the use of commonly agreed data. But its main point is that assessing the impact of vitality and viability is a very difficult business and is underpinned by subjective assumptions and criteria. The DETR have undertaken research into the possibility of a common or agreed approach to assessing retail impact. Called the Combined, Retail, Economic and Transport Evaluation (CREATE) it is not a model but a logical series of steps that aim to use a consistent range of data. The government consider that the CREATE approach has a number of advantages including:

- a clear step-by-step approach;
- the integration of retail and transportation retail impact assessments (in accordance with PPG6 and PPG13);
- survey based (reducing the need for unsubstantiated assumptions);
- a consistent framework for predicting the likely impact of edge-of-centre/out-of-centre foodstores; and
- sensitivity analysis of the principal variables to highlight the effects of different judgements about the likely trading pattern of a new store (DETR, 1998).

To the outsider (and sometimes those involved) the whole process of assessing the impact of new retail developments may seem to be an awful lot of effort to come to a conclusion that few people seem to agree upon. The question that arises next is: *Do new large food stores have an impact upon existing centres or not?*

EVIDENCE ON THE IMPACT OF LARGE FOOD STORES ON EXISTING CENTRES

There is a good deal of anecdotal evidence on this subject from residents of towns about how a certain new supermarket has led to the decline of the town centre while they are as likely as anyone else to jump in the car to go and shop there. As we have hoped to show above, it is difficult to come to an agreement on this objectively. Two questions arise from this: Do new food supermarkets have an impact on an existing centre? And if they do, Should we be bothered about it?

The scale of retail change in the past 20 years has been phenomenal. From 457 outlets in 1986 the major foodstores had 1102 in 1997 and while they accounted for 29.9% of food sales in 1987 that had risen to 53.7% in 1996. But the actual composition of this spend was changing too as food retailers began to increase the range of goods on offer to include pharmacy, dry-cleaning, non-food goods such as video cassettes and PCs, as well as financial services. This has started to further challenge the ability of traditional shopping centres to compete. The London Chamber of Commerce and Industry estimates that 14 000 of the capital's 20 000 independent confectioners/tobacconists, off-licences and convenience stores may close over the next 10 years in part because of the impact of large supermarkets. This challenge has been helped by the relaxation of Sunday trading laws that used to benefit the smaller traders over their bigger rivals.

But assessing the impact of new out-of-town stores on town centres is not simply a case of finding good data. There are a number of other problems including:

- there has been no attempt to define or classify market towns and district centres as a particular focus for analysis;
- the lack of before and after assessments means that conclusions as to the effect of large foodstores are rarely based on empirical research;
- there is no 'control scenario' to compare the effects of large foodstore development with the situation had no development taken place;
- there is no common methodology for assessing traffic and transportation effects of large foodstores and comparing findings on a consistent basis; and
- no concerted attempt has been made to effectively integrate retail and traffic impact assessments (DETR, 1998).

Neither is this lack of information helped by the reality that 20% of local authorities do not require retail impact assessments to be submitted with applications for out-of-town retail developments. The result of this is a lack of 'base data' from which to assess changes in retail turnover and consequently impact. Nevertheless, the DETR study estimated impacts of between 13% and 50% on food retailers within market towns and district centres as a result of large out-of-centre foodstores. The decline in market share of town centres due to the location of out-of-centre stores varied between 21% and 75%. One of the direct outcomes of this impact has been the closure of many town centre food stores. In some towns this has led to a 25% decrease in food retail stores and overall vacancy rates increasing by 33%. Impact was also found not to relate solely to food stores as out-of-centre stores also sold a wide range of other goods and services. Overall, the DETR study concluded that:

- The development of large non-central foodstores can lead to a decline in the turnover of town centre foodstores (38% impact in the case of Tesco in Cirencester). This can and has led to the closure of some town centre food retailers.
- There is no available 'benchmark' to determine what percentage decline in turnover will lead to an unacceptable fall in profitability. It will depend on the particular circumstances of individual retailers. A significant fall in turnover can have a disproportionately high impact on the profitability of stores, influencing the ability of retailers to reinvest in store improvements/refurbishment, and ultimately to continue trading. In other circumstances, a reduction in turnover has no adverse consequences.
- Impact is likely to be most significant for stores that are trading at marginal levels of profitability. Experience shows that foodstore retailers will review store

performance, and where stores are performing below a particular turnover/ profitability threshold, these stores will be closed. For example, in 1994 Safeway announced the closure of some town centre stores nationwide as part of a company-wide review of stores.

- Even where town centre food retailers suffer an impact, but do not subsequently close, there may still be a concern that this will lead to a general decline in activity elsewhere in the centre, and adversely affect the vitality and viability of the centre. This is likely to be most apparent in centres where the centrally located foodstore is the key anchor retailer in the market town or district centre.
- Research shows that market towns and district centres generally have small catchments, which will only support a limited number of large foodstores. Therefore the development of an out-of-centre or edge-of-centre foodstore represents a loss of potential investment in the town centre. New town centre foodstores can act as a catalyst for further investment in town centres.
- Where there is no capacity for additional retailing, the opening of an edge-of-centre or out-of-centre superstore is likely to lead to 'disinvestment' in the town centre (i.e. failure to reinvest in store refurbishments, etc.). This has implications for the future viability of the individual retailer, and investment in the town centre as a whole.
- Even the potential threat of an out-of-centre foodstore can adversely affect retailer confidence.

In addition to the impact on retailing, the study also found that out-of-town supermarkets attract a significantly higher proportion of car borne trade than town centre stores. But, the study also found that between 25% and 65% of car-trips to an out-of-town store also involve a visit to the town centre. In addition, if people have a car they are as likely to use it to shop in the town centre as they are to shop out-of-town. One argument that has been introduced in the light of the above is that of clawback. If all towns had their own out-of-centre convenience store, then residents of town A will be less likely to travel to town B to do their shopping thereby reducing distance travelled and the amount of spending that a town loses to another. It also reduces the impact of a proposed store as it gains expenditure from other out-of-centre stores rather than the town centre. The DETR study found that this argument does not hold good for all situations and any clawback will not be as significant as drawing trade away from town centres. However, the Secretary of State allowed an appeal in early 1999 for a new superstore in Cornwall after accepting the argument of the appellants that it would clawback trade from surrounding areas. The proposal involved a 3298 m^2 Tesco store in the town of Redruth, which has no main foodstore. It was estimated that residents spent £15m per annum in foodstores outside of the town. But because there was no suitable site for a foodstore in the town the developer was forced to look at an edge-of-town location (*Planning*, 5 February 1999).

THE GOVERNMENT'S JUSTIFICATION FOR SEEKING TO PROTECT EXISTING CENTRES AGAINST NEW RETAIL DEVELOPMENTS

The next question that arises relates to the reasons behind all of this effort: *Why protect existing town centres?*

> The importance of our town centres has always been acknowledged but is now firmly at the top of the political agenda. Town centres need to develop a clear strategy which embraces a positive approach to planning, public investment and good management (Donaldsons, 1995, p. 3).

> We want to focus new developments in town centres, to secure their revitalisation, to ensure greater social inclusion and to achieve environmental benefits, particularly less dependence on the car (Richard Caborn, former Minister for the Regions, Regeneration and Planning, Speech to the British Council of Shopping Centres Annual Conference, 5 November 1998).

The question that underpins the whole current approach to retail policy in the UK is the primacy given to the protection of town centres. It is easy to get caught up in the details of a retail impact assessment and miss the reason why. It is worth noting that there are no convincing economic arguments as to why town centres should be preferred over out-of-centre sites. What it really comes down to are cultural arguments, as set out in Box 5.

Box 5 *Why bother to protect town centres? (DETR, 1998)*

Market towns have historically been the social and trading focal point for rural England. Their legacy of ancient streets and buildings is a fundamental part of our national heritage. However, as some of their traditional functions are gradually being eroded, there is a genuine concern about their future viability. In particular, there is widespread concern about the effects of large foodstores, particularly in non-central locations, on the economic health of market towns.

District centres generally lack the historical associations of market towns, and often have a less clearly defined and established role. However, they also perform an important shopping and community function. A number of the challenges facing market towns, and in particular the growth of large food-stores, are also relevant to district centres.

In addition to this more 'cultural' argument are two other arguments for maintaining shopping in existing or traditional centres. First, there is the environmental argument concerning the increase in car-borne traffic, the associated increase in carbon-dioxide emissions and the loss of greenfield sites. Second, since out-of-town retail developments depend heavily on car usage they can exclude those who do not have access to a car (e.g. the young, old or poor). Although there have been attempts to tackle this situation through the provision of public transport links, town centres on the whole provide better public transport access to retail facilities. But, as Chapter 11 on town centre management makes clear, it is not simply a case of restricting out-of-centre development. What is also needed is a proactive strategy to make towns more attractive. This is not always directly related to planning as Box 6 points out.

Box 6 *Who will compete? The need for attractive town centres*

Brighton is an attractive town within commuter distance of London with some historic and popular retail areas within its centre. However, apart from these speciality shops its natural function as a regional shopping centre is being undermined by competition from out-of-town developments and the lack of attractive comparable facilities within the town. Churchill Square is typical of the 1960s brutal architecture tradition and was the town's answer until it was demolished in 1996. High parking charges also worked against the shopper using the centre but these were not in the council's control. The answer has been to put together a strategy that aims to challenge the growing dominance of the out-of-town competition by making the town more attractive and accessible. Park and ride schemes have been introduced along with the development of a new covered mall. A local retailers' forum provides a voice for shopkeepers and other attempts have been made to make the town centre more vibrant through pedestrianisation schemes and the encouragement of cafés.

The importance of being able to have a healthy town centre in terms of vitality and viability is not simply to enable them to compete with out-of-centre locations but it also becoming increasingly important in the investment decisions of the future. IPD is a company who analyse the return on investment in retail centres around the country and produce an annual league table of centres based on this. Table 2 shows the top and bottom five centres in 1998. This information is becoming increasingly important to large companies in deciding where to invest and can also be another factor to take into account in assessing the vitality and viability of a centre.

Finally, another victim of the shift to out-of-town retailing that has begun to receive attention recently is the plight of the village shop. The government's Rural White Paper was concerned with the decline of the village or community shop. These shops do not simply provide the daily retail needs of local residents but

Table 2 *IPD league table on percentage return per annum 1998*

Ranking	Local authority district	Total return 1994–1997 (% pa)	Ranking end 1994
1	Westminster	15.6	176
2	Manchester	14.2	19
3	Middlesbrough	14.0	12
4	Edinburgh	13.3	27
5	Kensington	13.1	102
247	Maidstone	0.3	178
248	Rochester	0.2	168
249	Watford	–0.6	248
250	Basildon	–0.7	63
251	Aylesbury	–1.1	190

often also function as a Post Office, which can provide financial services for isolated communities or less mobile residents. The loss of a village shop can have a disproportionate impact on the lives of villagers and the impact of any new out-of-town retail development should include an assessment of the affect on such premises.

The decline of the village shop is not simply a related to the growth in out-of-town shopping (though undoubtedly there is a relationship) but has a more complex origin related to increased mobility and the rise of commuting from once distant centres. However, a number of communities are stemming this decline by either taking over shops that are going to close or setting up their own. The residents of Cromhall, Avon, decided to run their own shop when their village Post Office closed in 1992. The sum of £14 000 was raised from the 150 residents which allowed them to buy a building and stock it with local produce. There is one paid employee but the rest of the staff are volunteers from the village. This is one of approximately 30 similar ventures around the country.

CONCLUSIONS

This chapter has mainly focused on the high profile and important question of out-of-town retailing and its impact on existing centres. While it is clear that there has been a U-turn in thinking on the issue of new out-of-town developments the focus is now as much on regenerating existing centres as assessing the impact of new developments (see Chapter 11 on town centre management). It should also be clear that assessing the impact of developments is not an easy matter. But this chapter does not even begin to address other impacts from multiplex cinemas, factory shopping outlets, combined retail/leisure schemes, restaurants, pubs, hot food outlets and other leisure schemes.

But what is important to note is that there is all party support for the presumption in favour of town centres and for encouraging a range of uses to improve its vitality and viability. As the former Government Minister in charge commented:

> Let me be quite clear, we are not trying to strike a 'balance' between town centres and out-of-town shopping. That would be the type of wishy-washy policy that means all things to all people. This Government – like the last one – has an explicit preference for encouraging retail development in existing town centres (Richard Caborn, Minister for the Regions, Regeneration and Planning, Speech to the British Council of Shopping Centres Annual Conference, 5 November 1998).

What is also clear is that even if the Government's policy is successful, out-of-town development is here, and it is here to stay. Out-of-town retail development now accounts for a third of all retail spending and this proportion is rising. Attention is now rightly turning to our town centres and how to regenerate and help them compete in order to provide a greater choice in retail provision as well as encouraging a more environmentally friendly form of development.

Glossary of Terms

This glossary covers both particular forms of retail development and types of retail location. Because retailing is dynamic, it should be noted that new forms of retailing may evolve which are inadequately described by current terminology.

Amusement centres – Buildings used for such activities as bingo halls and clubs, prize bingo centres, amusement-with-prizes machines (for example, fruit machines) and amusement-only machines (pin tables and video games).

Bulky goods – Goods generally sold from retail warehouses where the goods are of such a size that they would normally be taken away by car and not be manageable by customers travelling by foot, cycle or bus (flatpack), or that large, flat areas would be required to display them, e.g. furniture in room sets, or not large individually, but part of a collective purchase which would be bulky, e.g. wallpaper, paint.

Commercial leisure developments – Developments which need to be accessible to a large number of people, such as multi-screen cinemas and bowling alleys.

Comparison shopping – Other shopping not classified as convenience shopping, which the purchaser will compare on the basis of price, quality and quantity before a purchase is made, e.g. clothes, fashion, gift merchandise, electrical goods, furniture.

Convenience shopping – Broadly defined as food shopping, drinks, tobacco, newspapers, magazines, and confectionery, purchased regularly for relatively immediate consumption.

Cumulative impact – Combined effect of all out-of-centre developments, developed and proposed, on the town centre, or the effect of such developments on all strategic centres, including the town centre.

District centres – Shopping centres or groups of shops, separate from the town centre, usually containing at least one food supermarket or superstore and non-retail services, such as banks, building societies and restaurants serving sub-urban areas or smaller settlements.

Edge-of-centre – A location within easy walking distance of the town centre, and usually adjacent to the town centre, and providing parking facilities that serve the centre as well as the store, thus enabling one trip to serve several purposes.

Factory shop – A shop adjacent to the production unit and specialising in the sale of manufacturers' products direct to the public.

Factory outlet centres – Group of shops, usually in out-of-centre locations, specialising in selling seconds and end-of-line goods at discounted prices.

Multi-screen/multiplex cinemas – A development of a minimum of five screens.

Neighbourhood centres – Small groups of shops, typically comprising a newsagent, small supermarket/general grocery store, sub-post office and other small shops of a local nature.

Out-of-centre – A location that is clearly separate from a town centre but within the urban area, including programmed extensions to the urban area in approved or adopted development plans.

Out-of-town – An out-of-centre development on a greenfield site, or on land not clearly within the current urban boundary.

Regional shopping centres – Out-of-town centres generally of 50 000 m^2 gross retail area and larger, typically enclosing a wide range of clothing and other comparison goods.

Retail parks – A single development of at least three retail warehouses with associated car parking.

Retail warehouse – A large single-level store specialising in the sale of household goods such as carpets, furniture and electrical goods, and bulky DIY items, catering mainly for car-borne customers and often in out-of-centre locations.

Retail warehouse clubs (or discount clubs) – Generally out-of-centre retailers specialising in bulk sales of reduced price, quality goods in unsophisticated buildings with dedicated car parks. The operator may limit access to businesses, organisations or classes of individual through membership restrictions.

Supermarkets – Single-level, self-service stores selling mainly food, with a trading floorspace of between about 500 and 2500 m^2, often with their own car parks.

Superstores – Single-level, self-service stores selling mainly food, or food and non-food goods, usually with at least 2500 m^2 trading floorspace with dedicated car parks at surface level.

Town centre – The term 'town centre' is used to cover city, town and district centres which provide a broad range of facilities and services and which fulfil a function as a focus for both the community and public transport. It excludes retail parks, neighbourhood centres and small parades of shops of purely local significance.

Vitality and viability of town centres – Vitality is a reflection of how busy a centre is at different times and in different parts. Viability is a measure of its capacity to attract ongoing investment, for maintenance, improvement and adaption to changing needs.

REFERENCES

Department of the Environment (1993) *Planning Policy Guidance Note 6: Town Centres and Retail Development*, HMSO, London.

Department of the Environment (1994) *Vital and Viable Town Centres: Meeting the Challenge*, HMSO, London.

Department of the Environment (1996) *Planning Policy Guidance Note 6: Town Centres and Retail Development*, HMSO, London.

Department of the Environment, Transport and the Regions (1998) *The Impact of Large Foodstores on Market Towns and District Centres*, HMSO, London.

Department of Trade and Industry (1998) *Competitiveness UK. Our Partnership with Business*, HMSO, London.

Department of Transport (1994) Planning Policy Guidance Note 13: Transport, HMSO, London.

Donaldsons (1995) *Town Centre Health Checks*, Donaldsons, London.

Healey and Baker (1995) *Measuring Vitality and Viability – A Critical Analysis of the Tests of PPG 6*, Healey and Baker, London.

House of Commons Environment Committee (1994) *Shopping Centres and Their Future*, volumes 1 and 2, HMSO, London.

Scottish Office (1998) *National Planning Policy Guidance Note 8: Town Centres and Retailing*, Scottish Office, Edinburgh.

Thomas, K. (1997) *Development Control. Principles and Practice*, UCL, London.

UK Government (1990) *This Common Inheritance. Britain's Environmental Strategy*, Cm 1200, HMSO, London.

CHAPTER 9

PLANNING FOR TRANSPORT

Claire Carr and Iain Docherty

INTRODUCTION

The role of transport

> It is difficult to conceive of a situation where transport does not play a major role in
> the life of an individual (Robinson and Bamford, 1978, p. 3)

Transport is the essential mechanism through which people are linked together across space. The historic development of advanced societies and economies has only been made possible by improved transport technologies, which have minimised the time taken to travel between places and made it easier for us to interact with one another.

Clearly, modern economies require a transport system capable of moving both goods and labour efficiently between sites of production and exchange (Button and Gillingwater, 1986). But transport is also crucial for the individual's full participation in society. The ease with which we are able to access transport services and to travel between places plays a large part in shaping our quality of life. Indeed, transport can be said to 'create the utilities of place' (White and Senior, 1983, p. 1) since improved accessibility reveals the full range of social activities open to individuals (Table 1).

HISTORICAL CONTEXTS

Over time, changing patterns of land use have reflected the widening availability of transport, and its increased effectiveness in reducing the friction of distance. Before 1800, the land transport systems that provided the means of economic exchange between settlements were exclusively based on roads for the use of pedestrians and horse-drawn vehicles. However,

> Major changes in transport technology which began to emerge during the first quarter
> of the 19th century had a major influence on the growth of cities, the organization of
> their internal structure, and the supply, demand, efficiency, speed and opportunities
> for movement within them (Daniels and Warnes, 1980, p. 4).

The subsequent shift from 'foot cities' to 'tracked cities' (Schaeffer and Sclar, 1975) characterised by the horse, and later electric, tram, had profound impli-

Table 1 Classification of purposes of urban personal travel

Activity	Journey Classification
Economic	
Earning a living	To and from work
Acquiring goods and services	To and from shops and outlets for personal services
	In course of shopping or personal business
Social	
Forming, developing and maintaining personal relations	To and from homes of friends and relatives
	To and from non-home rendezvous
Educational	To and from schools, colleges and evening institutes
Recreational and leisure	To and from places of recreation and entertainment
Cultural	To and from places of worship
	To and from places of non-leisure activity, including cultural and political meetings

Source: Daniels and Warnes (1980, p. 20).

cations for urban form. For the first time, the separation of homes and workplaces became the norm, and so land use in cities became increasingly specialised. The development of the more efficient urban rail systems, including metro networks, of the early twentieth century further encouraged the dispersal of cities through the construction of large suburban communities at much lower residential density than the historic areas of the inner urban core.

But the 'tracked' era was to last little over 50 years. After 1920, transport in the UK, as in most countries of the developed world, was transformed by the introduction of motor vehicles, particularly the private car. Increasing disposable incomes allied to the liberal ideals of promoting personal choice (the 'car-owning democracy') and maximising physical mobility as a means to promote more flexible, responsive markets and economies (Meyer and Gomez-Ibanez, 1991), elevated the car to the centre-piece of transport provision.

However, adoption of the North American ideal of universal car ownership and use has been problematic. The car's voracious appetite for road and parking space has proved incompatible with our limited road infrastructure and relatively compact historic urban form (Starkie, 1982). Widespread congestion has arisen, resulting in the waste of non-recoverable resources and the production of both locally and globally harmful pollution. Westwell (1991) highlights the American influences on British planning experience, particularly the trend towards low density suburban sprawl and the rapid growth of satellite dormitory settlements around major cities, encouraged by a *laissez-faire* attitude to widespread car use.

These trends in land use and transport have reinforced each other over several decades, resulting in a situation whereby, for many people, high levels of mobility are not a matter of choice but of necessity. Several sections of British society appear to be locked into land-use patterns that result in car dependence. For example, in 1989, fully 82% of drivers agreed that it would be difficult to adjust their lifestyles to being without a car (Jones, 1992).

As late as the 1980s, both national and local transport policies were dominated by the pressure to build new and larger roads to meet ever-growing car ownership levels and the belief that improved mobility acted as a catalyst for economic development. The publication of the Department of Transport's *Roads for Prosperity* White Paper (DTp, 1989) illustrated the grandeur of this 'predict-and-provide' approach by promoting a £23 billion programme of road building. Projects that have since been completed include: the M40 between Oxford and Birmingham; two shorter 'missing links' in the national motorway network, the M3 Winchester bypass across Twyford Down in Hampshire and the M65 between Blackburn and the M6 at Preston; other trunk roads including the A34 Newbury bypass and the A14 route between Rugby and Cambridge which was seen to be a vital link in the strategic road network serving the east of England; and several smaller local bypasses of existing communities designed to provide relief from traffic congestion. However, many of these schemes were the subject of major protests from environmentalists and the wider public, with projects such as the M3 at Twyford down, the Newbury Bypass, the M11 extension in east London and the M77 in Glasgow attracting major media interest (Routledge, 1997).

Despite the continuation of a significant roads programme into the 1990s as early as the 1960s, the classic government-sponsored study *Traffic in Towns* (Buchanan, 1963) devoted much of its analysis to the investigation of traffic generation and its interrelationship with changing land-use demands. Almost 40 years later this debate has re-emerged owing to the growing concerns about the environmental impacts of a transport system dominated by the car, including the depletion of non-recoverable resources and the contribution of motor transport to greenhouse gas emissions and other gaseous and particulate pollution. Furthermore, the Standing Advisory Committee on Trunk Road Assessment (SACTRA) has concluded that there is little evidence to support the commonly held view that new roads uniformly promote economic development and regeneration. However, this is not to say that there will be no road building in future, as specific projects may continue to be justified on local economic or safety grounds.

Shifting Attitudes

In the 1990s there has been a major shift in policy direction, fuelled by the contention that to continue to meet the growing demands for motorised transport would stand in direct conflict with the objectives of sustainable development. At the global scale, the 1987 World Commission on Environment and Development defined 'sustainable development' as that which 'meets the needs of the present without compromising the ability of future generations to meet their own needs'. The government's 1990 White Paper *This Common Inheritance* (DoE, 1990) established the first comprehensive environmental strategy for the UK in response to the issues raised in the World Commission.

Further impetus to international cooperation in reducing transport-derived pollution was provided through the UN's Earth Summit held in Rio in 1992. At this meeting a framework for further action in each member state was agreed, of which the publication of the full UK strategy for sustainable development in 1994 formed part. This strategy, devised under the auspicies of the Royal Commission on Environmental Pollution (RCEP), endorsed the principles that planning and transport policies at all levels need to meet the objectives of sustainable development:

> There is now general recognition that a continuing upward trend in road traffic would not be environmentally or socially acceptable. The need is to find transport policies for the UK and Europe which will be sustainable in the long term (RCEP, 1994).

The aspirations of such strategies have also informed the development of a 'new urbanism' (Newman and Kenworthy, 1996) which recognises the need to better relate transport and land use if sustainability is to be achieved. Simply, it recognises that land-use planning is significant in the context of climatic change and that one of the strongest connections in this relationship is through the transport system. In particular, it aims to reduce the amount of urban travel by minimising the need for it. This can be sought particularly by a return to the development of higher-density, mixed-use areas around high quality transport systems rather than dispersed low-density suburbia, to provide a focused urban structure that can help to reduce car dependence.

THE CHALLENGE

GROWTH IN CAR TRAVEL

Despite a growing awareness of the significant environmental effects of transport and the re-focusing of policy at both the national and local levels, the growth in the demand for car travel continues. Over the last decade, energy consumed by transport has increased by more than one-third with people making more journeys overall and longer journeys.

Statistics published by the Department of Transport (DTp, 1993) emphasise the dominance of car travel relative to other modes. Whilst road-based travel increased from 180 billion passenger kilometres in 1952 to 638 billion passenger kilometres in 1992, bus and coach travel declined during the same period from 92 to 43 billion passenger kilometres. Car travel, on the other hand, increased from 58 billion passenger kilometres in 1952 to 585 billion passenger kilometres in 1992, a ten-fold increase in 40 years.

This dramatic increase in car-based travel is set to continue over the next 30 years. National Road Traffic Forecasts (NRTF) published by the Department of the Environment, Transport and the Regions (DETR) in 1997, for example, predict that traffic growth between 1996 and 2031 is likely to increase by as much as 60%. Whilst there is debate about the technical basis for these forecasts, given that car ownership per head of population is set to rise by 41% over the next 30 years, there is no doubt that without some intervention, be it fiscal, legal or in some other way behavioural, traffic will continue to grow.

The challenge facing planners today is therefore to ensure that this growth in car ownership is not simply translated into ever greater car use and car dependence. To do so will require policies at the national and local levels aimed at not only improving the provision of public transport or facilitating alternative modes such as walking and cycling but, independently, a variety of mechanisms for managing the private car. Also, and perhaps more fundamentally, for policies to be successful there will need to be a radical change in social behaviour and individual attitudes towards the use of the car.

The government's 1998 Integrated Transport White Paper, *A New Deal for Transport* (DETR, 1998), began the task of setting out such potential new policies in detail. Throughout, its aspirations for more sustainable future transport policies are focused on promoting a modal shift away from the car to public transport or the 'personal' modes of walking or cycling. Policy instruments that may be available to restrain car use are divided into two categories, sticks and carrots. The sticks available include: limiting the proportion of available road space allocated to the car through bus priority measures, pedestrianisation and the installation of cycleways; price measures such as congestion charging in the form of tolls, extended and increased parking charges, particularly for private non-residential spaces at workplaces; and speed policies incorporating general overall limits, particularly in residential areas, and other traffic calming such as speed humps and narrowing.

Carrots focus on improvements in public transport, including increased service frequencies, extended hours of operation, higher quality vehicles, enhanced integration and accessible real-time information. Other positive measures include support for walking and cycling by constructing dedicated cycle and pedestrian lanes away from other traffic and providing grants for employers to install storage and changing facilities for 'active commuters'. These measures are described at some length in the White Paper, being promoted to improve integration between different modes, and improve the safety, quality, reliability and comfort of public transport services to the extent that they provide a more attractive alternative to the car in terms of journey time, flexibility and convenience; and to allow for the provision of expanded and improved facilities for walking and cycling as key enhancements aimed at encouraging more sustainable travel patterns.

In many ways, the objectives set out in *A New Deal for Transport* are palliative rather than truly radical measures, designed to tweak our existing land-use and development policies in order to increase the proportion of trips captured by non-car modes. But if a significant shift away from the car is to be achieved in future, our re-appraisal of the ideal transport and land-use patterns must be more fundamental.

RE-INTEGRATING TRANSPORT AND LAND-USE PLANNING

If any significant impact is to be made on the dominance of the car in our transport system as a means to reduce its impact on the environment, it is likely that nothing less than a reversal in the post-war planning paradigm of accommodating urban dispersal will be required. Put simply, high quality urban public transport services that can rival the convenience of the car will only be rendered viable if a return to a more intensive, higher-density urban form is made.

The potential advantages of the 'compact city' (Jenks *et al.*, 1996) in reducing the negative externalities of car use were acknowledged by the previous government. That land-use planning decisions can exert considerable influence in reducing the need to travel was recognised in the joint DoE/DTp publication *Planning Policy Guidance on Transport* (PPG 13) (DoE/DTP, 1994).

The general thrust of PPG 13 (and its subsequent sister documents for Scotland, Wales and Northern Ireland), is that whilst transport is vital to economic well-being, forecast levels of traffic growth simply cannot be accommodated by our infrastructure, even if this were desirable from an environmental standpoint. It recognised that future demand for car travel must be managed by:

- promoting choice by increasing the relative advantage of means of travel other than the car, especially walking, cycling and public transport;
- reducing dependence on the private car; and
- increasing the competitiveness and attractiveness of urban centres against peripheral development.

The key aim of PPG13 is to ensure that local authorities carry out their land use policies and transport programmes in ways which help to:

- reduce the growth in the length and number of motorised journeys;
- encourage alternative means of travel which have less environmental impact; and hence
- reduce the reliance on the private car.

To achieve these aims, PPG13 gives advice on locational policies for development plans which encourage a more sustainable pattern of development. By influencing the location of development the need for travel can be reduced. In particular local authorities should be:

- promoting development in urban areas and within existing settlements;
- concentrating development in existing centres and at locations with good public transport links;
- maintaining and improving the choice of travel modes; and
- limiting parking provision.

The principles of PPG13 are firmly grounded in the need to discourage the use of the car and promote other travel modes including public transport, walking and cycling. These include:

- restraint measures to control the use of the car, such as parking policy, and reallocation of road space to favour other travel modes;
- fiscal and institutional measures to address the current low marginal cost of car travel and the relative cost disadvantages facing users of public transport;
- measures to improve the use of existing roads infrastructure;
- innovative measures to reduce car use, such as car share clubs and car-free developments; and
- measures to mitigate the adverse impacts of the car-such as traffic calming and local traffic management schemes.

The Role of Parking Policy

The provision of parking, its scale and, more importantly, its cost is known to have a major influence on car use. Although parking is increasingly seen as an instrument for restraining demand, the evidence to date seems to highlight only a very cautious movement in this direction and in contrast a number of examples where the exact reverse is happening.

For example, it is estimated that over 50% of employers give financial assistance towards car commuters' costs by providing of free parking, and a number of studies have suggested that a free car parking space is actually worth between £4000–£6000 to the employee. Conversely, only about 3% of rail commuters receive a subsidy from their employers.

Parking policy in the past has discriminated against city centres and this will need to change in a way which at the very least applies equally to all parking spaces whether in town or out of town.

Sustainable Transport in Cities

The key elements of an integrated urban transport strategy are:

- land use and transport need to be planned together;
- people need to be brought back into the city to live, work and play;
- provision needs to be made for essential traffic with a destination in the city centre;
- the provision of high quality and frequent public transport is critical – only towns and cities can provide the critical mass to allow the levels of investment to be sustained as opposed to dispersed to out-of-town development; and
- the creation of pedestrian friendly areas in towns and cities.

Since the publication of PPG13, further policy guidelines have been issued, including *A Guide to Better Practice* (DoE/DTp, 1995), which provides a useful guide for practitioners seeking to translate the concepts of PPG13 into real planning policies.

The remainder of this chapter describes how the principles of PPG13 have been applied to date through the consideration of a number of case studies of recent land-use developments and proposals located throughout the UK.

CASE STUDIES

The Gyle Centre, Edinburgh

The Gyle shopping centre opened on the western outskirts of Edinburgh in October 1993. The centre was the first of its kind in Scotland and comprises 300 000 ft^2 of retail floorspace in a covered shopping mall with approximately 3000 car parking spaces, including staff parking.

It is situated approximately five miles from the city centre adjacent to the Edinburgh City bypass which provides direct connections to the strategic road network. The Edinburgh to Fife railway line runs along its northern boundary with South Gyle station situated approximately 800 m from the centre. Covered facilities for buses and taxi drop-off and pick-up are situated immediately adjacent to its main entrance.

The Gyle was conceived back in the late 1980s as one element within a range of major developments in West Edinburgh proposed in the early 1990s. These included the extension of the M8 Motorway to the Edinburgh City Bypass which was completed late in 1995; the opening of the Hermiston Gait Retail Park in November 1995; major office development in and around the adjacent Edinburgh Park and South Gyle area.

There are a number of other transport improvements that are currently planned which will have an influence on travel patterns and accessibility in the west of Edinburgh. These include:

- The construction of the City of Edinburgh Rapid Transit (CERT) from Edinburgh Airport to the City Centre currently programmed for completion by the year 2000. This new transport link will also serve the Gyle.
- The proposed new railway station at Edinbugh Park with an interchange with CERT.

On opening in 1993 the Gyle centre was considered to be well placed in relation to the developing commercial area to the west of Edinburgh and to large parts of South East and Central Scotland.

In order to understand the potential retail and transport impact of the Gyle centre, a before and after study was commissioned by a group led by The Scottish Office. This study examined conditions prior to the opening of the centre and condition some 18 months after the centre opened. The key findings in relation to transportation emerging from this study can be summarised as follows:

- The Gyle is very well located in relation to the strategic road network; however, access by other transport modes is limited due to its remote location from residential areas.
- Access is dominated by the private car with 84% of shoppers arriving by car. Only 9% of shoppers travel by bus with a further 6% either walking or cycling to the centre.
- Traffic flows to the centre are relatively high for its size – on average traffic flows peak on a Saturday with some 16 000 vehicle arrivals.
- The car park operates close to its capacity, particularly at weekends.
- Travel by train is limited due the remote location of the railway station from the centre.
- The bus network servicing the Gyle has barely changed since opening with approximately 39 buses per hour during peak periods; however, the range of services has reduced with a limited bus catchment area.
- The Gyle makes a significant contribution to vehicle emissions and energy consumption resulting from shopping trips in the west of Edinburgh.

There are a number of important lessons that can be learned from experiences at the Gyle regarding the location of new development in relation to transport infrastructure. These are:

- The location of new development immediately adjacent to the strategic road network will encourage car-borne trips.

- This attraction is further increased by the availability of ample free car parking.
- The provision of facilities for buses on site is unlikely to significantly influence modal share if the services do not closely match the potential catchment for bus passengers, i.e areas of low car ownership.
- Similarly, the potential for shoppers to walk and cycle to the centre is limited due to its remote location from residential and built-up areas.
- The relatively remote location from the railway station is a missed opportunity for closer public transport integration.

Recently proposals were approved to extend the Gyle by an additional 60 000 ft^2. Attached to this approval were stringent conditions relating to improving transport links to the Gyle in order to address some of the above concerns. These transport improvements include:

- The provision of a local bus service linking areas to the north and west of the Gyle currently not served by public transport, with the service guaranteed for a period of 15 years.
- An annual leaflet drop to all homes within the city detailing public transport services to the Gyle.
- An electric bicycle recharging point for free recharging of these vehicles.
- The provision of improved pedestrian walkways to the proposed CERT halt on South Gyle Broadway and to South Gyle railway station.
- The development of a staff travel/green commuter plan for staff working at the Gyle which would include the provision of a staff bus and a reduction in the number of staff car parking spaces.
- The provision of a home delivery service.

These transport improvements reflect the shift in attitudes towards car-borne travel since the original consent was granted for the Gyle and, importantly, the need to guarantee the provision of public transport services over a period of time to enable more sustainable travel choices.

It will be interesting in the future to monitor the effects that the Gyle extension and further development in the area surrounding the Gyle with the proposed improvements to public transport have on the way in which people travel to the centre.

MANCHESTER MILLENNIUM

The work currently being carried out to reconstruct Manchester city centre after the devastating bomb explosion of 1996 provides an excellent example of the practical development of a more sustainable urban transport strategy.

Manchester city centre is faced with the same challenges relating to transport and out-of-centre development as many other cities and towns within the UK. However, in June 1996 an IRA bomb completely destroyed the city's retail and commercial core providing the catalyst for major refurbishment of the city centre.

The speed with which Manchester took up the challenge of rebuilding the city centre under the guidance of a task force known as the Manchester Millenium was impressive. The role of the task-force was – and still is – to coordinate and oversee the work, bring together the public and private sectors to manage the recovery and reconstruction of the city, and to support businesses unable to trade.

The first task was to assemble a masterplan for the city and an international urban design competition was launched and won by EDAW with a plan involving new public open spaces, an urban park and cultural area, a pedestrian friendly environment, major improvement to the retail centre of the city, major new leisure facilities and the reintroduction of residential properties to the core.

The need to rebuild the city created both the opportunity and a fundamental requirement to develop an integrated transport strategy for the city to ensure good accessibility by all travel modes. The key features of the strategy are to create an accessible city for all, provide real choice, reduce unnecessary traffic and encourage the removal of through traffic by planned coordinated investment, leading to a cleaner, safer and more attractive city centre.

The transport strategy will be developed over a 10-year period, with the key elements, for which funding is already in place, being delivered within the first three years of the rebuilding programme.

At present 60% of trips to and from the city centre are made by car and 40% by public transport. However, of the car traffic, 30% has no business within the city centre. In common with other cities and towns, Manchester suffers the problems associated with this through traffic of congestion during peak periods. If this situation is allowed to continue, then these congested periods will increase and activity will be driven away from the city centre.

Manchester is fortunate in so far as it has an extensive rail network, a modern street running light rail system and a comprehensive bus network. The foundations for developing a sustainable transport strategy are therefore already in place and it is recognised that transport accessibility to the city centre will increasingly depend on encouraging greater use of this public transport network and encouraging car owners to use public transport wherever possible and convenient.

The objective is to encourage a significant shift to public transport so that there are at least as many public transport trips as car trips. In addition, the strategy is also designed to discourage the through traffic, which has no business in the city centre, and encourage it to use other routes outside the city, so that traffic volumes in the centre can be reduced. The removal of extraneous through traffic will allow the introduction of significant environmental improvements thereby creating a more pleasant and attractive environment for pedestrians and cyclists.

In general, the approach taken towards the use of streets in the core area will be to ensure that they are pedestrian friendly, with buses having access during the day subject to satisfactory management and that general traffic should be allowed access to the core in the evening in order to create a sense of security and life and to avoid dead pedestrian zones.

The key elements of the strategy are:

- completion of the inner ring road to cater for through traffic and act as a distributor road for traffic seeking access to the city centre;
- a variable message signing system to direct traffic to the most appropriate car park with space availability;
- enhancement and refurbishment of core short stay city centre car parks to modern standards of safety, security, lighting and signage;
- two new metrolink city centre stations near the heart of the redeveloped area;
- the creation of pedestrian street, with partial closure of existing roads to traffic during the day (reopening at night) in pedestrian dominated areas;
- encouragement of park and ride at railway stations outside the city centre; and
- the development of bus quality partnerships between the city council, Passenger Transport Authority and bus operators in order to deliver high quality and reliable bus services.

PLANNING INQUIRIES – BARNET FOOTBALL CLUB AND GATWICK VISITOR ATTRACTION

Two development proposals which illustrate the application of the principles of PPG13 are described here.

A public inquiry was held into Barnet Football Club's proposals to relocate to a new stadium during the course of 1997. The proposals were supported by a transport strategy and detailed transport plan which aimed to encapsulate the principles of PPG13.

The transport strategy involves a package of measures based on: public transport, parking controls, traffic management, and pedestrians and cyclists. Key to the proposed strategy would be the provision of shuttle bus services on match days accompanied by limited car parking on the site and parking controls so that the use of the car is not encouraged and spectators do not park in residential streets. A programme of monitoring the effectiveness of these measures would be introduced so that modifications could be introduced if considered necessary; for example, the frequency and routings of bus services, together with the extent of parking control measures.

A decision is awaited on the proposals; however, the above highlights the need to incorporate a Transport Plan in the initial stages of the planning of a new development.

Approval has recently been granted for a proposed new visitor attraction at Gatwick Airport following a public inquiry in 1997. Gatwick Airport is already well served by public transport with some 960 trains stopping at the Gatwick Airport railway station over a typical weekday. Proposals also exist to upgrade this level of service and the destinations served with Thameslink 2000, improvements to the Gatwick Express service and options for linking Gatwick with Heathrow Airport. The visitor atttraction will be located within a few hundred metres of the railway station.

Pedestrians and cyclists would be catered for by means of a network of segregated routes within the airport which provide safe access to all parts of the airport. The needs of the mobility impaired will also be met by the existing high quality facilities at the airport.

The scale of this development was such that it was vital to ensure that its location was planned in close proximity to excellent and strategic public transport links.

CONCLUSION

Land-use patterns and transport systems are interdependent. Advances in transport technologies and the extent to which new transport systems are able to overcome the friction of distance has underlain the evolution of our urban form.

Until recently these advances have enabled people to become more and more mobile. Widening car ownership has increased the degree of personal choice available to individuals in their trip-making decisions, and generated more complex patterns of movement. Cities have decentralised and residential and other development diffused away from historic cores. However, dependence on the car as the dominant transport mode has now reached the stage where the negative externalities of car use outweigh many of its advantages. Some of these contradictions are easily visible: the congestion levels caused by over-use of the car reduce its ability to provide for flexibility in journey patterns. Others, although less visible, substantially degrade the environment and our quality of life, climate change attributed to greenhouse gas emissions representing the most cogent example.

In order to tackle the sustainability challenge, the role of the car, and the nature of the urban form associated with it, must be reappraised. It is likely that the compact city, where residences, employment and services are in close proximity will provide a solution by reducing the need to travel and maximising public transport's share of those motorised trips that remain. Although emerging from decades of decline, our historic cities are well placed to play an important role in the sustainable future, since they combine the capacity to accommodate a significant share of the forecast increase in household numbers with a legacy of substantial public transport infrastructure. PPG13 and the projects implemented to date under its guidance demonstrate that much can be achieved: the challenge is to expand and extend this approach to create truly sustainable cities and communities.

REFERENCES

Buchanan, C. (1963) *Traffic in Towns*, HMSO, London.

Button, K.J. and Gillingwater, D. (1986) *Future Transport Policy*, Croom Helm, London.

Daniels, P.W. and Warnes, A.M. (1980) *Movement in Cities*, Methuen, London.

DETR (Department of the Environment, Transport and the Regions) (1998) *A New Deal for Transport*, HMSO, London.

DoE (Department of the Environment) (1990) *This Common Inheritance*, HMSO, London.

DoE/DTp (Department of the Environment and Department of Transport) (1994) *Planning Policy Guidance on Transport*, PPG13, HMSO, London.

DTp (Department of Transport) (1989) *Roads for Prosperity*, HMSO, London.

DTp (Department of Transport) (1993) *Transport Statistics Great Britain*, HSMO, London.

Jenks, M., Burton, E. and Williams, K. (eds) (1996) *The Compact City*, Spa, London.

Jones, P. (1992) What the pollsters say, in: Whitelegg, J. (ed.), *Traffic Congestion: Is There a Way Out?*, Leading Edge, Hawes, pp. 11–31.

Meyer, J.R. and Gomez-Ibanez, J.A. (1981) *Autos, Transit and Cities*, Harvard University Press, Cambridge, Mass.

Newman, P.W.G. and Kenworthy, J.R. (1996) The land use–transport connection – an overview, *Land Use Policy*, **13**(1), 1–22.

RCEP (Royal Commission on Environmental Pollution) (1994) *Transport and the Environment, 18th Report*, HMSO, London.

Robinson, H. and Bamford, C.G (1978) *Geography of Transport*, MacDonald and Evans, Plymouth.

Routledge, P. (1997) The imagineering of resistance: Pollok Free State and the practice of postmodern politics, *Transactions of the Institute of British Geographers*, **22**, 359–376.

Schaeffer, K.H. and Sclar, E. (1975) *Access for All: Transportation and Urban Growth*, Penguin, Harmondsworth.

Starkie, D.N.M. (1982) *The Motorway Age*, Pergamon, Oxford.

Westwell, A.R. (1991) *Public Transport Policy in Conurbations in Britain*, Keele University Thesis, Keele.

White, H.P. and Senior, M. (1983) *Transport Geography*, Longman, London.

CHAPTER 10

TOWN CENTRE MANAGEMENT

Julie Grail

INTRODUCTION

The concept of Town Centre Management has arisen in response to the increasing competition that town centres are now faced with, together with the continuing desire for town centres to be the natural focus for their surrounding communities. Owing to changes in lifestyle, increased mobility and changes in retailing, in order to continue to be successful, town centres must be in a position to compete in the broadest sense with neighbouring town centres, out-of-town centres and other forms of retailing.

Town Centre Management is concerned with enhancing and maintaining the vitality and viability of town centres through a partnership between the public, private and voluntary sectors. The partnership is charged with developing a shared vision for the town which deals with both long-term aspirations and short-term achievable projects. In most cases, although not necessarily all, the implementation of this vision is co-ordinated by a Town Centre Manager.

In the majority of cases the role of the Town Centre Manager is one of co-ordinator and catalyst; however, it is evolving rapidly and has already in a short space of time developed from a fairly meager starting point of 'janitor' employed by the local authority. There are already many variations to the role but it is undoubtedly developing a significantly broader remit than merely janitorial functions and indeed in some of the more advanced examples the janitor role can be found within a subset of a total Town Centre Management team. In response to this evolutionary process the background and discipline of the Town Centre Manager is constantly developing. At the outset appointments were largely internal redeployments from within council departments and in many cases with a planning discipline. Since that time many professions have moved into the sphere of Town Centre Management including retailing, property, marketing and general management disciplines.

The aim of this chapter is to set out the key challenges facing town centres and in response to outline the fundamental structures within Town Centre Management and give a commentary on the growth of the concept throughout the UK. Two case studies will then be utilised in order to demonstrate Town Centre Management in practice and in particular to focus on the different approaches required to deal with different sizes and types of town centre. The chapter will then go on to consider the implications of Town Centre Management to planning, and address the issue of how planners in other fields can better understand and assist Town Centre Management .

THE CHALLENGES FACING TOWN CENTRES

It is increasingly being reported by many sources that town centres are facing external factors which are contributing to their decline. In addition, past planning policies allowing development on greenfield sites have exacerbated the problem. Nevertheless, in terms of national planning policy, planning for town centres has emerged as a key facet of planning sustainable development. The recent government guidance in PPG1, PPG6 and PPG13 has emphasised the important role that town centres play, particularly for concentrating development in areas well served by public transport, reducing trips, promoting mixed-use developments and in the reuse of brownfield sites (DoE, 1996, 1997). The revised PPG1 (*General Policy and Principles*) has been restructured to place greater emphasis on key policy messages. Incorporated into the document is a presumption to prefer urban rather than greenfield sites for housing and commercial developments, a renewed emphasis on quality of urban design and a commitment to mixed-use and sustainable development. With regard to sustainable development, the government is committed to concentrating development in areas well served by public transport, especially town centres. It encourages local authorities to include policies in their plans to promote and retain mixed uses, particularly in town centres. The revised PPG6 (*Town Centres and Retail Development*) also makes specific reference to the support for town centres. The government sets out its main objective as sustaining and enhancing the vitality and viability of town centres, and states that town and district centres should be the preferred locations for developments that attract many trips. The guidance also introduces the sequential test for development, which requires consideration for town centre sites as a priority followed by edge-of-town and only as a last resort out-of-town sites. In addition, PPG6 recognises the importance of the role of Town Centre Management.

It is useful at this stage to quantify the challenges to the traditional high street and to put these into context. Retail vacancies has long been a criterion for assessing the vitality of town centres. Between 1990 and 1994 the national average for retail vacancy increased from 7% to 13%. This increase can be attributed to a complex set of factors as follows. Retailing developments over the past decade have made a significant contribution to the change in the way the population shops. There are now six regional shopping centres either open or under construction, which account for over 5 million square feet of retail space. Out-of-town retail developments have cropped up throughout the UK, and despite the changes within PPG6 now favouring town centre developments, there is a further 91 million square feet in the pipeline. Factory outlet centres are a relatively new phenomenon which retail largely durable and comparison goods at discounted prices. There are now 20 planned or operating within the UK (Boots The Chemist, 1997).

Alternative forms of retailing are also increasing their share of the market. Petrol stations accounted for2 billion of retail sales in 1994, and currently account for 34% of all UK confectionary sales. Railway stations are also becoming a retail sales area in their own right: in Liverpool Street Station there are more office worker than rail traveller customers. Airports are also becoming contributors to retail sales, and in 1996 40% of BAA first quarter profits were from retailing. In addition, catalogue and electronic home shopping is reported to be on the increase. There are currently 300 000 Internet users in the UK and 30 million worldwide, and hence a number of retailers are trialling Internet shopping including Argos, Waterstones, Body Shop, Asda and Virgin. Nevertheless the success of this style of retailing is yet to be proved (Boots The Chemist, 1997).

Out-of-town shopping sales are said to currently account for 30% of total retail sales. This is largely due to the success of the major supermarket chains. In 1994 the major supermarkets accounted for 5% of all music and record sales, 13% of all newspapers and magazines, 20% of petrol and 21% of all health and beauty, cosmetics and medicines. In a survey in 1996 the success of supermarkets was demonstrated further: they accounted for 50% of all meat and poultry sales, 50% of fruit and vegetable sales, 30% of fresh fish, 75% of bread, and 30% of all wine sales (Boots The Chemist, 1997).

In addition to these staggering figures concerning retail sales there are other contributing factors to challenge the traditional high street. Between 1989 and 1994 it was reported by the *Financial Times* that two high street banks closed every day, and that between 1984 and 2004 half of the high street banks will have closed. Overall financial and professional uses are predicted to decline from 9% to 3% in the next 10 years. Retail uses (A1) are predicted to reduce from 65% of the high street to 30%. The areas of growth within the town centre are predicted to be food and drink uses (A3), expected to rise from 9% to 27% in the next 10 years, health and leisure from 17% to 30%, and residential occupation to rise from negligable to 10% (Boots The Chemist, 1997).

Demographic changes will also play a part in shaping the high street for the future. By the year 2010 it is predicted that there will be one million more retired people, three million more mature spenders (49–65 year olds), and two million fewer 19–40 year olds than in 1996. The consumer society is also expected to continue to demand extended opening hours including Sunday trading, with 33% of consumers already shopping on Sundays at least once per month (Healey and Baker, 1996).

What does all this mean for town centres in the future? It certainly means that for town centres to even begin to compete they must be well managed, well understood and have clear strategies for the future, taking into account these predictions.

TOWN CENTRE MANAGEMENT AS A RESPONSE

TOWN CENTRE MANAGEMENT – THE NATIONAL PICTURE

Town Centre Management has been presented as a response to and as a tool with which to tackle the problems of our declining town centres. However, the concept of Town Centre Management is still young and many variations exist throughout the UK. The earliest example of Town Centre Management was in 1986, and by 1991 35 Town Centre Managers had been appointed. At this time, the Association of Town Centre Management (ATCM) was established, which aims to represent Town Centre Management initiatives on a national scale, and to further the cause by lobbying relevant parties and particularly influencing government policy. There are currently just over 200 Town Centre Managers throughout the UK, although there are many more management initiatives which, for various reasons, do not have a specific Town Centre Management post associated with the partnership.

The concept is largely based on the American principle of shopping centre management where all key services and facilities are co-ordinated by a shopping centre manager and paid for by a service charge to tenants for the good of the whole. Up to this time town centres have been managed on a very *ad hoc* and disparate basis depending on the particular perceived problem or priority area. They have not considered the town centre as a single entity, and have not achieved the economies of scale which this approach would enable.

Styles and degrees of partnership vary throughout the UK, not only due to the varying maturity of initiatives, but also because of the varying needs and practicalities of different scales and locations of centres. Partnerships range from an informal gathering of interested partners meeting on an *ad hoc* basis to very formalised structures in a number of more advanced examples. Although in some cases this range of examples may act as a continuum upon which a town may begin somewhere at the lower end and advance towards the ultimate aim of a formalised structure, this is not necessarily the case. The advanced formalised structure will not necessarily be appropriate to all town centres, particularly those of a small scale and within a multi-centred district.

A recent publication by the ATCM in conjunction with Boots The Chemist, *Developing Structures to Deliver Town Centre Management* (1997) sets out a series of possible model structures to be used and adapted to suit the particular needs of a locality. There are nine models proposed as follows:

1. *A Town Centre Management Initiative.* This is a structure which is extremely flexible and informal and can be adopted with or without a Town Centre Manager in post. A forum, steering group and working groups meet on a regular basis with all the key players feeding into this process. *Examples* – Frome, High Wycombe, Wokingham.

2. *Shared Town Centre Manager.* This structure is similar to that above, but allows a Town Centre Manager to be appointed to work on more than one town within the same local authority area. Different Action Plans for those towns would be produced based upon feedback from the partnership groups. *Examples* – Hawick and Galashiels.

3. *Town Centre Manager.* This is found in larger towns where a steering group directs and supports a Town Centre Manager who is paid for by contributions from the private and public sectors. In many cases the Local Authority acts as the employer. Again working groups focus on key issues and key players feed in to the partnership framework. *Examples* – Kingston upon Thames, Nottingham, Hemel Hempstead.

4. *Town Centre Manager employed by a Chamber of Commerce.* This is similar to model 3 but the private and public sectors contribute to the Chamber of Commerce which in turn employs the Town Centre Manager. There are few examples of this structure; town centres tend to favour the Local Authority employment option, particularly in the short term, for the respectability and security of tenure which a Local Authority can offer. *Example* – Perth.

5. *Town Centre Management (Private Sector/Public Sector Co-ordinators).* A Local Authority officer co-ordinates the public sector management, whilst a private sector co-ordinator brings together commercial interests. Often the private sector post has some element of public sector funding. For this type of model to be successful the co-ordinators need close co-operation and to share the same objectives, priorities and timescales. *Examples* – Leeds, Gravesend.

5. *Local Authority Appointed Town Centre Manager (Private Sector Secondee working in Local Authority).* A large majority of Town Centre Managers are fully funded by the public sector. There are advantages in the more assured funding and knowledge and acceptance by officers and members of the council. Nevertheless this structure does carry the disadvantages of being viewed as a council employee by the private sector, and often the lack of support and funding from the private sector. *Examples* – Derby, Warrington, Kendal.

7. *Local Authority Officer working with Private Sector.* This structure allows for a Local Authority officer to act as a focus for town centre issues within the council and also as a link into the authority for the private sector, albeit within a rather loose structure. *Examples* – Birmingham, Enfield.

8. *City Challenge – Town Centre Manager.* There are some examples within the UK where a City Challenge initiative has funded the appointment of a Town Centre Manager. The advantage of such an approach is that the post is part of a regeneration process with considerable resources and influential support, but the Town Centre Manager is only part of a wider strategy and the funding is only short lived. *Examples* – Huddersfield, Brixton.

9. *City Centre Company*. This structure is based on North American examples where a company is set up to take over the management responsibility of a specific geographic area, employing staff and raising revenue. This model is seen as a progression from a strong partnership foundation between the public and private sectors. *Examples* – Bristol, Coventry.

As stated earlier these models merely provide a summary of the current examples within the UK; however, there is certainly no definitive model for a successful Town Centre Management initiative. As the concept matures lessons are being learnt and hence structures change. In terms of the key players in any initiative, the local authority must, and in the majority of cases does, take a leading role. Much of the work, certainly in the early stages, is about redefining and refocusing the local strategies and hence influencing the thinking and action within the key council departments. There is also, in many cases, quite a considerable culture difference between the public and private sectors and this requires a diplomatic and pragmatic approach. The current situation in the UK relies heavily on voluntary support from the private sector and in some cases this can mean considerable time and resources commitments. A problem inevitably associated with this is that the private sector representatives tend to come from the large corporations who can more easily afford to devote the time as opposed to a small sole trader. Depending on the size of the town the Chamber of Commerce can play a part in the partnership, but in many cases the retail element of a Chamber is weak and therefore fairly ineffectual. Many other partners are involved in partnerships throughout the UK, including the police, universities and colleges, the voluntary sector, and the churches, to name but a few.

Irrespective of style and scale of partnership, Town Centre Management initiatives must if nothing else have a strong commitment from a few and require at least one champion to further the cause in the local area, particularly given the still rather informal and immature nature of these partnerships. For example, under the vast majority of the current initiatives, although the private sector plays a part within the structure, there is no formalised method of ensuring a certain level of commitment and longevity to their involvement.

TOWN CENTRE MANAGEMENT IN PRACTICE

For the purposes of this commentary the Town Centre Management process is being subdivided into six steps which will be illustrated using the two different case studies of Frome in Somerset and Kingston upon Thames in Surrey. However, before launching into these six steps it is important to put into context the principles of Town Centre Management against the two case studies. The size, status and issues relating to the two case studies differ considerably and therefore warrant a quite different approach to management.

Figure 1 *Frome – Catherine Hill*

Frome is a historic market town dating back to 685 AD. It has a population of 25 000 with a rural hinterland of up to 70 000. Over recent years, but at least the last decade, the town has been experiencing a spiralling decline associated with a number of factors including the relocation of the Cattle Market to an out-of-town site, industrial decline in the town and surrounding area, the development of an out-of-town supermarket, increasing prominence of neighbouring retail centres due to major developments, in particular Trowbridge and the Shires development, and more widely the changing nature of retailing, shopping patterns, mobility and hence ultimately the face of the high street (see Figures 1 and 2). This impact adds up to a 25% vacancy of its total 100 000 ft^2 retail provision. One area, originally the main shopping thoroughfare but now very much marginalised, reported figures of 60% vacancy in 1995 (Mendip District Council, 1995, 1996).

In stark contrast, and at the other end of the retail hierarchy, is Kingston upon Thames, which also prides itself in being a historic market town (Figure 3). However, more appropriately and particularly in the context of its town centre, it

Figure 2 *Round Tower*

is better described as a major regional shopping destination. Kingston has a population of 140 000, but more relevant to its current status is a 750 000 person catchment within 15 minutes drive time. There is additionally an extremely strong catchment within one hour travel time, which is largely due to the strong retail mix and capacity of 3.5 million square feet of retail space, with negligible vacancies and close to 7000 car parking spaces. The scale of retail provision in Kingston has increased considerably within the last decade, largely due to a £20 million relief road and associated pedestrianisation scheme, rationalisation of the Bentalls site leading to a redevelopment of the Bentalls Department store and the associated development of a 600 000 ft^2 four-storey covered shopping centre (The Bentall Centre), plus the development of a 240 000 ft^2 flagship John Lewis store (Kingston Town Centre Management, 1997a, b).

Figure 3 *Kingston upon Thames Action Plan*

ENHANCEMENT SITES

1. Fife Road
Road resurfacing is planned for March 1997.

2. Castle Street
Street lighting improvements and general enhancement work required. Partnership funding to be sought.

3. London Road
General enhancement works planned including street furniture and signing improvements. Public Art Opportunities. Partnership funding to be sought.

4. Railway Station
General enhancement works required within and surrounding the site. Partnership funding to be sought.

5. Eden Street/Adams Walk
General enhancement works required. Partnership funding to be sought.

6. Clarence Street
Street furniture improvements required. Partnership funding to be sought.

7. Thames Street/Wood Street
Signing improvements required. Public Art Opportunities. Partnership funding to be sought.

8. Church Street/Union Street
Repaving planned. No funding identified to date.

9. Apple Market
Repaving works commenced in January. Design includes predetermined area of york stone paving and clay paviers to be used for street cafes.

10. Ancient Market Place
Identified as a site for revitalisation. Proposals to extend pedestrianisation and introduce diversity of uses including specialist markets and street cafes. Public Art opportunities. No decision to date. Partnership funding to be sought.

11. Riverside
Links to riverside require enhancement. Partnership funding to be sought.

12. St James Area
Enhancement works required including street cleaning improvements. Partnership funding to be sought.

DEVELOPMENT SITES

1. Charter Quay
Application submitted in January 1997 which includes a theatre, landmark apartments, restaurant and riverside cafes, retail, restaurant and leisure uses on the Market Place frontage and formation of the Thameside walk including a bridge over the Hogsmill. No decision to date.

2. Former Power Station
Development includes residential and 150 bed hotel. Permission granted. Residential development started. Site to link with proposed development on British Gas site by way of a new link road to Richmond Road.

3. British Gas Land
Proposals approved for 50,000 sq ft retail development (foodstore), 30,000 sq ft leisure development, residential, car parking and a new link road from Richmond Road to Skerne Road. Decontamination necessary.

4. Turks Boatyard
Development underway for a Passenger Boat Pier, bar and restaurant on the ground floor and flats on the first floor.

5. Sea Cadet HQ
Development for 30 flats and replacement 3 storey sea cadet building.

6. Vicarage Road/Water Lane
Identified as a development site. Appropriate uses include leisure, residential, retail and/or offices. No application to date.

7. Bus Station/Bentall Depository
Identified as a development site for mixed uses including leisure. No application to date.

8. Clarence Street
Permission recently granted for a Wetherspoon Public House, licence granted for one year.

9. Former C&A Department Store
Two permissions granted. Both include a restaurant/pub on ground and first floors, one has residential on upper floors and the other a health club.

10. Station Yard, Sopwith Way
Development underway for 139 one and two bed flats.

11. Post Office
Post Office facility is moving into a new 'Alldays' store at 28/30 Eden Street. Site is identified for development. No application to date.

12. Ashdown Road/Ladybooth Road
Site identified for development. No application to date.

Step One – Developing a Partnership Framework

Developing a partnership framework is an important first step and involves identifying key partners and organisations, creating or reviewing forums and working groups, and developing communication channels. In the example of Frome a wide-ranging town centre forum, known as the Taskforce, took the umbrella role incorporating key players from all levels of government and many other representatives from the public, private and voluntary sectors. The membership of this group is approximately 40 and although it has no powers and no budget the group proves a very influential means to communication and action. This is aided by the fact that the group is attended by the Chief Executive of the District Council and chaired by the Leader of the County Council. Kingston's situation is quite different, partly due to the large, urban nature of the town and the lack of residents within the town centre area. A Management Board directs the workings of the Town Centre Manager with representatives from the funding partners from both the public and private sectors, and is chaired by an elected member. Nevertheless no true town centre forum exists in the town, although many smaller specific working groups are present.

Step Two – Understanding the Current Status

It is important that in considering the future potential of an area the current status is fully researched and understood. A review of existing policy and survey material is important, as is a comprehensive strengths, weaknesses, opportunities and threats (SWOT) analysis, preferably undertaken with consultation. In many cases a town may be rich in information relating to key facts and statistics, yet may prove weak in terms of actual qualitative information from the users of the town. An exercise in both seeking general views and consulting on proposals is valuable to a longer term positive partnership. A User Survey is a project which can be relatively easily implemented through the Town Centre Manager. In Kingston such a survey was developed in month two of the contract period and implemented through businesses and their customers in months three and four. Similarly, having collected views on town centre matters, proposals in the form of a draft business plan were drawn up in Kingston and presented in organised public settings for consultation. The level of local commitment in Frome, most if not all those involved in the town actually live there as well, meant that consultation was on a considerably more specific level. In particular a Local Agenda 21 project, the Map of Frome, was used to encourage anyone to make their views known about the town by way of marking a flag on a map. This became an extremely valuable way of achieving emotive responses, albeit in some cases biased by respondents following a visible radical comment made earlier on the map.

Step Three – Formulating the Vision

Formulating a consensus vision for the future is a complex process and yet crucial to the success of any particular initiative. In Frome the view of many locally was one of disappointment that the town had appeared to fail against its neighbouring towns and ultimately failed against its proud history. The emotive response to this was to strive to 'return' Frome to its former glory. Inevitably, given the changing nature of town centres and understanding the future trends both locally and nationally, this was not achievable. As stated earlier in this chapter, with 30% of retail turnover currently being accounted for in out-of-town centres, with two high street banks closing per week, and with the nature of town centres changing such that A1 uses are increasingly being lost to A3, to name just a few trends, a return to the 1950s is not possible. The vision for Frome, as with many smaller towns, particularly those with strength of character, must be seen as one of differentiation as opposed to direct competition. Frome cannot begin to compete directly with Trowbridge, it is a no longer a level playing field, and not least the two towns share largely the same mobile catchment. The challenge for Frome is ultimately coping with a strategy that aims to contract the retail provision and enhance the unique features and the local distinctiveness, exploit the positive local community approach, consider other complementary uses particularly residential, and encourage a small and manageable quality environment as opposed to the current sprawling of vacant and derelict buildings with outmoded uses.

The challenge for Kingston in terms of a vision is quite different to the circumstances in Frome. The greatest current challenge to Kingston is overcoming complacency. The town centre is currently extremely successful and thriving, the view inevitably therefore is that no threats exist and no radical action is needed. The true facts are that changes are occurring so rapidly that Kingston could find itself in a position of decline much sooner that it expects if care is not taken to position itself correctly in the future market place. Consumers are increasingly demanding more and making harsh comparisons, particularly as mobility becomes more widespread. Clean, safe, attractive and accessible environments are expected.

Step Four – Establishing a Commitment to Funding

Step four represents the phase where visions are turned into reality. As discussed later in the chapter, the funding of town centre improvements is currently unreliable and unrepresentative. This issue will be debated in greater depth later, but it suffices to say at this stage that it is essential that financial contributions to the town centre are viewed as investment not expenditure. This said, the matter of complacency has implications on the level of funding achievable to deliver meaningful results. Ironically, the larger the problem and therefore the lower the vitality, the easier it becomes to encourage commitment to funds and support particularly from the public sector where it is seen as a political priority. Support to Town Centre Management is not only financial, however, and may come in other forms. To cite an example in Kingston, a secondee from Marks & Spencer was used specifically on a major Customer Care project. Support in kind was more forthcoming in Frome largely due to the sense of urgency with which people approached the problem of decline. Examples of such projects include accommodation, and facilities for the Town Centre Officer were provided by Boots The Chemist, design and promotional skills of a small number of key small businesses in the town were utilised free of charge for the good of the town, and a local printer was used to produce quality colour productions at little or no cost.

STEP FIVE – PRODUCTION OF A BUSINESS PLAN

It is an established procedure that a strategy in the form of a Business Plan is produced to set out the objectives of the town centre and Town Centre Management initiative; nevertheless the style and format of such a document varies according to the location and the desired target audience. The ultimate objective of a plan for Frome was consensus building, and as such the document was in the form of a brief manageable report covering the key target areas in the short-term and the long-term visions. In contrast, Kingston has a professionally produced 16 page full colour three-year strategic Business Plan together with a full colour annual Action Plan. The documents are making a very positive statement about the professional long-term approach being adopted, and ultimately seek to source further funding (see Box 1).

Box 1 *A sample business plan*

The contents and style of a Business Plan can depend on the particular focus within an area and indeed the maturity of the initiative. However, there are many common ingredients which are outlined below using the Kingston upon Thames example.

Business Plan
The Business Plan is a three-year strategic document which deals with the town centre strategy and vision for the three-year contract period. The strategy is divided into eight strategic objectives as follows:

Objective One – Access
To improve accessibility to, and within, the town centre. Particular emphasis will be given to the needs of public transport users, the management of private transport, pedestrians, cyclists and those with disabilities.

Objective Two – Business Viability and Innovation
To maintain Kingston's competitive edge by providing the conditions which enable town centre businesses to thrive and prosper and by developing innovative services to improve customer care.

Objective Three – Communication and Consultation
To maintain and improve communication between interested parties in the town centre and visitors to the town centre, and to inform and encourage involvement in Town Centre Management through various forms of consultation.

Objective Four – Environment
To create and maintain a clean and attractive environment in the town centre and to develop and enhance Kingston's unique character and riverside setting.

Objective Five – Investment
To maintain and improve the economic development of the town centre and to foster partnership working between public and private agencies in order to attract continued investment

Objective Six – Marketing and Promotion
To market and promote Kingston as a regional centre for shopping, leisure and entertainment, education and business.

Objective Seven – Security and Safety
To create and maintain a safe environment in the town centre both day and night.

Objective Eight – Monitoring
To monitor and report upon the performance of Kingston town centre and the Town Centre Management initiative.

Step Six – Monitoring

Town centres have traditionally been very poorly monitored. Some enlightened companies have undertaken specific exercises for their own purposes, but the town has not been viewed in totality. A major part of any Town Centre Management initiative is to create a robust monitoring and review procedure. Key performance indicators which can be used for this purpose include footfall figures, rental levels, turnover figures, vacancies and indeed mix of shops with particular attention to the number of discount and charity shops. A Town Centre Manager is well placed to co-ordinate this effort, as much of this information is already available within a town albeit concealed and disparate in nature.

TOWN CENTRE MANAGEMENT – FUTURE SCOPE

During the run-up to the general election of May 1997, the Labour Party produced a 'Ten Point Charter for Better Towns and Cities' as follows:

- Establish Civic Forums as partnerships between the local authority, public, private and community sectors to seek Civic Grants.
- Target dedicated public funds and specific grants for town centre improvement initiatives.
- Introduce stronger powers of land assembly for partnership organisations.
- Stimulate home building and develop creative ways of encouraging residents back into town and city centres – to help stimulate 24 hour cities.
- Promote the greater use of public transport – a greater integration of national retail and transport planning guidance.
- Strengthen the identity of individual shopping centres and key shopping streets with a view to enhancing the role of the town centre as the hub of economic and social life.
- Promote employment opportunities and endeavour to raise the status, conditions, professional training and skills of the people who work on the service frontline.
- Create greener towns and cities by revitalising and extending urban parks, commons and open spaces, and preventing the erosion of greenfield sites.
- Pay greater attention to both crime prevention and crime detection, including greater use of CCTV, better lighting and closer co-ordination between the police, local businesses and the public.
- Employ a manager for every town centre and provide support for local, regional and national co-ordination of town centre management, thereby bringing new life and hope to all our urban centres.

Many of the initiatives within this Charter are already being considered in towns and cities throughout the UK and as such are being incorporated as objectives within Town Centre Management Business and Action Plans. The key feature of concern within Town Centre Management which the Charter does not explicitly deal with is the funding of initiatives, and in particular the security of long-term funding.

Drawing from the recent publication by URBED for the ATCM (1997), *Town Centre Partnerships. A Survey of Good Practice and Report of an Action Research Project*, a number of key issues are being debated which could assist in the longer term resourcing of Town Centre Management initiatives. From the research study it was found that less than half of town centres have their own budgets, and the majority of these depend on raising contributions from the private sector. The main private sponsors of town centres, namely a few major retailers and one or two landowners, are keen to see a more robust funding mechanism which eliminates or at least reduces the need for the constant 'begging bowl' principle and in addition tackles the problem of 'free riders' currently widespread in town centres.

A number of possible options are being investigated, with some key research work being undertaken on the American Business Improvement District concept and the adaptation of this to a possible UK Town Improvement Zone (TIZ), and additionally the scope for a review of the current system of Business Rates and local authority finance.

BUSINESS IMPROVEMENT DISTRICTS

Business Improvement Districts (BIDs) have been set up in cities throughout the US and there are now well over 1000 examples in the US and Canada. They are created under state or city legislation to provide additional public services in retail or commercial districts, funded by a levy on property owners. In general they have been created in neighbourhoods that have suffered decline or risk doing so. BIDs are a vehicle by which property owners can invest in local improvements for long-term commercial gain. The BID structure allows private sector funds to be raised for public services to which all those who use the district have access. Nevertheless, despite the public nature of BID services, property owners benefit most as the services contribute directly to the value of their asset. As such, the private investment in public services is justified by the return it provides to property owners. There are two key characteristics which are central to the operation of the BID – the compulsory levy, and the voting rights. The principle of a compulsory levy (typically 5%) ensures that there is no 'free rider' element; that is, if payments were on a voluntary basis then each property owner would have an incentive not to contribute to the scheme and still derive benefit from the services provided. The levy is usually based upon the Rateable Value, although it may be set to ensure a maximum level for smaller businesses. In respect of the voting rights, all property owners have a vote in the management of the BID and the services it provides, usually requiring two-thirds support and becoming mandatory for a five-year period. As a private, not for profit organisation, BID members elect members of the board which holds the officers of the BID accountable.

With respect to the focus of the BID, given the long-term decline of public services such as street cleaning and maintenance and the increased fear of crime in most major US cities, it is not surprising that most BIDs focus their services around the concept of 'clean and safe'. Additionally, tackling the symptoms of dirty streets and the fear of crime within a limited geographical area readily lends itself to simple direct action at the local level. However, only about 80% of expenditure is now being spent on this particular theme, and as BIDs develop they are moving into promotional and business development programmes (Travers and Weimar, 1996).

TOWN IMPROVEMENT ZONES

In terms of the applicability of such an approach to the UK scenario, recent research (URBED, 1997) has considered the scope for the principle of a Town Improvement Zone (TIZ). It is now largely recognised that at present the system of funding town centres is both ineffective and unfair. Hence there is a strong case for a mechanism that enables all those who benefit from or with a stake in the town to contribute. Nevertheless this contribution needs to be seen as a charge akin to the service charge principle in shopping centres, not an additional tax over and above that of the current Business Rate. Current proposals on this matter suggest a designated area (typically part of a town centre in need of investment) which is managed by a limited company, or a Town Trust. The expenditure should be based on an agreed Business Plan deliverable in a five- to seven-year period and should be funded through a public/private partnership. A number of pilot studies are planned in order that the proposals can be tested out before legislation is enacted.

REVIEW OF THE CURRENT BUSINESS RATE STRUCTURE

The URBED (1997) study reported that over many years the amounts invested by local government in general have fallen. An earlier study had found that capital expenditure by local government as a proportion of national domestic expenditure fell from around 3.5% in the period between 1973 and 1976 to around 1% in the period from 1989 to 1992. One result of these successive cut-backs is that many authorities have little left over from running basic services to spend on lasting improvements. Despite the general support for the concept of a Uniform Busines Rate, which has the benefit of being predictable, businesses do complain about paying high levels of business rates without having any control over how the money is spent. Central government currently receives the Business Rate, and local authorities only act as the collectors. This concept inevitably creates confusion and conflict between the businesses and the local authority. Businesses see their local authority as the tax collector and therefore resent the poor value they receive in return. These two parties being working together for the good of the town, but there is no real incentive for local authorities to prioritise their resources towards town centres.

There is no doubt that the current situation is damaging to long-term sustainability both in terms of positive partnership working and ultimately in the longer term investment in town centres. URBED's study (1997) sets out a list of possible reforms for consideration as follows.

- Reducing the level of rates paid by small businesses through a lower rate per pound on smaller properties (as suggested in the RICS Bayliss Committee

Report, 1995) or through changes in the valuation process to ensure that rateable values reflect changing trading conditions and property values.

- Enabling local authorities to vary the rate per pound within limits of say, plus or minus 10%, possibly reflecting the capacity to pay (as with the 'Hardship' provision). This could perhaps be compensated for through a charge on car parking in out-of-town locations, as well as in town.
- Distinguishing between the property tax element, which goes to the government for redistribution, and the local service element, which should be related to the amount spent by the local authority on the town centre.
- Setting up arrangements whereby funds raised from the rates are available to match business contributions to a Town Improvement Zone.
- Implementing other proposals of the Bayliss Report, such as more frequent revaluations and a review of Empty Property Rates, and the need for local authorities to account for expenditures funded through rates.
- Reviewing the way the Standard Spending Assessment redistributes funds, for example by taking account of commercial floor space in town centres, and the costs of maintenance and security.
- Considering ways of reducing the overall level of commercial rates, particularly in areas that are economically disadvantaged, perhaps by bringing the level more into line with continental practice and raising business taxes in other ways, such as local taxes on payroll or VAT.
- Enabling supplementary levies on businesses to be used to fund higher standards of service, and to underpin the raising of capital through bonds.

CONCLUSION

Town Centre Management should be seen as a flexible framework to deal with the management of change in town centres. In some cases, change may mean substantial development and expansion; however, in others this may mean contraction of the traditional A1 retail uses and support for other uses such as A3 food and leisure uses or, indeed, residential. No one model exists in order to achieve this, and it is critical that each locality considers the reasons for establishing a partnership and the particular style based on local knowledge and implementation. A structure that may be suitable for a large urban centre is unlikely to be appropriate for a small rural town or a multi-centred district. A number of clear messages do prevail, irrespective of location. A partnership approach is vital with all key players signing up to the principle. This partnership must then develop a shared vision with which all partners feel some degree of ownership. However, added to this vision must be a clear focused strategy for action which is realistic, achievable and appropriate to the town centre in question.

Nevertheless arguably the key success for Town Centre Management to date has been the ability to sharpen the 'focus' on town centres, and encourage a holistic and committed approach to the town centre. This aspect had been lacking for many years and the results of this absence were very clear. Town Centre Management is only one mechanism, however, and in many cases is still truly only one committed individual. A major challenge to Town Centre Managers is to obtain committment from others to the principle of a shared vision and a co-ordinated approach. However, this is extremely complex to achieve and depends on good influencing skills and diplomacy to make things happen in partnership. Planners inevitably will find themselves somewhere within this partnership and will require a broad and clear understanding of their town centre in order to make a positive input. Many examples can be cited of days past, referred to earlier in the section on Town Centre Management in Practice, when problems have occurred or been created by a lack of cohesion, particularly between council departments and a generally fragmented approach. There is still a long way to go before the power and influence is there to convince the silent masses within a town centre to take part in some way, and apart from time and maturity perhaps the biggest stumbling block at this stage is the lack of a robust funding mechanism.

REFERENCES

Boots The Chemist (1997b) *Town Centre Facts and Statistics*, Boots The Chemist, Nottingham.

Department of the Environment (1996) PPG6, *Town Centres and Retail Development*, HMSO, London.

Department of the Environment (1997) PPG1, *General Policy and Principles*, HMSO, London.

Healey & Baker (1996) *A Review of Sunday Trading Patterns*, Healey & Baker, London.

Kingston Town Centre Management (1997a) *Business Plan 1997–99*, Kingston Town Centre Management, Kingston upon Thames.

Kingston Town Centre Management (1997b) *Action Plan 1997/98*, Kingston Town Centre Management, Kingston upon Thames.

Mendip District Council (1995) *Frome Town Centre Action Plan 1995/96*, Mendip District Council, Shepton Mallet.

Mendip District Council (1996) *Frome Town Centre Action Plan 1996/97*, Mendip District Council, Shepton Mallet.

RICS (1995) *Improving the Rating System – The Bayliss Report*, Royal Institution of Chartered Surveyors, London.

Travers, T. and Weimar, J. (1996) *Business Improvement Districts. New York and London*, LSE, Corporation of London, London.

URBED (1997) *Town Centre Partnerships. A Survey of Good Practice and Report of an Action Research Project*, HMSO, London.

CHAPTER 11

THE BUILT ENVIRONMENT AND DESIGN

Marilyn Higgins and Andy Karski

INTRODUCTION

The physical form and layout of our surroundings have a significant impact on people's everyday experience and quality of life. It is what most people see and understand about planning and planners. Although planners can have a great influence on the design of our environment, it is one area where planners need to work with a wide range of other professionals, organisations and the public to achieve success.

The purpose of this chapter is to explore the main issues relating to the role of design in planning practice. Design is becoming an increasingly topical issue at both national and local levels, having been left out in the cold for a number of years during the 1970s and 1980s. It has been receiving more attention in planning education, policy and practice during the 1990s.

The role of design within planning has gone through interesting historical changes and has at times been the subject of bitter controversy. It is a complex area and there are no easy answers or straightforward recipes. There are few absolute rights and wrongs. This chapter tries to help the reader's understanding of the role that design plays within the planning process in influencing results on the ground.

The next section explores the *meaning of urban design* in terms of process and product and sets its *context within the planning profession*. The following section discusses *design policy and tools* used at both a national and local level. Recent central government initiatives are explained and good practice in development plan policies, site-specific briefs and design guides discussed. The chapter then identifies key players within the process and sets out the roles of some *relevant organisations*. Examples of *positive initiatives* being undertaken by these agencies are given. The next section discusses one specialist area of particular importance, *sustainability*. We then use two case studies to illustrate many of the points made in the chapter. The final section provides an *evaluation* of the current place of design within planning, drawing conclusions based on earlier sections. It proposes likely future directions regarding priorities and practice within the profession.

Conservation issues are important in considering urban design in a planning context and they are discussed in Chapter 4 on Development Control.

THE MEANING OF URBAN DESIGN AND ITS CONTEXT WITHIN THE PLANNING PROFESSION

MEANING OF URBAN DESIGN

Urban design is a term that has come into increasing use. The term is notoriously difficult to pin down and often means different things to different people, although it always brings together many things. It is an analysis of the three-dimensional *relationships* between all the different elements within the environment, including buildings and the spaces between them, movement patterns, structures and landscape (Figure 1). It is strongly related to social, economic and cultural influences and cannot be separated from use and activity, since the 'people' element is central to the whole concept. All these elements could be said to make up the *character* of a place. However, the *process* is as much part of urban design as the *product*, and there is a close relationship between the two. Creating high quality environments in the public realm is as important as after-care and long-term management considerations. Views of the community, users and clients are important in informing this process from early stages. Different people have different design needs, and not everyone shares the same experience. Consultation can help ensure that the needs of people generally not in positions of power are taken into account, for example disabled people, ethnic minorities, women and children (see Chapter 15 on Participation and Equal Opportunities).

The *process* of urban design includes the notion of *control*, for example over planning applications, but it is helpful to think of it also as *encouragement*, for example in the awarding of prizes, the publicising of successful schemes and the way planning policies are written. Good design can also equate with good economics, in both the short and long term.

Although visual appearance lies at the heart of the concept, the other senses of touch, hearing, smell and sometimes even taste are also important in defining the character of places. Urban design also has to do with people's sense of well-being, and should strive for their comfort, security, health and pleasure. In sum, urban design has to do with a *sense of place*.

According to the Urban Design Group

> Successful urban design nurtures the essence of the places where people live and work and it creates places that people can enjoy and which refresh the spirit. Urban design is concerned both with processes and the three-dimensional products of change, at scales from a group of buildings to a city centre or a metropolitan area (Urban Design Group, 1996, p. 38).

Perhaps most importantly, the concept of design needs to be considered in a wide sense to deepen understanding of it. Design issues are relevant at many different spatial scales. They can be important in making judgements about the strategic layout of cities, the relationships between groups of buildings and spaces and the detailed design of individual buildings. Design considerations should be

Figure 1 *Covent Garden, London. Urban design involves relationships between people and all the different physical elements within the environment and can be used to create lively places where people want to come*

incorporated within the early stages of the planning and development process and not be seen as an after-thought.

Early consideration also applies to landscape issues. Landscape, like urban design, also has a very wide meaning and can cover *soft* landscape (trees, shrubs, anything that grows) and *hard* landscape (paving, seats, litter bins, lighting columns, signs, other street furniture) (Figure 2). Landscape can play many functional roles and can contribute to sustainability goals, as we shall see later in the chapter.

'Urban' should not be seen as too confining. By definition, planners are normally dealing with the created or built environment, in terms of design. Design issues are of undoubted significance in the countryside and there has been increased attention to this area recently. The look of new roads and bridges, the siting of development and village expansion patterns are all things that require an understanding of design issues. How the built environment impacts on and integrates with the natural environment is of crucial importance and design judgements have a role to play in determining the acceptability of proposed development.

CONTEXT WITHIN THE PLANNING PROFESSION

The role of design within the planning profession has gone through various cycles since the Second World War. There are relationships between its role in central government policy, planning education and practice.

Figure 2 *Glasgow Cathedral Precinct. An appropriate setting for this important building: simple, yet effective, use of hard and soft landscaping*

The post-war planning system largely addressed physical problems of urban areas. Most people who became planners in the 1940s, 1950s and early 1960s were architects or engineers. This was the era of grand masterplans, new towns, major infrastructure projects, modern architecture and comprehensive redevelopment. Architectural determinism (the idea that physical surroundings can be a pivotal influence in people's experience of life) was accorded considerable status.

A reaction against all of these things followed in the late 1960s, with a growing recognition of the importance of the social sciences and urban management. There was a growing awareness of economics, sociology and politics that led to an increase in social scientists entering the profession, influencing the content of planning courses in the 1970s. During this period, design was not a prominent issue in planning practice and most planners did not possess the relevant skills and awareness. This relegation of design was aggravated by the general election in 1979, when the Conservative government initiated a *laissez-faire* approach to planning generally, which included design issues.

The 1990s have finally seen a renewed interest in urban design, as the pendulum swings the other way. The *laissez-faire* approach is seen to have produced undistinguished environments. There is a growing recognition that planning practice should integrate the complexities of environmental, social and economic considerations in a collaborative way and not swing between polarities. This has been encouraged by a recognition that good design can improve the quality of people's lives. There are obvious links with environmental sustainability. Growing globalisation and competitiveness have meant that the quality of places is receiving increased attention in an attempt to achieve economic advantage. There are many more examples of urban design being an influence in planning practice, as we shall see in the following sections.

Summary

Urban design is the term generally applied to design considerations within the planning profession. Design issues need to be seen in their widest sense, at different spatial scales, incorporating the relationships between activities, movement and the three-dimensional form of places. It is a process as well as a product and should involve the wider community to ensure success. Planners have a role in encouraging good design as well as rejecting poor design.

There has been a recent resurgence of interest in urban design, partly as a reaction to undistinguished environments but also linking with concerns about sustainable environments.

Design Policy and Tools for Implementation

National Policy

Central government policy can be very influential in determining what happens on the ground. Government policy and guidance are especially important because the British planning system is 'discretionary', rather than being based on statutory codes or ordinances as in some other countries. In the case of design, which is not a clear-cut arithmetic exercise, planners often must be able to apply informed judgement in making and justifying decisions about the quality of proposed development.

There are long-running debates about planners having the power to reject architects' designs and the extent to which design is an 'aesthetic' matter. John Punter has written extensively on aesthetic or design control (see Punter, 1986–7 and 1994, for example). He argues that we are now trying to get away from seeing aesthetics as a narrow study of beauty and instead are relating good design to practical, everyday issues as well. Broadening concepts of good design to include wider environmental and human issues along with the more architectural ones gives planners a clear reason for being involved in design assessment (Punter and Carmona, 1997, pp. 69–70 and 200). It is possible to develop criteria to be applied when assessing design issues. Well-considered application of these criteria clearly related to the *context* of the area helps planners make informed judgements about the design of development proposals. This does not mean that all new development should ape its neighbours. Good modern design can result from a thorough analysis of context and be most appropriate, even though it breaks with traditional style.

Government policy over the last 20 years echoes these debates. When the Conservative government came to power in 1979, they adopted a hands-off approach to design issues and left it up to the 'market' and project architects. This was exemplified in DoE Circular 22/80 *Development Control – Policy and Practice*:

> Planning authorities should recognise that aesthetics is an extremely subjective matter. . . . This is especially important where a building has been designed by an architect for a particular site. . . . Control of external appearance should only be exercised where there is a fully justified reason for doing so . . . (DoE, 1980).

The Circular encouraged limiting design control to 'environmentally sensitive areas, such as national parks, areas of outstanding natural beauty and Conservation Areas' and discouraged intervention in design detail elsewhere, unless there were exceptional circumstances. Too often, using the word 'subjective' has deliberately discouraged discussion and has been used to say 'hands off' to planners.

The 1990s, however, have seen a steady shift towards planners having more control over design, starting in 1990 with the white paper *This Common Inheritance* (DoE, 1990). This accepted that many aspects of design are legitimate concerns of the planning system. A watershed occurred in 1992 with PPG1 *General Policy and Principles*. 'Annex A: Design Considerations' stated, 'The appearance of proposed development and its relationship to its surroundings are material considerations' (DoE, 1992a). For the first time, design was explicitly recognised as a 'material consideration', which is all-important in development control terms. In other words, design concerns carry sufficient weight to be legitimately used to refuse planning applications. Although there was still an emphasis on sensitive areas and the role of designers, recognition of the importance of the wider setting was clearly stated. Development plans and planning guidance were identified as providing guidelines about 'broad matters of scale, density, height, massing, layout, landscape and access, while avoiding excessive prescription and detail'. In Scotland, NPPG1 *The Planning System*, published in 1994, contained similar sentiments (Scottish Office Environment Department, 1994a).

Although PPG1 was a step forward, there were calls for government guidance that went even further. John Gummer, the Secretary of State for the Environment from 1993 to 1997, personally championed the cause of good design. The DoE (1994a) published *Quality in Town and Country: A Discussion Document*. It encouraged *quality* in design, mixed uses, lively town centres, sustainability, user-friendly transport, local distinctiveness and inter-disciplinary working (Figure 3). In short, it put urban design on the map. It also made the point that quality pays and is good economics, emphasising long-term issues of maintenance, adaptability and longevity.

Quality in Town and Country was closely followed by another initiative in 1995, *Quality in Town and Country: Urban Design Campaign* (DoE, 1995), seeking to encourage broad debate about urban design matters. The government

Figure 3 *Princes Square, Glasgow. The government is encouraging mixed uses and lively town centres, emphasising local distinctiveness*

invited local teams to prepare a site development brief and generate design solutions, involving the public during the process. Twenty-one schemes were chosen from the 106 submitted and received government funds averaging £30 000. Case Study 2 describes one of the schemes, in Wimbledon town centre.

Revisions to PPG1 in 1997 further strengthened the role of urban design, identifying sustainable development, mixed use and design as themes underpinning the government's approach to the planning system. By encouraging good design 'everywhere', guidance began to shift away from the previous 'two-tier' approach of thinking that design is important only in sensitive locations such as Conservation Areas. The revised PPG1 stresses the importance of the local context and movement and activity patterns. It identifies scale, density, massing, height, landscape, layout and access as issues to be carefully considered in attempting to achieve quality solutions, as well as a collaborative design process involving various parties. It still cautions against over-prescriptiveness and detail, but drops previous exhortations about the 'subjectiveness' of design. In 1999, the Urban Task Force chaired by Lord Rogers produced a major report criticising design standards and professional skills levels. Ensuing debates have highlighted the crucial role that design can play in urban regeneration initiatives (Urban Task Force, 1999).

A number of other government documents mention design. For example, DoE Circular 5/94 *Planning out Crime* (DoE, 1994b) and Scottish Office PAN 46 *Planning for Crime Prevention* (Scottish Office Environment Department, 1994b) discuss design issues in relation to layout, landscaping, lighting, access, parking, etc. PPG 3 and NPPG 3 in Scotland about *Housing* both discuss design issues, emphasising the need to ensure quality, including energy efficiency and relationship to the surroundings (DoE, 1992b; Scottish Office Environment Department, 1996). The Scottish Office has been particularly active in producing guidance about design in the countryside. They produced PAN 36: *The Siting and Design of New Housing in the Countryside* (Scottish Office Environment Department, 1991) which was followed by PAN 44: *Fitting New Housing Development into the Landscape* (Scottish Office Environment Department, 1994c). These documents emphasised such aspects as the importance of correct siting in relation to the surroundings, landscape setting, layout, materials and energy efficiency.

LOCAL POLICY AND DESIGN TOOLS

Development Plan Policies

The increasing recognition of design dimensions at central government level has thrown a spotlight on the policy aspects as expressed in development plans. PPG1 attempts to build in more *objectivity* as opposed to *subjectivity* in the design process and encourages the inclusion of relevant development plan policies based on area appraisals defining local distinctiveness. Underlying this is the idea that carefully thought out and clearly worded policies can help guide applicants for planning permission and set out the authority's policy framework, thereby promoting greater certainty, speed and efficiency.

It is worth emphasising how important it is for planners to carry out a proper analysis of the character of individual places. Every place and every site is unique, just as every person is unique, with his or her own distinctive marks. Given the way that the property market functions, there is a tendency for large volume housebuilders and national retail chains, for example, to build similar developments up and down the length of Britain. Planners need to make continual judgements about the appropriateness of proposed development and these judgements are best made if there is a systematic analysis of the 'sense of place' against which proposals are judged.

Any concept of 'good' design that is not significantly based on contextual issues is undoubtedly flawed. This is not to say that an emphasis on context means that new buildings need to slavishly mock their surroundings in terms of such elements as height, features and materials (Figure 4). Planners have been criticised for such simplistic notions. Good new buildings, spaces and structures can take clues from their surroundings but still be expressed in a modern idiom (Figure 5). Too often unhelpful arguments about architectural style dominate design debates. Style in itself does not matter as much as how new design is executed. What is appropriate for one location is not for another.

John Punter and Matthew Carmona have written a comprehensive book about design, particularly in relation to development plan policies, which is based on

Figure 4 Crowne Plaza Hotel, Edinburgh. The safe approach is a new hotel on the Royal Mile built to ape its neighbours

Figure 5 Museum of Scotland, Edinburgh. This new museum in the centre of Edinburgh in an unashamedly modern building, borrowing historic references from its surroundings, that makes a lively contribution to the townscape

research they carried out for the Department of the Environment (see Punter and Carmona, 1997). This is a very good source for those seeking more information about the role of design in planning policy and gives examples of good practice. One of their over-arching conclusions is that many areas lack effective design policies at both strategic and local development plan levels. Many plans contain vague statements about 'good quality design' which are toothless because they are not backed up with proper analyses or effective assessment criteria. Existing policies tend to be largely about physical appearance and ignore the wider aspects of urban design as defined in the previous section, including the functional, social and ecological aspects.

Strategic Policies

Because of their strategic nature, you would not expect structure plans or Part Is of Unitary Development Plans to contain detailed design guidance (see Chapter 3). However, especially with the increased emphasis on the importance of development plans since 1991, it is crucial to develop coherent policy frameworks about strategic design to guide local policy and action.

Examples of how this strategic scale of development plan might take design into account are:

- Broad Conservation Area or Listed Buildings issues: the Lothian Structure Plan 1997 emphasises the strategic importance of Edinburgh's historic core, including for tourism.
- Urban regeneration strategies: Birmingham has developed policies based on a study of its various urban quarters, each with its distinctive urban design characteristics and needs; the city has comprehensively improved public activities in the city centre, linking them with a strong pedestrian network and public open spaces.
- Important long views: successive strategic plans for London have safeguarded, for example, views of St Paul's Cathedral and Parliament from important vantage points by prohibiting building above a certain height inside specific cones of vision (Figure 6).
- High buildings: for some years, development plans for parts of London and Edinburgh have had policies defining where high buildings are appropriate and design considerations that need to be borne in mind.
- City centre improvements: the Strathclyde Structure Plan policies aim to stimulate interest and focus development activity on existing retail centres and away from edge-of-town greenfield development. Consultants have developed the Glasgow City Centre Public Realm strategy, already partially implemented (Figure 7), which aims to keep and attract lively uses and create pleasant pedestrian spaces (Gillespie's, 1995). It is a good example of strategic urban design worked through in detail.

Figure 6 *London. Strategic planning policies safeguard views of St Paul's Cathedral and Parliament from important vantage points*

Figure 7 *Outside the Italian Centre, Glasgow. Glasgow's Public Realm Strategy has created lively pedestrian spaces*

Local Plan Policies

Given that successful design happens on a site-specific basis, local plan policies assume great importance. Local plans have not had a strong tradition of effective, detailed design policies. A local plan can never be detailed enough to be specific about all sites within its boundaries and it is difficult to strike the right balance when choosing words to effectively guide development within a whole area while not being overly prescriptive in a blanket fashion. Too often policies have been too bland and not specific enough to be helpful to the planning application process.

Punter and Carmona argue for a hierarchical approach to design policies. Broad design objectives in line with the overall aims of the plan can be elaborated upon with more specific urban design principles and processes, criteria and standards, which in turn can provide the basis for more detailed supplementary design guidance. Some authorities divide local plan districts into smaller areas, each the subject of character appraisal and more detailed design policy. Birmingham's Urban Quarter strategy is based on urban design analyses of local areas, taking account of land uses and activities as well as physical aspects like topography and physical linkages (City of Birmingham, 1990).

It is important to be as explicit as possible in developing criteria and standards to elaborate a design strategy for an area as encouragement to 'good design'. The DoE document *Development Plans: A Good Practice Guide* (DoE, 1992c) argues for a topic-oriented structure for plans, with design treated in a discrete chapter, rather than dispersed throughout others. Illustrations can be useful in helping to explain design concepts and increase understanding.

Site Briefs and Design Guides

One of the most effective and detailed ways of guiding future development proposals for any given site is to prepare a brief specifically for it. Many planning authorities also prepare design guides covering various topics such as crime prevention, shopfronts, house extensions, child-care facilities and accessibility issues. These design guides cover the local authority area or sub-areas in a more blanket fashion than site-specific briefs.

While not having the same weight as statutory development plan policies and proposals, site briefs and design guides come under the category of 'supplementary planning guidance'. Government advice is that they should be rooted in development plan policy; greater weight is attached if they have gone through a consultation process and been formally adopted by a Council committee (DoE, 1997).

Authorities vary in their use of briefs, according to their priorities and local circumstances. There is a danger that in a time of declining resources, non-statutory activities such as this may suffer as staff are diverted to development control and development plan work. The nature of site-specific development briefs varies and they are referred to under several different names. 'Planning briefs' are usually the most general, covering aspects such as size, ownership, physical condition of buildings or land, land uses, planning policy and history, access, services, landscape and nature conservation. 'Developers' briefs' often provide similar information but go deeper into the financial and land management aspects. 'Design briefs' are the most specific on urban design issues. Most briefs deal with a level of detail relevant to planning issues when it comes to design: land uses, height, bulk, materials, access, parking, circulation, landscape framework, layout and building lines. The Royal Town Planning Institute (RTPI) published a Practice Advice Note on *Development Briefs* which gives guidance on their content (RTPI, 1990).

Some of the most difficult aspects of briefs are judgements about how prescriptively they should be written and how much flexibility to allow. Arguments can revolve around what aspects of local tradition should be promoted in new buildings, as opposed to allowing more freedom to express modern design.

Good practice is to include relevant information about the wider context of the area as well as issues about the site itself. It is important that briefs are kept up-to-date if they are to remain meaningful. Good graphic material can help provide clarity and enliven the document. Briefs usually include elements of both control and encouragement and can serve a promotional purpose; getting the balance right between being visionary and realistic is important. Careful choice of words is critical for clarity. Constraints and opportunities alike should be highlighted.

Edinburgh City Council has incorporated 'thumbnail briefs' for certain 'major development opportunity' sites within their Central Area Local Plan (City of Edinburgh Council, 1997). While not as detailed as a proper development brief, the statutory force of the Plan gives weight to 13 sites, which includes written material and diagrammatic site plans covering such items as pedestrian, cycle and vehicular connections and access; preferred land uses; Listed Building and Conservation Area issues; and strategic landscape framework.

Regarding more general design guides, most authorities have traditionally produced guidance about such topics as shopfronts and house extensions. Subjects vary according to the location; recent emphasis has been on improving the quality of design of new housing, crime prevention through design, energy efficiency in the layout and design of new development, barrier-free design allowing accessibility and child care facilities. Leicester City Council has produced *Design Notes for Major Developments* which advises on provisions for children and their carers (Leicester City Council, undated). Birmingham City Council has produced *Designing for Parent and Child Guidance Notes* and a *Car Park Design Guide* after consulting women during their preparation (Birmingham City Council, 1992, 1995).

A design guide for buildings was published in 1998 for the whole of the Chiltern hills area. What makes it unusual is that it spans all 13 planning authorities covering the Chilterns Area of Outstanding Natural Beauty. It was published by the Chilterns Conference, an advisory committee featuring representatives of local authorities, statutory agencies and voluntary groups, thereby also making it a good example of participative design guidance. This appears to be the first attempt in the UK to co-ordinate policy across such a wide area (Chilterns Conference, 1998).

Perhaps the best known area-wide design guide is the pioneering *A Design Guide for Residential Areas* (Essex County Council, 1973), which was updated in 1997. Drawing heavily on the 'townscape' principles of urban design, it was a reaction against quantitative standards and traditional highway standards and was an early attempt by a local authority to encourage good quality design respecting the character of the area. Its emphasis on context led to neo-vernacular styles, which were often unthinkingly replicated in other parts of the country (Punter and Carmona, 1997, p. 23). Interestingly, the new guide for Essex (Essex County Council, 1997), produced 25 years after its predecessor, is in line with 'The Quality Initiative' and sustainable principles, encouraging crime prevention, access for disabled, car-free zones, traffic calming, mixed uses, higher densities and flexibility.

DEVELOPMENT CONTROL

Because all the above tools are limited in their detail, it is usually left to the development control system to implement design considerations. This is where most battles are fought before any development appears on the ground (or doesn't!). Planning officers must work closely with elected representatives, who make the final decisions, other Council departments, a wide range of consultees and members of the public. Coordination skills are crucial, as are basic urban design skills and knowledge (see Punter, 1993, for a helpful discussion on what design skills planners working in development control require). Negotiation skills are also important, as considerable discussion between the planning officer and the developer often goes on both before and after a planning application is submitted.

Traditionally, it has been rare that major planning application decisions are made on design grounds alone and there has been a fear of appeal consequences on a topic where many planners feel exposed and unskilled (see Parfect and Power, 1997, pp. 22–24). Usually design objections have been accompanied by other grounds as well. Significant decisions taken on design grounds still have a tendency to make the headlines of the weekly planning journal! However, this is likely to change, strengthened by recent government guidance that will take a while to percolate through to local development control decisions.

SUMMARY

In practice, there is a hierarchy of design policy and tools. Central government guidance about the place of design in the planning system has become stronger in the 1990s and it is now explicitly a consideration when determining planning applications. A number of government publications refer to design considerations, but there are calls for the government to be even stronger and bring design guidance together in one document. National policy sets the context for strategic and local development plan policies, which remain an under-developed aspect of policy in many local authorities. Site briefs and design guides have played a role for some time, and are increasingly taking on board quality, sustainability and equal opportunities concerns. Planners working in development control are at the sharp end of implementing policies in statutory development plans and in supplementary planning guidance.

Organisations and Positive Initiatives

To help understand how urban design works in practice, in what follows we discuss key stakeholders in the design process.

Local Authorities

Local authorities are the key guardians of environmental quality and urban design strategy. They have a role both in the *encouragement* of creative, high quality solutions, and in *control*, ensuring that only appropriate change is allowed. They, like central government, should be good models in regard to the location and design of their own premises (which is not always the case!).

Although the planning service is the key player, it is crucial that planners are co-ordinating with all other service functions that also have a role in environmental concerns, which are virtually all other local authority departments. Most, but not all, planning departments employ specialists: urban designers, architects, landscape architects or tree experts. Many large departments have a Conservation and/or Design section. However, as budgets have been squeezed and more services are being bought in from outside, more authorities are buying in expertise as necessary. Along with the increased emphasis on urban design generally, there has been an increase in the number of urban design consultancies. It is essential, however, that planning authorities retain in-house expertise in urban design to inform the range of their functions, including development control, policy formulation, area regeneration and project implementation. Over the past few years there has been a growing number of job advertisements for planners with urban design expertise.

Urban Design Group

The Urban Design Group was established in 1978 and was the first multi-disciplinary forum set up in the UK to promote high standards of urban design to both professionals and the public. Membership (currently around 1000) is by subscription and there are lower rates for students. The Group produces *Urban Design Quarterly*, organises seminars and lectures and has instigated various other initiatives, including a good place guide. Recognising the importance of *process*, the Urban Design Group pioneered Urban Design Action Teams (UDATs) in the UK, which are founded on principles of participative design. Teams of urban designers work with local communities to try to find site-specific solutions. The Group has been awarded a grant from the Department of the Environment to explore the contribution that public participation can make to urban design.

URBAN DESIGN ALLIANCE

The Urban Design Alliance is a new grouping that formed in 1997. Seven bodies have combined to give a stronger voice to urban design, emphasising a multi-disciplinary approach: the Royal Town Planning Institute, the Royal Institute of British Architects, the Landscape Institute, the Royal Institute of Chartered Surveyors, the Institute of Civil Engineers, the Urban Design Group, and the Civic Trust. They began by meeting with the Department for Environment, Transport and the Regions and the All Party Parliamentary Group on Architecture and Planning to show how urban design can be incorporated effectively into govern-ment policies and programmes. Four subcommittees have been looking at the areas where urban design can have significant impact: transport interchanges as lively, mixed activity nodes; housing, including the issue of density; education within the professions; and multi-disciplinary town/city audits making urban design central to the process. The Alliance hold conferences and seminars aimed at various audiences and intends to carry out an audit of urban design practice.

ROYAL FINE ART COMMISSION/COMMISSION FOR ARCHITECTURE AND THE BUILT ENVIRONMENT

The Royal Fine Art Commission was established in 1924 (1927 in Scotland) to advise public agencies on the design of major development proposals all over the country. Commissioners were appointed by the Queen and were therefore inde-pendent of government, giving them freedom to comment without constraint. In 1999, it was replaced by the new Commission for Architecture and the Built Environment with a wider remit working with government, the private sector and the public to promote good design in England.

In 1990, the English Commission produced *Planning for Beauty* (Royal Fine Art Commission, 1990), arguing for more weight to be given to design and public realm considerations. The Commission in Scotland, which remains unchanged, in pro-ducing reports to Parliament about casework, includes illustrations of what, in its opinion, are the most successful modern designs all over Scotland, thereby trying to encourage designers and planners to raise their sights in aiming for high quality solutions. The English Commission's book *What Makes a Good Building?* is well illustrated with examples of new developments that relate well to their context. Based on long experience of commenting on cases, the book defines the main design criteria as: order and unity; expression of function; integrity or honesty; the relationship between plan, section and elevations; detail; and integration with the surroundings considering appropriate siting, massing, scale, proportion, rhythm and materials (Royal Fine Art Commission, 1994, pp. 69–79).

COUNTRYSIDE AGENCY: COUNTRYSIDE DESIGN SUMMARIES AND VILLAGE DESIGN STATEMENTS

The Countryside Agency (previously Commission) has been involved in recent initiatives aimed at raising awareness and increasing the quality of design in villages and the countryside. These initiatives arose out of threats to the quality of the English countryside and fears that rural areas were beginning to look alike and lose their distinctive character. In 1993 the Commission produced *Design in the Countryside*, setting out its approach with the underlying principles that new development should be harmonious with its setting and respect and sustain local diversity and distinctiveness (Countryside Commission, 1993). Much of this work was carried out for the Commission by consultants BDOR Ltd. Experimental work took place in 1994 on the new techniques of Countryside Design Summaries and Village Design Statements, the results of which were published in *Design in the Countryside Experiments* (Countryside Commission, 1994).

Countryside Design Summaries are advocated as useful pieces of supplementary planning guidance, fleshing out development plan policies, promoted by local authorities (Countryside Commission, 1996a). Each individual Summary would analyse the relationship between the landscape, settlement pattern and buildings, identifying principles appropriate to the particular locality which can be applied to development proposals. The Commission's publication *Countryside Design Summaries* gives practical information to implement the scheme.

Village Design Statements, in contrast, are produced by local communities, although local authorities may later adopt them as supplementary planning guidance. Again, the emphasis is on analysing local character and sense of place in determining *how* development should take place. Character is defined at three levels: landscape setting, shape of the settlement, and nature of the buildings. Principles for managing change are drawn up based on distinctive local character. This applies to the form and pattern of the settlement as well as the design detail of individual buildings. The document *Village Design* (Countryside Commission, 1996b) is a practical guide. Parish Councils, elected Members and planning officials become involved with local residents and business interests and wide consultation is built in to reach consensus. The Countryside Commission guidance provides examples where good modern architecture is achieved that does not merely copy the past.

One early example of a Village Design Statement is for Cottenham, near Cambridge, where 400 new houses are proposed in the local plan. The Statement (Cottenham Village Design Group, 1994) was written by the village design group, supported by the officers and members of South Cambridgeshire District Council. It has since been formally adopted as supplementary planning guidance by the Council. The Statement covers modifying and creating buildings as well as dealing with street furniture, rights of way and local highway standards.

ENGLISH PARTNERSHIPS: TIME FOR DESIGN

In 1996, English Partnerships (the government's urban regeneration agency) published *Time for Design: Good Practice in Building, Landscape and Urban Design*. This publication emphasised the importance of good design promoted by a major non-government agency involved in commercial and housing developments throughout England. The initiative stresses the economic significance of good design in the long term. It recognises the importance of good designers who can respond to the unique opportunities provided by every site while responding to the needs of building users. It gives examples stressing the importance of public art, the needs of people with disabilities, landscaping, security and energy efficiency. In schemes for which English Partnerships is the major funder, they expect designers to be selected through a competitive process and offer guidance on how to do so.

English Partnerships build design objectives into the grant application process, to add weight to the whole issue (Figure 8). The existence of a design briefing document needs to be discussed, as well as the process whereby designers are to be appointed. Architectural and environmental goals explicitly appear on the application form. Proposals specifically need to be shown in relation to their surroundings, and energy efficiency and disability access need to be described.

CIVIC TRUST AND LOCAL AMENITY SOCIETIES

The Civic Trust, which is the equivalent of a national amenity association, was set up in 1957 as a response to placeless post-war development. Initially, it campaigned for protection for the whole of the street scene, which resulted in legislation establishing Conservation Areas. The Civic Trust is primarily a conservation body and is the umbrella organisation for a large network of local amenity societies, normally comprised of lay people who lobby for good conservation

Figure 8 *Oxo Tower, London. English Partnerships encourages good design and assesses this when considering grand aid; Oxo Tower is a good example of a renovation creating a mixed-use building in the heart of London*

practice. The Scottish Civic Trust pioneered the concept of a Buildings at Risk register, publicising vacant Listed Buildings to potential new users. The Civic Trust more recently has set up an active Regeneration Unit. Civic Trust awards are one of the oldest award schemes in the country recognising design achievements in both new build and conservation projects.

ARCHITECTURAL PANELS

A small number of local authorities have their own local panels that review significant planning applications and comment on their design as part of the development control process. The Architectural Panel for the London Borough of Bromley is a good example. It was set up in 1995 and was initiated mainly because the Borough ceased to employ its own in-house architects. The Panel consists of six independent architects and landscape architects in private practice who are appointed by the local RIBA (Royal Institute of British Architects) chapter who give their time on a voluntary basis.

The Panel has been successful in effecting design improvements in several key cases, for example a major town centre insurance company headquarters. It has been most effective when it is consulted in good time, even before applications have been submitted, and not after decisions become hard set, as happened in comments about a town centre supermarket. The Panel has been active in considering the design of a major new leisure building on the site of the former Crystal Palace on a prominent site at the top of Crystal Palace Park. A good working partnership exists with the planning department. The Panel also writes an annual report for the Council and sees itself as contributing to the aims of the government's quality agenda and implementing the Council's Unitary Development Plan policies (London Borough of Bromley, 1996).

Summary

A number of statutory and non-statutory bodies exist at the national and local levels who both control and encourage design quality. Urban design should be a collaborative process, involving multi-disciplinary teams and local communities.

Designing for Sustainability

Sustainability in design combines enhancing people's quality of life in terms of environmental, economic and social benefits while at the same time minimising any damaging impact on the earth's resources in both the short and long term. It is therefore a study of relationships between different elements within an overall system, as discussed in Chapter 2. This philosophy fits neatly with the exhortation to 'think globally and act locally'. The location of activities, the design of neighbourhoods, the layout of new development and the detailed specification of new buildings, landscape and spaces all have design implications that can be assessed against sustainability criteria.

When we think about the links between sustainability and design, just as for planning generally, much of the current emphasis has to do with concepts that are not particularly new. For example, housing in the Scottish Highlands has recognised the importance of climate and microclimate for hundreds of years in siting and design detail, including materials.

Because there are so many elements to consider, it is helpful to think about sustainability and design issues in terms of different spatial scales: the region, the neighbourhood and the site. A very useful guide to the subject is *Sustainable Settlements: A Guide for Planners, Designers and Developers*, a joint publication by the University of the West of England and The Local Government Management Board (Barton *et al.*, 1995). The book is organised according to the various spatial scales and provides well-illustrated checklists and criteria against which to assess development proposals. It is especially appropriate for planners.

At the strategic scale, government guidance is now placing emphasis on sustainability as a planning consideration. Landform, vegetation patterns, natural resources, sources of pollution and existing infrastructure (roads, sewers, etc.)

Figure 9 *High Street, Edinburgh. Recent improvements to Edinburgh's Royal Mile have widened pavements, discouraged car use and employed high-quality materials*

should inform design considerations and can give clues about whether new development is appropriate or not. Wildlife corridors and green wedges, for example, should be evident at this scale and followed through in local plans and site briefs. Land subject to flooding or coastal erosion should be avoided.

At the neighbourhood scale, again, spatial patterns need to be thought through. It is generally recognised that most people are willing to walk up to around 400 m for many services, such as local shops and recreational facilities. Human needs and comfort should be taken into account for people of all ages and there is now a growing recognition of the role that mixed use areas can play in people's lives. There also needs to be a finer grain of consideration about the more precise location of such things as pedestrian routes, cycleways, roads and public transport stops (Figure 9). A hierarchy of passive and active recreational opportunities catering to different age groups needs to be developed, minimising potential conflicts of noise and disturbance. Not only safeguarding nature but also providing new opportunities for it should also be considered.

Climate and microclimate should be considered in terms of slopes, vegetation and orientation so that development can take advantage of solar gain and not be overshadowed. Landform and vegetation can provide shelter and the location of development should avoid frost pockets and sites suffering from too much exposure to the wind and driving rain. Locational factors such as these help to keep down future heating requirements and can make open spaces in the immediate environment more pleasant to use. The form of development should be considered; flats and terraces are more energy efficient than detached houses. The form of buildings has been found to influence heat loss by over 50% (Barton *et al.*, 1995, p. 25).

At the level of the individual site, it is critical to analyse carefully the exact location of all land uses and the size or density of each component and its relationship to other uses. Movement patterns, barriers and opportunities need to be examined. At this scale, mobility and accessibility issues need to be worked through in detail to help people with disabilities. Routes to schools need to be considered to satisfy safety concerns, thereby encouraging children to walk.

At the level of the individual site, microclimate, again, is very important, whether the site is in the Shetlands or the Isle of Wight or any point in between. Each site is a unique combination of influences. All the above issues are relevant and need to be worked out at the most detailed level of individual buildings and spaces. It is generally accepted that new development should be sited facing within 45 degrees of south, to take advantage of solar gain. Windows facing northwards should be smaller than those facing south, for fuel efficiency; the main living rooms should face south. Slopes, vegetation and the form of development should avoid overshadowing.

Hard and soft landscape and open space need to be integral to the design. Gardens and clothes drying areas need to be orientated with the sun's path and shelter taken into account. There needs to be a clear demarcation between public and private spaces to promote the sense of 'defensible space'. Privacy needs to be respected, but a balance needs to be struck with overlooking, for surveillance can help to increase security. Maintenance considerations need to be taken into account when designing in the first place. Ecological principles and nature conservation can be encouraged by planting native species. In hot climates, shade trees can be chosen and placed to keep the sun off outdoor spaces and windows. In windy parts of Britain, trees can be planted to give shelter to buildings and outdoor spaces (Figure 10). Trees can help shelter buildings if placed a distance up to six times their height away (Barton *et al.*, 1995, p. 158). They can also be at least partial screens for noise, fumes and particles. Shrub beds within 1–1.5 m of buildings can help to trap warm air. Recently there has been some experimentation with using natural materials for building, for example compacted earth. Other European countries are ahead of Britain in starting to plant on roofs. Tree Preservation Orders can be promoted on areas of value and any tree to be saved needs to be protected during construction periods.

Layouts and landscape can also be designed with security in mind. It is useful to have front and back entrances to houses overlooked, as for children's play areas and other open spaces (Figure 11). Design can be used to give an identity to places. Plant species and layout of buildings and spaces should be chosen to eliminate places where people can hide. Boundaries of gardens should be clearly marked and/or secure. Prickly shrubs can be used to deter intruders.

Movement systems can give priority to pedestrians and cyclists. Traffic calming measures to slow speeds are also more common but must be designed well to add

Figure 10 *The Meadows, Edinburgh. Trees bordering the Meadows help shelter the Royal Infirmary: this is especially important given the strong south-westerlies that whip across the large open space to the wards with balconies overlooking the park*

Figure 11 *Craigmillar, Edinburgh. Children's play areas should be overlooked and carefully sited in related to housing*

to, rather than detract from, the area. The Canmore Housing Association in Edinburgh has constructed a car-free development on a site well-served by public transport. This is an idea that started in Germany and the Netherlands and enables more space to be given over to housing and open space, since car circulation and parking do not need to be catered for. Edinburgh Council is also instigating a radical car-sharing scheme for residents of the city where people are able to book cars ahead. In addition to providing for a network of cycleways, some local plans are including policies for cycle parking within new development and cycle storage in flats.

Building construction and maintenance implications have major knock-on effects for sustainability issues. 'Building services consume approx. 40% of UK delivered energy and 50% of carbon dioxide emissions. . . . The benefits of energy-efficient siting and design of buildings are *economic* – saving money; *social* – reducing fuel poverty; and *ecological* – reducing resource exploitation and emissions' (Barton *et al.*, 1995, p. 25). Embodied energy is the amount of energy that goes into the making of new building materials, transport and construction on the site. This is a significant amount of energy consumption globally and is becoming an issue influencing construction. There are moves to re-use buildings rather than demolish them and to re-cycle redundant materials. The heritage industry and conservationists are finding common ground with environmentalists! Innovative ways of generating and conserving energy are continually evolving. There are likely to be more conflicts in the future between conservationists and environmentalists about whether to accept, for example, solar panels and non-traditional relationships between windows and walls within Conservation Areas and on Listed Buildings.

The entire lifecycles of buildings need to be considered, and not just in the short term, as has happened too often in the past. Medium- to long-term running and maintenance costs are just as important as initial costs in achieving sustainability gains. There is more attention to issues extending the usefulness of buildings by building in flexibility from the start. For example, room layout and sizes can take account of the growing number of people who are working from home, which new technology makes easier. Partitions can give flexibility to room sizes and the construction detail of roofspaces can ensure they could be used as a room in the future. Mobility and accessibility aspects such as avoiding steps, wide doorways and downstairs bathrooms can help ensure the 'life time homes' concept as people get older and experience more problems. Layouts of any building type could earmark room for potential expansion without having adverse impacts on the surroundings.

In line with the emphasis on seeing design as a process, an important component of sustainability is on the individual, human element, seeing how the environment influences people's daily lives. Brenda and Robert Vale in *Green Architecture: Design for a Sustainable Future* (Vale and Vale, 1991) provide useful illustrations of sustainable buildings from countries all over the world. Many of

Figure 12 New housing at Glenalmond Street, Glasgow, by John Gilbert, Architects. Designed with sustainability principles high on the agenda

their examples illuminate the principle of involving building users in the design from the outset. Although the focus is on individual buildings in relation to their environment, it is a useful guide showing real examples that can help raise expectations elsewhere. At all levels of spatial scales discussed above, it is important for planners to work with local communities to effectively gather their input into issues that will affect their future lives.

More authorities are now incorporating development plan policies governing design issues taking sustainability into account. Leeds City Council issued a *Sustainable Development Design Guide* in 1998 which is supplementary planning guidance rooted in Unitary Development Plan policies. The primary purpose is to provide a practical guide to encourage a reduction in adverse impacts and an increase in environmental gains when development is being considered. It provides illustrative examples of many of the principles discussed above.

In 1997, Scottish Homes, the national housing agency, promoted a competition for housing associations to design with innovation and quality in mind. Sustainability was one of the main quality themes that Associations were encouraged to address. Thirteen winning schemes were chosen across Scotland which are now built. One of the winners, by the Shettleston Housing Association in Glenalmond Street, Glasgow, used sustainability indicators as key drivers behind the scheme (Figure 12). There was consultation with user groups from the beginning and a partnering approach adopted. The brownfield site used to be an old laundry and some materials are being recycled for both the buildings and paving. The scheme is car free and house types have been selected to maximise energy efficiency. There are solar panels and a south-facing glazed atrium enclosing a semi-private open space for use by the residents. Landscape principles reflect the ecological theme of the whole scheme, including a pond and creepers up the walls. Water butts are provided to recycle water for garden use. An innovative geothermal energy system is proposed, which would extract heat from deep beneath the ground using water within former mine workings.

SUMMARY

Sustainability aims have to do with a complex web of global and local environmental, social and economic concerns. Design has an important role to play at regional, neighbourhood and local site scales and includes quality of life considerations. Government policy, development plans and supplementary planning guidance are beginning to take sustainable design issues on board.

CASE STUDIES

WEST SILVERTOWN URBAN VILLAGE

West Silvertown Urban Village is a major regeneration scheme in London's Docklands illustrating good practice in urban design as described in the rest of the chapter. The site of 11.3 hectares was formerly vacant and when complete should house about 5000 people. The chief principles adopted are ones that make up the Urban Village concept: mixed uses and tenures, urban density and human scale (for more information, see Aldous, 1992, 1994). The site is near employment opportunities and an international exhibition centre. There are many overlaps with sustainable development principles and design concepts have been chosen which are appropriate to London's East End.

Administratively, the site is within the London Borough of Newham's Unitary Development Plan (UDP) area, but the London Docklands Development Corporation (LDDC) has been responsible for development control and regeneration strategies. In the late 1980s Tibbalds Monro, a planning and urban design consultancy, was commissioned by LDDC to carry out an initial urban design appraisal and prepare a master plan. This fitted within a wider Development Framework (1992) prepared by LDDC. Previously, there had been considerable criticism about the lack of urban design considerations informing regeneration of the Docklands area.

In close collaboration with Newham Council, the strategic development and design principles were fleshed out following a major Planning for Real event involving the local community. These guidelines were incorporated into Newham's

Figure 13 *West Silvertown, London. Buildings orientated toward the public waterfront*

UDP and formed the basis for the development brief for phase one. In 1994 Wimpey Homes and Tibbalds Monro won the competition to masterplan phase one and develop the first parcel of the urban village, comprising around 1000 new dwellings, live–work units, shops, a village hall, pub, school, public open space and associated infrastructure. Partnership between a number of bodies has been at the root of the development, including the Peabody Trust.

The principles at the heart of the design were orientating the buildings and spaces towards the waterfront and integrating a simple vehicular and pedestrian circulation system with built form and open space, as well as mixed use and mixed tenure. Access to all parts of the site has been carefully thought through, allowing a fine grain of pedestrian routes around key nodes and axes. The waterfront is linked visually and functionally to the heart of the site; the dock-edge provides a hard landscaped esplanade open to all and accessible by foot from public streets and private courtyards. Perimeter blocks and courtyard development incorporate a variety of housing types in low, medium and higher buildings. There are central community uses and open space. Higher, more prominent buildings are located on the waterfront, around key nodal points and at gateways into courtyards (Figures 13, 14, and 15).

Affordable housing is provided, including homes for the elderly with shops on the ground floor. Social housing makes up about one-third of the stock and is scattered in pockets within the owner-occupied areas. Acknowledging that after-care is crucial, a management company and charitable trust has been set up to look after the village and support community initiatives. A document called *The Urban Village Design Codes: Ensuring Design Quality in the Future* has been produced to try to ensure that future development adheres to the urban design

274

Figure 14 *West Silvertown, London. Mixed uses, urban density and human scale along a spine road*

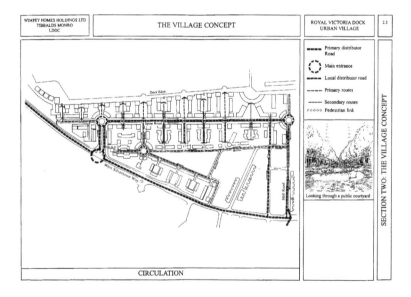

Figure 15 *West Silvertown, London. Simple circulation system makes use of key nodes and axes and a fine grain of pedestrian routes*

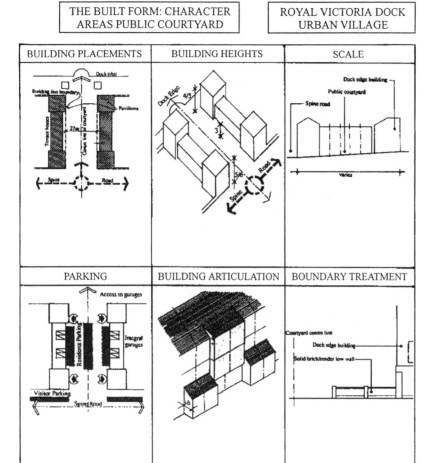

THE BUILT FORM: CHARACTER AREAS PUBLIC COURTYARD	ROYAL VICTORIA DOCK URBAN VILLAGE

BUILDING PLACEMENTS	BUILDING HEIGHTS	SCALE

PARKING	BUILDING ARTICULATION	BOUNDARY TREATMENT

Figure 16 *West Silvertown, London. An example of the design code*

concepts put forward initially (Figure 16). These codes have been adopted as supplementary planning guidance and are in a legally binding development agreement with developers in the area.

WIMBLEDON TOWN CENTRE

A second case study is a major site within Wimbledon town centre, which is one of the 21 sites picked as part of the government's Urban Design Campaign. Public

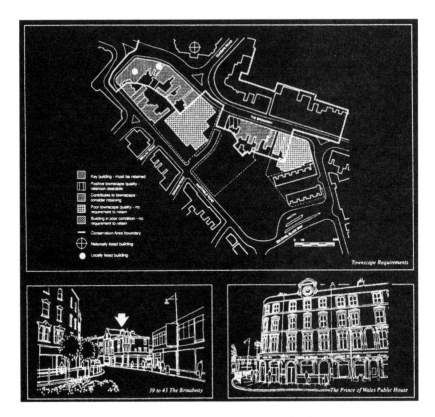

Figure 17 Wimbledon. Townscape analysis preceded the design process

participation therefore formed a major part of site briefing. Balancing the aspirations of local people with the commercial requirements of multiple land owners and developers is often a thorny issue in complex commercial centres. This was particularly so given the history of conflict on this site.

Tibbalds Monro worked closely with the London Borough of Merton to steer a course involving the wide community. Proposals were based on a rigorous analysis of the site in relation to its surroundings, including activities, quality and condition of buildings, movement patterns, historical development and the character of spaces and views (Figures 17 and 18). Part of the site is within a Conservation Area and UDP policies have provided a framework for the site. Public consultation helped feed local everyday experience into the debate (Figure 19). Three rounds of open workshop sessions involved various groups of people who were able to influence the objectives for the site and generate design development options. The first two rounds were focus groups of similar interests, whether land owners, local and national businesses, site occupiers, immediate neighbours, local residents or

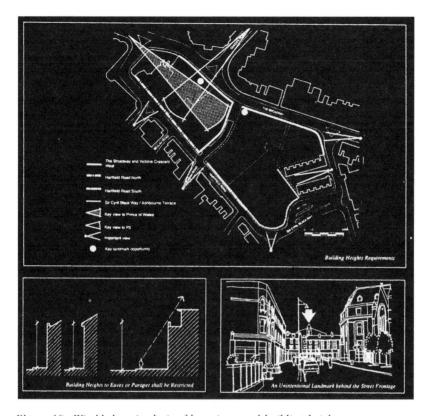

Figure 18 Wimbledon. Analysis of key views and building heights

amenity groups. Final sessions were mixed groups, to raise awareness of balancing different needs.

One danger of such participative methods is raising false hopes, and the consultants were careful to confirm that options were potentially viable, thereby ensuring realism. Design principles adopted were: mixed uses (supermarket, multiplex cinema, shops, outdoor cafes, market stalls, public hall, shoppers' car park), providing pedestrian links and usable spaces, development oriented toward the street, balancing the needs of cars and people, and concentrating activity around the most important pedestrian routes and spaces (Figure 20). Eventually six development options explored the way that different priorities may influence development and, hence, the Development Brief for the site (Figure 21). The Development Brief steered a middle course and provides a framework encouraging good design sympathetic to its context, without being overly rigid or prescriptive. This will become supplementary planning guidance, addressing such issues as land uses and activities, townscape issues including buildings to be retained, open space

Figure 19 Wimbledon. One of the public consultation meetings

and pedestrian access, accessibility and circulation, vehicular access and servicing, car parking and bus stops, building lines in relation to the streets and spaces, building heights and landmarks (Figure 22).

EVALUATION

SEIZING THE OPPORTUNITY

It is an exciting time, with the 1990s seeing a renewed interest in design within the planning profession; new organisations and initiatives have been set up to champion the cause of good design. It will be interesting to see how these initiatives are carried through in the future if they are to be meaningful. Appeal decisions should be monitored to establish the extent to which design considerations are influencing outcomes. Some local authorities have good records at being creative in seeking design quality, but others have not. Building sound systems is often difficult in a time of decreasing resources and time pressures and there is a long way to go.

Recent emphasis on sustainability has many overlaps with good design and the momentum from that quarter needs to be captured and focused explicitly on design issues. Authorities generally could be undertaking more policy development and monitoring strategic and area design policies and writing more site briefs with clear design considerations. All of this needs to be based on sound area appraisal, working with local communities and development interests. Planners need to be

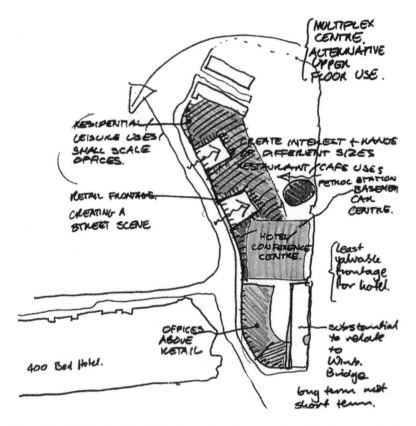

Figure 20 Wimbledon. Sketch design produced as an option following consultation

trained during both initial and continuing professional education and on the job in being creative in how design matters can be handled in their daily work to bring about real improvements for people on the ground; this includes gaining confidence in discussing design issues.

FUTURE DIRECTIONS: THE CHALLENGE AHEAD

Planners need to develop further their own understanding of the real meaning behind urban design so it is able to bear fruit in their work. Understanding the term in its wide sense is crucial, incorporating product as well as process, strategic as well as local issues, encouragement as well as control, the built environment as well as the natural. The emphasis on creating places that people enjoy makes the concept relevant for the daily jobs of most planners.

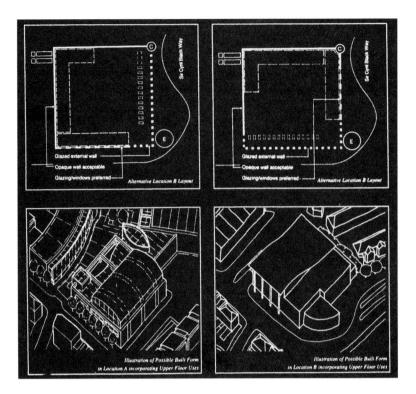

Figure 21 Wimbledon. Development options

Awareness needs to be raised about how design relates to sustainability issues at various spatial scales. The design aspects of policy development and individual development proposals need to be considered and progress monitored, including the achievement of sustainability objectives. This is a classic case where it is important to make connections between various issues and people. The development of explicit criteria would be helpful in achieving action. It is only comparatively recently that design and sustainability have become major issues and it is imperative that awareness is raised amongst planners, good examples publicised and good habits started. Involving the public in meaningful, timely and creative ways is a major challenge and we must seek ways in which to come to a deep understanding of the real meaning of good quality design.

ACKNOWLEDGEMENTS

Figure 12, © John Gilbert, Architects, reproduced with permission. Figures 13–22, © Tibbalds Monro, reproduced with permission.

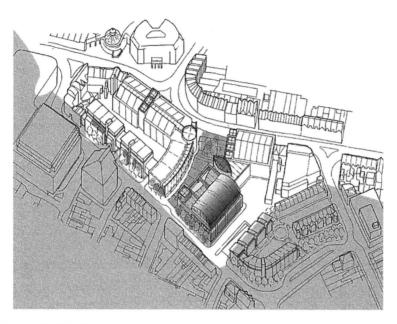

Figure 22 *Wimbledon. A final option for mixed uses, orientated toward street frontages and a new public open space*

REFERENCES

Aldous, T. (1992) *Urban Villages*, Urban Villages Group.

Aldous, T. (1994) *Economics of Urban Villages*, Urban Villages Forum.

Barton, H., Davis, G. and Guise, R. (1995) *Sustainable Settlements: A Guide for Planners, Designers and Developers*, University of the West of England and Local Government Management Board, Bristol and Luton.

Birmingham City Council (1992) *Car Park Design Guide*, Birmingham City Council, Birmingham.

Birmingham City Council (1995) *Designing for Parent and Child: Guidance Notes*, Birmingham City Council, Birmingham.

Chilterns Conference (1998) *Chilterns Countryside Design Guide*.

City of Birmingham (1990) *Birmingham Urban Design Study*, City of Birmingham Council, Tibbalds, Colbourne, Karski.

City of Edinburgh Council (1997) *Central Edinburgh Local Plan: Adopted Written Statement*, Edinburgh Council.

Cottenham Village Design Group (1994) *Cottenham Village Design Statement*, Countryside Commission.

Countryside Commission (1993) *Design in the Countryside*, CCP 418, Countryside Commission, Cheltenham.

Countryside Commission (1994) *Design in the Countryside Experiments*, CCP 473, Countryside Commission, Cheltenham.

282

Countryside Commission (1996a) *Countryside Design Summaries: Achieving Quality in Countryside Design*, CCP 502, Countryside Commission, Cheltenham.

Countryside Commission (1996b) *Village Design: Making Local Character Count in New Development*, CCP 501, Parts 1 and 2, Countryside Commission, Cheltenham.

Department of the Environment (1980) *Development Control – Policy and Practice*, Circular 22/80, Department of the Environment, London.

Department of the Environment (1990) *This Common Inheritance: Britain's Environmental Strategy*, HMSO Command 1200, London.

Department of the Environment (1992a) *General Policy and Principles*, PPG1, Department of the Environment, London.

Department of the Environment (1992b) *Housing*, PPG 3, Department of the Environment, London.

Department of the Environment (1992c) *Development Plans: A Good Practice Guide*, HMSO, London.

Department of the Environment (1994a) *Quality in Town and Country: A Discussion Document*, Department of the Environment, London.

Department of the Environment (1994b) *Planning Out Crime*, Circular 5/94, Department of the Environment, London.

Department of the Environment (1995) *Quality in Town and Country: Urban Design Campaign*, Department of the Environment, London.

Department of the Environment (1997) *General Policy and Principles*, PPG1, Department of the Environment, London.

English Partnerships (1996) *Time for Design: Good Practice in Building, Landscape and Urban Design*, English Partnerships, London.

Essex County Council (1973) *A Design Guide for Residential Areas*, Essex County Council, Chelmsford.

Essex County Council (1997) *The Essex Design Guide for Residential and Mixed Use Areas*, Essex County Council, Chelmsford.

Gillespie's (1995) *Glasgow City Centre: Public Realm: Strategy and Guidelines*, Strathclyde Regional Council, Glasgow.

Leeds City Council (1998) *Sustainable Development Design Guide: Supplementary Guidance No. 10*, Leeds City Council.

Leicester City Council *Design Notes 13: Major Developments*, Leicester City Council, Leicester (undated publication).

London Borough of Bromley (1996) *The Architectural Panel for Bromley: First Annual Report 1995–6*, Bromley Council.

Parfect, M. and Power, G. (1997) *Planning for Urban Quality: Urban Design in Towns and Cities*, Routledge, London.

Punter, J. (1986–7) A history of aesthetic control: The control of the external appearance of development in England and Wales 1909–1985, *Town Planning Review*, **57**(4), 351–381; **58**(1), 20–62.

Punter, J. (1993) Development design skills for development controllers, in R. Hayward and S. McGlynn (eds), *Making Better Places, Urban Design Now*, Butterworth Architecture, Oxford.

Punter, J. (1994) Aesthetics in planning, in H. Thomas (ed.), *Values in Planning*, Avebury, London.

Punter, J. and Carmona, M. (1997) *The Design Dimension of Planning*, E and FN Spon, London.

Royal Fine Art Commission (1990) *Planning for Beauty*, HMSO, London.

Royal Fine Art Commission (1994) *What Makes a Good Building?* HMSO, London.

Royal Town Planning Institute (1990) *Development Briefs*, Practice Advice Note No. 8, RTPI, London.

Scottish Office Environment Department (1991) *The Siting and Design of New Development in the Countryside*, PAN 36, HMSO, Edinburgh.

Scottish Office Environment Department (1994a) *The Planning System*, NPPG1, HMSO, Edinburgh.

Scottish Office Environment Department (1994b) *Planning for Crime Prevention*, Planning Advice Note 46, HMSO, Edinburgh.

Scottish Office Environment Department (1994c) *Fitting New Housing Development into the Landscape*, PAN 44, The Scottish Office, Edinburgh.

Scottish Office Development Department (1996) *Land for Housing*, NPPG 3, Scottish Office, HMSO, Edinburgh.

Urban Design Group (1996) *Urban Design Source Book 1996*, Urban Design Group, Oxfordshire.

Urban Task Force (1999) *Towards an Urban Renaissance*, DETR, London.

Vale, B. and Vale, R. (1991) *Green Architecture: Design for a Sustainable Future*, Thames and Hudson, Ltd, London.

Chapter 12

Planning to Conserve the Natural Heritage

Jeremy Raemaekers

Introduction

In this chapter we explore the contribution of the planning system to conserving the natural heritage. There is no simple definition of the natural heritage. We shall be pragmatic and take it to mean what falls within the remit of the government's natural heritage agencies, i.e. those whose titles specify nature, countryside and natural heritage itself. This covers two kinds of natural asset which British legislation has tended to treat separately:

- wildlife – including all kinds of non-domestic plants, animals and lower forms of life, both as single species and as communities of species;
- the cultural and aesthetic contribution of naturalistic elements to landscapes.

It excludes pollution, which falls within the remit of the environmental protection agencies, except in so far as it affects wildlife or landscape amenity in a fairly direct way.

In this sphere, as in many others, planning's contribution is patchy, yet the planner needs to have a broad grasp of the field in order to know when and how to act. In some circumstances the planner acts very directly, for example when deciding whether or not to permit a development that would destroy a local nature reserve. In others the planner plays the role of catalyst, for example in getting other parties around the table to produce an urban nature conservation strategy, much of which the planning system would have no direct part in implementing.

In order to contribute effectively, the planner needs:

- understanding of the rationale of conservation;
- knowledge of natural heritage assets and an appreciation of their local and wider values;
- understanding of the forces that threaten those assets; and
- knowledge of ways and means of conserving them in the face of those forces.

This requires a grasp of the fields of nature and landscape conservation, countryside recreation, and the primary industries of farming, forestry, mining and water.

The planning system carries the leading responsibility in none of these fields, but it impinges on all of them.

The next two sections of this chapter set the scene by considering why we should conserve our natural heritage, and how we assess its condition. The following two sections form the core of the chapter: how the heritage is protected and planning's role in that. We describe the relevant institutional and legislative framework, and identify the statutory and additional contributions of planners. We then move on to explore, through practice case studies, three arenas of conservation and the role within them of the planner: urban nature conservation, recreation in a sensitive landscape, and forestry. In the final section we evaluate how well, given its potential and limitations, the planning system is performing in conserving the natural heritage.

WHY CONSERVE OUR NATURAL HERITAGE?

It is common to speak of a 'conservation ethic', but what does this really mean? In truth, very divergent reasons can be advanced for conserving the natural heritage, and they can also be placed in different value systems. It is important that you have some awareness of these, not only because you may meet them in cases involving conservation issues, but also because you need to be conscious of what drives your own approach in such cases.

At one extreme, *religion* is a value system which has much to say concerning the relations between humans and nature (Brown, 1990). For example, environmentalists argue about whether the Judaic tradition is inherently unfavourable towards environmental sustainability, because it appears to sanction an exploitative approach to nature. In a society in which religion is less explicitly a guiding force than it used to be or than it still is in many other cultures, we are not always aware of its influence on our ways of thought. For example, the concept of stewardship of the Earth is often cited in expressing the idea of sustainable development. In fact, this is originally a religious metaphor, meaning that God has given us the job of stewarding life on earth, i.e. looking after it on his behalf.

Whether or not you link it directly to religion, you might argue that there is a *moral* or ethical reason for conserving life. The human species is in a position of immense power over other forms of life, is able to realise what effects it has on them, and is in principle able to control those effects. You could argue that this confers a responsibility on us to look after other life. This is an altruistic reason, because it is not based on any material advantage to us.

A more selfish, i.e. human-centred, reason is that the natural heritage brings much pleasure to many people. This *aesthetic* justification is so obvious that it does not really require concrete measures to demonstrate it, but here are a few anyway:

- many millions of people in Britain watched the television series *Life on Earth*, which has also been sold to many television networks abroad;
- 60 million visitor days were spent in England's National Parks in 1994;
- the Royal Society for the Protection of Birds has 1 million paid-up members.

A third and diverse set of reasons is *utilitarian*. The world's biggest industry, tourism, in many ways exploits natural assets, be it the attractiveness of the scenery, the quality of beach and sea in coastal resorts, or the wild animals in a game reserve. For example, a 1995 survey estimated that hill walkers and moun-taineers in the Highlands and Islands of Scotland spent £164m supporting over 6000 jobs, in an area inhabited by only 200 000 people. Wild animal tourism in Scotland is estimated to generate £60m and support 10 500 jobs (Scottish Tourist Board, 1996).

Many forms of wildlife have direct food value; worldwide, we take nearly 100 million tonnes of wild fish from the seas each year. In a less direct but even more important way, wildlife also remains the essential underpinning of farming. Any farmer or gardener knows the value of earthworms for soil fertility, and the experience with modern pesticides has revealed clearly the contribution of natural predators to keeping down the pests of farm crops. Even in the age of biotech-nology, the ultimate source of new genetic material for improving domesticated plants and animals remains their wild relatives (Prescot-Allen and Prescot-Allen, 1988). Wild plants are also the essential sources for many medicinal drugs (Myers, 1983).

These utilitarian values also underpin the concept of sustainable development, explored in Chapter 2. Apart from the individual benefits which natural assets may supply, such as those listed above, sustainable development recognises that each natural asset is part of a larger web of life, which includes life support systems on which we, like any other organism, ultimately depend. A recent estimate of the economic value of services to humankind provided by the sum total of ecosystems all around the globe is between US$16 trillion and US$54 trillion – compared with the current US$18 trillion GNP of all the world's nations (Holmes, 1997). It is interesting to note that the most valuable ecosystems in this sense are coastal ones, on which the planning profession has only recently begun to focus attention. As yet, we still tend to undervalue such ecological services and therefore to allow them to be damaged.

This strategic but pragmatic justification of conservation was eloquently pre-sented in the *World Conservation Strategy*, the definitive ecological statement of the need to conserve renewable living resources (International Union for the Conservation of Nature and Natural Resources *et al.*, 1980). This set three great objectives:

- maintain essential life support systems, such as the climate regulation function of forests or the water purification and supply functions of aquifers;

- preserve genetic diversity, for example through nature reserves and gene banks;
- use species and ecosystems sustainably, for example do not run down fish stocks or interfere with the role of estuaries as breeding and feeding grounds for fish.

The message of the *World Conservation Strategy* underpins the Biodiversity Convention agreed at the Rio Earth Summit (see Box 2 in Chapter 2). The official British response to that convention is *Biodiversity: the UK Action Plan* (UK Government, 1994a). This sets out the government's policy on the conservation of biodiversity, i.e. the variety of wildlife and the communities it forms.

The different sorts of reason given above can also be expressed in the language of economics, which classifies the value of goods and services into use, option and existence. Use value is that which you derive from direct use; option value is that which you place upon retaining the asset in case you should wish to use it in the future; and existence value is that which you place upon something you may never expect to use, but which you nevertheless wish to retain because it means something to you. Thus you might buy a ticket to enter a nature reserve, which represents the reserve's use value to you. Or you might pay an annual subscription to a wildlife trust giving you free entry to all its reserves, in case you should wish at some time in the year to go there, representing their option value. Or you might take out a life membership of the trust, even knowing full well that you will never visit any of its reserves, just because you like to know that the wildlife is protected there, which represents its existence value to you.

MEASURING THE STATE OF OUR NATURAL HERITAGE

We have looked briefly at why we should conserve the natural heritage. In the two sections that follow this one we will look at how planning is involved in conserving it, but we consider first how to establish the condition of the heritage and to monitor changes in it. Knowledge of status and trends should, after all, underpin a rational approach to action.

At the national scale, it seems to be commonly assumed that the quality of our natural heritage is deteriorating. Motorways and bypasses are driven through sites of natural interest and scenic beauty; intensification has driven wildlife off the farm; oil spills threaten our shorelines; human-induced global warming is altering the climate, raising sea levels to threaten coastal habitats and shifting the distributions of wildlife populations. It is very easy, however, to be misled by headline-grabbing events. A motorway driven through a scenic area will attract protest actions and be widely reported; the creation of a nature reserve will not. We therefore need to dig behind the headlines and establish what changes truly are taking place. We also need to decide what are good and bad changes, and which ones really matter.

Practical and cost limits mean that we cannot monitor everything, and even if we could, the overload of information would be more an obstruction than a help. In consequence, a whole new discipline of environmental indicators has grown up in recent years (MacGillivray and Kayes, 1994). To be useful, an indicator:

- needs to be a good proxy for other components of the environment, i.e. it must make ecological sense;
- should have readily available data, i.e. it must be practicable; and
- should strike a chord in the imagination of ordinary people, i.e. it must make social sense, being easily communicated and representing something people care about.

Indicators can be of different types. The land-use planner needs to know three things: what is changing and how much, why it is changing, and how effective are measures taken in response. As a result, it is common to distinguish three types of indicator:

- those that track pressures on the environment, such as the growth in mountain recreation;
- those that track the actual state of the environment, such as hedgerow loss; and
- those that track the success of actions taken to counteract pressures, such as the rate of damage to designated sites of natural value.

For example, provided that the records exist and that we can access them, we could count the population size of a butterfly. We might then be able to show a correlation between this state of the environment indicator and a pressure indicator, such as a change in the proportion of grassland cover types, which could account for it beyond reasonable doubt. A relevant response indicator might then be the uptake of a farm grant intended to promote retention of the grassland type which supports that butterfly. Try the example in Box 1.

Box 1 *Trends in UK bird populations: human causes and effects?*

Of the 105 species of bird regularly monitored, 34% are decreasing, 31% are increasing, and 35% show no consistent trend. Ten out of 12 seed-eating farmland species are declining, but some woodland species have greatly increased.

Now look at the following indicators. Do they suggest how human influence on land use might account for these trends?

- Species diversity (of all forms of life) across principal habitats in Great Britain increased between 1978 and 1994 in moorland, but fell in upland grassland mosaics, woodland, semi-improved grassland, improved grassland and arable fields.

- Forest cover in Great Britain more than doubled from 1905 to 1991; since 1947 the area of conifers has increased four-fold, but that of broadleaved trees has risen only slightly.

- From 1945 to 1990, in England the proportion of urban land rose by a half, woodland rose by a half, managed land (mainly arable fields and grassland improved for pasture) fell slightly, and rough grazing (i.e. semi-natural open country) fell by over a quarter.

Sources: MacGillivray and Kayes (1994), Department of the Environment (1992a), UK Government (1994a).

Some elements of the natural heritage, such as those in Box 1, are in principle measurable in an objective way. This is the case for wildlife, the first component of the natural heritage as we defined it in the Introduction; but the second component, landscape, does not so readily lend itself to being classified and counted. Of course there are separable components of landscape which we can measure, and we may value them individually. But we certainly also react to and value a total landscape as we view it, which is much more than the sum of those individual parts. This is a very complex phenomenon, and moreover changes according to the context: people are sentimentally attached to what they are familiar with, and that changes over time, even within the same person (try it out with your own experience).

One approach to monitoring landscape change is to admit that we cannot cope with the complex whole, and to break it down to its objective component parts, such as field size, length of hedges and density of tree features. This is itself a major project that has been attempted more than once. These days it is made more feasible by advanced airborne and satellite imaging, and digital data storage, handling, retrieval and analysis. The *Countryside Survey 1990* is a recent effort to collate information of this sort (Department of the Environment, 1993; a revision is currently under way). It can be argued that this is all we need do in order to inform policy-making: we identify that people are concerned about the status of hedges, we show that hedges are being lost at a certain rate, and we pass legislation to reduce further loss.

But it would also be desirable to approach more closely the meaning to people of changes in *whole* landscapes. Behavioural studies can establish how people react to quantified changes in the presence of measurable components within whole landscape views. What is needed is an intermediate framework that would allow us to extrapolate from such behavioural studies to the nationwide monitoring of measurable components. Such a framework could be provided by *The Character of England*, published by the government's agencies for the English countryside (Countryside Commission and English Nature, 1996). This map classifies the countryside into nearly 200 landscape character areas as objectively as possible. By relating both the behavioural studies and the surveys of measurable components to landscape character areas, it would be possible to build up a picture of how people are likely to feel about change in each area and even, by extrapolating the survey data, to predict reaction to future changes expected from given policies.

The Countryside Survey, *The Character of England*, and their equivalents, have been carried out by national agencies primarily to inform those agencies' policies at national and regional levels. They are certainly useful to local planning authorities as guidance and background information to help formulate general policies for their territories, for example indicating which landscape types are disappearing fastest and should be prioritised for protection. But the planning authority also needs to know how common a given type is within its own territory, whether and how fast it is declining locally, and exactly where it is to be found. National surveys are usually of little use for this, because they do not provide that level of local detail. It would in principle be feasible to carry out surveys at a sampling intensity high enough to serve more local information needs as well as higher level ones, but the national agencies lack the massive resources required to do that. Moreover, local variations would often require adaptation or subdivision of national categories. In practice, therefore, the collection of much local information has to be locally organised, though it is always desirable to maintain compatibility with higher level approaches and classifications if possible, as a means of extending the local penetration of higher level databases and enabling comparisons between local areas.

Local authorities obtain the requisite local data from a variety of sources. They will know of nationally important sites because these have been designated by the relevant national agencies (see below). Many locally important sites will be brought to their attention by voluntary organisations, such as county naturalist trusts or advisory groups of academic experts in nearby universities, and they may sponsor, commission or directly carry out their own surveys. Using air photographs, maps and ground survey, many authorities have mapped natural habitats throughout their territories on at least a presence–absence basis using the National Vegetation Classification, and many have also carried out landscape character surveys.

An accurate and comprehensive survey is, however, expensive, especially when repeated at intervals to monitor trends and to keep site-specific information up to date, and is therefore vulnerable when authorities are looking for activities to cut in order to find savings. Development planning and control may also have been at best only one consideration in their design, so that the information may not be of the most useful type or in the most useful form for the planner. Moreover, they tend not to provide an integrated overview of the territory's natural heritage.

An interesting experiment which sought to address all three problems of cost, appropriateness and integration is *Assessing the Natural Heritage Resource*, the results of which were published as a guidance note for Scottish local planning authorities (Scottish Natural Heritage, 1996). Pilot assessments were made for two local authority territories, gathering information to identify the key characteristics and qualities of the natural heritage, considering how and why they are changing, and identifying the effects of changes in a systematic and integrated way which spans ecology, landscape and amenity. It is not a site-by-site assessment and is not intended to substitute for a comprehensive habitat survey, for example, but rather gives a strategic overview of the territory which allows policies to be made that are sensitive to local assets, pressures and preferences. It is intended mainly to contribute to making the Development Plan, but can also feed into other environmental initiatives, such as Local Agenda 21.

The territory is broken down into working areas defined by natural systems, such as river catchments, modified where appropriate in very 'humanised' landscapes by human influences. For each working area a schedule of key characteristics and features is drawn up by a team including an ecologist, a landscape architect and one or more locally knowledgeable planners. For each feature, the schedule describes in a paragraph its contribution to the working area's ecology, landscape and amenity; past, present and likely future changes and their effects; suggested aims for the natural heritage which may be considered alongside other planning and land management aims; how to implement them; and possible indicators of environmental change thrown up by the assessment of that working area. An example of a couple of rows from such a schedule is given in Table 1.

THE LEGISLATIVE AND INSTITUTIONAL FRAMEWORK

The purpose of this section is to take you on a tour of relevant law, institutions and land designations. You need to have a grasp of the main features of this framework to make sense of the different ways in which planners interface with it. How they do so is outlined at the end of this section and explored through case studies in the next section.

THE NATURAL HERITAGE AGENCIES

As indicated in the Introduction, nature conservation has historically been treated separately from landscape conservation and recreation in the UK. The foundation of modern legislation and institutions for both are the 1949 National Parks and Access to the Countryside Act and the 1967/8 Countryside Acts, which institutionalised the split by creating separate agencies for the two functions. This split is still reflected in England, where there is a national agency for the former function,

Table 1 Extract from natural heritage resource assessment of West Lothian. Source: Scottish Natural Heritage (1996)

Area 2
COASTAL
Sheet 1

NATURAL HERITAGE RESOURCE ASSESSMENT WEST LOTHIAN

Key characteristics and features	Contribution (Qualities)	Changes and effects	Suggested aims	Implementation	Possible indicators
Landform Undulating coastal area with rocky outcrops	Gently undulating countryside rising up to the west from the tidal zone and levelling out to the east. Highly visible from major east/west routes (M9/A904). Landform reflects local geological variations. Midhope Burn bisects area as it flows through to the tidal zone. Some rock outcrops provide natural features in the landscape.	Robust landform that is unlikely to change much even in the long term as a result of natural processes. Sandstone quarrying has taken place in the past and pressure for new extraction must remain a possibility.	To protect natural processes and to control mineral workings and engineering projects to sustain and where possible enhance landform features.	AGLV and other Local Plan policies. Control of mineral workings; well located and screened proposals may be acceptable if no significant impact on landscape.	Monitoring planning permissions and review of aerial photographs would indicate changes over appropriate time-scales.
River and drainage systems Midhope Burn, high water quality. Ponds.	The whole area drains north to the Firth of Forth via the Midhope Burn and its tributaries. Midhope Burn water quality generally good, supporting salmonids.	Watercourses vulnerable to pollution due to intensive agricultural production, particularly stock-rearing and dairying.	To sustain natural form of river systems and drainage patterns. To protect from pollution using precautionary principles, especially for ponds.	Development control and consultation on drainage and water course improvements. Conditions on new agricultural and any industrial development. Integrated pollution control.	Water quality of the burn could be monitored using standard water quality indicators, together with salmonid populations.

continues overleaf

Table 1 (*Continued*)

NATURAL HERITAGE RESOURCE ASSESSMENT WEST LOTHIAN

Key characteristics and features	Contribution (Qualities)	Changes and effects	Suggested aims	Implementation	Possible indicators
	Several small permanent and seasonal ponds. Some artificial and ornamental, others resulting from quarrying or mineral subsidence. (See target noted sites in Phase 1 Habitat Survey.)	Threat of drainage and infilling of ponds always present and lack of management may result in long-term decline in the ecological value of the ponds, a diminishing resource.	To protect all permanent and seasonal ponds as far as possible. If losses inevitable, to seek to ensure replacement ponds are constructed and biota are translocated. To enhance ponds by encouraging ecologically sound management.	Promotion of value of small water bodies. Management agreements. Development control use conditions and S.50 agreements to protect and enhance survival of ponds, etc.	The number, distribution and water quality of ponds could be used as indicators of change.
Land cover and the Landscape Patchwork of well-tended-fields	Patchwork of cereal crops, bright green grazing swards and woodland of various types, creates mosaic of colours and textures at most times of the year. Gives a well-cared-for appearance.	Land cover highly modified due to farm and forestry management. Areas of woodland generally well fitted into the landscape. Due to high land quality very little has been left undrained or unmodified in some way.	To sustain the distinctive estate character whilst enhancing ecological value and ensuring sustainable woodland and forestry enterprises.	Forestry strategy. Management agreements. AGLV policy. However, local authority would have limited direct influence.	Estate 'character' is difficult to monitor but woodland size, type and distribution could be used as indicators of change.

English Nature, and one for the latter, the Countryside Agency. In Wales the two functions were united under the Countryside Council for Wales by the 1990 Environment Act, and in Scotland they were united under Scottish Natural Heritage by the 1991 Natural Heritage (Scotland) Act. The Joint Nature Conservation Committee coordinates the three countries in matters of UK-wide and international importance to nature conservation, but there is no such body for landscape conservation.

These national bodies are not departments of central government, but arm's length agencies whose governing boards are appointed by central government and which are funded by it. Their status gives them a degree of independence in policy-making, but ultimately they are answerable to government, if only through its direct control of their funding.

The functions of nature and landscape conservation differ in two important ways. First, although both functions make wide use of grants and of agreements, with or without financial compensation, only nature conservation involves the direct management of some land by the state natural heritage agencies through ownership or lease. Second, nature conservation was viewed originally as the province of science and not concerned with public access or enjoyment, whereas landscape conservation was from the outset teamed with public access for the enjoyment of the countryside, initially through National Parks and later more widely. Thus the nature conservation function has had a unitary remit – protecting the assets – whereas the landscape conservation function has always had a binary remit, balancing the interests of conservation and recreation. It follows that the two functions have rather different cultures.

NATIONALLY DESIGNATED AREAS

Nature Conservation Designations

A prime function of the natural heritage agencies is the identification and designation of protected areas. The sectoral split between the nature and landscape conservation agencies is reflected in the designations. The main nature conservation designation is the Site of Special Scientific Interest (SSSI). These have been identified by the nature conservation authorities (English Nature, Countryside Council for Wales and Scottish Natural Heritage, respectively) and their predecessors in a huge survey effort over the past 40 years. There are now over 6000 of them, ranging in size from a few hectares to thousands, and occupying a sizeable proportion of the land and freshwater surface (Table 2).

SSSIs may be designated for their biological or earth science interest. The designation does not alter ownership – the land stays in the hands of whoever happens to own it – and it does not automatically guarantee total protection from actions that would damage the interests for which it was designated. It is a statement of conservation importance.

Table 2 *Sites of Special Scientific Interest, 1993*

	Number	Area ('000 ha)	% territory
England	3759	886	7
Scotland	1364	846	11
Wales	876	206	10
Northern Ireland*	46	48	3
Total	6045	1985	8

* In Northern Ireland they are called Areas of Special Scientific Interest (ASSIs).
Source: UK Government 1994b.

From their inception in 1949, SSSIs were offered strong protection from development under the planning acts. A planning authority must consult the nature conservation authority if it proposes to grant permission for a development that would affect an SSSI. The nature conservation authority may ask the Secretary of State to call the case in for his determination if the planning authority intends to grant permission despite an objection from the nature conservation authority.

It was however not until the passing of the highly contentious 1981 Wildlife and Countryside Act that protection was afforded from farming and forestry operations, which do not fall under the planning acts, but have proved to be the greater threat. You need to know about this, because it highlights a critical difference in the way built development and other land operations are treated. Under this Act, the nature conservation authority can make a management agreement with the owner or occupier of the land not to undertake operations specified in the designation of the SSSI as potentially damaging to its natural interest (Figure 1).

If the occupier is unwilling, cash compensation can be offered for profit foregone (agreements were in fact introduced under the 1968 Countryside Act, but only became common under the 1981 Act). If the occupier still refuses, there is a last resort power of application to the Secretary of State for a compulsory purchase order, but this is never invoked, and an obdurate owner could go ahead and perform the damaging operation. Thus there is, in effect, no guarantee of protecting the public interest against that of the owner or occupier.

This system is based on the voluntary principle of willing cooperation by landowners and occupiers, but it infuriated many farmers, who saw it as an infringement of their right to use their land as they wished. It also infuriated many environmentalists, who saw it as a surrender to the landowners. Where is the justice, they cried, in wildlife law allowing the occupier to claim compensation for refusal to plough a meadow, when planning law allows refusal of permission to build on the same meadow without compensation? Moreover, compensation was paid for loss of farm grants for operations like grubbing up hedges – yet legally the grants were discretionary, depending on the public interest, and not an automatic entitlement at all. To cap it all, compensation had to be paid from the limited budget of the nature conservation authority, not the vast coffers of the agriculture department.

Figure 1 *An example of what the Wildlife and Countryside Act tried to control: 'Prairie Farming' in the Carse of Stirling, Scottish Central Belt. Source: Jeremy Raemaekers*

There was public outrage at sums sometimes in the millions being paid to landowners *not* to do something – and indeed in some cases plainly something they had never intended to do before compensation became available. Yet, despite the headline-grabbing cases, the truth is that the vast majority of management agreements, now covering a total of 100 000 hectares, are reached with no fuss. Even more to the point, these days most payments are not purely compensatory, but include also reward for *positive* actions to help the natural interest of the site. This is more in tune with a modern partnership approach to development and conservation.

The issue is highly significant for planners because it goes to the heart of land-use rights. The attempts to reform the European Community's Common Agriculture Policy in 1986 and 1992 to be more environmentally friendly drew attention away from the issue, but it has returned as a result of the European Habitats Directive 92/43. The directive is hugely important, because it required member states

- to encourage *generally* the management of features of the landscape which are important to wildlife, such as hedgerows (Article 10);
- to identify *specifically* by 1998 a network of Special Areas of Conservation (SACs) to protect natural habitats of European importance, to secure their effective protection, and to compensate for any losses to the network by identifying new sites (Article 6). The measures apply also to Special Protection Areas (SPAs) designated under an earlier European directive on wild birds, 79/409.

All SACs and SPAs are or will be SSSIs, and they will in effect be an upper tier of SSSI. Damage to sites will be allowed only if no alternative solution can be found and there is an overriding public interest. For priority habitats identified by the European Commission itself, damage will be allowed only if justified 'in the interests of human health and public safety, benefits of primary importance to the environment itself, or, following an opinion from the Commission itself, other imperative reasons of overriding public interest'. In effect, this forces the UK to move from the voluntary principle to something close to guaranteed protection of key sites. Moreover, it does so for the marine environment, which was not effectively protected under the existing regime, because planning law does not reach below the low water mark and because the basis of SSSI designation cannot apply in the context of sea law.

Like SSSI designation, SAC and SPA designation impinges directly on planners, both through consultations by the nature conservation authorities on site designation, and through planners' duty to protect the sites. This includes powers to remove the permitted development rights of statutory undertakers, and to revoke existing but unfulfilled planning permissions, with compensation for the permit holder. The general duty under Article 10, interpreted via national planning guidance, also requires planning authorities to include policies in their Development Plans that will give it force (PPG9, *Nature Conservation*, Department of the Environment, 1994).

In addition to SSSIs, the nature conservation authorities also designate National Nature Reserves (NNRs) under the 1949 Act. These are managed directly by the authorities, either through ownership, or through a lease, or through a nature reserve agreement with the owners. There are just over 300 NNRs (Figure 2); from the point of view of the planning authorities, the important point is that they are also SSSIs and have to be treated as such.

Landscape Conservation and Recreation Designations

Whereas the nature conservation designations apply throughout Britain, the landscape and recreation ones do not. In England and Wales there are 10 National Parks, covering 9% of the land area. These were designated during the 1950s under the 1949 National Parks and Access to the Countryside Act by the National Parks Commission, the predecessor of the current countryside agencies (Figure 3).

The purposes of the Parks, restated under the 1995 Environment Act, are 'to conserve and enhance the natural beauty, wildlife and cultural heritage of the area' and 'to promote opportunities for the understanding and enjoyment of the special qualities of those areas by the public'. In line with sustainable development, where the two purposes conflict, greater weight is attached to the former. The Parks coincide with the finest areas of upland and coast in England and Wales. It is important to appreciate that the British Parks are very different from the original National Parks in the US, which are wilderness areas expropriated by the state and

Figure 2 *Ariundle National Nature Reserve, Strontian, west Scotland – a West Coast Oakwood. Source: Jeremy Raemaekers*

run by it exclusively for conservation and recreation. Britain has little wilderness, and its National Parks are inhabited by a quarter of a million people, are not owned by the state, and are run by authorities representing predominantly local rather than national interests. You would not necessarily realise that you were in a National Park unless you happened to notice visitor management features which say so (Figures 4, 5, and 6).

Two of the original 10 parks (Lake District and Peak District) were created as independent planning authorities, and under the 1995 Environment Act all will become so; park-wide Local Plans are already required under the 1991 Planning and Compensation Act. A small but significant planning measure in National Parks is the revocation of permitted development rights, allowing more control over minor alterations and operations which could affect aesthetic appeal or the natural interest. The same measure is applied to two lowland areas, the New Forest Heritage Area and the Norfolk and Suffolk Broads; the Broads are regarded as the 11th National Park (PPG7, Department of the Environment, 1997), and there is now an intention to designate the New Forest and the South Downs as National Parks.

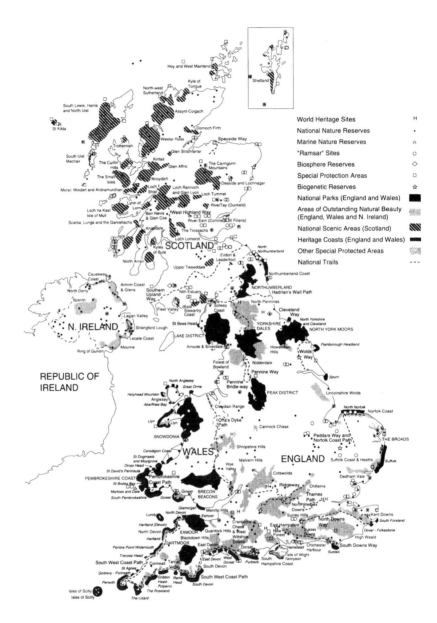

Figure 3 *Protected arease in the UK. Reproduced with permission from Digest of Environmental Statistics 1998, no. 20, Figure 8.4*

Figure 4   Helvellyn, Lake District National Park. Source: Jeremy Raemaekers

Figure 5   Helm Crag from Heron Pike, Lake District National Park. Source: Jeremy Raemaekers

Alongside National Parks, the 1949 Act also enabled the National Parks Commission and its successors to designate 48 Areas of Outstanding Natural Beauty (AsONB) in England, Wales and Northern Ireland (where the Department of the Environment for Northern Ireland is the designating body) (Figures 7 and 8); they cover 13% of the land area of England and Wales (Figure 3). They differ from National Parks in three ways. First, they are designated for landscape beauty alone and not for recreation. Second, whereas the National Parks lie in the uplands, the

Figure 6 *Hadrian's Wall, Northumberland National Park. Source: Jeremy Raemaekers*

Figure 7 *Tors on Bodmin Moor, an Area of Outstanding Natural Beauty. Source: Jeremy Raemaekers*

Figure 8 *South Downs, an Area of Outstanding Natural Beauty. Source: Jeremy Raemaekers*

AsONB lie in the lowlands. Third, even though they are considered in landscape value as the lowland equal of the upland National Parks, they lack the administrative structures of the Parks. They do benefit from extra funding, and most of the permitted development rights removed in the Parks are also removed in them, but the Countryside Commission (now Agency), which is responsible for them, is campaigning for more money and for stronger administrative machinery to prevent their decline (Countryside Commission, 1997).

A different kind of designation is the Environmentally Sensitive Area (Figure 3). This is an agricultural designation under the Agriculture Act 1986, but it is made on the recommendation of the natural heritage agencies. It is not a planning designation, but deserves mention, both because it is often mistaken for one, and because it has been one of the more effective environmental tools for influencing what happens to farmland. Environmentally Sensitive Areas are intended to conserve attractive farmed landscapes by offering farmers within them the opportunity of entering an agreement which supplies a package of grants to help preserve traditional landscape, natural and archaeological features in return for conforming with certain practices. Entry to the scheme is entirely voluntary, so success obviously depends on uptake.

There are also grants available for similar purposes to farmers outside Environmentally Sensitive Areas, administered by the agriculture departments, the natural heritage agencies and the Forestry Authority. Some of these apply everywhere, while others target landscape features characteristic of certain areas (summarised in UK Government, 1994b, chapter 15). Such grants must be seen in the context of the exceptional postwar state support of the farming industry, which has tended to increase intensification and mechanisation at the expense of the natural heritage (see, for example, Nature Conservancy Council, 1991; Lowe, 1986; Shoard, 1980). Spending on environmental measures within the farming support budget has increased greatly under the Agriculture Act 1986 and the 1992 Agri-Environment Regulation of the Common Agricultural Policy, but it still amounts to only 4% of it.

Coasts have also received special attention. One-third of the English and Welsh coastline is designated as Heritage Coast by the countryside agencies, and much of this receives extra protection and management input because it also lies in National Parks or AsONB, or is owned by the National Trust, which has bought nearly 1000 km of coastline in its Enterprise Neptune project. Planning guidance has been issued which in essence argues that, in hitherto undeveloped areas, development which does not need to be on the coast should not be permitted there (PPG20, Department of the Environment, 1992b).

Scotland

With the exception of Environmentally Sensitive Areas, Scotland has gone its own way on landscape and recreation designations. Until now there have been no National Parks in Scotland, where a coalition of landowning, local authority and Hydro Board interests rejected them, and where recreational demand was in any case light in 1949. It also has no AsONB. There are instead 40 National Scenic Areas covering 13% of the land (Figure 3), which are mostly upland and coastal, and in which planning controls are tightened. The 70-year debate over National Parks in Scotland ended with the government's announcement in September 1997 that Scottish Natural Heritage should bring forward proposals for creating National Parks. Loch Lomond and theTrossachs has been cited as the first candidate area, and the Cairngorms as the second. The former is currently one of four Regional Parks, created under legislation unique to Scotland and managed by the local authorities with grant aid from Scottish Natural Heritage. They have a primarily recreational, rather than conservational, purpose.

There is also provision for the designation of Natural Heritage Areas, an integrated designation intended to apply over a large area of outstanding wildlife and scenic value subject to multiple demands, such as the Cairngorm Mountains. This has however been criticised for being a toothless concept depending on goodwill rather than powers, and the provision has never been activated since its enactment in 1991. There is no equivalent in Scotland of Heritage Coasts, although Scottish Natural Heritage defined marine consultation areas in response to the fish farming boom, in which it asked planning authorities to consult it on applications. Planning guidance sends the same message about coastal development as south of the Border (Scottish Office Development Department, 1997b).

In September 1998 The Scottish Office (1998) issued a consultation paper proposing that, when new SSSIs are put forward for designation, occupiers should be

Figure 9 *Straiton Pond, Local Nature Reserve, Edinburgh. Source: Jeremy Raemaekers*

given the opportunity to enter a management agreement with incentive payments for positive actions; the controversial compensatory agreements under the 1981 Act would be abolished.

LOCAL DESIGNATIONS

In addition to the numerous national designations, there is also a plethora of local designations by local authorities. Again these are separate for nature and landscape conservation. A great deal of effort is put into identifying and protecting sites of local interest (see, for example, Collis and Tyldesley, 1993). Nevertheless, only one local designation is statutory, the Local Nature Reserve (LNR), which can be designated by a local authority under the 1949 Act. It is a useful means of conserving sites which, while of modest scientific value, nevertheless have a value to the local communities which can readily gain access to them for pleasure and education (Figure 9). The local authority will usually own the site, giving it total control over its fate. There are over 240.

The other designations are non-statutory, and their effect is limited to including policies in the Development Plan which afford them some extra protection from built development compared with the rest of the countryside; there is no protection from farming or forestry. There is often a lack of coordination between neighbouring authorities, with the result that a designation halts at the administrative boundary although the scenery marches on.

THE CONTRIBUTION OF PLANNING AUTHORITIES

Having outlined the framework of natural heritage conservation, we can now set out the range of roles which planning may play therein. We shall then explore in the next section some examples of these roles. It is useful to think of roles in three categories: duties which planning authorities must perform, specific powers laid down by statute which they may exercise at their discretion, and additional activities which they may undertake but which are not specified in any statute.

The 1968 Countryside Act laid a general duty on local authorities 'to have regard to the desirability of conserving the natural beauty and amenity of the countryside' in exercising their functions relating to land (section 11). Natural beauty includes flora, fauna and physiographic features as well as landscape, and amenity – an ill-defined term – means something like affording pleasure. This can be seen as the legal basis for all planning authority activities to conserve the natural heritage. It is now backed by the requirement of Article 10 of the European Habitats Directive to encourage the management of countryside features important to wildlife, and of the Town and Country Planning (Development Plan) Regulations 1991 to have regard to the environment in the preparation of Structure Plans.

More specific duties are set out in national planning guidance (PPG7, Department of the Environment, 1997, and PPG9, Department of the Environment, 1994; NPPG14, Scottish Office Development Department 1999a; Welsh Office, 1996). The guidance requires Structure Plans and part 1 of Unitary Development Plans to identify key sites, such as SSSIs and AsONB, to establish a strategic natural heritage conservation framework for the territory. They should include policies in respect of sites which reflect their relative importance (international, national, regional, local). Local Plans and part 2 of Unitary Development Plans should interpret these in detail, and should set out the criteria against which applications affecting sites will be judged. The surveys which local planning authorities are statutorily bound to undertake in order to inform the drawing up of Development Plans should cover the natural heritage. Detailed procedures are set out in planning circulars for handling applications in designated sites.

In addition to these duties, planning authorities can exercise a number of relevant powers specified in legislation. These include:

- making byelaws, e.g. to control recreation on a beach, and which may sometimes be necessary to secure the protection required by the Habitats Directive;
- issuing Tree Preservation Orders to save valued trees or groups of trees;
- designating Local Nature Reserves;
- making access agreements or orders under the Countryside Acts to enable public access to the countryside; planning units are also often involved in footpath work alongside the Highways Authorities responsible for establishing rights of way;

- making management agreements under the Countryside Acts – a wide-ranging power which is seldom exercised because of cost.

Other contributions which planning authorities may make include:

- promoting where appropriate natural heritage conservation and enjoyment as an end use for reclaimed mineral workings or industrial land, or as an interim use for temporarily vacant land;
- leading and coordinating local nature conservation strategies (see the next section), and ensuring that the relevant parts of these are incorporated in Development Plans;
- promoting nature-friendly management of land by other local authority departments such as highways (e.g. not mowing road verges until flowers have set seed), parks (e.g. more naturalistic growth) and education (e.g. nature projects in school grounds);
- promoting surveys of the natural heritage over and above the basic requirement for Development Plan making, e.g. by funding voluntary bodies to do them;
- hosting liaison groups between the public, private and voluntary sectors.

Although we have placed a lot of emphasis in this section on statutory functions in natural heritage conservation, it is fair to say the non-statutory roles as catalyst and information clearing-house are among the most effective that planners can play. They form a particularly large part of their role in urban areas, where there are inevitably few sites of national importance, but where 80% of the population lives.

THE VOLUNTARY SECTOR

We have described above the governmental systems for conserving the natural heritage, but the voluntary sector is also a major player. There are powerful lobby groups like the Council for the Protection of Rural England, which apply pressure at parliamentary and policy-making levels, and there are organisations which directly manage a large amount of land and water to conserve the natural heritage. For example, The National Trust, which has 2.5 million members, owns many properties of natural heritage value, including 770 km of coastline; the Royal Society for the Protection of Birds has a million members, is a major owner of nature reserves, and increasingly plays a national policy lobbying role; and there is a comprehensive network of county naturalists' trusts which own reserves or manage them for owners. These trusts are also an example of voluntary organisations that exercise influence as non-statutory consultees of local planning authorities at both Development Plan and development control levels.

Case Studies of Practice

Having set out in the previous section the framework for natural heritage conservation, we can now explore examples of how it works in practice and how the planning system is involved. This section presents three case studies which, between them, cover different aspects of the natural heritage, different arenas of action, and different types of planning work. The first case concerns the making of an urban nature conservation strategy, the second a development control conflict between conservation and recreation facilities, and the third the origin and testing of a type of forestry strategy.

Nature Conservation and Planning

The Case Study

As indicated in the previous section, one of the voluntary actions local planning authorities may undertake is a local nature conservation strategy. Such strategies are good examples of positive planning, and show the authority playing both a formal role as plan-maker and development controller, and an informal one as catalyst and coordinator of other agents. Many authorities have now made strategies, particularly for urban areas. The example below is that of my home town, Edinburgh, but it is repeated in many places.

Edinburgh Council published its strategy in 1992, drawing on a survey of the city's wildlife begun in 1987 (City of Edinburgh District Council 1992a, b, c). The survey examined over 1000 sites and revealed that almost 40% of the land area within the city bypass is green space capable of supporting wildlife, even excluding private gardens, which themselves must cover a substantial proportion of the other 60% and are a very rich wildlife habitat. Such high proportions of habitat in urban areas are in fact common; our towns are often more welcoming to wildlife than our fields.

The survey, however, also revealed threats both from pressures and from neglect. Half of the 31 most important sites identified were threatened by potential development, and many of these were not protected in the Local Plans, indicating an important task for the planning authority. No less than 26 of these 31 sites were unsympathetically managed, and half of all the woodlands examined showed no sign of regeneration at all, being doomed to die off unless actively managed.

The vision is that:

> Armed with this strategy we can be sure that decades from now Edinburgh will still be full of green places and our open spaces and parks will be known for their variety, interest and richness of wildlife. We will still need the blaze of colour from a formal flowerbed and the plain green functional football pitches but we will have much more. Meadows full of wildflowers, quiet corners where the wild birds can nest in safety and

trees in abundance. Here will be the green, fascinating areas where the city dweller can wander in peace and where children will have the opportunity to see for themselves the beauty and wonder of nature (City of Edinburgh District Council, 1992a, p. 1).

The survey and subsequent strategy are typically a joint effort, led by the city's planning department, but also involving the then regional council, the government heritage agency Scottish Natural Heritage, and voluntary groups at international (World Wide Fund for Nature), national (Scottish Wildlife Trust) and local (Edinburgh Wildlife Group) levels. The general ecological approach was to identify Urban Wildlife Sites (the most valuable sites), wildlife corridors which allow plants and animals to migrate and interbreed between sites, and at least two Neighbourhood Nature Areas in each ward which, though of lesser importance, could be used to encourage local communities to become involved in site planning and management.

The strategy objectives are to:

- protect important wildlife sites;
- encourage the sympathetic management of existing and newly created habitats;
- encourage the creation of habitats for the benefit of both wildlife and people; and
- involve people in urban wildlife and the care of their local environment.

A test of the first objective arose soon after adoption of the strategy. A supermarket chain applied to develop an Urban Wildlife Site lying at the end of one of the identified wildlife corridors. The council refused permission. As it turned out, the company did not appeal against the refusal and later withdrew because it was granted permission to develop a much larger site elsewhere in the city, but the point remains that the site's integrity was upheld because of the policy in the strategy, even though it had not yet been incorporated in the relevant statutory Local Plan.

Incorporation into the Local Plan, however, accords the policy more muscle, and the strategy states at the outset that the intention is that the council will do so. The three Local Plans since produced in Edinburgh have duly incorporated such policies, identifying the Urban Wildife Sites and protecting them from development. A policy in one Plan requires applicants for development permission to submit 'an environmental assessment quantifying the impact of their proposals on the nature conservation value of the site' (policy RE15, City of Edinburgh District Council, 1993).

The second and third objectives are only partly within the council's control, since much of the land is owned by others, but the strategy includes a policy committing the council to 'prepare management plans for urban wildlife sites in its ownership, and take full account of wildlife in managing its other lands', in addition to a policy to encourage others to do likewise. By 1997 the council had produced management plans for half the Urban Wildlife Sites in its control, and had succeeded in getting owners of some of the other sites to produce them too. For example, producing one was made a condition of planning permission for a university to redevelop a former mental hospital site with wooded grounds.

The last objective seeks to build on existing community nature conservation projects. An example is Meadows Yard Neighbourhood Nature Area, a derelict allotment which passed to council ownership with a view to built development. Owing to physical constraints development proved not to be feasible, and the site languished until the nature conservation strategy. Under the strategy it has been taken into management by a committee of the council's strategy officer (a qualified planner located in the planning department), a representative from the voluntary Scottish Wildlife Trust and six residents of the area. Residents have surveyed the wildlife of the site; undesirable plants are being controlled; access, a footpath and signage have been put in; trees have been planted and a pond made. A newsletter written by the strategy officer goes to the nearest 300 houses.

Lessons

The most important lesson is very simple: have a strategy. With a strategy, it is possible to catalyse and coordinate actions by diverse bodies and people. With a strategy, it was possible to argue successfully for resources to get Neighbourhood Nature Areas off the ground. With the strategy as justification, a site was effectively defended even without a policy in the statutory plan. If you can back your stance on a particular case with a general policy that is part of a document in the formulation of which you have consulted other interests, then it will carry more weight. This principle has been codified in national planning guidance on another topic, supplementary design guidance on buildings (PPG12, Department of the Environment, 1992d).

The strategy also primes the council to take advantage of any opportunities that may arise in the future. This is what has happened with the city's parallel urban forestry strategy. This lay dormant for want of funding, but when the Millenium Forest Fund was established with National Lottery money, a successful application was made for funding and the strategy sprang to life. It will considerably expand the city's stock of woodlands by planting 100 new clumps of trees in much less time than originally envisaged. Four officers have been taken on for the project, based in the planning department. Similarly, following the agreement of the Bio-diversity Convention at the 1992 Earth Summit, an opportunity has arisen to apply for funding from the European Union to extend the city's nature conservation strategy by pioneering an urban biodiversity action plan, focusing on species and habitats rather than sites.

The strategy officer also points to more specific lessons. One is to beware of ranking sites by importance. While the logic seems indisputable, in practice it means that sites ranked as of strictly local importance are likely to be offered up as sacrifices, with the result that in the long term only the most important sites are protected, and there seems little point in having identified the others in the first place. Another lesson is to avoid unnecessary prescription in the wording of policies. For example, inserting a standard, such as a minimum percentage of tree cover in a policy to encourage developers to plant trees, would give the developer something specific to dispute, and no incentive to plant more than the minimum prescribed.

RECREATION VERSUS CONSERVATION

The Case Study

For this case we move from the city to the opposite extreme, one of Britain's highest mountains, on the edge of its largest wilderness. The case concerns an application to erect a funicular railway and a visitor centre on Cairn Gorm in north-east Scotland. It is a good case study for three reasons. First, it is a micro-cosm of the classic planning conflict between development of a natural asset for its recreational value and conservation of the asset for its heritage value. Second, it involves planning from the national level down to the local level. Third, it addresses the interaction between a natural heritage agency and a planning authority.

Cairn Gorm is the most popular of the five downhill snow skiing centres in Britain. It lies on the upper flank of the famous mountain of that name, and its development has the been the focus of much controversy over the years (Figure 10). The Secretary of State for Scotland has twice rejected attempts to expand the site, in 1981 and 1990. Such has been the controversy here and at other skiing centres that the Scottish Office issued a National Planning Guideline on skiing developments in 1984 and a replacement in 1997 (Scottish Development Department, 1984; Scottish Office Development Department, 1997a).

The present application sought to upgrade the existing site by replacing the open chair lift to the top station with a funicular railway, which could carry more people and operate in all weathers. It would carry not only skiers in winter, but also sightseers in the summer. The top station, presently a small restaurant, would be much expanded into a visitor centre. The idea was to boost the summer trade to help fund the skiing enterprise.

The local authorities and the government's development agency, Highland and Islands Enterprise, have always favoured expansion of the site; indeed, their predecessors largely funded its development. The tourism and leisure industry is a vital employer in the Highlands, where job opportunities are few and young people tend to migrate out in search of jobs. Tourism is however primarily a summer industry, and the development of skiing has been seen as an important way of generating winter jobs in the industry. Scotland-wide, skiing is said to generate

Figure 10 *Glenshee – one of Scotland's downhill skiing stations. Source: Jeremy Raemaekers*

over £20m a year and to support 1500 winter jobs directly and indirectly. Apart from the value to the local economy, the promoters of the development can also point to the national importance of the ski centres in meeting national sporting demand. The five centres together attract 200 000–650 000 skier-days a year, Cairn Gorm itself being the leader. The skiing lobby claims that demand exceeds the supply of facilities.

Unfortunately, four of the five ski centres lie in environmentally sensitive sites. The Cairn Gorm site itself lies adjacent to a proposed Special Protection Area (SPA) under the European Birds Directive and a proposed Special Area of Conservation under the European Habitats Directive, is in a National Scenic Area (NSA), and is one of only three proposed natural World Heritage Sites (designated by the United Nations) in the UK. This meant that when the planning authority as required consulted the natural heritage agency, Scottish Natural Heritage, on the proposal, the latter was very concerned about both the scenic impact of the proposal and the physical impact of delivering a large number of summer sightseers to within a short walk of the summit. The summit plateau has the most extreme climate in Britain, and its arctic-alpine vegetation is especially sensitive to trampling, taking up to a century to regrow once damaged.

But Scottish Natural Heritage wished to avoid the expensive Public Inquiry which an objection to the proposal would cause, and wished to avoid being seen locally as obstructive. Hence it approved the development in principle, even though the visitor centre would clearly impact on the view of the NSA. The national planning guidance (in draft at the time) allows development in designated sites of *national* importance when

> exceptionally, any significant adverse effects on the environmental qualities for which the site has been designated are outweighed significantly by the scale of the social, recreational and economic benefits that would arise (Scottish Office Development Department, 1996, para 32).

At a pinch, this could be interpreted to let the development go ahead. However, the guidance cannot be so flexibly interpreted with regard to the SPA and proposed SAC. It states that, in such a case, development can go ahead only if there will be no adverse effect on the interest of the SPA or SAC, or there is an overriding public interest and no alternative solution. In this instance, the visitor pressure clearly would threaten the interests of the SPA and SAC; there are alternative ski centres; and the proposal could hardly be classed as a matter of overriding public interest. On nature conservation grounds, therefore, Scottish Natural Heritage could not approve the proposal. Caught on the horns of a dilemma, the compromise it came up with was to accept the proposal for the building on scenic grounds, but only subject to the agreement of a visitor management plan which would protect the birds and vegetation.

The plan eventually agreed requires all visitors to be kept inside the visitor centre. But what then, you will ask, is the point of driving half way up the mountain, then paying to go to the top, if you cannot get out when you arrive? That in turn calls into question the attraction of a visitor centre on top of the mountain and thus the financial viability of the entire proposal. In this circumstance, the precautionary principle to which government subscribes surely calls for refusal of the proposal, but it was approved by Highland Council subject to the agreement of the visitor management plan to Scottish Natural Heritage's satisfaction. Nobody is happy with this outcome.

Lessons

Do you think this case shows the planning system in a good light? It highlights the recreation–conservation conflict and within it the tension between local and national interests. It reveals the difficulty faced by the national natural heritage agency, with a multiple remit tied to policy which is tougher in one sphere (wildlife) than another (landscape), merely because the European Union happens to have issued a directive on one but not the other.

But the lessons go deeper than that. Why has the case dragged on for so long and caused such bitterness when there is specific national planning guidance which should show the way? Arguably, the national planning guidance has failed, because it has not sent clear signals (Raemaekers, 1991, 1996). You could also argue that the Cairngorm massif, split between several local authorities, is a prime candidate for a national park-type of institution which would have produced strategic policy obviating such a controversy. Ironically, not long after the funicular case was decided, the government announced the intention to designate the massif as a National Park (see previous section).

PLANNING AND INDICATIVE FORESTRY STRATEGIES

The Case Study

This case study differs from the recreation one in two ways: in the role played by the planning authority and in the type of issue at stake. In the recreation case the planning authority is the decision-making body, and the natural heritage agency is its consultee. In this instance, the roles are reversed, and planners can obtain results only by persuading another powerful government regulatory body, the Forestry Commission. The recreation case study is about whether to allow built development in a wilderness, but this one explores a decision about the environmental benefit of retaining a working countryside in one primary use, farming, or allowing it to be converted to another primary use, forestry. Depending upon the circumstances, either could be interpreted as more environmentally friendly. In order to understand the case, we need first to outline the afforestation debate.

Government has promoted tree planting throughout this century because Britain is so deforested compared with other European countries: 5% tree cover in 1919, 11% now compared with the European average of 25%. You will probably agree that felling or planting a wood is a major and long-lasting land-use change; after all, trees take 30–70 years to grow to harvestable size. Yet forestry, like farming, was almost entirely excluded from planning control by the 1947 Town and Country Planning Act. It follows that someone can be refused permission to build a small house in the countryside, yet the landscape for square miles around that same site can be entirely felled or planted up without planning permission.

To fell more than a few trees, you do need permission, but it comes from the Forestry Commission, which is a national government body, not from the locally elected planning authority. To plant trees requires no permission, although you do need approval of your planting plan by the Forestry Commission if you want its grants. In practice, this gives the Forestry Commission control, because few people find it financially viable to plant without grant. The Forestry Commission was also itself a major planter until the 1980s. It regulates itself, although in 1992 the Commission was split into an operational arm, the Forest Enterprise, and a separate regulatory arm, the Forestry Authority, which now regulates the Enterprise as well as the private sector.

Many people have complained about the lack of local planning control over planting and felling. The debate came to a head during the 1970s and 1980s when the overall tax regime, specific tax rebates on planting, and planting grants, together promoted a wave of private sector planting, mostly with foreign species of conifers, often in large uniform blocks which look ugly and harbour limited wildlife. Much of that planting took place on open moorland, especially in Scotland and in the uplands of England and Wales, but not uncommonly on the sites of previously standing mixed woods of natural, scenic and cultural interest, which were felled to clear the land for planting.

In response to such concerns, planners sought to exercise some control over forestry. In 1974 the Forestry Commission began to consult local planning authorities on the applications it received for felling licences and planting grants. This helped, especially as the Commission tried its best to accommodate planners' views. But the planning authorities lacked strategies equivalent to the Development Plan to guide their responses, so they were reacting case by case and not necessarily consistently. Moreover, they had little information on either the existing forest stock or trends, and the Forestry Commission was reluctant to divulge data. Calls were made for 'indicative forestry strategies' (IFS) to fill the policy gap.

The first was published by Strathclyde Regional Council, the Structure Plan authority for a vast swathe of western Scotland, in 1988. It was concerned at the transformation of the landscape wrought by conifers spreading at the rate of 8000 hectares per year. The planners consulted with bodies representing heritage, water and land-use interests, mapped these interests, and drew up a 1:250 000 scale strategy map taking account of them. It showed where they would welcome planting, where they would accept it, and where they would oppose it (Goodstadt, 1997).

The Scottish Office subsequently produced a planning circular endorsing IFS in the style of Strathclyde's, and requiring any made to be included in the Structure Plan (Scottish Development Department, 1990 – later emulated in England and Wales, Department of the Environment, 1992c; Welsh Office, 1992; since revised in Scotland, Scottish Office Development Department, 1999b). This gives the strategies some legitimacy, even though in law forestry remains outside planning control. Eight Scottish regional planning authorities and at least four English county planning authorities have produced IFS (Royal Society for the Protection of Birds, 1996).

An early test of the effectiveness of the strategies was a 1991 proposal to plant 230 hectares of hill sheep land, at Muirhill on the Campsie Fells north of Glasgow. The Campsies were zoned as sensitive in the then brand new Central Regional Council IFS, meaning that there was a presumption against further extensive planting. A more detailed local forestry framework also zoned the site as unsuitable for planting because it is a water catchment and of wildlife interest. When consulted by the Forestry Commission on the proposal, the planning authorities opposed it on

316
———

these grounds. A failure of coordination between the district and regional councils, however, weakened their case, and the Forestry Commission's regional advisory committee, which arbitrates in forestry disputes, recommended approval of the proposal. The Central Region planners upheld their objection, pointing out that approval would ignore the newly minted IFS, which would be seen to be worthless if it were flouted at the first test. The matter was referred up to the Forestry Commissioners themselves. They, possibly on the instructions of the Secretary of State for Scotland – who oversaw both the Commission and the planning regime – overturned their regional advisory committee's recommendation and rejected the proposal. The decision was seen as a political one endorsing the principle of IFS.

Lessons

The IFS story shows how the planning profession, perceiving a widespread change of rural land use with major impacts on the natural heritage, but over which it has no statutory control, contrived to exercise some influence over it. Strathclyde Regional Council, by putting together a strategy, in effect bounced the Scottish Office into issuing a planning circular sanctioning IFS. The importance of making a strategy is clear, as it was in the urban nature conservation case study – and as it was in the ski centre case study, where the continuing absence of a strategic framework has led to repeated tussles and an unsatisfactory outcome.

The Muirhill case is a success story from the planning authorities' point of view, but IFS have been strongly criticised in some quarters. When planners venture into unfamiliar territory occupied by other professionals, such as land agents, foresters and landscape architects, these may view the new arrivals as bureaucrats interfering in what they are not equipped to understand (Watson, 1995; Murray, 1994). Two of the criticisms are also worth mentioning here because they raise issues of general importance in planning.

The first is that the strategies ignore commercial reality: what is the point of zoning lots of land as preferred for planting if it is financially unattractive? The planners involved are conscious of this, but would counter that commercial land values are unstable, depending on the relative subsidies to forestry and to farming, which could change unpredictably; that such values are not their business; and that in any case the planning authority would be accusable of exceeding its powers if it published a policy map in effect identifying the commercial value of land and thus affecting the land market.

The other criticism is that the strategies zone swaths of land as sensitive to planting using existing natural heritage designations, which are not necessarily a good guide to whether and how the landscape can absorb tree planting. The zoning approach fails to differentiate between different types of forestry, such as blanket conifers versus selective broadleaved cover, and the strategies essentially deal only with new planting on bare ground, rather than management of existing forest. In the face of these complications, some argue that planners should abandon drawing 'go' and 'no go' zones on maps. They should focus instead on developing a set of design guidelines. Provided there were sufficient information about the values and needs of the surrounding area, such guidelines would permit decisions more appropriate to the individual case, and would allow a shift of emphasis from saying yes or no, towards a positive design approach.

IFS are not the only type of plan through which town and country planning can be involved in forestry. They are a specific response to a specific concern. There are many informal forestry and countryside strategies made by English and Welsh councils. There are also positive plans for the National Forest and the 12 Community Forests in England and the Central Scotland Forest. These are all about enhancing landscapes by positive programmes of planting.

EVALUATION: THE ROLE AND PERFORMANCE OF THE TOWN AND COUNTRY PLANNING SYSTEM

THE LIMITS OF THE PLANNING SYSTEM'S ROLE

We have seen in this chapter that there are many ways in which the local planning authorities can contribute to natural heritage conservation, both statutory and non-statutory, and both regulatory and promotional.

There are, however, limits to the scope of the planning system to contribute to natural heritage conservation. The one most frequently cited is the exclusion from the planning system of the major primary land uses of farming, estate management and forestry. Although we have seen that there are ways in which planning can make inputs, especially in forestry, ultimately it has little power to shape the direction of policy in these fields or to prevent specific actions detrimental to the natural heritage. Thus planning has been able to do little, beyond information collation and exchange and lobbying, to moderate the massive impact of agricultural intensification through land drainage, ploughing of meadows, reclamation of moorland, loss of field boundaries, application of agrichemicals and the like. A recent exception to this is hedgerow protection under the Environment Act 1995. This requires those intending to remove a hedge over a certain age to notify the planning authority, which can then prevent removal if it can show that the hedge has a certain heritage value (but imagine the amount of data, communication and enforcement this will need to be effective!).

A similar limitation is the cessation of planning control at the low water mark, below which a very large part of our natural wealth lies. An example of a resulting anomaly is that a planning authority regulates the landing station for a fish farm, but not the farm itself floating just offshore in a sea loch. Many environmentalists would argue that the wave of concern for the environment in the last few decades has paid too little attention to marine conservation.

Thirdly, planning can do a limited amount about pollution, on which attention is increasingly focused as a threat to the natural heritage. Within its own territory, a planning authority can protect amenity locally by controlling where potentially polluting developments go. It can do nothing, however, to prevent pollution entering its territory from outside by river or air transport. Long-range acid air pollution from industrial and vehicle emissions is implicated in needle drop and death among coniferous trees and in the extinction of life in naturally acidic water bodies. Thus, remote areas like the Cairngorm Mountains may suffer from pollutants emitted hundreds of miles distant.

How is the Planning System Performing?

Accepting these limits to the role of the planning system, how is it performing within them? We can approach the question by applying the principles of environmentally sustainable development as criteria.

The planning system has historically sought to balance conservation and development. Thinking on sustainable development argues that this is no longer enough. The system must be more rigorous in its approach, and must:

- identify critical natural assets that must be preserved at any cost;
- seek compensation in kind for those non-critical assets that are lost to development, in order that the total stock of assets is not reduced;
- always seek opportunities to enhance existing assets or to create new ones; and
- always seek ways to minimise damage to the heritage.

The latter three criteria are arguably nothing new to the planning system. The second has long been met at the level of the individual application through planning agreements and obligations, and is now beginning to be applied at the level of the Development Plan through environmental appraisal. It is reinforced by Article 6 of the Habitats Directive. The third criterion is met through such positive initiatives as the nature conservation strategy described in the previous section, and the fourth through development control, stiffened by the introduction of environmental impact assessment in 1988 (see Chapters 2 and 13). These three criteria between them account for the great mass of planning decisions and actions with implications for the natural heritage, and there can be little doubt that, at the level of the individual case, the trend is upward.

However, the sheer pressure for development – for example a projected 3.8 million new English homes 1996 to 2016 – means that even good performance according to these criteria is unlikely to prevent further erosion of the current heritage. It is this perception that focuses attention on the first of the four criteria listed above, which is new to planning. The intrinsic problems of identifying critical assets have been pointed out in Chapter 2, and the government's heritage

Table 3 Number of Sites of
Special Scientific Interest damaged:
government version

Year	Number of sites
1990–1	233
1991–2	183
1992–3	129
1993–4	117

Table 4 Number of Sites of Special Scientific Interest damaged: Friends of the Earth version

	1991–2	1992–3	1993–4	1994–5	1995–6
England	272	200	142	134	147
Wales	41	165	165	171	198
Scotland	no data	18	17	28	no data
Total	313	383	324	333	345

Source: SCENES October 1997 from Friends of the Earth's website.

agencies are not as keen on the concept as they were (CAG Consultants and Land Use Consultants, 1997). The case study of the ski centre in this chapter is an example of the kind of dilemma that can arise when seeking to apply the principle – in this case due to the different status of scenic and biological designations in international agreements.

Nevertheless, we can take Sites of Special Scientific Interest as one of the least contentious approximations of the nation's critical natural assets, and look at our success in protecting them. According to the government damage is falling (Table 3). Unfortunately, Friends of the Earth do not agree, especially in the case of Wales (Table 4)!

Most of the damage is short term and reparable, caused by farming operations. Most of the *irreparable* damage is however due to planning permissions. The worst offenders are big government-sponsored projects, like the M3 at Twyford Down, the Newbury Bypass or the Manchester Airport second runway. This is not surprising, if you think about it, because it is more likely that the natural heritage interest will be overriden where the competing interests are deemed to be of regional or national importance. Unfortunately, it also inevitably sends the signal that central government is prepared to sacrifice critical natural assets where the price is right. While this would have been acceptable under traditional planning thought, it is not so under 'strong' sustainability. The Habitats Directive should in future force us towards protecting critical assets. Once again, Europe is the driving force behind progress on the environment.

320

REFERENCES

Brown, S. (1990) Humans and the environment: changing attitudes, in: Silvertown, J. and Sarre, P. (eds), *Environment and Society*, Hodder and Stoughton for the Open University, Sevenoaks, pp. 238–279.

CAG Consultants and Land Use Consultants (1997) *What Matters and Why – Environmental Capital: a New Approach*. Report to Countryside Commission, English Nature, English Heritage and the Environment Agency, CAG Consultants, London.

City of Edinburgh District Council (1992a) *An Urban Nature Conservation Strategy for Edinburgh*, The Council, Edinburgh.

City of Edinburgh District Council (1992b) *An Urban Nature Conservation Strategy for Edinburgh, Urban Wildlife Site Descriptions*, The Council, Edinburgh.

City of Edinburgh District Council (1992c) *An Urban Nature Conservation Strategy for Edinburgh, Technical Report*, The Council, Edinburgh.

City of Edinburgh District Council (1993) *South West Edinburgh Local Plan: Written Statement: Adopted*, The Council, Edinburgh.

Collis, I. and Tyldesley, D. (1993) *Natural Assets. Non-Statutory Sites of Importance for Nature Conservation*, The Local Government Nature Conservation Initiative.

Countryside Commission (1997) *Improving the Funding and Management of Areas of Outstanding Natural Beauty, Consultation Paper*, The Commission, Cheltenham.

Countryside Commission and English Nature (1996) *The Character of England: Landscape, Wildlife and Natural Features*, The Countryside Commission, Cheltenham and English Nature, Peterborough.

Department of the Environment (1992a) *The UK Environment*, HMSO, London.

Department of the Environment (1992b) PPG20, *Coastal Planning*, HMSO, London.

Department of the Environment (1992c) Circular 29/92, *Indicative Forestry Strategies*, HMSO, London.

Department of the Environment (1992d) PPG12, *Development Plans and Regional Planning Guidance*, HMSO, London.

Department of the Environment (1993) *Countryside Survey 1990 Main Report*, Department of the Environment, London.

Department of the Environment (1994) PPG9, *Nature Conservation*, HMSO, London.

Department of the Environment (1997) PPG7, *The Countryside – Environmental Quality and Economic and Social Development*, HMSO, London.

Goodstadt, V. (1997) Environmental sustainability and the role of indicative forestry strategies, *Scottish Forestry*, **150**(2), 77–84.

Holmes, R. (1997) Don't ignore nature's bottom line, *New Scientist*, 17 May, 11.

International Union for the Conservation of Nature and Natural Resources, United Nations Environment Programme and World Wildlife Fund (1980) *World Conservation Strategy*, IUCN, Morges.

Lowe, P. (1986) *Countryside Conflicts: the Politics of Farming, Forestry and Conservation*, Temple Smith/Gower.

MacGillivray, A. and Kayes, R. (1994) *Environmental Measures. Indicators for the UK Environment*, Wildlife and Countryside Link et al.

Murray, J.S. (1994) Indicative forestry strategies – a critique, *Scottish Forestry*, **48**(1), 16–21.

Myers, N. (1983) *A Wealth of Wild Species*, Westview Press, Boulder, Colorado.

Nature Conservancy Council (1991) *Nature Conservation and Agricultural Change*, The Conservancy, Peterborough.

Prescot-Allen, R. and Prescot-Allen, C. (1988) *Genes from the Wild*, Earthscan, London.

Raemaekers, J. (1991) Piste control: the planning and management of Scottish ski centres, *The Planner*, 15 November, 6–8.

Raemaekers, J. (1996) Slippery slopes of downhill guidance, *Planning Week*, 4 April, 14–15.

Royal Society for the Protection of Birds (1996) *Forestry Plan Scan '96. A Review of Indicative Forestry Strategies*, RSPB, Edinburgh.

Scottish Development Department (1984) *National Planning Guidelines 1984: Skiing Developments*, Scottish Office, Edinburgh.

Scottish Development Department (1990) *Circular 13/90 Indicative Forestry Strategies*, Scottish Office, Edinburgh.

Scottish Natural Heritage (1996) *Assessing the Natural Heritage Resource. A Guidance Note for Local Authorities from Scottish Natural Heritage*, Scottish Natural Heritage, Perth.

Scottish Office (1998) *People and Nature. A New Approach to SSSI Designation in Scotland*, Scottish Office, Edinburgh.

Scottish Office Development Department (1996) *Draft NPPG Skiing Developments*, Scottish Office, Edinburgh.

Scottish Office Development Department (1997a) NPPG 12, *Skiing Developments*, Scottish Office, Edinburgh.

Scottish Office Development Department (1997b) NPPG 13, *Coastal Planning*, Scottish Office, Edinburgh.

Scottish Office Development Department (1999a) NPPG 14, *Natural Heritage*, Scottish Office, Edinburgh.

Scottish Office Development Department (1999b) *Indicative Forest Strategies*, Circular 9/1999, Scottish Office, Edinburgh.

Scottish Tourist Board (1996) *Tourism in Scotland 1995*, The Board, Edinburgh.

Shoard, M. (1980) *The Theft of the Countryside*, Temple Smith.

UK Government (1994a) *Biodoversity: The UK Action Plan*, Cm 2428, HMSO, London.

UK Government (1994b) *Sustainable Development: The UK Strategy*, Cm 2426, HMSO, London.

Watson, A. (1995) Indicative Forestry Strategies – a costly con trick, *Ecos*, **16**(1), 52–58.

Welsh Office (1992) Circular 61/92, *Indicative Forestry Strategies*.

Welsh Office (1996) Planning Guidance Wales – *Planning Policy; and Technical Advice Note (Wales) – Nature Conservation and Planning*.

CHAPTER 13

PLANNING FOR MINERALS, WASTE AND CONTAMINATED LAND

Jeremy Raemaekers

INTRODUCTION

There are three regimes of environmental regulation in the UK: the town and country planning system, the natural heritage protection system, and the environmental protection or pollution control system. The present chapter addresses the interface of the first and the last, but there is not space to cover the entire environmental protection system. We therefore focus in this chapter on certain parts of it, with which planning has a fairly clear interface – minerals, waste and contaminated land.

Minerals are defined in the planning acts as 'all substances of a kind ordinarily worked for removal by underground or surface working'. This definition focuses on extraction, omitting subsequent processing except where this is on the site of extraction and of a fairly simple kind – e.g. the crushing of rock or the washing of coal. We shall exclude oil and gas, the extraction of which, in the case of the UK, is nearly all off shore and therefore not under planning control, and the processing of which on land is not considered a primary industry in the way that mining and quarrying are.

Wastes are hard to define. The obvious definition of waste is a by-product of no commercial value, but in practice there is much effort to recycle 'wastes', which by definition then must have value. It also seems logical to include under wastes emissions to air and effluents to land or water from industry and transport, which we commonly call pollutants. But again in practice these are considered separately, and we shall generally not deal with them here. Waste planning is a current topic in which planners are trying to define their role under a new legal regime.

Contaminated land is the legacy of past failure to protect the environment through inadequate waste management and pollution control. A whole section of the chapter is devoted to it because, like waste planning, it is a current topic in which planners are faced with a new legal regime.

As we shall see below, there is a further and pragmatic reason for dealing with minerals and wastes in the same chapter, namely that Britain disposes of much of its waste in the holes ('voids') left by aggregate and rock quarrying.

MINERALS

THE PECULIARITY OF MINERALS AND MINERALS PLANNING

From the standpoint of the planning system, minerals differ from other development. First, mineral extraction does not add something to the environment (except in so far as it requires buildings on site and produces wastes), but rather removes something from it. Secondly, as a corollary of this, minerals can be developed only where they naturally exist, whereas in principle most forms of development could go anywhere. Thirdly, the extraction process at a given site tends to continue for a long time, sometimes decades; whereas the construction phase of most developments, which produces similar environmental challenges, lasts just a few years. One might tentatively add a fourth characteristic, that, more than most development, minerals extraction is the necessary supply base of much other economic activity. Land-based mining and quarrying contribute over £4 billion annually to the national economy, and employ some 50 000 people, mostly in rural communities (Census of Production, cited in Confederation of British Industry, 1998).

Minerals planning has become a specialism within town and country planning, almost a profession within a profession. This is reflected in England in a separate series of 15 mineral planning guidance notes (MPGs), the requirement to produce separate Minerals Local Plans, the existence of the professional journal *Minerals Planning*, and the advertisement of job vacancies specifically for minerals planners. It is therefore surprising that it barely features as a specialism in planning courses accredited by the Royal Town Planning Institute (Royal Town Planning Institute, 1997). A good general account of minerals, their extraction and the abatement of its environmental impacts is given by Blunden (1996), who takes an international view. Owens and Colwell (1996) review minerals planning from the standpoint of sustainability. Planning viewpoints can also be found in special issues of *Planning* (23 January 1988) and *Scottish Planner* (February 1994).

THE GOVERNMENT'S APPROACH TO MINERALS PLANNING

Given that minerals underpin so much of the nation's economic activity, the government not surprisingly insists in its national planning guidance that planners must not stand in the way of adequate supply:

> The level of minerals production is a consequence of customer demand in response to the needs [of providing for homes, jobs, shops, food, transport, fuel, building materials and recreation]. The level of minerals production is therefore essentially a matter for market forces . . . The determination of the best means of meeting the demands of the market is not an objective of the planning system: such decisions are best left to the

commercial judgement of the minerals industry (NPPG4, *Land for Mineral Working*, Scottish Office Environment Department, 1994).

This view accepts that the level of demand is set by the market rather than attempting to manage demand. This contrasts with the spreading acceptance of demand management in transport, energy production, waste management, and now even housing provision, in tune with the government's espousal of sustainable development.

Notwithstanding the above, the government tries to set out a 'sustainable framework for mineral extraction'. This is in principle not strictly feasible for resources such as minerals, since the supply is finite, but the next best principles of using as little as possible and of minimising the environmental impacts of extraction are applied instead:

- To conserve minerals as far as possible, while ensuring an adequate supply to meet the needs of society for minerals.
- To minimise production of waste and to encourage efficient use of materials, including the appropriate use of high quality materials and recycling of wastes.
- To encourage sensitive working practices during minerals extraction and to preserve or enhance the overall quality of the environment once extraction has ceased.
- To protect designated areas of critical landscape or nature quality from development, other than in exceptional circumstances where it has been demonstrated that development is in the public interest (*Sustainable Development: the UK Strategy*, UK Government, 1994; these principles are also included in mineral planning guidance).

There is a hint of limiting supply also in the policy in the 1994 version of NPPG4 for Scotland. That sets a limit of four coastal superquarries up to the year 2009 to supply demand from outside the region, especially from Southeast England, which cannot supply its own demand. This is in reality, however, more likely the result of a political tussle between the Scottish Office and Southeast England, than a manifestation of sustainable development thinking. We shall return to this case later in this section.

The government's assertion that market forces should determine supply does not mean that the state refrains from intervening in minerals markets. As in most countries, the state has intervened heavily in the energy market and, since coal historically provided most of Britain's energy, the coal industry has been a part of this. Around 1900 coal mining employed a million people and entire communities existed purely because of mines. The industry was later nationalised, and a special relationship was established between it and the nationalised electricity generating industry, which was a key customer. Then in the 1980s, for both economic and political reasons, government orchestrated the demise of the deep-mined coal industry and incidentally the concomitant rise of the opencasting of coal (Hills, 1984; Rydin, 1993, chapter 13).

Figure 1 *Craig Park crushed rock quarry, Ratho, Edinburgh. Reproduced by permission of Alan Prior*

ENVIRONMENTAL IMPACTS AND THEIR CONTROL

There are many kinds of minerals, but those in the UK can be grouped into dimension rock for building; aggregates (crushed rock, sand and gravel) for all kinds of foundation work and especially roads; raw materials for chemical processes like cement making, fertiliser production and ceramics; metal-bearing ores; fuels like coal; and peat. Environmental impacts vary according to the nature of the mineral and whether or not it is extracted on the surface or underground (Figure 1). In Britain the chief concerns are numerous surface quarries for rock and for sand and gravel, as well as opencast coal pits; only a handful of deep coal mines still operate. Nobody would question that extraction is an unsympathetic neighbour, and since mines and quarries often lie either close to habitation or in scenic landscapes, they pose planners with a classic jobs versus environment tradeoff.

Most mineral extraction in Britain is of low value materials, which have to be transported in bulk and which, because of their low value per tonne, are generally confined to local markets. To put it the other way around, the aggregates for road building, for example, will have to be found within a radius of some tens of kilometres of the building site. This adds an extra twist to the planning constraint that 'minerals have to be mined where they occur'. It produces enduring conflicts in sensitive areas, for example the quarrying of limestone in the Peak District National Park to feed steel furnaces and power station sulphur scrubbers, because there simply is no other source within economic distance.

On-site impacts vary, but noise, blasting and dust are typical. In some cases there is considerable modification of the landscape, whether in removing

Figure 2 *Coal bing from a deep coal mine, east Lothian. Source: Jeremy Raemaekers*

overburden to reach a seam in surface mining, or in the permanent dumping of waste, e.g. from underground mining of coal. *Waste tips* in intensively mined areas can come to dominate the local landscape, for example near St Austell in Cornwall where china clay is mined, coal bings in deep coal areas like the 'Valleys' of South Wales, or slate in Snowdonia, North Wales (Figure 2). Historical tips can come to be valued as the essence of the local cultural landscape, as with the red oil shale bings in West Lothian, Scotland, where some are positively protected. This raises an interesting debate about the origin of landscapes, their relative value as cultural and natural heritage, and their value as heritage against the value of the land in new uses.

In addition to such waste material extracted in removing the product from the ground, there are also in some processes 'tailings' – material left over after primary processing. These are often stored behind a dam to prevent leaching of toxic substances, e.g. acid runoff resulting from exposure to oxygen. Tailings are often in the form of ponds, because the process leaves a wet waste, or simply because the dam traps water. Occasional failures of tailings dams can cause considerable ecological damage, such as the disaster on the Cota Doñana in Southern Spain in the spring of 1998, where a unique coastal nature reserve is threatened by a massive outflow of tailings laced with heavy metals (MacKenzie, 1998).

The chief off-site impact of extraction is *transport*. A sizeable pit will generate hundreds of lorry trips daily. Typically, this imposes a traffic load which is inappropriate to small country roads and detrimental to the amenity of nearby residents, being noisy, dusty, muddy and a threat to safety. The requirements of correct loading and wheel washing before leaving the site help abate dust and mud. Ideally, the product is taken away by rail in the first instance, or by ship if on the coast, but of course these options are seldom available. (Ironically, most of the small railways of the nineteenth century were built for mineral movement, not people movement, but have long since closed down, and building a new railway would pose big planning problems as well as a high cost. Inspection of the Ordnance Survey 1:50 000 scale maps of old mining areas will reveal a web of 'tk of old rly' or 'dismantled railway'.)

One of the chief planning issues is *restoration and aftercare* of the site after working ceases (see MPG7, Department of the Environment, 1996). Sites are often bought by the extractor from the landowner, although the extractor may simply buy the mineral rights or lease the land for the duration of the work. In the former case the extractor is then free to sell the site back or sell it on to another party. The extractor is not however wholly free to leave the site in whatever condition he or she pleases; the conditions imposed by the planning authority will include restoration conditions.

Typically, sites are on farmland and are restored to farmland, sometimes improved beyond their original condition. But they can be restored to other purposes, for example recreation: a sand or gravel pit can readily be landscaped to produce a park and a lake for watersports. Closed opencast coal mines are a valuable source of sites for tree planting in the new forest initiative areas (e.g. the National Forest in the Midlands, the Community Forests near major conurbations and the Central Scotland Forest between Glasgow and Edinburgh).

Hard rock quarries by their nature are not wholly backfilled unless there is a convenient and cheap source of material, or unless they are used as waste landfills (some companies operate as both mineral extractors and waste disposers). When they are not wholly backfilled, worked out quarries leaving behind walls can still have value for nature conservation, once plants colonise (especially basic rocks like limestone, on which flowers flourish), or perhaps for rock climbing.

Underground mines pose different after-care issues. Generally they are out of sight and therefore out of mind, but they can pose two problems: outflow of polluted water and subsidence. *Polluted outflows* have become a topical issue following the closure of over 100 deep coal mines in the last 15 years or so. The empty mines fill with water, which leaches iron and other metals from the shaft walls; unless a mine is pumped continuously to prevent filling, it eventually overflows into the nearest water catchment, polluting the streams. But if I no longer own a closed mine, and if I met the environmental standards of the time at which I owned it, is it fair to expect me to rectify the problem now? Special regulations have had to be made to cope with the problem retrospectively.

Subsidence can be a severe planning constraint locally. Removal of entire coal seams, especially where there are several above each other, inevitably leads to settling of the land surface above. In heavily mined areas up to two-thirds of buildings may be affected, although the proportion severely damaged is only a few percent. The problem is mostly a historical one now, but cooperation between miners and planning authorities can minimise future problems by seeking not to place development directly above seams to be mined, and leaving coal in place where overlap is unavoidable.

Applications for mineral extraction are by their nature subjected to close environmental scrutiny by the planning authorities. Environmental impacts can be mitigated through planning conditions, and over the years the standards required of operators by the planning system have increased (the Town and Country Planning (Minerals) Act 1981 was a significant milestone). A typical planning condition for a quarry would carry several tens of conditions. In England, the series of MPGs offer detailed guidance on this; in Scotland and Wales the guidance is much more compact, though planners often refer to the English MPGs for further advice.

It has also been common since the introduction of the *Environmental Assessment* Regulations in 1988 to require an Environmental Statement from the applicant. Indeed, the revised European Directive on Environmental Assessment 97/11/EC, which came into force in 1999, makes assessment mandatory for quarries and opencast mines over 25 ha and for peat extraction over 150 ha. The Environmental Assessment system is outlined in Chapter 2. As indicated there, a huge literature exists on the subject, including a good practice guide by the Royal Town Planning Institute itself (Royal Town Planning Institute, 1995). Selman (2000, pp. 266–288) gives an accessible account of EA, focusing on mineral extraction. To give you an idea of the issues, Box 1 reproduces the contents of a statement submitted with an application for a modest extension to an opencast coal mine.

Box 1 *Subject contents of an Environmental Statement for extension to an opencast coal mine: Blindwells East, East Lothian, Scotland*

Note: this omits background, existing situation, details of the proposal, non-technical summary; and, for each subject, discussion and mitigation proposals.

Visual impact
   baseline landscape context
   visual analysis
Ecology
   soil descriptions
   soil nutrient status
   land capability classification
   soil-handling recommendations
   drainage
   habitat survey
Archaeology

Hydrogeology (note: this is probably the most complex issue in opencasting)
    ground conditions
    groundwater rebound
Noise
    measurement of levels
    prediction of levels
    rating of levels
Dust
    effects of dust
    potential dust sources
    climatic conditions
    areas adjacent to site
Blasting
    ground-borne vibrations
    air-borne vibrations

Source: Scottish Coal (nd).

Negotiating with the applicant about what the statement should cover (known as 'scoping'), and assessing it when it has been submitted, can be quite a challenge for the planner, unless s/he is familiar with mineral matters. A revealing account of coping with the unexpected is given by Egerton (1994), who was landed out of the blue with the first application for a gold mine in the Highlands of Scotland.

Forward Planning

At the national level, there have in the past been national plans for the then nationalised coal industry, with production targets. Since privatisation of the industry, there has been no government plan for it. The Department for the Environment, Transport and the Regions employs consultants to estimate future demand for aggregates, and the information is used by regional aggregate working parties (RAWPs), which bring together the industry and planners, to identify demand in each region and how it is to be met (see MPG6 Aggregates). No such regional framework exists for non-aggregate minerals. Regional planning guidance (RPGs) should in principle set out a regional framework for minerals generally, but this has usually in practice been little more than reiteration of national policies in the MPGs.

The Environment Act 1995 places mineral planning authorities under a duty regularly to review all mineral extraction permissions in their territories. They should also safeguard important mineral deposits from development which might sterilise them. The Planning and Compensation Act 1991 also requires mineral planning authorities to produce Mineral Development Plans which show where working may occur, where mineral wastes should be deposited, where the 10 year landbanks of valid planning permissions are located which ensure that future demand can be met, and which contain policies for development control, restoration and aftercare. The exact form of these plans varies (see Box 2).

Box 2 *Minerals and waste disposal policies in Development Plans*

Under the Planning and Compensation Act 1991 responsibility in England and Wales is assigned as follows (PPG12 *Development Plans and Regional Planning Guidance*, Department of the Environment and Welsh Office, 1992, para. 3.13):

Wales: Local Plans to contain policies. Now UDPs to contain policies.
English metropolitan areas: Borough UDPs to contain policies.
English shires: Counties to produce separate or joint minerals and waste Local Plans.
National Parks: NP Authority to prepare separate or joint minerals and waste Local Plans or to incorporate policies in parkwide Local Plan.

In *Scotland*, the Town and Country Planning (Scotland) Act 1997 includes a requirement for policies on waste installations in Development Plans. NPPG 4 *Land for Mineral Working* 1994 and NPPG10 *Planning and Waste Management* 1995 spell out that the Structure Plan should set the strategic context for a region, interpreted through Local Plans. Local Subject Plans devoted to minerals or waste could be prepared, but none exists for waste and only three for minerals.

EQUITY ISSUES

As mentioned above, mining and quarrying applications tend to pose the planning authority with a trade-off between local jobs and damage to local amenity. A surface quarry or mine in fact employs few people (typically a few tens), since it is largely mechanised – a necessity given the need to move a lot of material to win a small amount of product. Nevertheless, to a small community in the countryside which has few other job opportunities, even a few jobs can make a lot difference, especially as they are year-round, and also because they are for men, many of whose former sources of employment have declined. The down side is that local residents have to put up with the impacts outlined above.

A particular problem arises where a community is subjected to the *cumulative impact* of prolonged working at one site or at a succession of sites in the neighbourhood. This has been the case with opencast mining in Tyne and Wear, for example (Clough, 1993). Each application is judged on its merits but, even with

Figure 3 *Open cast coal mine, Midlothian. Source: Jeremy Raemaekers*

the best working practices, the ceaseless disturbance will grind people down and also blight the area, making homes hard to sell and deterring inward investment. Yet it may seem unfair to an applicant that they are turned down because of their addition to the cumulative effect, rather than because of the impacts of the individual project, which may be no worse than those of others previously granted permission.

Opencast coal mining (Figure 3 and 4) has been painted as particularly damaging, to the extent that the Labour manifesto for the 1997 general election included proposals that would severely constrain it, and which were then written into revised planning guidance, in particular requiring that a proposed development must yield a net benefit to the local community in order to gain permission (Scottish Office Development Department, 1999; Department of the Environment, Transport and the Regions, 1999a; see Chapter 2, for a discussion of the significance of the new policy). Opencast coal mining turns over some 10 000 ha of land a year (Blunden, 1996), and may in some cases even threaten the health of nearby residents (Edwards, 1997). However, there is often some *planning gain* secured from the development through site restoration. Some of the possible outcomes were mentioned above. Others are that the site may rework an earlier coal mine, which is cleared away as part of the restoration of the new one; or land may be stabilised to allow house or road building where it was not previously possible without extra investment. The deal might actually involve the building of, say, an access road to an adjacent housing estate which needed one. Such deals are struck under section 106 of the Town and Country Planning Act 1990 (in Scotland

Figure 4 *Open cast coal mine, East Lothian. Source: Edward Williams*

section 75 of the 1997 Act, or section 69 of the Local Government (Scotland) Act 1973) (see Chapter 4).

An equity issue of a different sort has arisen at inter-regional scale. In the late 1970s it was proposed that very large crushed rock *coastal superquarries* could be developed on the coasts of Norway, Scotland and Spain, able to profit from economies of scale in extraction and in transport by sea, and able to serve distant markets. One such quarry operates at Glensanda in Loch Linnhe on the west coast of Scotland. This option has come to the attention of Southeast England, which is unable to supply its own demand, being densely populated, with a high demand but few potential supply sites which are not firmly constrained by proximity to settlements or valued environmental areas. It was therefore proposed, and incorporated into MPG6 *Aggregates* in 1994, that Scottish superquarries might be developed to supply Southeast England. The Scottish Office responded in its 1994 NPPG4 *Land for Mineral Working* with a long deliberative text, eventually concluding with the statement that up to four such quarries might be permitted to the year 2009 on the north and west coasts of Scotland. An application was made to develop one at Lingerabay on the Isle of Harris off the west coast, which became a *cause celèbre*. The case went to a public inquiry which lasted a long time, and the inquiry reporter (equivalent of inspector in England) reported to ministers in April 1999, but her recommendation was not yet known at the time of writing in February 2000.

How do you view this application? You could take a national view, which says that it is entirely sensible because the Southeast is tightly constrained while Harris is remote and little populated: demand will be met with disamenity to the fewest people. But you can also view it as the unfair export of environmental costs from the Southeast to a distant and weak region – just another manifestation of Sassenach imperialism. This view gains strength from the designation of Lingerabay as a National Scenic Area, which would be severely modified. There are also worries about incoming ships' ballast water being unloaded, bringing with it exogenous species of sea life which would impact on the local marine ecology. What is most interesting is that the people of Harris, represented by their local council, at first supported the application for the jobs it would create, yet later did a U-turn to oppose it, partly on environmental grounds *per se*, and also on the grounds that it would damage environmental tourism, which is itself an important and potentially longer term employer.

A third equity issue of a still more different sort is the proposed *quarry tax*. The European Union has a policy to shift the burden of taxation on industry and commerce from taxing employment to taxing resource consumption. The rationale is that this will help both employment and the environment at the same time. The UK Government introduced such a tax in late 1996, the landfill tax, described in Box 3 below. In the March 1999 budget, the government announced that it would impose an analogous tax on quarrying unless the minerals industry produced a voluntary package of proposals to improve its environmental performance.

A specific purpose of the tax would be to act as an incentive to better environmental controls, and specifically to promote the use of recycled minerals (which would be tax free) in lieu of primary ones. The Confederation of British Industry raises several queries about the proposal, a couple of which are clearly valid (Confederation of British Industry, 1998). First, many minerals are traded internationally (unlike the waste subject to landfill tax), and the UK industry would be at a competitive disadvantage against countries not subject to such a tax (to which one might counter that it should be a European Union tax anyway). Second, the aim of increasing recycling is already addressed in part by the landfill tax. Moreover, most of the viably recyclabe mineral wastes already are recycled, and a tax at the rate envisaged of £1–2/tonne sold would not be much of an incentive, because the raw mineral itself makes up only a small part of the cost of whatever it is eventually used for (Bate, 1998). The CBI also point out that, since the public sector accounts for 40% of the custom of the industry, the public sector will itself be hard hit! This is of course more a threat than a valid objection, since the public sector just as much as the private sector should minimise resource use.

EVALUATION

Minerals differ from other development under the planning acts in several ways, not least of which are that they underpin much of our economic activity, and that they have to be developed where God, not the planning authority, chose to put them. Minerals face planners with hard choices.

Winning minerals is a messy business, yet as a densely populated and industrialised nation, we need a lot of minerals, including high bulk/low value ones which realistically must be obtained near the point of use. Unfortunately, that same high population density places a premium on countryside and residential amenity, to which mineral extraction is detrimental. We have limited scope to export abroad the environmental costs of winning minerals, except in the case of low bulk/high value ones, such as uranium, gold, diamonds and the like. We have also been lucky enough to find oil and gas offshore rather than onshore.

Minerals, being finite, cannot be used sustainably in the strict sense. Nevertheless, the UK has tried to limit the damage done locally by extraction, both by enforcing generally applicable good working practices, and by seeking to protect cherished landscapes from minerals development. We do not suffer from the excesses of strip mining seen in much of the New and Old Worlds. Nevertheless, we do not, and probably cannot, hope always to succeed, as witnessed by communities driven to distraction by successive opencast mines on their doorsteps, and by continuing extensions granted to quarries in National Parks.

As planners, we need also to be aware that big shifts can occur in the markets for fuel minerals in particular, with the result that the range of planning issues raised can change dramatically over the time it takes an undergraduate student to complete a course and acquire his or her initial practice experience. In part this can arise from technological breakthroughs, as with North Sea oil and gas. But it can also arise from government intervention. It would be fair to say, for example, that the major planning issue raised by coal is not mineral working at all, but how to regenerate entire villages and districts left without employment by the wholesale closure of deep mines.

WASTE

THE PROBLEM OF WASTE

We live in a society that produces and consumes a lot of goods, and it follows that we produce a lot of waste. Waste is the unwanted by-product of industrial (some of which we have looked at above), commercial and domestic activities or anything otherwise discarded; it can be gaseous, liquid or solid. The amount and variety of waste has risen greatly in the last half century, raising at least three environmental concerns:

- The supply of natural resources is ultimately limited and its extraction and processing into goods affects the environment; we could reduce the drain on resources and the impacts of it by creating less waste in the first place, and we could recover more of what we do produce.
- The disposal of waste can pollute the environment in various ways and, as pollution control standards are tightened, it is becoming harder to find acceptable sites for disposal facilities.

Table 1 *Waste arisings in the UK.* (Figures are estimates for a year in the 1980s. Note the distinction between controlled and other waste)

Sector	Annual arisings (million tons)	Total arisings (%)
Household	20	5
Commercial	15	3
Construction and demolition	70	16
Other industrial	70	16
Sewage sludge	35	8
Dredged spoil	35	8
Total controlled	**245**	**56**
Mining and quarrying	110	25
Farming	80	18
Total all waste	**435**	**100**

Source: Department of the Environment and Welsh Office (1995a).

- Waste treatment and disposal facilities are generally regarded as bad neighbour developments, and this too makes it harder to find acceptable sites for them.

For these reasons, the search is on to find ways of minimising the amount of waste we produce in the first place, recovering what is produced in some way, and disposing of what is left over in a way that achieves a socially acceptable balance between cost and environmental protection.

Table 1 shows the waste produced. Two points jump out at you from the table. First, the sheer quantity – half a *billion* tonnes of it every year. Second, whereas most of us equate waste with what we put out in our domestic bins, that actually accounts for a very small proportion of it – even less than the sludge left over from the treatment of sewage! The table does not show special waste, which is toxic or a fire hazard; this accounts for 5% of all controlled waste. It also excludes the small quantities of radioactive and explosives waste, dealt with under dedicated legislation.

What the table does not reveal is that, in the words of a parliamentary committee, 'the continuing lack of information in government is extraordinary' (House of Commons Environment, Transport and Regional Affairs Committee, 1998, p. lxxi).

WASTE MANAGEMENT OPTIONS

What options are available for dealing with the waste? The Enviromental Protection Act 1990 put in place a sound regime for regulating waste management, but

Table 2 *Waste disposal in the UK*

Sector	Landfill (%)	Incineration (%)	Recycled/reused (%)	Other
Household	90	5	5	0
Commercial	85	7.5	7.5	0
Construction and demolition	30	0	63	7
Other industrial	73	2	21	7
Total controlled	**70**	**2**	**21**	**7**

Source: Department of the Environment and Welsh Office (1995a).

there was still no strategy to address the big issues outlined above, under which the regime would operate. The UK Sustainable Develoment Strategy (UK Government, 1994) began to address this by establishing a *waste management hierarchy* to move waste disposal towards a more environmentally sustainable pattern. This reflects the policy of the European 5th Action Programme on the Environment (Commission of the European Communities, 1992). The hierarchy, from most to least desirable, is:

- *Reduce*: reduce production of waste to the minimum compatible with economic sustainability.
- *Reuse*: put objects unaltered back into use (e.g. milk bottles).
- *Recover*: *Recycle*: put materials back into use, e.g. cullet from bottles;
  Compost: process organic waste to produce soil conditioner or growing medium;
  Energy: burn waste and recover the energy content of it, or collect landfill gas for burning.
- *Dispose*: last choice; ensure disposal is environmentally sound (generally in a landfill – dumping at sea is being phased out).

The policy is to shift overall management practice up the hierarchy. But how do we perform at present? Table 2 shows that we overwhelmingly use the least desirable option in the hierarchy, landfill. The figures need some interpretation; for example, those on industrial waste almost certainly underestimate recovery of the end products of processes, which are sold on or become feedstock in some other part of the same company, and so are not counted as waste. The figures on household and commercial waste, which together form what is called municipal solid waste (MSW), are real enough, however, and differ greatly from those of some European nations, which achieve much higher rates of recovery and/or favour incineration over landfilling of what can be burnt.

In order to move waste management from the position shown in Table 2 up the hierarchy set out above, a national waste strategy has been produced (Department of the Environment and Welsh Office, 1995b; a separate one is being made in

Scotland, Scottish Environment Protection Agency, 1999). We shall return to this below, but shall first look at the implications of waste management for the planning system.

THE IMPLICATIONS OF WASTE MANAGEMENT FOR THE PLANNING SYSTEM

The two management options with the biggest land-use impacts are landfill and incineration. *Landfilling* has hitherto dominated in Britain because it is cheap, because many areas have suitable ground conditions of impermeable clay, which seals sites against leaching of effluent, and because there are lots of old quarries which make convenient and generally impermeable holes. Landfilling a quarry with waste is also an effective way of restoring the landform, killing two birds with one stone.

Until recently there were some 5000 landfill sites in the UK, a figure that is comparable with the number of substantial industrial sites, and would make landfill a significant use of land, even without amenity and environmental issues. The trend is now towards fewer but better run sites, as controls are tightened to implement the European Directive on the Landfilling of Waste. The European view is that landfilling is basically undesirable, and the directive reflects the waste management hierarchy set out above. A particular bone of contention is that the UK operates co-disposal of MSW and some hazardous industrial wastes, relying on the former to biodegrade the latter. The European Commission disapproves of this and would rather see separate toxics-only sites, but the UK argues that it works well at the 300 sites licensed to do it, and has won the right to determine practice on this aspect at the national level.

The other pressure bearing down on landfilling is the landfill tax, introduced in October 1996. This levies charges to encourage other management options in keeping with the waste management hierarchy. It is hitting the councils responsible for waste disposal hard in the short term, until they find ways of passing on the cost or other management options (Box 3).

Box 3 *The landfill tax*

The landfill tax was introduced in October 1996 under the Finance Act 1996. It was hailed as the UK's first green tax, with the purpose of shifting the tax burden from employment to natural resource use (actually, this is not strictly true, since the rise in VAT on fuel is a green tax too). The landfill tax is fiscally neutral, being compensated by a 0.2% fall in national insurance payments. Its objective is to reduce the amount of waste going to landfill, thereby reducing the risk of pollution from landfills, through reducing the amount of waste arising in the first place, e.g. by recycling, which also reduces the call on primary resources. The tax is £2 per tonne of inert waste such as builders' rubble, and £7 per tonne for biologically or chemically active waste such as MSW (£10 from April 1999). Some wastes are exempt, such as harbour dredgings, quarrying waste, and some contaminated soils stripped from contaminated land.

An associated scheme of environmental bodies is further intended to use part of the income generated by the tax to fund local projects beneficial to the environment, preferably but not exclusively with regard to waste management. Thus there should be a 'double whammy': the tax reduces waste and potentially funds projects which also further that goal. This is as near as the government will come to a hypothecated tax, i.e. one that is dedicated to activity which it taxes. Under the scheme, the landfill operator (who actually pays the tax and passes the cost on to his customers in higher charges) can reclaim up to 20% of his tax liability as a rebate, provided it is paid into environmental bodies. The rebate can count for up to 90% of the money paid into a body, with the remainder being paid in by the landfill operator direct. A regulator, Entrust, has been created to license such bodies.

First, the good news. In its first year of operation, the tax raised £420m for the Treasury, and paid between £26m and £40m into trusts, depending whose figures you accept. Again according to whose figures you accept, there were 400 or over 1000 such trusts a year and a half down the line. Some waste generators have reduced their arisings in response, and the waste management companies are finding a new line of business in advising their customers on how to do so.

Now the bad news: there are big question marks over the tax's realisation of its main objectives. Different interested parties give different stories, but all seem to agree that a lot of waste has 'gone missing' in some way – active waste has been relabelled as inert to attract a lower rate of tax; or to avoid tax altogether inert waste has been retained by generators in unnecessary landscaping on golf courses, road schemes, house foundations and so forth, or waste has been illegally fly-tipped.

Ironically, the reduction in inert waste going to landfills has created a problem for the landfill operators, who are now short of material to seal and landscape their tips; some even resort to buying in primary quarry products to compensate! In response, inert waste used for landfill restoration was made tax exempt from 1999, but not material used for *sealing* landfills.

All this suggests that the tax is having, if anything, the opposite effect from that intended. Perhaps it is set too low to bite anyway – less than 1% of the turnover of a typical firm generating wastes. However, commentators agree that the idea is right, and that it is now a matter of fine-tuning the system.

Sources: Pearce (1998), Farrar (1998), Dudgill (1998), House of Commons (1998).

Table 3 *Incinerators in the UK in 1991*

Type	Number
MSW	30
Sewage sludge	6
Clinical waste	700
Hazardous waste	4
Chemical companies' in-house plant	40

Source: Royal Commission on Environmental Pollution, cited in Department of the Environment and Welsh Office (1995a).

The advantages of landfilling were mentioned above. The disadvantages include the potential for release of pollutants, mainly by leaching into ground water and by landfill gas generation. Leaching is addressed by lining and draining sites (but it does not always work – see Box 4 below), and gassing by gas extraction for energy recovery, turning a problem into a profit. Installation of gas recovery plant is subsidised by the government under the non-fossil fuel obligation (NFFO), which forces the regional electricity companies to buy some of their electricity from renewable energy sources even though they cost more than conventional ones. Other aspects which planners must take into account in considering the siting of landfills are smell, wind-blown rubbish, dust, noise and the heavy traffic of lorries to and from the site, which may amount to hundreds of loads each day. One way of reducing this traffic is the use of rail within the chain from collection via transfer (sorting and compacting) stations to disposal sites, and this could be an important factor in siting.

Incineration is not a common method of disposal in this country (Table 3), but has generated a lot of planning interest. Specialist high-temperature incineration is an effective means of disposing of clinical waste and many toxic wastes. There have in the past been many publicised cases of alleged – but never proven – health impacts in the vicinity of such incinerators, notably those operated by Rechem in Scotland and Wales.

Mass-burn incinerators are used to dispose of MSW, sewage sludge, carcases and the like. There used to be more of these in the 1970s, but by December 1996 all but six had been forced to close by higher emission standards introduced to comply with European Directive 89/429/EEC on incineration. A handful of new ones have and are being built to the new standards (89/369/EEC), generally with energy recovery incorporated in order to make them financially more viable through the sale of electricity (e.g. Edmonton in London). This also renders them eligible for subsidy under the NFFO. A revised European Directive with still tighter standards is in preparation.

The environmental advantages of incineration are:

- reduced production of methane (a greenhouse gas and an explosion risk) from decomposition of waste in landfill;

- energy recovery from burning, either as electricity or as combined heat and power;
- reduction of the volume of final waste for disposal (as ash) by 90%;
- preemption of the pollution risk from landfilling the waste.

The disadvantages are:

- it remains costlier than landfill, though the gap is narrowing as landfill grows more expensive;
- MSW incinerators are big investments which, once made, tie up one's options for waste disposal;
- there can be a conflict between incineration and recycling for some materials like paper (if paper is removed from waste, the heat yield of the waste drops);
- some emissions remain, e.g. heavy metals.

Modern mass-burn incinerators should produce little smoke and grit pollution, but they will generate as much traffic as a landfill. The august Royal Commission on Environmental Pollution (1993) favours them, but this cuts no ice with the public, who remember the dirty old incinerators and do not distinguish between mass-burn and high-temperature incinerators. They are seen as bad neighbour developments, shunned by residents, commerce and clean industries anxious to project a high amenity image. Planning blight is therefore a big consideration in determining an application for an incinerator, and such applications take eight to ten years to determine.

This raises an important general issue: the demarcation between the planning and pollution control regimes. Research for the government found that planners see central pollution control authorities as 'too close to industry' and concerned that pollution control powers do not protect against cumulative pollution by successive developments in one locality (Department of the Environment, 1992). Moreover, planning decisions are made by a democratic process which cannot ignore the reality of planning blight due to people's perceptions, whatever the facts of the case. The pollution control system is, in contrast, more technocratic, and less immediately exposed to the local political process, especially since the recent centralisation of pollution control functions.

The result is that planners may seek to control pollution through planning conditions. This is exceeding their powers, and the government has had to step in with planning guidance to try to define the regimes' relative roles. PPG23 (Department of the Environment and Welsh Office, 1994a) tried to resolve the tension by encouraging consultation between the two regimes and suggesting simultaneous, rather than sequential, application for emissions licences and planning permission. But it accepted that matters relevant to a pollution control authorisation may also be taken into account in a planning decision, and that development that satisfies pollution control authorities may still be deemed by the planning authority to

——

present an unacceptable risk in planning terms. In short, an incinerator that passes its emissions test will not necessarily get planning permission. New English planning guidance for waste requires planning permission to be obtained before the waste management licence (PPG10, Department of the Environment, Transport and the Regions, 1999b).

PLANNING FOR SUSTAINABLE WASTE MANAGEMENT

On a more positive note, planning guidance sets out what the planning system can contribute to the achievement of more sustainable waste management under three broad headings (NPPG10, Scottish Office Development Department, 1997):

- implementing the Waste Management Licensing Regulations 1994;
- applying the principles of sustainable development;
- implementing the national waste strategy.

The *Waste Management Licensing Regulations 1994* implement the waste pro- isions of the Environmental Protection Act 1990. The regulations bring in many new provisions, which put into effect the EC Framework Directive on Waste 75/442/ EEC, as amended by 91/156/EEC. This is a typical example of UK law being triggered by the requirement to implement European law to which the country is party. The directive requires *planning* measures for waste management. This is interpreted as requiring Development Plans to set out strategic and detailed policies and proposals for making sites available for treatment and disposal facilities. Box 2 explains where in the scheme of Development Plans these should appear.

The principles of *sustainable development* which the planning guidance wishes to see applied fall into two groups:

- general ones, but which have specific applications in waste management – best practicable environmental option (BPEO), the precautionary principle, and the polluter pays principle (PPP);
- those specific to waste management – proximity and regional self-sufficiency.

The BPEO is the option that yields most benefit or least damage to the environ- ment in the long term and at acceptable cost. BPEO can operate at any level, but its particular application to waste management is the very complex appraisal of what, at national and regional scales, is the best mix of waste treatment methods.

The precautionary principle states that where there is good reason to fear an environmental impact from an action, you should err on the side of caution even if the evidence is not conclusive.

The PPP seeks to ensure that management options bear their full environmental costs, and that those responsible for pollution are the ones that pay them. The landfill tax is an example, as is ensuring that conditions attached to planning permission for a facility place on the developer the cost of environmental care and site restoration.

The proximity and self-sufficiency principles are themselves in a sense applications of the PPP, since the former requires that waste be dealt with as close as possible to its source, encouraging communities to take responsibility for their own waste. Self-sufficiency is one means of achieving proximity, requiring groups of waste disposal authorities to deal with their waste within their own borders (in Scotland specifically within Structure Plan areas), rather than exporting the problem.

The *national waste strategy* (*Making Waste Work*, Department of the Environment and Welsh Office, 1995b), seeks to apply these principles through the waste management hierarchy (a draft review was published in July 1999, Department of the Environment, Transport and the Regions and Welsh Office, 1999). The 1995 strategy sets a number of targets which the planning system will have a role in achieving, among them:

- to reduce the proportion of waste going to landfill from 70% to 60% by 2005;
- to recover value (in one way or another) from 40% MSW by 2005; there is already a target of recycling 25% of household waste by 2000, which there is no hope of even approaching, since councils average around 6% (Table 2).

Boxes 4 and 5 illustrate efforts by regions at opposite ends of the country and opposite extremes of population density to plan strategically for waste management. Read and consider them from the standpoints of the sustainable development principles, the waste management hierarchy and the national strategy targets set out above.

Box 4 *Waste strategy for the Scottish Highlands*

The main method of waste disposal in the Highlands, as elsewhere, is landfilling. The population is small and very dispersed, which means that either you run many small landfills, or you opt for a few big ones but accept inefficient long distance transport of waste along country roads. The small dump option is increasingly ruled out by the rising cost of landfilling due to tax and stricter standards. Existing dumps do not meet the new standards, so will be forced to close, and are running out of space anyway. Nor is incineration a viable alternative to landfilling, because modern incinerators able to meet strict new emissions standards are expensive investments, and require a very large concentrated source of waste nearby to pay their way. Even recycling requires a high density of population to make sense financially. It seems to be very difficult indeed for such a region to move up the waste management hierarchy.

Experience bears this out. The region was faced in 1994 with an acute shortage of disposal sites. The then district councils, as waste disposal authorities, were fast running out of places to put their waste, but the then regional council, as planning authority, was failing to find new sites locally acceptable in planning terms. The region proposed as the solution two new regional super-dumps. One, in the far north, already existed and would be expanded to take rubbish from the whole northern area. Unfortunately this site, completed only four years earlier as a supposedly impermeable landfill, was already leaking leachate, which was not a good omen for expansion. The other site had yet to be found, in a strategic location accessible by the two biggest roads in the region, the A9 and A96. The potential savings of the superdump approach are considerable: the two strategic sites were calculated to cost £17m over the period 1997–2010, as against £27m to maintain local sites.

But, of course, a regional superdump is inevitably subject to the NIMBY ('not in my back yard') effect: although everybody produces waste, nobody wants their own, let alone the rest of the region's, dumped near them. Nor is this only a matter of aesthetics: the Highlands economy depends much on tourism income derived from its scenic beauty, and a landfill in the panorama will clearly not help local tourism. Every proposal attracted vehement protest.

The new unitary Highland Council has found a stop-gap solution until a strategic one can be reached, by extending the life of the Longman waste tip at Inverness to 2002. But this cannot be a longer term solution, because the tip borders a Site of Special Scientific Interest and would therefore not be granted a further expansion.

Sources: Cramb (1994), *SCENES* October 1997.

Box 5 *Waste strategy for the Southeast*

The shire counties of the English Southeast region have to deal with the waste of their own dense populations in often high amenity landscapes, and historically they have also taken large amounts of London's waste. In 1997 SERPLAN, the standing conference of local planning authorities in the region, published a waste planning strategy approved by its member authorities. The strategy runs to 2010. It compares the current and projected new void space for landfilling with the projected waste arisings, based on assumptions about the minimum feasible reductions in waste.

In the case of inert waste (builders' rubble, etc.), a reduction of 50% from current volume would be achieved by waste minimisation, reuse, and recycling. This is claimed to be achievable because the landfill tax is a strong incentive to recover inert waste. If it is achieved, there will still be enough void space for inert waste – all of which is landfilled – by the end of the strategy period at 2010.

In the case of MSW, the assumed reductions by 2010 from current levels are 35% of commercial and 30% of household wastes (currently 6%). These are claimed to be achievable because the producer responsibility regulations will force recovery of commercial and household wastes. In addition to reduction, there is the possibility of diverting the remaining MSW from landfill to incineration or other forms of treatment, like composting, which reduce it to residues of 15% or less of its original volume. Assuming only diversion capacity already existing or committed (mostly incineration), then space for MSW will expire between 2005 and 2010.

To avoid a crisis, it will therefore be vital that more diversion capacity comes on stream during the plan period. Indeed, the proposal is that all the authorities should be landfilling only residues of MSW by 2010. In keeping with the national waste strategy, each county and London should also be self-sufficient in dealing with MSW by that time. That means London will have to shift from exporting 7m tonnes a year to the surrounding counties to zero, in just 13 years!

The SERPLAN strategy respects all the principles of sustainable development and the waste management hierarchy, taking advantage of the economies of scale in the region. The question is, whether it can be made to stick, or whether irresistible pressure will be put on the counties to find more landfill space.

Source: SERPLAN (1997)

EVALUATION

We have benefited historically in this country from benign conditions for the dumping of waste in landfills. Changing perceptions, driven in the background by our membership of the European Union, are forcing a reorientation towards a new way of thinking, under which landfilling is the least desirable option for dealing with waste.

Willy-nilly, planning is required to play an important role in that reorientation. Policy is requiring planners to shift from identifying sites and approving applications for landfills and transfer stations to catering for other types of facility such as incinerators, to which the public objects just as strongly. Now they must plan actively to implement locally a clear set of national principles, and they must work more closely with the waste and pollution control authorities. In the past some planners may have felt they could sit back and leave the decisions largely to those authorities; for example, mid-1990s Scottish Development Plans said very little about the subject (Raemaekers, 1995); others in contrast sought to poach on those authorities' territory. The Environment Act 1995 removed waste regulation from local government to the national environmental protection authorities, and this may in the short term distance the two regimes, rather than draw them closer together. Planners themselves feel short of relevant specialist training, and not one planning school offers a specialism in waste planning (Royal Town Planning Institute, 1997).

There is no doubt that habits will change, but we still seem to be a very long way from meeting the targets. We are going to be filling holes in the ground for a long time to come.

CONTAMINATED LAND

INTRODUCTION

We have considered so far what to do with the waste being produced now, in order to minimise future problems caused by its treatment and disposal. But we are also faced, unfortunately, with the legacy of waste from our industrial past, which has contaminated land. It has particular import for planning, not only because development control is the means by which much remediation of contaminated land is triggered, but more widely because of its effect on the market for land in urban areas and thus on regeneration. The problem has come to the fore only in the last 20 years or so, partly as old dirty industries close down, and is the last major domain of pollution to be addressed. You could often smell, see or feel pollution of air or water, but what was in the ground was out of sight and therefore out of mind, until a handful of dramatic incidents thrust it into the public gaze.

INTO THE LIMELIGHT

The most infamous of these was at Love Canal, by Niagara Falls in the US (Newson, 1992, pp. 164–169). Here a chemical company had dumped chemicals over 10 years in an unfinished canal. In 1953 the dump was closed and the site sold; a school and housing were built beside the closed dump. In 1978 chemical leakage from the dump led to the first US federal declaration of emergency for a man-made disaster and partial evacuation of the area. Clean-up took 10 years, cost US$250m, and even then only two-thirds of the site was declared habitable. Although the health impacts remained unproven, the incident precipitated the so-called Superfund Law of 1980, which sought to create a fund and mechanism for identifying the extent of contaminated land and cleaning it up. A similar case at Lekkerkerk in the Netherlands in 1980 brought the issue to attention in Europe.

Origin and Extent of Contamination

Where does the contamination come from? The answer is almost any kind of industrial and trading activity, ranging from the obvious ones like chemical works to the less obvious like scrapyards or dockyards. Mining and quarrying, described earlier in this chapter, can contaminate extensive areas. Old works using coal to produce town gas, coke, cold tar and other chemicals often cause trouble, as do disused gasometer sites. Often, however, the cause is the deliberate disposal of waste: closed sewage works have built up concentrations of heavy metals, and closed landfill sites may burn, settle, leach pollutants into ground or surface water, and leak gas (House of Commons Environment Committee, 1990). The extent of potentially contaminated sites is simply not known: possibly 100 000 sites covering 200 000 ha in the UK. The potential cost of clean-up is massive, in the tens of billions of pounds for even a conservative strategy. Government currently spends £250m a year on clean-up, and the private sector as much again, to remedy just a tiny proportion of the sites (Department of the Environment and Welsh Office, 1994b).

The Meaning of Contaminated Land

Of course, how much contaminated land there is depends on how you define it. The definition has proven to be highly contentious, because it both reflects and determines what land is designated as contaminated and what is done about it. The Environment Act 1995 put in place for the first time in Britain a unified regime to address contaminated land by inserting Part IIA into the Environmental Protection Act 1990 (National Society for Clean Air and Environmental Protection, 1996, pp. 263–272). If land is identified as contaminated, then it must be cleaned; if it is not so identified, no action need be taken. The Act defines contaminated land as:

> land which appears . . . to be in such a condition, by reason of substances in, on or under the land, that –
> (a) significant harm is being caused or there is a significant possibility of such harm being caused; or
> (b) pollution of controlled waters is being, or is likely to be, caused (Environmental Protection Act 1990, Part IIA, section 78A(2)).

The definition turns on the meaning of *significant harm*. This is not given in the Act, but in guidance subsequently issued by the Environment Agency. 'Harm' can be to human health, to protected habitats (why not other ones?) or to property. 'Significant' requires that a link can be demonstrated between the pollutant and something that can be harmed, e.g. a chemical can be shown to migrate out of a closed landfill through ground water into a drinking water well. If there is no such link, then there is no risk of harm, and the land is deemed not to be contaminated. Risk is the critical criterion in reaching the decision.

This overturns the previous approach, which set prescriptive levels for individual contaminants or classes of them, for a given use of the land (known as ICRCL trigger values – ICRCL stands for Interdepartmental Committee on the Redevelopment of Contaminated Land). Because ground conditions are so variable, because there are so many contaminants, and because they can interact in so many ways, the prescriptive approach proved too inflexible, sometimes prescribing action not well suited to the individual case (see, for example Box 6 below). In particular, it might often trigger clean-up even though there was no real risk, and clean-up can be hugely expensive.

But you might counter that the new approach is itself open to question. It requires individual interpretations of risk which are consistent from one part of the country to another, and which err on the side of safety in case of doubt. It is also open to silly side-effects, like a site dropping in and out of designation as contaminated land according to the state of repair of its fences and therefore of its risk to the public.

The Suitable for Use Approach

We have looked at what is identified as contaminated land, triggering clean-up. The next question is, how well does it have to be cleaned to be useable? The British approach to this question is that it should be suitable for use; this sets the level of cleanliness required according to the use to which the land is put. If you want the plot for a car park rather than for housing, then you need not clean it up as much, saving a lot of time and money. This is a decidedly pragmatic view, and reflects the UK government's emphasis on cost-effectiveness in environmental protection as a whole:

> Action on the environment has to be proportionate to the costs involved and to the ability of those affected to pay them (UK Government, 1990, para. 1.24).

Not everyone has taken such a pragmatic view. The Dutch have operated a 'multifunctionality' approach, which holds that the land must be returned to its pristine condition, enabling it to be used for any purpose, whatever might be the intended use. What is more, the presumption is that the soil must be decontaminated on site, not simply removed to a dump elsewhere. This very strict approach, much admired by environmentalists, can be explained in part by the country's high water table, permeable soils, and 80% sourcing of water from the ground.

Why has the UK government adopted the suitable for use approach? Because the experiences of the US and the Netherlands, and of its own abortive earlier proposals, have shown the very real dangers of aiming too high. The American system is underfunded and bogged down in legal wrangling, with little clean-up actually occurring. The Dutch government in the summer of 1997 abandoned the multifunctional approach as simply too expensive to finance overall, and because it can actually prevent rather than facilitate a given site being redeveloped, because the standards imposed are too costly to make the development financially viable (ENDS Report, 1997).

The UK government's previous proposals under the Environment Protection Act 1990 were for registers recording all sites which had been put to a *potentially* contaminating use at any time in the past. This turned out to be a disaster, both because of the monumental costs of surveying land, and because the rules required that land designated remain forever on the register regardless of action to clean it up. This would have blighted great swathes of urban land, stifling the market in brownfield (previously developed) sites, many of which are potentially contaminated.

This was unacceptable to the powerful development industry, which rebelled, forcing the government to withdraw the proposed registers. It was also directly contrary to the government's commitment to recycling brownfield land, both to stimulate urban regeneration and to reduce pressure on greenfield (undeveloped) sites, both of which are key planning objectives. The purpose of the 1995 regime is to remove the threat of blight by focusing on those sites that need action: the new definition of contaminated land reduces the amount of land designated to just 10%–15% of that under the 1990 proposals – maybe 5000 to 20 000 sites (Coleman, 1996; Baker and Harvey, 1997).

Operation of the Contaminated Land Regime

How then will the new regime operate? The Act places a duty on the local authority to look for and identify contaminated land, to publish a strategy showing how it will secure remediation of it, and to keep a register of its regulatory actions. The environmental protection agency (Environment Agency or Scottish Environmental Protection Agency) is on hand to provide expert advice to the local authority, and is directly responsible for 'special sites', being those that are most problematical. It also polices the local authority's discharge of its duties.

In keeping with the 'polluter pays principle', primary responsibility for contaminated land lies with the polluter, on whom the local authority can serve a remediation notice requiring clean-up. If the polluter cannot be found, then the current owner or occupier is liable. This may seem unreasonable, but it is a logical extension of the age old principle of *caveat emptor* – 'let the buyer beware' – which governs British land transactions. The owner should have checked that the land was clean before buying it, and protected themselves against unforeseen contamination by taking out insurance. The reality is that most contamination is historic and the polluter will not be found, rendering the owner liable. If the polluter or owner are unable to afford clean-up, then the authority may do it, and the government is making supplementary credits available to that end. If the responsible party refuses to act, then the local authority can itself have the job done and bill the responsible party.

The above is what *should* happen in theory but, as with all such regimes, practice may fall short of theory. The local authorities with contaminated land in their territories will have to acquire the necessary expertise, and the environmental protection agencies will have to organise themselves to be able to provide advice on demand. Moreover, the minefield of assigning responsibility and of pursuing defaulters through the courts, with no certainty whatever of eventually recouping costs, will be a strong disincentive against local authorities actively going out to find troublesome sites.

THE PLANNER'S ROLE

Serving a remediation notice is however intended only as a last resort, to be used where nuisance law or the planning system fail to secure clean-up. It applies only to land that is a threat in its *current* use, and therefore does not apply to land subject to a planning application for change of use or redevelopment. It is in fact expected that most cases of clean-up will be triggered by the planning system as applications come forward. The application site will be vetted by planners as part of development control and, if contamination is found, clean-up will be secured through planning conditions or s106 agreements (s75 in Scotland). If negotiation to secure clean-up fails in a planning case, then the remediation notice regime will come into play as a last resort when the application lapses or is withdrawn, if the land is still deemed a threat in its current use.

Planning guidance on contaminated land has recently been revised, but the essence of the planning system's role remains what is was before the introduction of the new regime (PPG23 in England – Department of the Environment and Welsh Office, 1994a; unified planning guidance note in Wales – Welsh Office, 1996; and PAN 51 in Scotland, Scottish Office Development Department, 1997). The guidance advises that few sites are so badly contaminated that they are unusable, and that Development Plans should contain policies for reclamation and possible use of contaminated land.

Contamination is a material planning consideration, and Local Plans and Unitary Development Plans should contain detailed criteria for determining applications on land known to be or which may be contaminated. If the authority receives an application to develop land known or strongly suspected to be contaminated, it should require a site investigation by the developer before determining the application; if there is only the suspicion of contamination, it may grant permission on conditions. The authority should seek expert advice in such cases from the environmental protection agency. Notwithstanding the authority's role, responsibility for safe development lies with the *developer* – the authority cannot be held liable for permitting development on what later proves to be an unsafe site.

The question remains, however: How many sites will be coming forward to planners for redevelopment? As was said above, the new regime is intended to facilitate a market in contaminated land, but there are doubts about how successful it will be in this. Research on attitudes has produced conflicting findings about the willingness of funding institutions to back development of contaminated land (Wilbourn, 1997; Joseph Rowntree Foundation, 1997). Developers vary in their attitudes too, with housing associations more prepared to buy and develop old industrial sites than are private house builders. Developers complain about inconsistency of approach between local authorities, and that it is unclear whether planners, environmental health officers or environmental protection agencies are responsible for deciding whether a site has been cleaned to a standard suitable for use.

It is to be hoped that such problems will fade as the guidance on the operation of the regime is firmed up and experience is gained of its operation. An example of what should be happening is given in Box 6. This example illustrates the vital role often played by the regeneration agencies in returning to beneficial use sites that would not be a commercial proposition without state intervention, and might therefore lie unused.

Box 6 *Reclamation of contaminated land: Bede Island, Leicester*

Bede Island is a city centre site with a lot of contamination, which is being reclaimed to develop a 13 000 m^2 business and science park, offices, 200 homes, 240 student flats, a 2 ha park, and a row of shops. The £15m reclamation is being carried out as part of Leicester City Challenge, funded by City Challenge and English Partnerships, as well as private investors. The city's planning and environmental health departments are closely involved in the design process.

The 13 ha site previously held a dyeworks, railway yards, oil and coal merchants, scrapyards, warehousing and a small power station – a typical range of sources of contamination of urban sites. The resulting contaminants included mineral oils, polyaromatic hydrocarbons (PAHs), heavy metals, polychlorinated biphenyls (PCBs), and there is also inert fill including ash, bottles and wood. The contamination needed to be dealt with not only to reclaim the site for beneficial use, but because it is bounded by a river on one side and a canal on the other, which need to be protected from migrating pollutants.

Reclamation took nearly two years, and 20 000 soil samples were chemically analysed. The ICRCL trigger values for clean-up proved to be inflexible, particularly because the land was to be put to several different uses, and a new-style risk-based assessment was undertaken in cooperation with the Environment Agency.

Source: Cockman (1997).

EVALUATION

The debate over the abortive 1990 proposals achieved one important success, that of highlighting contaminated land among the property development industry. Developers, their backers and planners are now aware of potential contamination and liabilities, such that contamination is likely to be identified and treated in the event of a land transaction. The fear is, however, that this very awareness will cause the industry to stay away from contaminated land, to the detriment of urban regeneration and greenfield protection policies. The jury is still out on how effective the 1995 regime will prove in overcoming this reluctance and promoting a market in contaminated land. It is likely that, one way or another, a good deal of public money will have to be pumped into reclamation. You could in any case argue that, since the problem arises from earlier times when the public as a whole did not require such strict environmental standards, it is only fair that the public purse should contribute to solving it now.

Looking back, we can see that the approach to contaminated land has evolved rather rapidly from ignorance and *laissez faire*, through a strong but unrealistic environmental backlash, to a regime which we might term an 'enlightened pragmatic approach'. Objections are raised by environmentalists that it does not in practice guarantee that contamination will be identified and remedied on sites which are not subject to a planning application – that it relies on a degree of proactivity by local authorities which they may not exhibit, because they lack the will, funds and expertise. Pragmatists can counter that 'the best is the enemy of the good', because holding out for too high an environmental standard is self-defeating, and that even the Netherlands have abandoned their purist regime as unsustainable.

CONCLUSIONS: MINERALS, WASTES, CONTAMINATED LAND AND SUSTAINABLE DEVELOPMENT

This chapter has looked at certain aspects of the interface between planning and environmental protection. Environmental regulation of minerals extraction is a comparatively old field but has been much tightened up in the last 20 years; serious waste regulation dates from the 1974 Control of Pollution Act; and, while how to deal with and redevelop contaminated land is not a new issue, it is only since 1990 that an effort has been made to produce a dedicated legal and institutional framework to address it.

Nor has regulation simply been tightened in these three fields. A new theme runs through policy and practice in all three fields: sustainable development, the attempt to produce a conscious framework within which we can address the classic dilemmas of development and environment. We are seeking to produce more quality of human and other life from less consumption of the natural resource base – you could even borrow Mies van de Rohe's architectural dictum that 'less is more'!

In the first section on minerals we looked at one of the two 'outer limits to growth' – primary resource consumption. In the second section on wastes we looked at the other one – the ability of the environment to absorb the side-effects of that resource consumption and the activities based upon it. Both these sections are intrinsically future-orientated. In the third section on contaminated land we looked at a legacy of the past as a possible constraint on future development.

But we also inevitably encountered 'inner limits to growth', social, economic and political constraints on development. For example, we saw that there are enough aggregates within the UK to meet the local shortage in Southeast England – i.e. there is no outer limit for the foreseeable future. The true constraint is the inner limit – who will pay the environmental costs of supplying it?

But are we making progress in these fields towards the goals of sustainable development? Superficially, perhaps we are; but wastes outputs are still rising, 90% of controlled wastes are still landfilled and recycling of domestic wastes is typically 6% or less. A piece of good news is that we do at least now have in place a wastes regulation and pollution control regime to prevent the creation of more contaminated land.

REFERENCES

Baker, W. and Harvey, C. (1997) Signs of life in the contaminated zone, *Planning*, 29 August, 20–21.

Bate, R. (1998) Taxing times ahead for the quarrymen, *Planning*, 23 January, 16–17.

Blunden, J. (1996) Mineral resources (ch. 4) and The environmental impact of mining and mineral processing (ch. 5), in: Blunden, J. and Reddish, A. (eds), *Energy, Resources and Environment*, 2nd edn, Hodder and Stoughton, London.

Clough, B. (1993) Nature conservation and environmental impact. Strategic issues in minerals planning, *The Planner*, May, 14–16.

Cockman, R. (1997) Bede Island, Leicester, *Planning*, 29 August, 21.

Coleman, A. (1996) Passing the muck, *Planning Week*, 21 November, 12–13.

Commission of the European Communities (1992) *Towards Sustainability. A European Community Programme of Policy and Action in Relation to the Environment and Sustainable Development* ('5th Action Programme'), COM(92) 23 Final – vol 2, The Commission, Brussels.

Confederation of British Industry (1998) *Briefing: Quarry Tax*, CBI, London.

Cramb, A. (1994) Hole lot of trouble for the Highlands, *The Scotsman*, 5 September, 4.

Department of the Environment (1992) *Planning, Pollution and Waste Management*, HMSO, London.

Department of the Environment and Welsh Office (1992) PPG12, *Development Plans and Regional Planning Guidance*, HMSO, London.

Department of the Environment and Welsh Office (1994a) PPG23, *Planning and Pollution Controls*, HMSO, London.

Department of the Environment and Welsh Office (1994b) *Paying for Our Past. The Arrangements for Controlling Contaminated Land and Meeting the Costs of Remedying the Damage to the Environment. Consultation Paper*, DoE and WO, London.

Department of the Environment and Welsh Office (1995a) *A Waste Strategy for England and Wales. Consultation Draft*, DoE, London.

Department of the Environment and Welsh Office (1995b) *Making Waste Work. A Strategy for Sustainable Waste Management in England and Wales*, Cm 3040, HMSO, London.

Department of the Environment, Transport and the Regions (1999a) MPG3 (Revised), *Coal Mining and Colliery Soil Disposal*, HMSO, London.

Department of the Environment, Transport and the Regions (1999b) PPG10, *Planning and Waste Managemnet*, HMSO, London.

Department of the Environment, Transport and the Regions and Welsh Office (1999) *A Way with Waste. A Draft Waste Strategy for England and Wales*, DETR and WO, London.

Dudgill, G. (1998) Ploughing landfil tax back into cities, *Urban Environment*, **47**, 8–9.

Edwards, R. (1997) Under a dark cloud, *New Scientist*, 27 September, 20–21.

Egerton, D. (1994) Gold mining – the Tyndrum experience, *Scottish Planner*, **37**, 8–9.

ENDS Report (1997) Dutch in policy retreat on contaminated land, *The ENDS Report* 269, June, 46.

Farrar, J. (1998) Seminar on the landfill tax, Royal Town Planning Institute Edinburgh and Lothians chapter, Edinburgh, 11 November 1997.

Hills, P. (1984) Planning for coal: issues and responses, in: Cope, D., Hills, P. and James, P. (eds), *Energy Policy and Land Use Planning*, Pergamon, Oxford.

House of Commons Environment Committee (1990) *Contaminated Land. Volume 1*, HMSO, London.

House of Commons Environment, Transport and Regional Affairs Committee (1998) *Sustainable Waste Management*, HMSO, London.

Joseph Rowntree Foundation (1997) The redevelopment of contaminated land for housing use, *Joseph Rowntree Foundation Findings Housing Research 225*.

MacKenzie, D. (1998) Doñana damned, *New Scientist*, 2 May, 12.

National Society for Clean Air and Environmental Protection (1996) *1996 Pollution Handbook*, NSCA, Brighton.

Newson, M. (1992) *Managing the Human Impact on the Environment*, Belhaven, London.

Owens, S. and Colwell, R. (1996) *Rocks and Hard Places: Mineral Resource Planning and Sustainability*, Council for the Protection of Rural England, London.

Pearce, F. (1998) A wasted chance, *New Scientist*, 30 May, 22–23.

Raemaekers, J. (1995) Scots have way to go on strategic planning, *Planning*, 17 February, 24–25.

Royal Commission on Environmental Pollution (1993) *Incineration of Waste*, 17th Report, Cm 2181, HMSO, London.

Royal Town Planning Institute (1995) *Environmental Assessment. Practice Advice Note 13*, RTPI, London.

Royal Town Planning Institute (1997) *Minerals, Waste Management and Environmental Protection: Education and Training Needs*, Report to the Institute by Heriot-Watt University.

Rydin, Y. (1993) *The British Planning System. An Introduction*, Macmillan, London.

Scottish Coal (nd) *Blindwells East Proposed Opencast Site. Environmental Statement*, Scottish Coal, Edinburgh.

Scottish Environment Protection Agency (1999) *Draft National Waste Strategy: Scotland. A Blueprint for Progress*, SEPA, Stirling.

Scottish Office Development Department (1997) PAN51, *Planning and Environmental Protection*, Scottish Office, Edinburgh.

Scottish Office Environment Department (1994) NPPG4, *Land for Mineral Working*, Scottish Office, Edinburgh.

Selman, P. (2000) *Environmental Planning*, Sage, London, 2nd edn.

SERPLAN (1997) *Revised Waste Planning Advice. A Sustainable Waste Planning Strategy for the South East 1996–2010*, SERPLAN (The London and South East Regional Planning Conference), London.

UK Government (1990) *This Common Inheritance. Britain's Environmental Strategy*, Cm 1200, HMSO, London.

UK Government (1994) *Sustainable Development. The UK Strategy*, Cm 2426, HMSO, London.

Welsh Office (1996) *Planning Guidance (Wales): Planning Policy*, Welsh Office, Cardiff.

Wilbourn, P. (1997) Final touches to the ground rules, *Planning*, 29 August, 8–9.

CHAPTER 14

TOURISM AND LOCAL ECONOMIC DEVELOPMENT

Tim Shaw

INTRODUCTION

Tourism, and its impact upon both national and local economies, has become an increasingly important feature of modern-day life in both developed and emerging nations. The growth of tourism has been particularly marked in the period since the end of the Second World War. During this period in the UK there has been a marked movement away from the traditional seaside holiday at home towards international tourism. More recently there has been a revitalisation of tourism in this country but it is now far more diverse and geared to cater for both overseas visitors as well as the domestic market.

All over the world countries are striving to make the most of their tourist potential as a means of generating much-needed wealth (especially overseas currency) and providing employment. Tourism has been developed in different ways, initially along the lines of the international resort – characterised for so many decades by the developments along the French and Spanish Mediterranean coasts and the Alpine ski resorts – but more recently with a greater understanding of and commitment to the notion of 'sustainable tourism'. This is an approach advocated by the UK government (Department for Culture, Media and Sport (DCMS), 1998).

Although tourism is a matter of international importance, this chapter focuses attention on tourism and local economic development in the UK. Particular attention is given to the role of statutory planning process in influencing the way in which tourism has been and is likely to be developed in the late part of the twentieth and the early part of the twenty-first centuries.

Tourism has been defined in many ways but perhaps a simple definition is the one suggested by the Tourism Society:

> the temporary short-term movement of people to destinations outside the places where they normally live and work and the activities during their stay at these destinations (in DoE, 1992)

This was further amplified by the Department of National Heritage (DNH) (1997):

. . . all aspects of the visitor experience, whether the visitor is on a day trip, a short
break or a long holiday, visiting for leisure or business, from this country or overseas.

Within the UK, perceptions of 'tourism' have changed dramatically during the
course of the twentieth century and this is a reflection of changing opportunities
and changing social trends. Greater personal affluence, the gradual acceptance of
holidays as part of contracts of employment (particularly paid holidays), improved
public and private transport, together with the growth of holiday resorts, all
contributed to the expansion of tourism in this country.

Whereas the 1950s were perhaps best characterised by a week's family holiday
'at the seaside', subsequent decades saw considerable growth of the overseas
package holiday. Inevitably home-based tourism was severely affected but during
the past decade the home market in all forms of tourism has expanded rapidly.
Although not all the traditional resorts have survived, many have and have done so
by adjusting to capitalise on new opportunities. Throughout the country it appears
that tourism, in all its different forms, is making a significant contribution to the
generation of wealth and the creation of jobs.

Although the internationalisation of tourism resulted in major decline in many
of the traditional coastal resorts, the same trends that took UK citizens in search of
foreign adventures brought overseas visitors flocking to the UK. In the 1960s it
seemed as though all roads led to London when the capital witnessed considerable
growth in tourism based not only on its heritage, but also on its image as the
centre of the 'swinging sixties'. It was not simply London that benefited; there was
a 'ripple-out effect' as overseas visitors travelled further afield to capture the
splendour of ancient cathedral cities such as York and Durham, the grandeur of
historic cities like Edinburgh and the magnificent countryside to be found in
places like the Cotswolds and the Highlands of Scotland.

The ability to respond to changed circumstances depends on a number of key
factors: vision, individual flair and entrepreneurship are essential. These may be
found at the level of the individual enterprise, in local trade associations and in
tourist board offices run by local councils. But no matter how good the product
and its marketing, it is difficult for local groups to prosper without the aid of
outside organisations. National and regional tourist boards have produced helpful
advice and guidance to individuals and associations, as well as providing marketing
at home and abroad.

Government help, often through the tourist boards, can also be of great
importance in helping to stimulate tourism. Grant-in-aid, such as that made
possible through the provisions of the 1969 Development of Tourism Act, has
helped to boost tourism. It is unlikely that such support would have been forthcoming if tourism had not been seen as making an increasingly significant
contribution to both local, regional and national economies.

From the 1960s onwards the economic importance of tourism has been highlighted by the tourist boards and government departments. As early as the 1967

Agriculture Act, the Ministry of Agriculture was viewing tourism as a means of broadening the base of the rural economy. Elsewhere, the Highlands and Islands Development Board were convinced that the development of tourism should play a major part in the restructuring of the Highland's economy. Today, there is an even stronger belief that tourism has a major role to play; this is noted in the White Paper, *Building Partnerships for Prosperity* (Department of the Environment, Transport and the Regions (DETR), 1997).

Thus, today, tourism in the UK accounts for 7% of the nation's jobs, in excess of 5% of the Gross Domestic Product (GDP) (with some figures indicating that the total economic impact of tourism could be as high as 12% GDP). So important has tourism become that it now accounts for 25% of the nation's overseas earnings in services and the World Tourism Organisation places the UK fifth in the league table of international earnings from tourism. (Statistics from the DNH, 1997.)

There are clearly two facets to tourism as a component of local economic development: job creation and wealth generation. The two are obviously linked but each represents the motivation behind the key players in the game of tourism development. Entrepreneurs are primarily concerned with generating profits. To them employment is a secondary consideration. The work-force is a necessity but will be cut if the enterprise can operate more efficiently and effectively with fewer employees. On the other hand, local government is keen to see the development of tourism primarily, though not exclusively, from the standpoint of creating employment for local people. Central government and tourist boards are aware of both dimensions and keen to see tourism flourish.

During the past decade the overriding interest in jobs and earnings has been tempered by growing environmental concerns. Tourism has been the subject of much debate about its environmental credentials. Although much of this has focused on the fragile and invaluable ecosystems of developing nations, at home there has been concern that tourist developments have subjected parts of the natural environment to damaging pressures. Some tourist activities are in danger of destroying the very resource which attracted visitors in the first place (Edwards, 1991). Land use planning has an important role to play in the future development of tourism.

It is important to acknowledge the role for planning, not only in helping tourism to flourish, but also in ensuring that tourism conforms to national planning policies, regional guidance and to more localised development plans. Given the growing emphasis on sustainable development, land use planning has a pivotal role in ensuring the coherent development of tourism.

However, planning must not underestimate the economic contribution made by tourism and as such must be sensitive to the particular characteristics and needs of the tourist industry. In June 1998 planning was severely criticised for its seeming lack of understanding about leisure and tourism (National Planning Forum, 1998) It would appear that there is a need for an improved and more effective working relationship between planning and the tourist industry.

THE ORGANISATION OF TOURISM

The 1969 Development of Tourism Act did much to establish a framework for the organisation of tourism in the UK. Until 1969 the tourist industry had to a large extent taken care of itself with local authorities and local chambers of commerce undertaking some tourism promotion. The desire to bring more organisation and structure to the industry was a reflection of the decline in the UK tourist industry in the face of growing competition from international tourism.

The legislation established a hierarchy of boards with responsibility for the development of UK tourism internationally, nationally and regionally. Funded in part by national government, in part by local government and in part by the tourist industry itself, the boards were charged with the more effective development of tourism within the UK. These included the British Tourist Authority, the four national tourist boards and a larger number of regional tourist boards within each of the home countries.

CENTRAL GOVERNMENT

Central government plays a key role in establishing the framework for tourism in the UK. The appropriate Secretaries of State are responsible for the co-ordination of government policy on tourism. In Scotland, Wales and Northern Ireland it is the Secretary of State for those countries and in England it is the Secretary of State for Culture, Media and Sport (Secretary of State for National Heritage until 1 May 1997). England is used by way of example, but what happens here is replicated to a large extent in the other home countries.

Throughout the 1990s there was growing interest in tourism. This culminated in a Strategy Document issued by the DNH (1997) outlining a way forward for the development of tourism. It contained the following mission statement:

> To develop tourism as a high-quality, profitable partnership of the industry, govern-
> ment and the tourist boards, so as to realise the growth potential of the industry and
> the associated social and cultural benefits for the nation

There has been no lessening of interest in tourism by the new Labour government, with the DCMS issuing a Consultation Paper on sustainable tourism in the UK in April 1998.

Other government departments have also expressed an interest in tourism. In 1992 the Department of the Environment issued Planning Policy Guidance (PPG) 21 on *Tourism*. This reflected the government's growing interest in the topic from the points of view of economic significance and impact upon the environment. Thus, PPG 21 clearly stresses 'its [tourism's] importance in land use planning'.

PPG 21 makes it clear that because some tourist developments do not differ markedly from other forms of development it is not possible to 'regard [tourism] as a single or distinct category of land use'. But PPG 21 goes on to say:

> But the demands it makes on land resources and its impact upon the environment mean that it is a subject that should be addressed in preparing or revising development plans, and one that will often feature in development control decisions.

It is acknowledged through this PPG that in 'dealing with a rapidly developing and innovative industry [tourism], there must be provision for assessing new and unfamiliar types of project.' It is also noted that the 'planning process can assist tourism' but that it must do this within the context of 'other related policies'. Thus, although the government's advice to local planning authorities is clearly that of emphasising the importance of tourism, it does not expect tourism to be considered in isolation from other planning principles and areas of land use activity for which planning policies exist.

PPG 21 sets out some of the clear benefits to be derived from tourism, especially economic growth and employment generation and that future trends provide considerable cause for optimism. What also emerges is the government's equal commitment to the environment. This PPG contains four principles that the government would use in its support for tourism. These are:

- supporting the development of the industry in ways which contribute to, rather than detract from, the quality of the environment;
- promoting the understanding of environmental quality concerns within the industry and of the need to improve the quality of its service and its products;
- ensuring through the regional tourist boards and Training Enterprise Councils that managers of tourism adopt visitor management techniques that can mitigate the impact on the environment; and
- encouraging those types of tourism which in themselves aim to safeguard the environment.

Such thinking must have been influenced in part by the Earth Summit in Rio which reflected a growing international commitment to environmental protection. Such issues were revisited by the Conservative government (DNH, 1997) and by the new Labour administration (DCMS, 1998).

In 1997 and 1998 the DETR issued a number of documents which may well influence the development of tourism well into the twenty-first century. These included: a White Paper, *Building Partnerships for Prosperity; Sustainable Growth, Competitiveness and Employment in the English Regions* (DETR, 1997), a Consultation Paper, *The Future of Regional Planning Guidance* (DETR, 1998a) and a Policy Statement, *Modernising Planning* (DETR, 1998b). These documents, although wide ranging, highlight issues of employment and environmental protection and sustainable development, all of which are important in the effective planning and management of tourism in the UK.

British Tourist Authority

The British Tourist Authority (BTA) was given prime responsibility for the promotion of British tourism abroad. It continues to promote British tourism with some of its promotional material being drawn from both national and regional tourist boards. Given the high cost of such overseas activities it was and remains sensible for the bulk of the promotional work to be undertaken by a single body rather than being duplicated by each of the other tourist boards. In short, the BTA is able to go for the 'big brand image'. It is better to present a robust and understandable view of the UK rather than dwell on the fine-grain detail which would inevitably emerge from regional tourist boards. Many overseas visitors (particularly those making their first trip) will have little knowledge of anything other than major centres such as London, York and Edinburgh.

It is likely that responsibility for the overseas marketing of British tourism will remain with the BTA, though the Scottish Tourist Board has been given permission to undertake a limited amount of overseas marketing.

National Tourist Boards

There are four main national tourist boards: England, Scotland, Wales and Northern Ireland. They have a number of broad functions. For example, they promote home-based tourism throughout the UK and provide an umbrella organisation for the various regional tourist boards within their national boundaries.

These national tourist boards have provided essential guidance for both the public and private sector in improving tourist development. In addition to the grant-in-aid to regional boards, they provide help and guidance with market research, project management and the development of new initiatives, all of which have made a marked contribution to the delivery of a better tourist product regionally and locally.

These boards are funded largely by central government. In Scotland, Wales and Northern Ireland this funding comes via their national government offices; for example, the Scottish Office, whereas in England the English Tourist Board (ETB) receives its income from the DCMS. In this chapter emphasis is given to the ETB.

The aims of the ETB (DOE, 1992) are:

To stimulate the development of English tourism by:
- the provision and improvement of facilities for tourists in England
- raising the profile of the industry through national campaigns

---

The English Tourism Council (ETC) was launched in July 1999 as a radical transformation of the English Tourist Board (ETB).

- facilitating a network of tourist information centres
- undertaking research on all aspects of tourism
- providing advice and support for local area initiatives
- providing advice and guidance to government, public and private sector bodies on tourism-related issues.

The ETB is constantly looking for ways in which it can improve tourism. The ETB's Annual Reports (for example, ETB, 1997a) give an indication of the way in which its activities have developed over time. But in 1997 the ETB embarked upon a major new initiative designed to ensure that tourism in England is in the best possible condition for the new millennium. This initiative started as Agenda 2000 and has now developed into Action 2000.

This initiative started in February 1997 with work on the 'formulation of a practical and commercially-effective action plan to revitalise domestic tourism' (ETB, 1997b). This reflects the ETB's view that there is a need constantly to review the contribution that tourism can make to the economy. Agenda 2000 was an opportunity for all those with an interest in UK tourism to offer suggestions and help set the agenda for exploiting the country's full tourism potential and, in particular, to help 'combat the threat of increasingly intense overseas competition'.

Action 2000 (ETB, 1997c) has emerged with a clear set of objectives:

- Accommodation schemes and quality standards
- Promoting England
- Trade communications
- Market and product intelligence and research
- Tourism training
- Market access and information

Although these six policy objectives are primarily concerned with addressing the main cause of concern – that tourism for the domestic market is suffering from considerable competition from overseas – they are also designed to improve the tourist experience for all visitors whether they be from home or abroad. To achieve this, considerable effort needs to be put into reversing a trend which started in the 1960s. The package holiday business has gone from strength to strength (and no longer just to the Mediterranean) and experience and confidence has led growing numbers to seek out more exotic, distant holidays overseas.

It may well be the case that, despite the best efforts of Action 2000, growing numbers of people will continue to take their main holidays overseas; this will be a hard trend to reverse. However, Action 2000 provides a basis for persuading more people to spend time and money on holidays within England (as well as attracting more overseas visitors). Greater affluence and a more leisured society has opened up new possibilities for additional holidays at home such as weekend breaks and half-term holidays.

The implementation of Action 2000 should give a considerable boost to the home tourist industry. This will include improving the quality of provision, offering greater choice and providing a more effective and efficient service, all backed by improved promotion and publicity. All are essential prerequisites for a dynamic tourist industry.

However, there appears to be a cloud looming over the future of the ETB. Pierce (1998) notes that the future of the ETB is under threat. His report in *The Times* newspaper suggests that Chris Smith, the Culture Secretary, is to abolish the ETB as part of the Treasury's demand for cuts in government spending. Ken Robinson, chairman of the Tourism Society is quoted as saying:

> It is illogical, unjustified and a *non sequitur* to all the good work that the department [DCMS] is doing. The money being saved is peanuts in the context of government spending, but the consequences of doing away with the ETB are catastrophic for the tourism industry.

It appears that the tourist boards for the other home countries are not under threat, though ironically England accounts for 85% of the £40 billion spent on tourism in the UK. There is concern that the existing high level of expenditure on tourism and the number of jobs (estimated at 500 000) in the industry will be threatened if the ETB is abolished. Although no time-scale has yet been announced, the likely success of Action 2000 must now be in doubt.

It may be that the activities of the ETB could be absorbed into the BTA, though this hardly seems logical if the other home nation tourist boards are to be retained. It is possible that its activities could be absorbed into the DCMS itself, though this would seem unlikely in the current climate of 'down-sizing'. Whatever the outcome, there is a generally held view that the loss of the ETB will be very damaging for the longer-term, strategic planning of tourism in England.

REGIONAL TOURIST BOARDS

The regional tourist boards (RTBs) are the organisations 'on the ground' providing advice and guidance on a wide range of issues to their members. Membership is broad-based and includes local authorities, businesses with an interest in tourism, trade associations, guides and consultants, together with a large number of providers ranging from larger hotels to camping and caravanning enterprises. They liaise with local authorities, government departments and quangos such as the Countryside Commission and the Sports Council. Although not statutory consultees, they are often consulted by local authorities on tourist and tourist-related development projects. Sometimes they are invited by central government to vet specific projects

Each of the national tourist board areas is divided up into a number of regions. For example, in England there are 11 RTBs. In this chapter particular reference is made to the activities of the Northumbria Tourist Board (NTB). This board operates in an area covered by the counties of Northumberland, Tyne and Wear, Durham and Tees Valley (which comprises the former Cleveland County Council and the Borough of Darlington).

Like all tourist boards, the NTB has a set of clearly defined functions. These include marketing, development, information and planning, together with finance and administration. Although its activities are wide-ranging, the full-time staff complement is only 27.

Funding for the RTBs comes from a variety of sources. In Northumbria the most recent annual figures show funding from:

Europe	£350 000
Local authorities	£280 000
ETB	£216 000
Membership subscriptions	£100 000
Commercial activities	£500 000
Total	£1 446 000

Although both staffing levels and budgets are low, such measures of size should not be used to belie Northumbria's regional significance. The RTB provides an important forum in which a wide range of interested parties can be brought together to debate both strategy and tactics as well as providing help and advice for members.

The RTBs perform an invaluable service through the development of Regional Tourism Strategies. These seek to provide a framework for tourism promotion and development within the region, bearing in mind both regional needs and opportunities as well as national policies such as those reflected in Policy Statements like *Success through Partnership: A Strategy for Tourism* (DNH, 1997) and *Tourism: Planning Policy Guidance 21* (DoE, 1992).

A Strategy for Tourism in Northumbria 1998–2002 (NTB, 1998) serves as an example of the strategies that are now influencing tourism development at the regional level. The document contains underlying principles, strategic aims and specific action points. The Strategy is underpinned by five principles. These are:

1. Competitiveness
2. Sustainability
3. Distinctiveness
4. Inclusiveness
5. Co-ordination

Out of these five principles have emerged seven strategic aims which have been developed:

- to build upon Northumbria's cultural and environmental inheritance and promote the sustainable development of tourism;
- to improve the performance of tourism enterprises and skills of people working in tourism, to exceed the expectations of visitors;
- to encourage the development of the region's tourism products, strengthening Northumbria's distinctive qualities in response to market needs and opportunities;
- to improve communication with visitors, facilitating access to products, easier bookings and better visitor management;
- to stimulate demand for tourism across Northumbria over a longer season, through improved awareness of the region as a quality destination and targeted and co-ordinated marketing activities;
- to encourage greater use of public and private sector partnership approaches to the development and marketing of tourism;
- to improve the measurement and monitoring of the progress of tourist development and its contribution to the economy and quality of life of Northumbria.

As 'grass roots' organisations, the RTBs provide a conduit for advice and guidance coming from the higher echelons of the tourist board organisation and from the government, as well as channelling ideas and concerns from within their areas back to the ETB and beyond. It is of interest to note the degree of overlap between the strategic concerns of the ETB and those of the RTBs, clearly indicating the symbiotic relationship that exists between these two tiers in the tourist board hierarchy.

Although there appears to be no immediate threat to the future of the RTBs in England, it is likely that the emergence of the Regional Development Agencies (RDAs), as outlined in the White Paper (DETR, 1997), will bring their role into sharp focus. The RDAs also have a remit to consider tourism, so the RTBs will have to decide how they can best work in tandem with the RDAs without duplication of function and ensuring that their long experience and accumulated wisdom can best be used within the region as a whole.

LOCAL AUTHORITIES

Many local authorities have developed a tourism function, often under the umbrella of an Economic Development Department. They maintain close relationships with their RTBs (and indeed are usually members) to ensure that they make the most out of tourism. Their aim has always been to exploit tourist potential to the full. The main thrust of their activities varies depending on the nature of the tourist potential. For example, a seaside town such as Blackpool (Blackpool Borough Council) devotes considerable time and resources to ensuring that tourism, the town's main economic activity, flourishes. Tourist accommodation, the famous Tower, beaches and the Pleasure Beach all feature in its promotional literature. By contrast, an authority such as South Tyneside, with a far less grand tradition of tourism, attempts to capitalise on what unique characteristics it has. These include its Roman and religious heritage, but primarily its association with the novelist Catherine Cookson. 'Welcome to Catherine Cookson Country' adorns road signs on the main points of entry into the Borough.

Local authorities are constantly looking for new opportunities for tourism. Bradford Metropolitan Borough Council is an area characterised by the heritage of a nineteenth century woollen town set against a backdrop of outstanding Pennine countryside. The local authority has worked hard to capitalise on both its urban and rural heritage. For many years visitors have come to Howarth, the home of the Brontës but this is now marketed as 'Brontë Country'. Similarly, the authority has highlighted its historical position at the centre of the Yorkshire woollen industry with most attention focused on the famous Bradford Wool Exchange. More recently the city of Bradford became custodian of the National Museum of Photography, Film and Television, a centre which attracts many thousand of visitors each year. Other attractions include the Worth Valley Railway, a railway line restored to full steam working.

But, however important any one visitor attraction might be, it is equally important to make linkages between all the locations on offer. Each individual attraction will carry publicity and promotional literature about others in the same area. In this way an authority is able to present a more impressive range of attractions to potential visitors. The more there is to see in an area, the greater the likelihood that visitors will stay overnight, thus boosting expenditure on tourism.

Whereas many local authorities are anxious to boost tourist numbers, some see this as a mixed blessing. Nowhere is this more strongly felt than in the National Parks. They are charged with improving public access, but all too often the visitors have become the problem (Edwards, 1991). Visitors come in larger numbers and in private cars. Not all come for quiet enjoyment but rather to engage in highly damaging and intrusive pursuits, such as motorised off-road driving. None of this was envisaged when the Parks were established. Certain parts of the National Parks are not capable of withstanding the physical pressure exerted by tourists, their cars and coaches.

However, some local residents are enthusiastic about encouraging more tourism in the Parks. Given the decline in the rural economy, catering for visitors offers the prospect of greater prosperity, which may come from increased pub and café sales, bed and breakfast accommodation or activity-based holidays. Commercially minded people feel there is a need for National Park authorities to relax their 'stranglehold' and for tourist development to be given a higher priority (Tourism and Recreation Research Unit (TRRU), 1981).

Here there is a unique challenge to be faced by planning. Balancing economic, social and environmental considerations will be an important task to satisfy the conflicting interests of those who consider themselves stakeholders in the countryside. Getting the most out of tourism will require planning and management of the highest order if conflict and alienation are to be avoided. The call for planning to play an improved role is at the heart of the Countryside Commission's (1998) Policy Statement, *Planning for Countryside Quality*.

Within local authorities, tourism is also a matter of concern for statutory planning. Development plans frequently contain a section on tourism. The level of detail varies considerably, normally reflecting the level of existing tourism and the potential for future development. Since the issuing of PPG 21 (see Central Government, above), local authorities have been provided with a fresh approach to tourism and ideas of how to incorporate appropriate strategies within their development plans. In a plan-led planning system the content of the development plan then influences development control.

All proposals to develop tourism are likely to be considered by the development control section of the local authority. As noted in PPG 21 there is no 'single or distinct category of [tourism] land use' and thus decisions to grant or refuse planning permission for tourist projects are made largely in the light of development plan policies and national planning policies.

Regional Planning Guidance (RPG) statements have existed in England since the late 1980s but many believe that these are inadequate and little more than a rehash of national planning policy as expressed through the PPGs. New versions of RPG statements will be published in the coming years and they may well have greater credibility in the light of the government's evolving ideas about regional planning and development (DETR, 1997). Local government within the regions has been far more active in its contribution to the RPG process. The North of England Assembly of Local Authorities (1996) has produced a *Review of Planning Guidance for the North East*. The review includes topic papers on tourism and they note that

> The tourism industry has become an increasingly important section of the regional economy and, despite the impact of recession and competition from other destinations, has potential for major growth in the future. As an important generator of income in the North, tourism has a key role to play in regenerating the area.

The challenge set for planning is

> Structure Plans and Urban Development Plans should consider the prospects for attracting developments of national or regional importance to the region, and identify possible locations for such developments.

If this is the strategic, longer-term role for planning, then the more immediate one is that

> . . . tourist attractions are managed in a way that minimises any potential conflict . . .

There is an important role for planning to play in the future development and management of tourism. Hopefully, improved approaches to regional planning will provide a more effective context for long-range planning and strategic investment in the tourist industry. Also, improved knowledge and understanding of the environment will enable local planners to work more effectively with the tourist industry to ensure a sustainable future for tourism.

THE COMMERCIAL SECTOR

As part of their promotional and development activities, many companies involved with tourism will find it advantageous to become members of their RTB. This helps to guarantee the flow of advice and guidance and may also help them with publicity. It also helps to bring them into closer contact with local government policy making and planning.

The nature of marketing in the commercial sector is very much conditioned by the resources available to individual companies. A small bed and breakfast enterprise may be able to afford no more than a notice-board outside the property or a listing in a local accommodation guide, whereas at the other end of the spectrum, national and international companies, such as Oasis and Center Parcs, are able to bear the cost of expensive television publicity campaigns.

Most commercial companies are sensitive about their image and seek to promote themselves in the best possible light. This may include the quality of the environment where their facilities are located, the quality of the facilities they offer and the level of customer care. Where tourist firms have come in for criticism, as, for example, on BBC Television's *Watchdog* programme, they have invariably moved quickly to 'damage limitation' to ensure no lasting harm to their reputations.

Although there appear to be some major tensions between planning and the tourist industry at the present time (National Planning Forum, 1998), planning engages most frequently with the commercial sector when dealing with applications for new or extended tourism developments. Even though the economic reasons for granting planning permission might appear overwhelming, commercial proposals must be viewed in the wider context of local planning policies. It may mean that considerable debate has to take place between the developer and the planner as well as with statutory consultees and local residents. This could require a public consultation exercise. Depending upon the nature of the proposals, there may also be a need for an environmental appraisal of the project. This was the case when Oasis wanted to develop a new enterprise in Cumbria not many miles away from the Lake District National Park.

When seeking planning permission, commercial companies may well stress the beneficial impact upon the local economy. Whereas this is not an unimportant consideration, there is no guarantee that the local area will benefit substantially from higher levels of employment or expenditure. This aspect is explored later.

However, different types of tourist enterprise will confer varying degrees of benefit on the entrepreneur and the local community.

SUSTAINABLE DEVELOPMENT

Growing global environmental concerns from the 1980s were brought to a head at the Rio Environment Conference in 1992. After Rio many nations incorporated the concept of 'sustainable development' into their policy making. In the UK this concept has pervaded many areas of planning and planning-related policy making. Tourism is no exception, as illustrated by the DCMS (1998) consultation paper on sustainable tourism. During the past decade a considerable literature has built up about sustainable tourism. In some cases this idea has been taken a stage further and the concept of ecotourism has emerged where the relationship between tourists and the natural environment is carefully controlled.

Great concern has been expressed about the threats posed by tourist developments to communities and habitats in this country and throughout the world (German Federal Agency for Nature Conservation, 1997). One of the great challenges for the twenty-first century will be the development of strategies which allow for the development of tourism in ways that permit countries and communities to capitalise on economic growth but without offending against the fundamental principles of sustainability (Pretty, 1998).

The World Tourism Organisation has described sustainable tourism as 'tourism that meets the needs of present tourists and host regions while protecting and enhancing opportunity for the future'. This definition clearly has its origins in the notion of sustainability advanced in the Bruntland Committee Report (World Commission on Environment and Development, 1988). The DCMS's Consultation Paper on sustainable tourism in the UK (1998) draws heavily on the principles derived from the 1992 Rio Declaration on the Environment by the World Tourism Organisation, the World Travel and Tourism Council and the Earth Council. Included in these principles are the following:

- Travel and tourism should assist people in leading healthy and productive lives in harmony with nature.
- Travel and tourism should contribute to the conservation, protection and restoration of the Earth's ecosystem.
- Travel and tourism should be based upon sustainable patterns of production and consumption.
- Nations should co-operate to promote an open economic system in which international trade in travel and tourism services can take place on a sustainable basis.

Far more progress has to be made before much of the world's tourist activities can be described as sustainable. Sustainable tourism is unlikely to be achieved in

Table 1

Non-sustainable tourism	Sustainable tourism
Rapid development	Slow development
Short term	Long term
Unstable	Stable
Quantitative	Qualitative
Remote control	Local control

Table 2

Non-sustainable tourism	Sustainable tourism
Development without planning	First plan, then develop
Intensive development in areas of finest landscape	Fine landscapes conserved
Tourism development everywhere	Developments only in suitable places and where local services already exist
High-tech mechanised installations	Selective mechanised low-tech development favoured

Adapted from Hardy *et al.* (1991).

the short term but progress must be made now if future generations are to benefit from sustainable tourism policies throughout the next century.

From a planning perspective, sustainable tourism is something that should not be a matter of local concern alone. Although the management of specific tourist projects is important, there is also a need for a broader, longer-term, strategic view of tourist development. As such, the principles of environmental sustainability need to be enshrined in national planning policy, regional planning guidance and structure plans. As more regional guidance and more structure plans are made the subject of environmental appraisal, there is a greater likelihood that future tourist developments will conform with the principles of sustainable development.

Lane (1991, 1993) attempts to highlight the difference between sustainable and non-sustainable tourism. It is evident that the general features of the two are markedly different, as too are the development strategies which bring them about. In a series of contrasting tables Lane highlights some of these differences (see Table 1). In examining different features within development strategies, again Lane highlights key differences between the sustainable and non-sustainable approaches (see Table 2).

Planning's future role in achieving sustainable development is made clear by the DCMS (1998) under 'Planning Imperatives':

> The decisions taken now about the design and development of new tourism facilities and infrastructure will play a key role in dictating the value and volume of tourism to the UK economy and society.

ECONOMIC DEVELOPMENT

Any overview of tourism must consider two issues: employment and income generation. Tourist boards and local government are much concerned by these issues as too is central government. Successive governments have expressed a need to capitalise on the opportunities provided by the development of tourism to maximise both job creation and income generation (DNH, 1997; DETR, 1997).

EMPLOYMENT

There has been a considerable amount of speculation as to the precise number of jobs created by tourism. However, it is estimated that 7% of the nation's jobs are in tourism (DNH, 1997). In recent years there has been a marked increase in the number of people estimated to be employed in tourism. Labour Market Trends (Office of National Statistics) indicate an increase approaching 10% in the period between 1989 and 1996 in the number employed in tourist-related industries. In some sectors increases have been even more pronounced. For example, in restaurants, cafés and in hotels the increase has been in the order of 20% and for travel and tour agents the increase has been over 30%. Clearly, these are important trends and provide part of the explanation of why the ETB is so keen to develop its Action 2000 strategy; there is potential for further growth in the tourist industry.

This growth is not simply a feature of the more famous tourist locations; there is growing evidence that tourism and related activities are of increasing importance to the economy throughout the country. For example, in the area covered by the NTB, tourism is now one of the major employers, outstripping other sectors such as construction, metal manufacturing and fabrication which only a relatively short time ago were so dominant within that region.

Although a considerable number of people are employed in tourism, it is important to realise that not all of these are in permanent jobs. There is a high degree of seasonality within the industry. Equally, within that season, many of the jobs will only be part-time. However, it is probable that the total number of people employed in tourism is higher than official estimates since the number of part-time and seasonal workers may not be officially recorded. This may also be the case for those working within family businesses. The position is further clouded by those for whom tourism may only comprise a small proportion of their working lives; for example, a farmer who does bed and breakfast as a sideline or a restaurateur whose business may include only a few tourists.

Not all jobs in tourism are filled by local people. Some job vacancies, especially seasonal ones, are often filled by student or migrant workers (including those from overseas) for whom the anti-social hours, low pay and limited job security are a small inconvenience when set against the opportunity to earn money. The larger part of their earnings may well be lost to the local economy. This is often a cause of local concern but it is extremely difficult to stipulate that tourist employment should be for local people only. Certainly it is not a part of planning's remit.

Job creation is also a function of the type of tourism. Fully serviced accommodation such as hotels and bed and breakfast tend to be relatively labour intensive whereas camping and self-catering are not. Similarly, the number of jobs associated with different types of activity holiday vary. For example, direct and indirect employment in pony trekking will be substantially greater than for fell walking. Such comparisons can be made throughout the tourist industry.

There are geographical variations in the numbers of people employed in tourism. However, there is a need for all those involved with the tourist industry to work together to ensure that as many self-sustaining jobs as possible are created if the industry is to make a worthwhile contribution to reducing unemployment and improving local economic conditions.

INCOME

The DNH (1997) estimated that tourism accounted for 5% of GDP but that the figure might be as high as 12% if factors such as hotel construction and car hire were taken into account. Approximately 4% of overseas earning came from tourism, more than that derived from North Sea oil, with the value of inbound tourism amounting to £12.1 billion.

Of the £40 billion income from tourism in the UK in 1997–1998 about 85% of this was spent in England. The ETB (1997) estimated that the amount spent by the British in England was steadily rising – a 5% increase from £10.86 billion in 1996 to £11.2 billion in 1997. This increase in expenditure was accounted for by a 6% increase in visits from 104.1 million to 110 million. This was an impressive growth in domestic tourism. Statistics at the regional level also indicate a growth in expenditure on tourism. For example, the NTB area, whose tourism is dominated by day visits, witnessed a 50% increase in tourist spending in the period from 1991 to 1996. By 1996 the value of tourism in Northumbria had risen to £818 million.

The tourist industry is committed to increasing the numbers participating in tourism within the UK and thus increasing levels of expenditure. Tourism is becoming less of a summer season activity and in some areas, especially the big cities, it is becoming an all-year-round business. More leisure time and greater affluence are allowing more people to enjoy tourism throughout the year.

Prolonging the 'season' is a major activity for the tourist industry supported by the statutory and non-statutory bodies. In major centres such as London the wealth and diversity of opportunities means that tourism can flourish throughout the year. By contrast, similar opportunities are less obvious in the older resort towns. But even in these places there have been major attempts to extend the season. Some resorts have taken advantage of conferences. Places such as Blackpool and Bournemouth frequently host the main political party conferences in the autumn at the end of their main holiday period. Similarly, the teachers' unions have traditionally chosen Easter as the time for their conferences, before the holiday season begins.

Generating income from tourism is about matching a market and a product. With so many options available to those looking to spend money on tourism, it is important that the product is attractive and of good quality. It is vital that the standard of hotels, the general environmental character of the area and any products associated with the venue meet the visitors' expectations. To this end, Action 2000 (ETBb, c, 1997) is focused upon improving the quality of all aspects of the tourist industry.

BUSINESS TOURISM

Not all benefits from tourism come from those projects developed to cater for specific groups of tourists. Business tourism is a case in point. This is a loosely defined term which relates to the wider benefits and experiences of business people visiting an area, particularly where this includes overnight stops and weekends. Clearly, business people do engage in activities outside the workplace even though they may be work-related.

Business visits to an area will generate expenditure in hotels and restaurants and may include visits to events in the locality such as the theatre or sporting fixtures. Whether visitors or hosts are paying is immaterial; money is being spent. The rise in 'corporate hospitality' in the past 25 years has become a feature of many sporting and cultural events. Sometimes this hospitality is designed as a 'reward' for existing customers or may be used as a basis for encouraging further inward investment.

In terms of local economic development the distinction between tourism and business tourism is perhaps unimportant in that they both make a direct contribution to the local economy. However, in planning the future development of towns, cities and countryside, it is essential to realise that there are many linkages between tourism, leisure and business, all of which may help to generate new economic activity.

ACCOMMODATION

Tourism makes its greatest contribution to the local economy when visitors make overnight stays. Not only does this mean that they pay for beds, but it is likely that they will spend additional money in restaurants and perhaps on entertainment. This pattern of expenditure is far more lucrative for the host area than when people make day trips and bring a picnic.

However, it is important to distinguish between the different types of tourist accommodation. It has already been noted that in terms of job creation, different types of accommodation generate different levels of employment. Because of the numbers employed in fully serviced accommodation, the price will be substantially higher for the visitor than if using self-catering or camping. Not everyone can afford the more expensive forms of accommodation and, if the tourist potential of an area is to be fully realised, then it will be necessary to ensure that a wide range of accommodation types is available.

Even though some visitors will use accommodation which makes only a small contribution to the local economy, two facts must be acknowledged: however little they pay, it is a contribution and, secondly, the longer they remain, the greater the likelihood that they will spend additional money in shops, pubs or entrance charges to local attractions.

Goodall (1989) highlights a range of accommodation types from the fully commercial hotels to the quasi-commercial Youth Hostels and to the non-commercial options such as second homes or staying with friends. All of these have different implications for the local economy. Depending on location, some forms of accommodation will have an all-year-round use whereas some will only be seasonal.

The nature of tourist accommodation has wider implications and can be a cause of friction between local people and the tourist industry. Although the local community may welcome the employment prospects that come from providing tourist accommodation, they are less enthusiastic when tourism competes for homes. The growth of second homes and the purchase of property for holiday lets has made it difficult in some areas for less well paid and young people to find property to rent or buy (Shucksmith, 1981). Tourism has greatly inflated the prices, especially in rural locations.

SKILLS AND TRAINING

As the tourism industry has developed there has been wide recognition of the need to provide all sectors of the business with a better range of skills. The thrust of Action 2000 is about improving the skills of all sectors of the tourist industry from international marketing to the level of individual customer care. This scale of training requires a concerted effort and, although parts of the industry will be able to provide 'in-service training', there is a role to be played by the Training and Enterprise Councils (TECs) as well as the education sector.

URBAN REGENERATION

Urban regeneration might seem somewhat removed from tourism but throughout the post-war period there has been a growing belief that tourism can benefit from, and indeed contribute to, urban regeneration. The Festival of Britain in 1951 was in part a demonstration of the nation's commitment to post-war reconstruction and it attracted many people to the capital city to enjoy the wide range of activities that comprised this major event. In a similar way, the Garden Festival programme of the 1980s and 1990s made a commitment to land reclamation as a means of encouraging urban regeneration and brought many thousands of visitors to Liverpool, Stoke-on-Trent, Glasgow, Gateshead and Ebbw Vale. Without these Festivals there would have been no reason to visit nor to spend money.

This trend continues on the Greenwich Peninsula (East End of London) with the construction of the Millennium Dome and Village which, although designed to celebrate the new millennium, also represents a significant regeneration of derelict urban land. It is expected that many hundreds of thousands of people will visit this location spending a considerable amount of money through travel, entry, subsistence and the purchase of mementoes. As with the Garden Festivals, many short-term and some long-term jobs will be created.

Although it is almost impossible to quantify the longer-term benefits of such tourist-related regeneration projects, Garden Festivals were successful in raising the profile of these areas. Gateshead has become famous for its Metro Shopping Centre and, more recently, its Angel, but the Garden Festival helped to put the town on the map. In part, the same was true in Liverpool and Glasgow.

Law (1991) refers to the Chairman of the Merseyside Urban Development Corporation:

> The development of tourism has been a necessary precursor to other forms of investment. The city has a negative image. If people increasingly visit Liverpool they will realise it is a nice place to live and work (Philip Carter).

Tourism can be seen as a focus for urban regeneration. For example, on Teesside (the area covered by the Urban Development Corporation) many of the new developments have a strong orientation towards the development and promotion of tourism. The revitalisation of Liverpool Docks, with the Albert Dock complex as its centrepiece, has become a major tourist attraction within the North West of England. Similarly, in the Castlefield area of Manchester/Salford, urban regeneration has been a major catalyst for the tourist industry (Law, 1991).

Within the Castlefield area there is now a complex of developments which attract many visitors to the area. These include the famous Granada TV studios and the G-Mex Concert Hall as well as a Museum of Science and Technology and the Air and Space Gallery. Castlefields also boasts the site of a Roman Fort and, from the industrial revolution, other points of interest such as Bridgewater House and the Merchant's Warehouse. Although each of these individual sites represents a point of interest, the combination of such a range of attractions generates higher levels of tourist activity.

Where such attractions exist in close proximity to one another there are considerable opportunities for joint marketing and publicity, and even joint ticketing, to offer attractive packages to those wanting to visit a number of the sites. Such approaches to marketing do not need to be confined to any one location; opportunities exist at the regional scale. Visitors to the Castelfield location may expect to find forward publicity for locations such as the Albert Dock in Liverpool and Wigan Pier.

However, it is not simply in the larger metropolitan areas that a link exists between tourism and urban regeneration; it happens in smaller towns too. Scarborough on the Yorkshire coast is a case in point. With funding from the Single Regeneration Budget, Scarborough has been able to develop a strategy for the improvement of its Castleside Ward which includes the heart of the town's tourist attractions.

The background to this initiative is rooted in high unemployment rates, large numbers of houses in multiple occupation (once providing accommodation for traditional seaside holidaymakers), dependency on fishing and seasonal tourism, rundown physical fabric and appearance in the centre of the resort and a concentration of social and economic problems (Castle Pride Partnership, 1995)

To attempt to address these problems the Borough Council and the North Yorkshire TEC formed the 'Yorkshire Coast Economic Development Partnership' in 1994. They were assisted in their work by the County Council and the Rural Development Commission. The fact that two of the main activities in this area, tourism and fishing, were no longer prosperous made it essential to breathe new life into the area through the encouragement of inward investment and the improvement of the physical environment. In itself this was a prerequisite for stimulating interest in this part of the town.

Thus, included in the aims of the Castle Pride Initiative was the idea of utilising 'the natural and built heritage of the Old Town, Castle and Harbour to provide a high quality and up-to-date tourist destination'. Following from this, one of the strategic objectives of the Partnership was to 'develop the visitor potential of key tourist destinations . . .'. Although tourism was not the only focus of attention, it was seen as an important part of the overall strategy.

In some cases, urban regeneration, although not driven primarily by tourism, has helped to provide a context for a potential expansion in tourism. This has proved so on Newcastle upon Tyne's Quayside. The redevelopment of the city's river front has resulted in new hotels (primarily to serve a business community) and a range of pubs, restaurants and cafés. An ambience has been created which has proved very attractive to local people, business visitors and tourists to the city and region.

Opportunities for developing the tourist potential of Newcastle's Quayside will come from the redevelopment of the Baltic Flour Mill (on the Gateshead side of the Tyne) into the Centre for Contemporary Art funded by the National Lottery. This will certainly have local and regional significance but may also attract wider attention, drawing visitors in from many parts of the UK and overseas. A new footbridge to be constructed across the Tyne will link Gateshead's new Arts Centre with the Newcastle Quayside.

It is clear that urban regeneration can influence the development of tourism directly and indirectly. In addition to creating specific attractions, it provides a much-needed infrastructure through accommodation, leisure and entertainment venues as well as creating an ambience which is welcoming and pleasing to those who visit.

PARTNERSHIPS

The Castle Pride Partnership in Scarborough was an example of how a multi-agency approach to a problem was better able to marshal the necessary expertise and funding to embark upon a major regeneration project. It is unlikely that the initiative would have been as successful had it been left to the local authority alone. Although tourism was not the only point of focus in the Castle Ward area of Scarborough, it was seen as an important component of the overall regeneration strategy.

Partnerships are not always urban-based. In North Yorkshire, for example, the Esk Valley railway line is being promoted by a consortium of the County Council, Scarborough District Council, the National Park and Regional Railways. Of paramount importance is ensuring the line stays open. It is hoped that the line will be used more heavily by tourists, a contribution to sustainable tourism, linking the Cleveland conurbation to the North Yorkshire Moors National Park and to the Yorkshire coast around Whitby. But it is not just tourism that will benefit; local communities along the line will also benefit by the retention of a major public transport link to both Middlesborough and Whitby. Again, investment in tourism can benefit the wider community and vice versa.

Although this partnership is about a railway line, some partnerships are more broad-based. The North Pennines Tourism Partnership is a case in point and is

> . . . a partnership of private, public and voluntary sector organisations in the North Pennines which aims to strengthen the rural economy and care for the countryside.

Partners include the constituent county and district councils, the two tourist boards and agencies such as the Countryside Commission and the Rural Development Commission, as well as a range of representatives from local groups active within the area. This represents a powerful grouping of expertise able to address a wide range of problems and tackle a multitude of initiatives. This will help bring greater prosperity to the area as a whole. Being able to draw on the management and organisational expertise of its members, the partnership has been able to secure funding from the European Regional Development Fund.

Throughout the country there are many such partnerships, wholly or in part driven by a tourism agenda. In Northumbria there are seven such partnerships, some, such as the North Pennines, taking a broad geographical approach, whilst others, such as the Hadrian's Wall Tourism Partnership, focus on the benefits that are to be derived from visitors to the Roman heritage.

Partnerships do not come about by chance. Rather they are the result of an overriding policy to co-ordinate and bring together the agendas of authorities, agencies, private groups and individuals for the common good of an area. It is likely that major tourist initiatives will be based on partnerships in the future. There is a role for planning within these partnerships since future tourist developments have to be set within the context of wider land use planning policies and that includes achieving sustainable development.

THREATS TO TOURIST GROWTH

The major threat to the growth of tourism in the UK is competition from other countries. Failure to capture an increasing share of the domestic and international market for tourism will have an adverse impact on job creation, income generation and the ability to re-invest in the industry as a whole. Although there is now a support infrastructure for the industry, through central and local government departments, tourist boards and a range of quangos, much of the funding required to maintain investment in tourism must come from the industry itself. Although the support infrastructure will provide some funding, this will only ever represent a small proportion of the money needed to grow the business.

It is to ensure that tourism does not go into decline that initiatives such as Action 2000 have been launched to highlight just what is expected of a modern tourist industry. The ideas being generated by the ETB, for example, are increasingly reflected in the strategies being formulated at the level of the regional tourist boards. It is now very much a buyer's market; tourists are now generally more sophisticated, better informed and more affluent and as such are in a strong position to exercise choice. The range and quality of opportunity will influence the choices that the tourist makes.

This increased awareness of the threats posed to the future development of tourism has prompted positive responses from the tourist boards. For example, the NTB (1998) has undertaken a major 'SWOT' analysis to help it identify the range of strengths, weaknesses, opportunities and threats to tourism in Northumbria. As far as weaknesses and threats are concerned, many of the issues raised are things that can be countered. Poor perceptions can be changed by effective marketing and product development, whereas environmental damage at major attractions can be reversed by more effective management. The key issue is that any failure to identify problems will make it more difficult to capitalise on the best that the region has to offer.

Good intelligence provides the basis for more effective forward planning and this comes mainly from a careful analysis of problems and opportunities. Turning problems into opportunities requires skill and time. This will be the case in persuading people that their perceptions of an area are wrong and that there are, in fact, a wide range of places to visit and things to do. The scale of the problems will vary considerably. For example, Northumbria suffers from remoteness and lower levels of funding as well as competition from Scotland. In an unfair world it simply means that areas like Northumbria have to devote more time and effort to building a base for tourist growth.

THE WAY FORWARD

With investment in tourism so crucial to the success of the industry, the government's proposals to introduce Regional Development Agencies (RDAs) in the English regions is highly significant. This measure (DETR, 1997) indicates the creation of an agency in each of the regions which will, in part, amalgamate the activities of English Partnership and the Rural Development Agency, two major players associated with inward investment and economic development in both urban and rural areas. The government is not unaware of the relationship that exists between tourism and the future prosperity of many areas and as such expects considerable interplay between the various tourist boards and the new RDAs.

> . . . the creation of RDAs offers a real opportunity to bring a greater degree of cohesion into regional economic planning and programme delivery, and for tourism to play a key role in regional regeneration (ETB (in DETR, 1997)).

The DCMS (1998) also refer to the significant role to be played by the RDAs as providing 'a strategic focus for economic decision-making at the regional level'. In recognising the 'important contribution of tourism to regional economies and the key role the sector has to play in the regeneration of the regions' the DCMS highlights the DETR view that the 'RDAs will work in close partnership with Regional Tourist Boards on the development of strategies for tourism in the regions'.

With the ETB rolling forward its Action 2000 programme better to prepare the tourist industry for the next century and with the RTBs fine-tuning their own strategies, there would appear to be every prospect of success for the industry, especially with such strong support from central government. The accumulated knowledge and understanding of tourism in the UK must be harnessed. The coming together of representatives from different public, private and voluntary sector organisations to develop strategy within the tourist boards is vital. In a similar way, the bringing together of representatives from a range of organisations has helped to launch specific tourist partnerships that have already proved they can 'make a difference' on the ground.

CONCLUSION

There is a buoyant future for the tourist industry in the UK. Current levels of activity would seem to indicate a trend of increasing participation in those activities which make up tourism in this country. This appears to be confirmed by statistics at both national and regional levels. The strategies of the BTA, national and regional tourist boards are designed to ensure that larger numbers of people from home and abroad take their holidays in the UK. The various action plans of these boards will help to improve accessibility to the tourist market through improved marketing and publicity, and to improve the quality of the tourist experience by paying more attention to training and product development.

Successive governments have placed considerable store on the importance of tourism to both the national, regional and local economies through the generation of income and employment. By any measure, tourism now makes a significant contribution to the GDP and one that politicians cannot afford to ignore. Tourism has come of age; it has lost its 'candyfloss' image (Williams and Shaw, 1988). In areas which have undergone major economic upheaval during the past 20 years, such as the areas covered by the Urban Development Corporations, tourism might not represent the only solution to economic revitalisation but it has made a significant contribution. Equally, in areas of the countryside where changing national and European policies have caused economic problems, tourism has gone some way to providing a broader base to the rural economy.

The UK has much to offer the tourist: the great diversity of its countryside and the variety of its urban areas which include the traditional resorts, historic market towns and capital cities. Within this country of dramatically contrasting environments there is a wide range of opportunities to cater for those seeking both passive and active experiences. But as a result of a well-developed infrastructure system, the range of tourist opportunities is highly accessible and it is possible for a number of events and activities to be incorporated into the same holiday.

In looking to the future, the government has made it clear that there is a role for land use planning within the development of the UK tourist industry. Although the tourist industry has sometimes been critical of the lack of sympathy and understanding shown by planners to new tourist developments, tourism has to be set within the wider pattern of land use activities. Only statutory land use planning can effectively achieve this. Notwithstanding the growing significance of tourism to the economic and social well-being of the nation, it cannot be allowed to ignore the longer-term strategic aims of the land use planning system.

It is therefore worth stressing the increasing significance of sustainable development as an organising framework for all future development. Developments in tourism are no exception; they must be planned within the context of sustainable development strategies.

REFERENCES

Castle Pride Partnership (1995) *The Castle Pride Initiative, Scarborough, A Submission by the Castle Pride Partnership for Challenge Funds under the Government's Single Regeneration Budget*, The Partnership, Scarborough.

Countryside Commission (1998) *Planning for Countryside Quality*, CCP 529, Countryside Commission, Cheltenham.

Department for Culture, Media and Sport (1998) *Tourism – Towards Sustainability: A Consultation Paper on Sustainable Tourism in the UK*, DCMS, London.

Department of the Environment (1992) PPG21, *Tourism*, HMSO, London.

Department of the Environment, Transport and the Regions (1997) *Building Partnerships for Prosperity: Sustainable Growth, Competitiveness and Employment in the English Regions*, DETR, London.

Department of the Environment, Transport and the Regions (1998a) *The Future of Regional Planning Guidance: Consultation Paper*, DETR, London.

Department of the Environment, Transport and the Regions (1998b) *Modernising Planning: A Statement by the Minister for Planning, Regeneration and the Regions*, DETR, London.

Department of National Heritage (1997) *Success through Partnership: A Strategy for Tourism*, DNH, London.

Edwards, R. (1991) *Fit for the Future: Report of the National Parks Review Panel*, CCP 334, Countryside Commission, Cheltenham.

English Tourist Board (1997a) *Annual Report*, ETB, London.

English Tourist Board (1997b) *Agenda 2000, Brief*, ETB, London.

English Tourist Board (1997c) *Action 2000, Brief*, ETB, London.

German Federal Agency for Nature Conservation (1997) *Biodiversity and Tourism: Conflicts on the World's Seacoasts and Strategies for their Solution*, Springer, Berlin.

Goodall, B. (1989) Tourist accommodation, *Built Environment*, **15**(2), 75–77.

Hardy, S., Hart, T. and Shaw, T. (eds) (1991) *The Role of Tourism in the Urban and Regional Economy*, Regional Studies Association, London.

Lane, B. (1991) Will rural tourism succeed?, in: Hardy, S., Hart, T. and Shaw, T. (eds), *The Role of Tourism in the Urban and Regional Economy*, Regional Studies Association, London.

Lane, B. (1993) Sustainable rural tourism strategies: a tool for development and conservation, in: Bramwell, B. and Lane, B. (eds), *Rural Tourism and Sustainable Rural Development*, Channel View Publications, Clevedon.

Law, C.M. (1991) Tourism as a focus for urban regeneration, in: Hardy, S., Hart, T. and Shaw, T. (eds), *The Role of Tourism in the Urban and Regional Economy*, Regional Studies Association, London.

National Planning Forum (1998) *Planning for Tourism*, Local Government Management Board, London.

North of England Assembly of Local Authorities (1996) *Review of Regional Planning Guidance for the North East, Topic Reports: 4 Economic Development and Tourism; 5 Sport, Recreation and Tourism*, North of England Assembly, Newcastle upon Tyne.

Northumbria Tourist Board (1998) *A Strategy for Tourism in Northumbria 1998–2000*, NTB, Durham.

Pierce, A. (1998) England singled out to lose its tourist board, *The Times*, 30 May.

Pretty, J. (1998) *The Living Land*, Earthscan, London.

Shucksmith, M. (1981) *No Homes for Locals?*, Gower, Farnborough.

Tourism and Recreation Research Unit (TRRU) (1981) *The Economy of National Parks*, TRRU, Edinburgh University.

Williams, A.M. and Shaw, G. (1988) Tourism: candyfloss industry or job generator?, *Town Planning Review*, **59**(1), 81–103.

World Commission on Environment and Development (1987) *Our Common Future*, Bruntland Committee Report, Oxford University Press.

CHAPTER 15

PUBLIC PARTICIPATION, EQUAL OPPORTUNITIES, PLANNING POLICIES AND DECISIONS

Roy Darke

INTRODUCTION

Public participation in the planning process in Britain has long been practised in one form or another. Participation is considered to be one of the three main ideologies of planning law (McAuslan, 1980) alongside property and the public interest. Greater weight was given to participation in planning in the late 1960s–early 1970s when citizen involvement in development plans was introduced as a statutory requirement in the Town and Country Planning Acts of 1968 and 1971. A number of principles for public participation in planning practice were laid down at that time. Since then official requirements have been relaxed and more discretion has been given to local planning authorities about whether or not they involve people directly in the planning process. Despite the recent relaxation of requirements the government and many local planning authorities remain strongly committed to the idea (the Department of the Environment, Transport and the Regions (DETR) *Planning Policy Guidance Note 1*, para. 41, notes five objectives of the plan-led system including 'securing public involvement in shaping local planning policies'). The Labour government elected in 1997 began to 'modernise' local government by streamlining political management structures. At the same time local authorities are being encouraged to develop stronger links with their electorate, and to enhance public participation in policy and implementation.

The purpose of this chapter is to consider various types of public participation in theory and practice, and to look at where and how citizens can best engage with land-use development and the planning process. Some examples of recent good practice are given to illustrate the possibilities and forms of public involvement in planning.

Public participation in the policy-making process is easier for some groups in society than for others. Questions of equality of information or access to public goods are concerned with much more than making a personal choice about becoming involved in the policy process; there can be official insensitivity to the needs of some groups, even systematic exclusion or institutional blockages to the participation and visibility of some people. Particular groups (defined by gender, race, disability and so on) are considered to suffer from a more deep-seated lack of opportunity to play a full part in British society because of the prejudice and discrimination they face from individuals, organisations and institutions. It is for this reason that legislation and codes of practice have been devised to promote equal opportunities in work, in other spheres of daily life and in use of the environment. Dealing with equal opportunities in town planning is included in this chapter as a particular case of planning for people.

The idea of public participation is considered in the following section and placed into the context of democratic principles and different forms of government.

A listing of the various aims, types and techniques of public participation follows, including consideration of the design and assessment of comprehensive, integrated 'packages' of citizen involvement on planning issues.

The fourth section moves on to consider the formal requirements for participation in planning practice. Although the legislative requirements for public participation are now relatively limited (particularly in England and Wales), many planning authorities have introduced participatory initiatives and innovations based on local political and professional commitment. Some noteworthy examples are briefly discussed.

The final section of the chapter considers equal opportunity policies as a means to enhance the participation and involvement of specific groups in the mainstream of social, economic and political life, and planning policy. The section covers legislation and good practice in equal opportunities.

The Idea of Public Participation

Participation in government by adults is an aspect of democracy. The right to vote for those whom we want formally to represent us in parish and town councils, community councils, local authorities and parliaments (regional, national and European) is enshrined in the representative form of government in Britain. We can easily forget that the right to vote was extended in British society only after hard-fought struggles by those previously disenfranchised. In the early part of the nineteenth century the right to vote was largely limited to men who held 'substantial' property holdings. Working men got the vote later in the nineteenth century, but most women did not gain the right to vote until well into the twentieth century.

The representative principle of government is built on the assumption that it is difficult, if not impossible, for the public to take part in making the decisions that crop up every day in government and administration. It is often said that people do not want to get involved in politics on a daily basis. Turnouts at local elections are normally around 40% of those eligible to vote; a lot of people prefer to stay at home during elections and just get on with their lives. Some writers have argued that this is an advantage of representative democracy, and that popular involvement in policy-making would lead to poor decisions because 'uneducated' people lack judgement, and they have warned against the 'tyranny of the mob' (Burke quoted in Williams, 1976, p. 85). Others have suggested that powerful groups, even if in a minority, will always promote their own interests above all others. Political self-interest has included, in the past, aristocratic opposition to popular participation in order to ensure the continued right of a traditional élite to rule over the majority.

Despite strong attachment to the representative principle by many politicians there are circumstances when governors believe that people should have the opportunity directly to take part in decision-making rather than rely on MPs or councillors to take decisions on our behalf. The referendums in Scotland and Wales in 1997 when Scots and Welsh electors had a direct opportunity to vote for or against a national assembly are examples of a more direct form of citizen involvement in policy-making.

A crucial distinction has been made between politics and government (Jones and Ranson, 1989). Politics is an activity where the merits of alternative forms of action to deal with problems in the public sphere can be publicly debated as a prelude to choice. 'It is a way individuals and groups in society put their opinions onto the agenda for collective action by government' (Jones and Ranson, 1989, p. 5). Government, on the other hand, is where decisions are formally made on behalf of all. In a representative democracy, policy decisions are made by elected politicians who work to consider and reconcile the varied views and opinions held by the public prior to making those choices.

Participation in planning, therefore, can span a spectrum of consultation and debate, where the public is engaged in discussion but has no right to decide policy (politics), through to more direct forms of decision-making about planning and environmental issues (government). In specific circumstances members of the public may be involved in formal decision-making itself.

Arguments for a more general extension of politics and public participation beyond use of the ballot box at periodic elections are usually made on the basis that: society and public opinion is becoming more diverse; government procedures have severe shortcomings; profound changes are occurring in all spheres of life (work, leisure, religion, community); and politicians and professionals cannot keep abreast of the growing diversity of needs and interests within the population. Recent writers on the state of Britain say that social divisions have widened over the past 20 years (Hutton, 1995) and that many people at the bottom of British society are living in poverty, forgotten by those who are relatively well-off. It is argued that one way to get the views of the poorest groups more fully incorporated into the policy process would be to extend their opportunities for participation in politics and government.

Others make a special case for public participation in planning and environmental policy saying that decisions about physical development are much too important to be left solely to elected politicians in the seclusion of Westminster or council offices in the face of massive questions that face us all, such as global resource depletion and environmental degradation. World leaders attending environmental summit meetings have affirmed the need for public participation as a means to secure popular commitment and to extend 'ownership' of the radical measures now needed to safeguard the environment for future generations. Local Agenda 21 is an example of a world-wide programme intended to extend citizen involvement in environmental politics (Raemakers, Chapter 13, this volume, has a broader discussion of Local Agenda 21).

Public participation in planning as defined and used in this chapter, therefore, means the range of opportunities and mechanisms for the public to engage directly in the land-use and environmental policy process, either as a form of politics or as a limited form of direct engagement in government. Some people may consider this not to be radical enough as an agenda because public participation is defined on terms decided by the government and existing decision-makers. Nevertheless, providing formal opportunities for people to have their say directly about planning policy or development proposals would move the official policy process closer towards the idea of participatory democracy and away from the representative principle along one of the major dimensions of democratic theory (Arblaster, 1987; Held and Pollitt, 1986).

Restricting the definition of public participation in planning to these formal channels of engagement in the policy process is not intended to suggest that informal or 'unscripted' action by members of the public is not legitimate. The protests and direct action by environmental campaigners over major road building, airport extensions, nuclear energy sites and other developments are manifestations of a much broader principle of freedom of expression and voice which is part of British political and civic history and culture. Direct action not only brings attention to the loss of countryside, trees and woodland, natural habitats and wildlife, but also asserts a much more fundamental political right of protest. Direct action may be: a last resort; an expression of frustration when the official channels appear to be closed or politicians and officials appear deaf or impervious to argument; a manifestation of deeply held views and beliefs about issues considered profoundly important which drives people to unofficial acts; or a fundamental statement of distrust / non-acceptance of the right of the governors to govern. Ultimately direct action can be an expression of desire for a wholly different form of society and politics which has been an important element of British history and social change. We should not condemn it lightly.

TYPES AND FORMS OF PUBLIC PARTICIPATION IN PLANNING

There is quite wide variation in the ways that local councils engage the local population about planning issues. This variety is reflected in listings of forms or types of public participation. A well-known typology of public participation in planning appeared in the 1960s at a time when there was a broader, world-wide eruption of interest in citizen involvement and political action intended to make governments sit up and listen (anti-Vietnam War demonstrations in the US, student and worker protests in France and Britain in 1968). Arnstein's (1970) ladder of citizen participation (Figure 1) has frequently been reproduced or adapted since it first appeared (1969).

The ladder of participation has shortcomings, not least its apparent elevation of one set of interests ('the public') in the policy process above all others. Another criticism is that it fails to distinguish between politics and government (a distinction introduced in the previous section). Later writers have adapted the ladder of participation and added qualifications to the original idea (Burns *et al.*, 1994). A main value of the typology is to show that public participation initiated by government can include public relations and manipulation with no release of power to the public. But we should also remember that there can be numerous interests or groupings (or stakeholders to use the currently fashionable term) involved in the planning process and that there is no automatic right for the views of one group (say, local residents) to be given precedence in debates about planning policy. If participation is intended to open up the policy process to ordinary members of the public, then why not to all other groups? The list of stakeholders involved in planning includes: developers (individuals and organisations); neighbours; civic societies and local interest groups; the local planning authority dealing with policies or planning applications; other 'interests' within local councils (including politicians and officials representing education, social services and other committees); neighbouring councils; district and strategic planning authorities (district/county or regional bodies); utility companies (water, gas, electricity); national bodies (such as the Environment Agency) linked to government; the DETR; local voluntary organisations and national bodies not linked to government (Landowners' Associations, Friends of the Earth); and so on. Of course, many of these 'interests' are automatically involved in planning issues (through statutory consultations, as initiators or arbiters of development). However, the list helps to emphasise the point that 'the public' is but one, admittedly important, interest in town planning. All the bodies on the list consider that they have a legitimate place in the planning process and several consider that they represent the 'public interest' and bring a wider perspective to planning matters than provided by the views of local residents. Local public opinion can be parochial and not always in the broader interest, such as NIMBY ('not in my backyard') protests against, say, the provision of new affordable housing in country towns and villages.

Attempting to understand Arnstein's approach to public participation introduces the idea of power within the policy process: an important component of the 'politics of planning'. Individual and group participants in the planning process have different amounts of power. Power is a complex and contested concept (Lukes, 1974; Clegg, 1989) but a simple definition suggests it is 'getting your own way'. A number of case

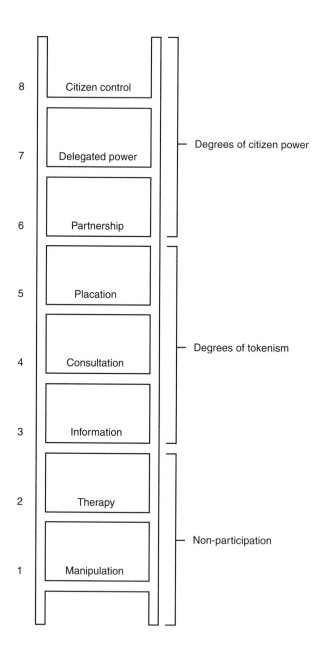

Figure 1 *Arnstein's ladder of public participation*

studies (Blowers, 1980; Simmie, 1981) have shown that the British planning process is dominated by powerful developer interests. Healey and colleagues in their study of British planning (1988, p. 245) concluded that farmers, minerals extractors, industrialists, established and profit-seeking property developers and land owners have moulded the planning system to work for their benefit. The development industry (builders and substantial land owners/developers) has been particularly influential and successful in developing a 'pro-development' approach within government circles in the recent past. The last Conservative government (1979–1997) was very positively disposed towards development not only because it believed strongly in the idea of economic growth (where physical development creates jobs and wealth) but also because its members were opposed to what they saw as excessive 'red-tape' and the thwarting of free enterprise by planning controls, rules and regulations (Thornley, 1991). Some more radical writers have even suggested that the planning system will *inevitably* reflect the interests of the most powerful and wealthy groups (Kirk, 1980). Development *is* an engine for the creation of jobs and wealth and may be in everyone's interest but that is not an argument for stopping debate and discussion about development proposals. It is because of the uneven distribution of power in British society that public participation remains an important principle for town planning and democratic politics.

Public participation in planning before the 1970s was usually organised for instrumental purposes (corresponding to the bottom rungs of the ladder of participation). Public opinion was used to support and legitimate the planners' ideas about future plans and policies. Public participation was intended to secure public approval for political and professional proposals. A good example of this narrow approach can be found in the government's *The Future of Development Plans* (Ministry of Housing and Local Government Planning Advisory Group, 1965, para. 7.42) which considered public participation principally as a vehicle for publicity and 'public relations'. However, growing levels of public protest about planning policies and proposals in the 1960s created momentum for an extension of the idea and processes of public participation in planning and led to legislation requiring local authorities to engage the public in the planning process.

A useful categorisation of the aims of public participation in planning has been provided by Hampton (1977). He identified two major objectives behind the introduction of greater public participation in planning in the late 1960s. First, policy-making and decisions can benefit from better information about public preferences and residents' concerns. Members of the public can also gain information from engagement in public participation around planning matters, helping them better to understand the reasons for planning policies and better to judge the implications and consequences for them and their communities from implementation of planning policies and proposals. Participation can also help the public to make better informed assessments and choices from a number of policy alternatives. Secondly, public participation can draw people more fully into a stronger and longer-term relationship with government and enhance their current and future ability to play a significant role in policy-making. Hampton called this 'enhancing citizenship' and it can be seen as a broader democratic objective alongside the more instrumental objective of making better plans.

From this analysis Hampton went on to develop a 'schema of participation', proposing that planning authorities should consider the means and techniques of public participation in the planning process in terms of three separate aims:

- dispersing information to the public
- gathering information from the public
- promoting interaction between policy-makers and the public.

He built on an important idea from the government's Skeffington report (1969) on public participation in planning which noted that there is no single or simple category of 'the public', rather that there are many separate publics. The Skeffington report distinguished between 'joiners' and 'non-joiners' being, respectively, those who are active in civic affairs (members of action groups, environmental protection societies, preservation trusts and the like) and those who are not members of any local organisation. An implication from this distinction is that 'joiners' will willingly engage with the planning process, say, by attending a public meeting on planning matters in the Town Hall on a cold winter night. However, if planners want to find out what 'non-joiners' think about a planning proposal they will have to use different techniques. The Skeffington Committee concluded that planning authorities need to be pro-active when seeking the views of non-joiners and it suggested using community workers to engage the majority of people in their own neighbourhoods, at the shops or in the pubs.

Hampton used this observation about the variety of groups and interests in local communities to suggest that planners should distinguish between *major élites* (such as local business groups, major employers, Chambers of Commerce, trades unions), *minor élites* (such as local interest groups, community associations, action groups), and, thirdly, the broad mass of the public as a *collectivity of individuals*. Combining the three elements: different objectives and aims of public participation in planning; different publics (major and minor élites and the public as a collection of individuals); and the various forms or techniques of public participation and information exchange (such as public meetings, exhibitions, focus groups, technical reports) creates a matrix of possibilities for the planning authority seeking to interact with the public (Figure 2). The analysis is valuable in pointing out that to achieve differing aims with different groups requires a variety of methods of public participation. Using the matrix can help planners in devising programmes of participation and consultation tailored to local needs and circumstances.

If a planning authority wants to achieve *all* the three principal aims of public participation (dispersing information, gathering information and promoting a dialogue with members of the public) it can only do so effectively by developing a varied package of techniques and types of participation. For example, a common

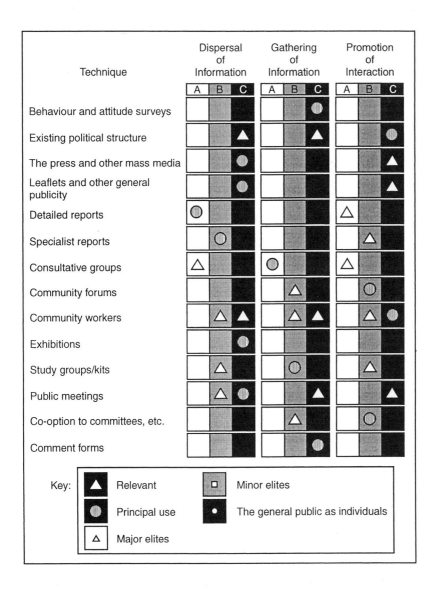

Figure 2 *The relationship of specific techniques to subsidiary objectives in public participation*

(but limited) package adopted by structure plan authorities in the 1970s during plan preparation was:

- a social survey of a random sample of households using a questionnaire;
- public exhibitions showing existing planning policies and environmental issues;
- a number of public meetings intended to spell out the possible issues and policies that could go into the plan.

In retrospect, this package was limited because it only:

- collected information from a random selection of households (representing a collectivity of individuals);
- gave information to those individual members of the public who decided to study the exhibition when placed in public libraries or shopping centres;
- gave information to the individuals and minor élites who bothered to turn up to the public meetings.

This commonly used package failed to provide serious opportunities for dialogue between planners and public (as a whole) and neglected the views of many local groups. To achieve broader coverage and aims would have required expanding and extending the package to include other targets and other participation techniques.

Bishop and co-authors (DoE, 1995) have also distinguished between one-way and two-way or interactive methods of public participation. Their classification updates the Hampton approach. Other recent work has updated the range of participatory methods available to town planners (Environmental Trust Associates, 1994; Wilcox, 1994). Environmental Trust Associates (1994, p. 7) say that '(i)nvolving communities is a process. An approach [to public participation in planning] based on a "quick fix" without asking key questions will be headed for failure'. Key questions that should be asked at the outset include: 'Why should we involve people?' 'Who should be involved?' 'How?' and 'When?'

Some tools are more suited to certain tasks than others, but the principal lesson for practice is that it is extremely unlikely that one technique will be appropriate as the basis of a public participation programme on a major planning issue. Another key to successful public participation is the way that the tools are used rather than the merits of the tools themselves (Wilcox, 1994). What is meant by this is that people are canny and will see when they are simply being asked to legitimate the planners' pet schemes and when they are genuinely being asked to make a contribution to the policy process. Another principal lesson for planners is to be straight with people and to be clear from the outset about what is open for full discussion, where policy can be changed, and what aspects of planning policy and proposals are already committed. Where the local planning authority has firm, decided policies a task of public participation is to tell people clearly why this is the case.

A key principle raised by all these recent writers on public participation in the policy process is that citizen involvement should not be treated as a brief episode where planners descend from their offices into the local community once in a while to use a few randomly selected techniques for collecting or giving information. Done well and with proper preparation and forethought, public participation can: be integral to the policy process and local politics; develop trust and respect between politicians, planners and the public; aid community development; raise public awareness of existing policies and future options; add to the quality of the end product (plans and planning policies); enhance the political process; and be enriching for all, including the policy-makers.

Nevertheless, there is dispute in planning circles over whether public participation, particularly when done fully and well, is worthwhile. This is a matter for individual planning authorities, politicians and planners to assess in the light of their capabilities, resources, ideologies and values. A common viewpoint is that public participation in planning extends the amount of time for making decisions when there is persistent pressure to speed up the planning process. Evidence on this question is mixed. Bishop's (DoE, 1995) review of participation in planning suggests that effective public participation does not extend the time for making decisions. A case study of local plan preparation in Sheffield, where the programme of public participation was particularly informative and interactive, shows that when the plan went on deposit for public inspection there were only two objections: one was based on a misunderstanding and was quickly withdrawn; the other comment was accepted by the planners and the deposit plan changed. The upshot was that there was no need for a public inquiry on the local plan and considerable savings were made in time and money (Darke, 1990).

STATUTORY AND RECOMMENDED OPPORTUNITIES FOR PUBLIC PARTICIPATION IN PLANNING

We mentioned earlier that the government introduced a statutory requirement for public participation in the development plan process during the late 1960s. The 1968 and 1971 Town and Country Planning Acts contained the requirement that the public be given an opportunity, first, to indicate the matters they felt should be included in the development plan (local and strategic) and, secondly, to have an opportunity to make representations on any matters contained in the draft plan prior to its submission to the Secretary of State for the Environment for scrutiny, review and public inquiry. Objectors were able to submit comments on the planning document and a public inquiry (examination in public in the case of structure plans) was required to be held. Structure plan authorities were also required to show how, when and in what ways the public had been consulted and engaged in the process of plan preparation and development by means of a formal document, 'the participation statement'.

This statutory approach towards public participation in the development plan process remains broadly intact today. However, there was never whole-hearted official acceptance of the expansion of public participation in planning. Ministers and MPs, civil servants and professionals were already saying that 'participation causes delay' in the early 1970s. Many local politicians also felt that their representative role and power was threatened by wider participation. The period since 1970 has, therefore, been one of reduced government commitment to the idea and relaxation of many of the intentions and requirements for public participation in planning which were strongly held at that time.

Legislation passed in the early 1990s relating to the preparation of development plans (the 1990 and 1991 Planning Acts in England and Wales) contains no requirement for public consultation or participation *prior* to placing draft plans on deposit for public inspection. At the point when local planning authorities put the draft plan on deposit they are required to take account of public representations and give a formal opportunity for members to record their views. In addition to placing the draft development plan on deposit (in publicly accessible locations) the local planning authority has to provide a statement of the publicity it has undertaken to increase public access to information about the plan. The statement of publicity is a weaker version of the participation statement originally introduced by the 1968–1971 legislation. The Secretary of State for the Environment, Transport and the Regions can require councils to further publicise the plan and opportunities for public comment if s/he thinks that the original publicity is inadequate. This provision has not been used since 1990, in comparison with a number of high-profile occasions during the 1970s and early 1980s (under the earlier legislation) when some county authorities were required by the Secretary of State to go back and provide evidence of further consultation and participation on the plan and its policies. The public inquiry (PLI) on the local plan is to hear all and every objection to the draft document, whilst the examination in public (EIP) on draft structure plans/ unitary development plans pursues inquiries into those specific aspects of the plan where the panel (chaired by a member of the Planning Inspectorate) requires further elaboration or clarification. The EIP panel also selects the parties to give evidence; there is no automatic right for all objectors to appear. Participants and topics at the EIP are, therefore, determined before the examination opens as a means to focus the discussion and complete the inquiry within a known timescale.

The rationale for the careful programming and selection of EIP topics and participants was the government's reponse to a number of large development plan inquiries in the 1970s (notoriously the public inquiry into the Greater London Development Plan). These inquiries became bogged down by the very large number of objections, all of which had to be heard despite much repetition and, sometimes, the orchestration of delay by objectors. This process can be very costly (witness the inquiry into the fifth terminal at Heathrow in the late 1990s) and can also be unfair (where development interests are able to sustain a presence and influence at the inquiry over a long period, whereas ordinary folk cannot afford the time or loss of earnings to do so). In a statement on 'Modernising the Planning System' in 1998 a Minister of State in the DETR indicated that the government would be seeking to introduce similar measures into the PLI (determination of topics and participants) in order to speed up the process.

Thomas (1996) has provided a 'map' of public participation in development plan preparation (based on government information) currently in force in England and Wales (Figure 3).

The requirements for public participation in development planning in Scotland differ slightly from the position south of the border. Before starting work on a structure plan (or its alteration) the planning authority must advertise the initi-ation of the process, explain the reasons, set out a programme of work and invite public comment. Key public and private sector interests and community groups should be identified and their active participation encouraged. The formal exist-ence of Community Councils in each Scottish local authority area provides a valuable bedrock for participation and consultation on planning policies and plans. Recent advice (Scottish Office, 1996b) suggests early involvement of key players and a partnership approach to structure plan preparation. In this respect (public involvement at the start of and during plan preparation) Scottish procedures differ significantly from those current in England and Wales. The procedures for plan approval and Examination in Public are largely the same across the British Isles.

The position with respect to local plans in Scotland is that local planning authorities are required to ensure that public interests are taken into account. The rationale for this is built around the principle of keeping plans relevant and effective. Specific provision in the Scottish Office advice on the local plan process (Scottish Office, 1996a) includes: the public right of access to information; preparation of simplified versions of plans for particular communities and general distribution; preparation of a charter for local planning; wide consultation and consultation tailored to the interests of particular groups; and public consultation concentrated at the draft plan stage. Further differences between the English/ Welsh and Scottish approaches to participation in local planning become apparent from these descriptions. Whereas the government seems to be taking a minimalist approach to participation in development plans in England and Wales a much more inclusive and open approach (particularly in the early stages of strategic planning and in local planning in general) seems to be officially welcomed and encouraged in Scotland.

In addition to opportunity for general public comment during the development plan process and on draft and final proposals in development plans, local planning authorities must undertake formal consultations with statutorily defined bodies (neighbouring councils, official and national bodies dealing with planning and the environment) during plan preparation. Local planning authorities take the views of formal and statutory consultees very seriously because, first, consultees are considered experts in aspects of planning and the development process and their evidence can signal flaws or difficulties in planning policies and their

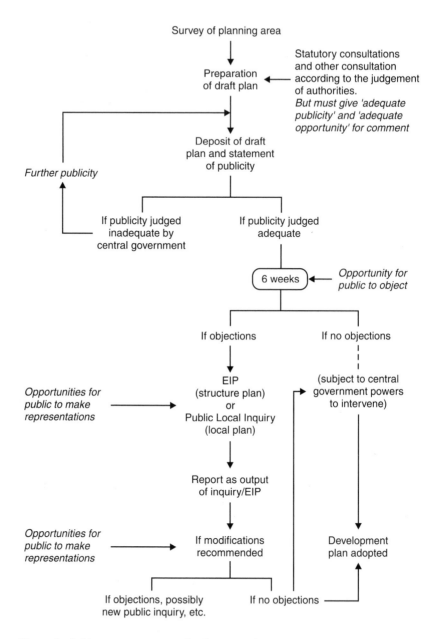

Figure 3 *Public participation in development plan preparation*

implementation and, secondly, opposition to the draft plan by such bodies at the subsequent public inquiry/examination could be very damaging to the credibility of the plan. However, other consultations (with most 'minor élites') are at the discretion of English and Welsh planning authories: these councils can decide whether or not to engage the public in planning policy discussions prior to deposit of the draft plan (compared with the explicit encouragement of community council, local group and public engagement in planning matters in Scotland).

At this stage it is worth making the point that consultation has sometimes been seen as a relatively 'weak' form of public participation (equivalent to the middle rungs of Arnstein's ladder) when used outside the framework of statutory consultation. However, some local planning authorities have used their discretion to undertake much more extensive public involvement and have included 'stronger' forms of dialogue with the public. An example (Box 1) is where local politicians held very strong views about the need for public participation and the involvement of previously poorly represented groups on planning matters (Darke, 1990).

Box 1 *A City Centre for People*

Sheffield City Council took proposals for the central area a stage further with a draft local plan in 1986. Entitled 'A City Centre for People' it was intended as a vehicle for investment tempered by community needs. Explicit policies of positive action included: space for community groups; child-care provision; improved disabled access and facilities; a safe environment for women; re-introduction of housing; and priority to pedestrians and public transport. Within this framework of policy parameters the Council was committed to significant community participation on plan preparation, particularly for groups not normally heard in commercial developments.

The public participation programme included widespread publicity and opportunities for comment. Councillors identified 12 groups they wanted to see specifically involved in the programme of participation including: women; young parents; elderly; people with disabilities; unemployed; low paid; young people; Asian and African–Caribbean groups.

A set of principles was applied at the outset of the participation programme. They were:

- clarity about the aims of participation from the start
- politicians to play a central role throughout
- linkage of motives, objectives, intentions with appropriate techniques/tools
- clear interpretation of policy and implications for specific groups
- identified procedures for evaluating and acting on the public's views.

A wide range of community organisations were invited to nominate representatives for the 12 advisory groups meeting over a number of weeks.

The groups set the agenda, nature, timing and location of the meetings and decided the response they would make. Two planners were used as facilitators for each group. The programme was made clear at the start. Funds were made available to allow the groups to meet and carry out their own programme of fact-finding. For example, the groups of people with disabilities visited a number of other cities to see how other councils dealt with planning their centres.

The planners began the sessions by explaining the process, the nature of the draft plan, and the policies already in place or proposed. As the groups developed their own confidence and momentum the planners took on a role of servicing the group (organising typing, getting and checking information, arranging rooms and child care). Features of the advisory groups were their informality, flexible approach and sensitivity to the different ways of working of members. Most groups met several times over a period of three months for sessions lasting about two hours. Only one of the groups (the unemployed) failed to produce a final report.

The groups reported to a group of councillors from the Planning Committee in an all-day Saturday 'informal hearing' at the Town Hall (with crèche and lunch provided). A wide variety of proposals and requests were made in a set of well-produced written and spoken presentations. Most proposals were in the form of planning policy guidance (about access to shops, availability of facilities in the city centre – such as child care for shoppers, baby changing rooms, disabled access, etc.). The councillors took all the findings away for comment and responded to every point made. Many suggestions were built into planning advice notes and briefings for developers.

Almost all participants felt that the advisory groups had been worthwhile and enjoyable. Elected members were particularly positive about the constructive and practical outcomes. There were some snags and failings. The unemployed group felt that they had no money to spend and nothing to offer the city centre planning process. Young people did not like the formality of (informal) meetings. Asian women did not get involved. But overall it was a successful programme of participation.

Lessons from the advisory group process were that:

- A clear strategy and objectives at the start helped to involve councillors and groups.
- Flexibility and scope for change of approach is essential to cope with different group needs.
- Politicians and planners need to be flexible and prepared to develop and learn new skills.
- Public participation done well has significant resource implications.
- Direct contact between participants and power-holders is essential to commitment and success.

A significant outcome was that when the comments on the draft plan were
collated at the end of the statutory period for representations, only two were
negative and these were resolved without the need for a public inquiry.

Source: Alty and Darke (1987), Darke (1990).

Another major element of the statutory planning process where public participation is officially required is in control of development. Central government
requires that local planning authorities publicise planning applications received
(under an amendment to the 1990 Town and Country Planning Act contained in
the 1991 Planning and Compensation Act) within the General Development Order
provisions. These regulations state that publicity is intended to allow neighbours
and other interested parties to make known their views about applications for
planning permission. The government's advice and recommendations (contained
in circulars from the DETR and Scottish Office Development Department)
schedules the prescribed forms of publicity for planning applications. Some
specific types of development require specialist consultations. Developers are also
required to notify land-owners/tenants of applications for planning permission on
land which is not owned or held by them. The General Development Order makes
provision for three types of publicity about planning applications: notices in a
newspaper circulating in the locality; the placing of site notices, visible to the
public; and neighbour notification (usually by letter) to occupiers and owners of
adjoining property. The advice has detailed requirements according to the circumstances and kinds of development but for most applications the local planning
authority can require a site notice or send out neighbour notifications dependent
on past practice and the nature of the site. There is some discretion available to
councils over the form of publicity required according to whether the planners
consider the principal interested parties live in the vicinity (when neighbour
notification is favoured) or where there is lack of clarity on who might be
interested (when a site notice is more appropriate). Other forms of notification and
publicity may be used by councils such as regularly sending lists of applications to
parish/town councils, or posting lists in public places (libraries, community
centres). A 'map' of the development control process is set out below (Figure 4)
showing the key points of publicity and consultation.

The position on publicity for development and neighbour notification in
Scotland is somewhat different (from that in England and Wales). The Scottish
system of neighbour notification requires that adjacent owners, occupiers or
lessees of non-domestic property be notified where they can be identified from the
valuation roll (including the requirement that the developer send notices to the
owner/occupier/lessee if they cannot be named). The position on neighbour
notification for adjacent domestic property has recently become more complicated
because the domestic valuation roll ceased to be updated after the introduction of

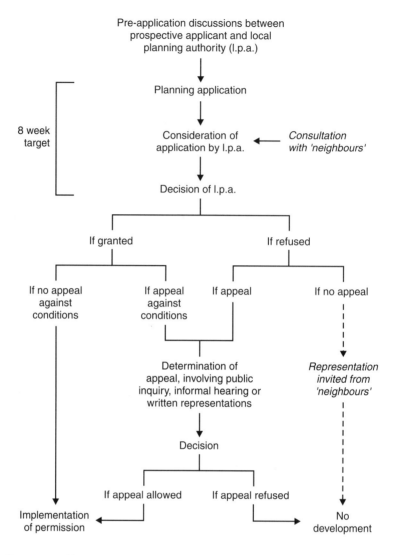

Figure 4 *Public participation in the development control process*

the community charge in 1989–1990. The charge/council tax register no longer contains information on ownership of domestic property so a procedure for sending two notices to residences adjacent to a development site was introduced in the early 1990s, addressed to 'owner' and 'occupier' respectively. Developers are required to include an annotated location plan with the application for permission to develop in order that the Scottish local planning authority can identify neighbouring properties that have not been informed of the proposed development.

There has been some recent discussion about third parties' rights in relation to applications for planning permission. There are two main elements to this discussion. The first concerns the right of third parties to speak and provide information during the determination of applications, which goes beyond current provisions in legislation and government guidance. A significant number of councils (about 40% of authorities in England and Wales at the most recent estimate) now allow members of the public to speak about planning applications and planning issues at the local authority committee meeting where applications for planning permission are to be determined. This is a relatively recent development (mostly since the early 1990s). Councils that allow public speaking in committee (and some also allow public speaking at formal site visit /site inspections by planning committee) normally have defined procedures and rules to ensure fairness and control over the process. A common set of rules allows both developers and residents, respectively, to have a specified time (three or five minutes) to address the committee. The rules normally include a requirement that the chairperson of the committee is informed by those persons wishing to speak before the meeting begins. Public speaking at planning committee appears to be popular with members of the public and has been well used when introduced. Experience has shown that this discretionary provision for public participation does extend the time taken to get through planning committee business (and this is one of the strongest objections to the practice). On the other hand, it does seem to enhance public interest in local planning matters as shown by the increased numbers of people attending planning committee meetings in councils where it has been introduced. An implication for planning practice is that planning officers attending committee may have to respond to new information on the spot and advise the committee on the implications for their previous recommendation (Darke, 1999).

A second element of recent debate about third-party involvement in relation to planning applications concerns rights of appeal. It has been proposed by some politicians and professionals that third parties (the local planning authority and the developer being the 'first and second parties') be able to appeal against the granting or refusal of planning permission. The arguments made for this right are mainly on the grounds that members of the public (principally neighbours) will bear many of the 'costs and benefits' of development and their lives can be deeply affected. It is suggested, therefore, that members of the public should be able formally to initiate a public inquiry if they feel aggrieved at a decision to refuse or permit a development. It is argued that if a developer is able to appeal a decision to refuse a development on grounds of loss of development rights, then so too should local people be able to appeal the granting of permission on grounds of their loss of amenity. In this debate on third-party rights of appeal, official arguments against change in the system have outweighed arguments in favour of extending rights. The principal argument against the extension of rights of appeal to third parties is that the Inspectorate and the local planning system would become overloaded with challenges to council decisions, causing undue delay and expense to developers and to government (local and national) who would automatically have to appear, yet third-party appellants would incur very little cost. The intention by the government to recover the costs of public inquiries from appellants against development control decisions signalled in July 1998 shows a further hardening of official attitudes against appeals (by making written representations more attractive) and delays in planning. On the other hand, there has been a third-party right of appeal in relation to development decisions in the Republic of Ireland for some years.

The other principal activity that local planning authorities have responsibility for, and where public participation can be a significant consideration, is enforcement. Recent government advice to councils has been to take a more pro-active role in enforcing planning controls and legislation. However, enforcement is a discretionary function for local councils. Difficult cases of enforcement are expensive of officer resources and can take a very long time to resolve. Councils often do not have the capacity to take a more active role in chasing down those who fail to obtain permission for development or do not meet the conditions of planning approval. A pragmatic assessment of the costs and benefits of whether to pursue enforcement by planning committees and officers is often the starting point for action (or inaction). However, the public can play a crucial role in advising local councils of development where permission has not been obtained. Strength of public opinion can be a powerful reason for a council to pursue enforcement action.

Public participation to achieve community benefit can be achieved through the mechanism of planning obligations (s. 106 of the 1990 Town and Country Planning Act and s. 52 of the 1991 Planning and Compensation Act: still called planning agreements in Scotland under s. 75 of the 1997 Act). Open public discussion of, or wider public involvement in, the negotiation of planning obligations is rare, although there are exceptions. Normally, planning obligations are thrashed out behind closed doors and only involve the developer and planning officers. A case where a set of community benefits was negotiated after a particularly thorough and innovative public participation programme was in relation to the development of a site in Liphook (Box 2). The third report of the Nolan Committee on Standards in Public Life (Nolan Report, 1995) (which considered probity in local government and town planning) recommended that information about planning obligations should be in the public arena, even if the main parties only want full disclosure after the completion of negotiations. Public knowledge of, and involvement in, the negotiation of community benefit and planning obligations may become a stronger feature of planning practice in the future.

Box 2 *Community planning in East Hampshire*

During 1996–1997 East Hampshire District Council faced development pressure on a former Ministry of Defence depot within the envelope of Liphook (population c. 7000 with a hinterland of c. 18 000). Sainsbury's, the retail chain, had purchased the site with conditions of sale including a requirement that the local community be involved in helping decide the form and nature of development. The County and District Councils were producing a local plan. The District Council had marked the site as suitable for a supermarket plus other development.

The Community Planning Programme was begun in 1997 entitled 'Liphook 2000'. A consultant specialising in community planning was used to provide a strategic framework for the programme, to train planning staff in community participation methods and skills, and to facilitate the main elements of the programme. After initial publicity, preliminary consultation with local people began in July. This stage saw community representatives agreeing the detail of the Council's guidelines for the planning process and preparation of an extensive programme of community participation from September.

A three-day event in September in the school/community centre included:

- an exhibition giving and asking for information (on residents' wants and needs, and ideas for the site)
- briefings from Sainsbury's about their ideas and needs
- small participatory workshops led by planners on
  - developing the local economy
  - traffic, movement and transport
  - community facilities
  - village design and site layout

The workshops lasted about 90 minutes and small groups of residents (not all of whom knew each other) spent most of the time working together on the key issues that they were interested in or concerned about. The Council staff served to focus the discussions and give specialist advice when asked. They were briefed to ensure that the workshops did not turn into question–answer sessions and were not confrontational.

Over 10% of local people got involved in this event. The findings and information gained were consolidated into briefings for a later event (early in 1998) when community representatives spent a day preparing a draft development brief and specific layouts for the site using the community design specialist as facilitator. The negotiated outcome included development of the supermarket, housing (including a proportion of affordable units intended for local residents), and a community hall.

Lessons from this programme of community planning include:

- the confirmation that public participation is a process that has to be planned and staged over time;
- local planning staff can play a central role (given training and development of political and facilitative skills) adding to the participatory ethos and culture of the department;

- a high proportion of local people can be involved if events are well planned and accessible;
- local political representatives can play a key role (at public events, specialist workshops and in negotiating community benefit).

Source: Details of the programme from East Hampshire District Council.

Examples of local planning authorities that have gone further than official guidance and advice from the government by undertaking substantial programmes of public consultation and participation show that citizen involvement is an extremely important consideration for some councils, planning authorities and developers. This extends beyond public participation in planning. Some progressive councils (such as Basildon District Council) have introduced wider innovations in public participation, including open question-and-answer sessions before formal committee meetings begin to give the public opportunities to quiz members and officers on any relevant issues.

Despite the apparent coolness shown by the last government towards public participation in the planning process the Labour government, elected in 1997, is not continuing this 'hands-off' approach. A number of Consultation Papers early in 1998 and the subsequent legislation and advice for modernising local democracy includes wide-ranging proposals to involve local people and communities much more directly in local debate and decision-taking. The government seeks more active searching out of the views of citizens (by citizens' juries, focus groups, conferences and opinion polls) and direct involvement in decisions (by permanent citizens' panels, forums, referendums), and suggesting that local councils introduce and use new forms of interactive communication between the public and their council representatives and officials (Internet, e-mail and so on). Some councils (such as the London Borough of Wandsworth) have already installed Internet sites in public libraries giving on-line information and direct interaction with the council and council personnel as part of its Charter Mark initiative and efforts to promote 'Best Value'.

EQUAL OPPORTUNITIES

There are two main ways in which town planners need to address equal opportunity issues in their professional work and practice. First, discrimination by employers and organisations (such as local authorities) is prohibited by law. Legislation applies to all employing bodies that provide goods and services, and that includes organisations in the private and public sectors. To comply with a raft of anti-discrimination legislation (equal pay, special provisions against discrimination on grounds of sex, race and disability) employers must adopt policies relating to recruitment, training, promotion and monitoring to ensure that equal opportunities apply to all members of the workforce. This set of provisions may seem unrelated to the mainstream of planning practice but it is increasingly recognised that planning education needs to address issues of management, and that includes managing the planning organisation, among other things, as an equal opportunities employer. After a relatively short time in professional life, recent graduates assume managerial responsibilities and need to be aware of their legal and professional duty to promote equal opportunities. Employers have to take great care in advertising posts and recruiting staff, in training programmes, in selection for promotion, and in dealing with complaints and breaches of good practice in employment. We might say that this aspect of equal opportunities relates to the 'internal' activities of the organisation.

Secondly, organisations that provide goods and services have responsibilities to ensure that they deliver these on the same basis to all, irrespective of the sex, race and other circumstances of clients, customers and users. This responsibility can be said to be particularly important for public organisations because they deal with a wide cross-section of people and are always in the public eye. Equal opportunities in service delivery also has a legal basis insofar as employers need to ensure that no part of their activities for users is discriminatory under the law. For example, the Disability Discrimination Act made it illegal to run a service that is impossible or unreasonably difficult for a disabled person to use. Access to buildings (such as public libraries or planning offices) is one element of this requirement for equal treatment. However, equal opportunity questions go beyond simply conforming to legislation. Planning organisations provide a wide range of services with the public interest in mind. The range of policy issues and groups that planners are required to consider is wider than covered in the statute book (including the elderly, young people, travellers, minority interest groups and so on). Employers and professionals are responsible for ensuring that they confront discrimination and inequality whenever it appears in their dealings with clients and users. Participation in the planning process should be equally available to all and the practitioner will have to work to that end. An example might be where a planning officer experiences, say, racist and exclusionary behaviour by some people towards others at a public meeting. Good practice and professional integrity requires that the officer confronts such unacceptable behaviour in an assertive yet diplomatic way. This is another example of the need for managerial skills in planning practice where knowledge and experience of conflict resolution, mediation and political skill are essential. We might say that this aspect of equal opportunities relates to the 'external' activities of the organisation.

The legislative framework for employers includes: the Sex Discrimination Act 1975; the Race Relations Act 1976; the Chronically Sick and Disabled Person Act 1970; the Disabled Persons Act 1986; and the Disability Discrimination Act 1995. All of these statutes outlaw discrimination and seek to promote equal opportunities and good relations within the community. The legal framework is backed by a number of national bodies and organisations which work with the intention of investigating and reporting on breaches of the law (such as the Equal Opportunities Commission; the Commission for Racial Equality). Other areas of official legislation and guidance which help to promote equality include, for example, the Building Regulations system which includes measures to ensure easy access to buildings for people with disabilities.

Many organisations have adopted equal opportunities guidance and policies relating to both these (internal and external) aspects of good practice. The Royal Town Planning Institute (RTPI) promotes anti-discriminatory action and behaviour in the Code of Professional Conduct and has produced several advisory booklets and papers on the topic (RTPI, 1992, 1995). Most organisations have their own guidance and good practice policies. The fine detail of this kind of guidance cannot be covered here but there is a specialised literature which should become known to all planning practitioners and students (Gilroy, 1993; Thomas and Krishnarayan, 1994a, b; Brennan/Local Government Management Board (LGMB), 1991).

Some examples will help to illustrate the kinds of questions and issues that town planners need to address in implementing an effective approach to equal opportunities in their professional work in the community. Advice about equal opportunities practice can be of two basic kinds: procedures for dealing with planning for special groups; and about the kinds of issues that need to be addressed in equal opportunities work for planning.

The first kind of advice is about procedures: how to make planning practice more sensitive to the needs of particular groups. There is a strong case for saying that professional planners should not compartmentalise community needs into separate boxes or categories. It has been said that planners should be responsive to all needs and all people (Gilroy, 1993, p. 41); planning is for people. A good procedural principle for planners is to learn from the experience of client groups directly and without preconceived ideas about what groups and communities might wish from the environment and from planning policies. Dexter duBoulay (Thomas and Krishnarayan, 1994a) records the intention by Coventry City Council in the 1980s to encourage greater dialogue between the planning officers and the black community through a city-wide Forum and a series of seminars. A list of issues that would form the agenda at the first Forum meeting was drawn up by planning officers. An assumption was 'that all the ethnic minorities were disaffected in the same way and would naturally come together to put forward a black view' (Thomas and Krishnarayan, 1994a, p. 53). In fact, the people who attended the Forum felt that they were being used to rubber-stamp the activities of the Planning Department rather than be involved in meaningful dialogue. They also felt they were being stereotyped as unable to contribute to discussion of planning-related issues without extensive prompting by the professionals. Instead of accepting this subservient role the participants at the Forum tore up the predetermined agenda and wrote a new prospectus on their own terms.

Thomas and Krishnarayan (1994a, p. 19) present survey evidence from a number of local planning authorities which studied the local institutional response to working with the black community. Their findings suggest that dealing with equal opportunity issues for this group 'is not at the forefront of practice'. They go on to say that institutional constraints appear to limit awareness and activity among planners of the needs of the black community and they had found a general lack of senior commitment to making equal opportunities central to departmental practice. They conclude that advice and action is needed at national and local level to encourage and guide equal opportunities practice in town planning.

There is advice and evidence on good practice. *The Good Equal Opportunities Guide* (Brennan/LGMB, 1991) covers both employment practice and service provision advice with respect to: disability; gender; race; gays and lesbians; part-time and casual workers; age; gypsies; and children. A series of conditions for the success of equal opportunities practice within local authorities are identified. They include:

- having long term goals
- developing and implementing practical action plans
- staying open to learning from experience
- maintaining and developing good relationships between members and officers as a basis for policy, strategy and institutional development
- maintaining a positive attitude towards fellow workers and service users
- dealing effectively with attacks
- encouraging and empowering (Brennan/LGMB, 1991).

The second kind of advice for equal opportunity practice is substantive; about issues and topics. However, this kind of advice always has to be seen as contingent on the specific circumstances of the planning task at a particular time and in a particular place. For example, Gilroy (1993, pp. 41–42) includes a range of issues that *may* be relevant to discussions between planners and particular groups in the community but she qualifies her advice by stating that this is merely a checklist and that the 'needs of a particular community or group . . . cannot be reduced to a shopping list'. The list is included here as a taster for the kinds of issues that town planners currently face in practice and *not* as a definitive checklist set in stone (Box 3).

Box 3 *Planning for people: Some equal opportunity issues facing planners*

Race

- hot food take-aways
- places of worship
- single-sex recreation facilities
- house extensions

- slaughter houses
- burial grounds

Women

- safety issues in transport management
- child care/support
- location of shopping
- housing layouts

Disabled

- pedestrianisation versus orange badge holders
- building design
- transport design and affordability
- recreation facilities

Elderly

- need for local shopping
- street furniture
- location of health facilities
- energy policies for low-income users

Source: Gilroy (1993, pp. 41–42).

CONCLUSION

In many ways the sorts of advice about good practice in equal opportunities work overlap with advice about effective public participation practice. Alty and Darke (1987) offered five key principles for good practice in public participation in planning. They are:

- be clear about the aims of participation at the outset;
- ensure that local politicians have a central role in the programme;
- link the motives, objectives and intentions of the public participation pro-gramme with the appropriate techniques and attempt to make the programme as comprehensive and consistent as possible;
- interpret the nature and implications of (existing and possible future) policies and plans for users/participants;
- where information is sought and collected from the public be sure that pro-cedures have been previously identified for evaluating and acting on the response.

These principles can be applied equally to equal opportunities practice and public participation in the policy process. The principles were developed from experience of public participation in planning in the 1970s when mistakes were made. When public participation in planning came to the fore in the late 1960s many planning organisations and professionals were enthusiastic but uncertain about how to go about setting up and managing citizen involvement. The public was sometimes offered a 'blank canvas' on which they could design the neighbourhoods of their dreams. What was not made clear was that such open-ended fantasies could never materialise (because of already established policies which would have been contravened, technical difficulties or lack of resources). These early programmes of public participation were often officer-led exercises rather than being seen as part of a political process. Politicians were sidelined and resented their marginalisation. Techniques were limited and opportunities for meaningful dialogue and interaction were absent, either because of lack of information, inappropriate techniques or inexperienced planning officers who were not used to acting as facilitators of group discussion. This lack of forethought on the part of the planners designing participation programmes and events also extended to how the information collected from the public was to be handled and fed into the policy process. Frequently information was collected from the public and then never used in policy-making.

Public participation in town planning and planning for equal opportunities are practices that need as much care and forethought as any other professional activity in the planning office. We have argued above that public participation needs careful design and prior consideration of purpose, aims, techniques, timing and use of results. It requires full knowledge and experience of the array of techniques and tools for involving and informing the public. Above all, the practice of planning for people requires the political skills of listening, responding to ideas and working in partnership to create policies and environments that will be inclusionary and popular as well as principled.

REFERENCES

Alty, R. and Darke, R. (1987) A city centre for people: involving the community in planning for Sheffield's central area, *Planning Practice and Research*, **3**, 7–12.

Arblaster, A. (1987) *Democracy*, Open University Press, Milton Keynes.

Arnstein, S.R. (1970) A ladder of citizen participation in the USA, *Journal of the American Institute of Planners 1969*, reproduced in *Journal of the Royal Town Planning Institute*, **57**(4), 176–182.

Blowers, A. (1980) *The Limits of Power: The Politics of Local Planning Policy*, Pergamon Press, Oxford.

Brennan, R./Local Government Management Board (1991) *The Good Equal Opportunities Guide*, LGMB, Luton.

Burns, D., Hambleton, R. and Hoggett, R. (1994) *The Politics of Decentralisation: Revitalising Local Democracy*, Macmillan, Basingstoke.

Clegg, S. (1989) *Frameworks of Power*, Sage, London.

Darke, R. (1990) A city centre for people: popular planning in Sheffield, in: Montgomery, J. and Thornley, A. (eds), *Radical Planning Initiatives*, Gower, Aldershot, pp. 172–189.

Darke, R. (1999) Public Speaking Rights in Local Authority Planning Committees. *Planning Practice and Research*, 14(2), 171–183.

Department of the Environment (1995) *Community Involvement in Planning and Development Processes*, HMSO, London.

Department of the Environment, Transport and the Regions (1997) *Planning Policy Guidance Note 1: General Policy and Principles*, HMSO, London.

Department of the Environment, Transport and the Regions (1998) *Modernising Local Government*, Consultation Paper, DETR, London.

Environmental Trust Associates/Local Government Management Board (1994) *Creating Involvement: A Handbook of Tools and Techniques for Effective Community Involvement*, LGMB, Luton.

Gilroy, R. (1993) *Good Practices in Equal Opportunities*, Avebury, Aldershot.

Hampton, W.A. (1977) Research into public participation on structure planning, in: Coppock, J.T. and Sewell, W.R.D. (eds), *Public Participation in Planning*, Wiley, New York, pp. 27–42.

Healey, P., McNamara, P., Elson, M. and Doak, J. (1988) *Land Use Planning and the Mediation of Urban Change*, Cambridge University Press, Cambridge.

Held, D. and Pollitt, C. (eds) (1986) *New Forms of Democracy*, Sage, London.

Hutton, W. (1995) *The State We're In*, Jonathan Cape, London.

Jones, G. and Ranson, S. (1989) Is there a need for participative democracy?, *Local Government Studies*, **4**, 1–10.

Kirk, G. (1980) *Urban Planning in Capitalist Societies*, Croom Helm, London.

Lukes, S. (1974) *Power: A Radical View*, Macmillan, London.

McAuslan, P. (1980) *The Ideologies of Planning Law*, Pergamon Press, Oxford.

Ministry of Housing and Local Government Planning Advisory Group (1965) *The Future of Development Plans*, HMSO, London.

Nolan Report (1995) *First Report on the Committee on Standards in Public Life*, Cm 2850, HMSO, London.

RTPI (1992) *Ethnic Minorities and the Planning System*, The Royal Town Planning Institute, London.

RTPI (1995) *Women and Planning, Practice Advice Note 12*, The Royal Town Planning Institute, London.

Scottish Office, Development Department (1996a) *Local Planning, Planning Advice Note 49*, Scottish Office.

Scottish Office, Development Department (1996b) Structure planning, *Planning Advice Note 37*, Scottish Office.

Simmie, J. (1981) *Power, Property and Corporatism: The Political Sociology of Planning*, Macmillan, London.

Skeffington Committee (1969) *People and Planning*, HMSO, London.

Thomas, H. (1996) Public participation in planning, in: Tewdwr-Jones, M. (ed.), *British Planning in Transition: Planning in the 1990s*, UCL Press, London, pp. 168–188.

Thomas, H. and Krishnarayan, V. (eds) (1994a) *Race Equality and Planning: Policies and Procedures*, Avebury, Aldershot.

Thomas, H. and Krishnarayan, V. (1994b) 'Race', disadvantage and policy processes in British planning, *Environment and Planning A*, **26**, 1891–1910.

Thornley, A. (1991) *Urban Planning under Thatcherism*, Routledge, London.

Wilcox, D. (1994) *A Guide to Effective Participation*, Delta Press, Brighton.

Williams, R. (1976) *Keywords: A Vocabulary of Culture and Society*, Fontana/Croom Helm, London.

CHAPTER 16

ETHICS AND TOWN PLANNING

Alan Prior

PLANNING AND THE MORAL MAZE

In a world of intensely conflicting interests and great inequalities of status and resources, planning in the face of power is at once a daily necessity and a constant ethical challenge (Forrester, 1989, p. 3).

Without going into a detailed discussion of ethics as a branch of philosophy, we can say that ethical decisions are moral decisions. Planning, involving decisions about where development should take place, and in seeking to balance the general public interest with the individual interest of the applicant for planning permission, or the objector, could be said to involve moral dilemmas. Cook (1994) advocates a logical and reasoned approach to resolving such dilemmas:

- identify and consider all the relevant factors
- identify and prioritise the important principles involved
- devise and classify relevant aims and objectives
- review possible alternative courses of action and related choices
- take account of the perspectives and viewpoints of others who may have an interest in the outcome

From the preceding chapters on development plans (Chapter 3) and development control (Chapter 4) in particular, you can see how this approach fits with the requirements in statute and policy guidance for preparing and reviewing development plans, and for making decisions on planning applications.

In preparing development plans, members of the public have a right to be informed and have their say before the plan is finalised, and planning authorities have to publicise these requirements and allow time for them in the plan-making process. Policies and proposals in the plan must, by law, be accompanied by a *reasoned justification*. In determining planning applications, only matters relevant to planning may have a bearing on the decision. The planning authority must, by law, *have regard to the development plan, and to any other material considerations*, including objections and other representations from individuals and organisations, and must publish the *reasons* for their decisions (i.e. the reasons for refusal, or for conditions to a grant of approval of planning permission). Ironically, what are popularly termed 'moral' issues should not come into the determination, i.e. it is not the planner's task to approve or refuse use of a building as a betting shop, or sex shop, or public house *per se*, though its use may be material in the sense of appropriateness to the locality (disturbance, etc.).

The doctrine of a rational and accountable basis for planning decisions, for example, in development control, requires that reasons for decisions must be clear and relevant, that these must be planning reasons, and that they are open to challenge in the courts if they are not. This applies to all planning determinations, including acquisition of private property by compulsory purchase, enforcement action to resolve a breach of planning control, and the preparation of development plans.

THE MORAL AUTHORITY OF THE PLANNER AND THE STYLE OF PLANNING

If you take the view of Forrester cited at the beginning of this chapter, i.e. that planners do not work on a neutral stage in which all interests have equal voices, can there be fundamentally right and wrong ways to plan? If there are, who should decide between right and wrong? If there are not, how do we know how to behave professionally? Does the planner, as someone who is employed to 'plan ahead', and to balance competing claims on the use of land, have the *moral authority* to do so?

We tend to accept the views of recognised experts in many spheres of life; for example, the doctor or the teacher. In thinking of them as moral authorities we do not have to think of them as infallible, as incapable of poor judgement or error. It is enough that they are reliable and inspire confidence. There are disagreements among physicists over the origins of the universe, so should we be surprised if there are differences between planners on the best way to plan, or what to include in the plan? The decisions of government are often challenged by opposition parties, or by individuals through the courts, so should we be surprised that the decisions of planning authorities are challenged by developers or aggrieved individuals? An expert may be wrong on particular matters within his/her field of expertise, but he or she may still be a more reliable and informed judge than the average member of the public.

Town planners, like other professionals, lay claim to a field of expertise that is accessed through gaining appropriate qualifications and membership of their professional Institute, and keeping the knowledge and skills required of a planner up to date in order to continue to lay claim to the professional expertise in the 'art and science of town and country planning'. However, there has been a recent critique of moral authority from a number of different standpoints.

First, there is the view that all moral judgements are, ultimately, *subjective* judgements of personal taste. As such, there is no arguing about them – what appeals to one person does not appeal to another, and that is the end of the matter. This view would argue that town planners, and the councils they work for, are in no better position to judge whether the design of a new building is appropriate for its location than the architect who designed it, the developer who built it, or the organisation or individual that eventually occupies it.

A variant of this view is that judgements of taste are culturally defined and, since most western countries are multi-cultural, there is no uniform culture, therefore no uniform taste. All judgements are therefore *relative*. In town planning, this perspective can be brought to bear on the attempt to impose vernacular styles of design on new infill buildings or shop fronts, which purport to determine taste in the use of external colour finishes. Another example would relate to religious differentiation, where sometimes planning authorities attempt to impose uniform parking standards on buildings to which the public have access, such as churches, but without taking account, in the case of mosques, of the Islamic tradition of walking to worship.

Thirdly, there is the view that there are no experts on morality, because there is, literally speaking, nothing to know about right and wrong conduct. Thus, claiming that cheating in any situation is 'wrong' says nothing about the activity of cheating, since there is no such property as 'wrongness', and therefore *no universal truths* about wrongness. Such views express attitudes rather than stating facts.

So, on what basis does the professional town planner claim moral authority?

In the 1950s, town planners could claim to expound and implement planning *principles* universally and unquestioningly. Today we are more likely to accept that there are no universal principles of good planning, only theories and policies which are open to debate and alteration. 'Good practice' in planning, as extolled in the Scottish Office Planning Advice Notes, or, for example, the Department of the Environment's *Good Practice in Development Plans* guide (Department of the Environment, 1994), merely reflect conventional wisdom rather than universal objective truths. Otherwise, such guidance would hold good for all time and would never be updated or replaced.

All of this causes problems for the 'art and science' of town planning, and for those who practise it. The art suggests something mysteriously intuitive and creative, while the science suggests the pursuit of objective facts. In contrast, some would claim that town planning is *neither* an art *nor* a science, but rather a form of social action.

Such challenges to the domain of expertise of town planning have been followed by the inevitable changes in view about the knowledge and skills that planners require. In the 1950s it was the design-based skills and aesthetic appreciation of the planner–architect. The principles of good planning were defined by planners themselves, regarded as self-evident, and therefore of no great ethical or political dispute (see, for example, Keeble, 1959). Consensus about the ends and means of planning was assumed. Therefore the ends sought by planning action were assumed to be in the public interest. Planners knew the kinds of environments that most people wanted: they were the kinds of environments that planners themselves regarded as being good environments. Planners and other public officials knew what was best for people. After all, they were the experts.

From the end of the 1950s, town planning began to be influenced by the disciplines and theories of geographers, economists and sociologists. Town planning activity began to be seen as intervening in how wealth and power were, and should be, distributed in society (e.g. through regulating land use). In this perspective, the judgements of town planners were fundamentally judgements of *value* about appropriate locations for development and, ultimately, the kinds of environments we want to create or conserve. By the end of this period, it was being realised by some commentators that:

> Plans are policies and policies, in a democracy at any rate, spell politics. The question is not whether planning will reflect politics, but whose politics it will reflect. What values and whose values will planners seek to implement? (Long, 1959, p. 159).

From the 1980s, the public interest became synonymous with the operation of the market mechanism. The role of town planning was to assist the operation of the market, and hence development. Protection of private property rights came to be seen as a purpose of land-use regulation, with the town planner mediating in neighbour disputes, or refereeing conflicts between developers and neighbours. It was during the 1980s that the rights of the individual as citizen and consumer were reasserted. In the 1990s, planners have had to address these rights in the contexts of environment and quality of life in general, and quality of planning services in particular.

From all of this has developed an ambiguity in the scope and purpose of town planning practice – is it a practice requiring specialist substantive technical knowledge and skills, or is it about political choices and the values that underlie these? The latter view rejects the notion of the town planner as someone who is specially qualified to make 'better' decisions about land use and environmental change. What is 'better' is a matter of judgement, based on one's values, and planners have no superior expertise in making such judgements. However, as Taylor (1998, p. 161) states, 'the view is still taken that the town planner possesses some specialist skill, namely skill in managing the process of arriving at planning decisions'. The emerging role for the planner, therefore, seems to be someone who identifies and mediates between different interests in land development. In this view, the town planner is someone who assists others in identifying and realising their environmental aspirations, rather than defining and assessing these aspirations. Here the town planner is not a technical expert, but a facilitator or enabler of others. Some have labelled this a 'communicative', rather than authoritative, style of planning.

JUDGEMENTS BY AND FOR WHOM?

A profession could be said to be characterised by a common set of expert knowledge and methods, professional autonomy, and internal control over the certification and disciplining of colleagues. It also shares a set of ethics, which inform its standards of entry and code of behaviour. At the heart of the practice of town planning has been the notion that town planning is an activity, and hence the activities of town planners, serve the public interest. This was the prevailing view in the immediate post-war years following the establishment of the comprehensive planning system in the 1947 Town and Country Planning Act. Yet, since the 1960s, commentators have challenged the premise of the public interest as simplistic and naive. Serving the public interest may clash with the planner's obligation to serve the client, the profession, or his or her own sense of personal responsibility. Such principles do not always coincide with what Campbell and Fainstein (1996, p. 477) call the '*competitive and messy political realities of planning*'.

Judgement therefore permeates planning. We are all concerned about achieving quality environments, but who defines what is quality? Who decides what is 'good' planning? The fundamental questions facing any planning exercise are questions about what it is best to do. Deciding what is best to do is therefore fundamentally about questions of values. Town planning action can significantly affect the lives of large numbers of people. It can be a very powerful activity. But different individuals and groups may hold different views about how the environment should be planned, based on different values and interests. Town planning is therefore now generally regarded as a political activity, involving choices about the *ends* of planning, and about the best *means* to achieve those ends.

So, whose values should prevail – the values of the planner, as the *technical expert*, who produces the plans or the report on the planning application? Or the values of the council, elected to, amongst other things, provide a planning service to the local community? Or the values of local communities themselves? Or the values of individuals in those communities? The question of '*whose values?*' strikes at the heart of the role of the professional town planner today.

STANDARDS IN PUBLIC LIFE: TOWARDS A NEW ETHICAL FRAMEWORK FOR PUBLIC SERVICE

Many professional planners work in local and central government. Britain's system of local government is founded on principles of *representative democracy*. In this context, the long-held traditional view is that elected members provide the *policy direction*, and paid officials *implement the policies*. Although the functions of a council rest with locally elected councillors, the management and running of these activities is delegated to paid officers. Officers are responsible to the council. Their job is to give advice to councillors and the council, and to carry out the council's work under the direction and control of the council, their committees and sub-committees. Officers may also make policy decisions delegated to them by councillors. Over the years there have been concerns generally about the role of the elected politician, and the role of the appointed professional (town planners and others) in taking decisions, and therefore applying judgements based on values, on planning and other aspects of local government.

The Committee on Standards in Public Life (the Neil – originally Nolan – Committee) was set up following an announcement by the Prime Minister in the House of Commons on 25 October 1994. It is a Standing Committee charged with examining key areas of public life and, if necessary, making recommendations designed to ensure that the highest standards are maintained, and are seen to be maintained. In its third report on local government (Committee on Standards in Public Life, 1997) it calls for 'a radical change in the ethical framework within which local government operates'. It has particular concerns about town planning, which it regards as 'probably the most contentious matter with which local government deals'. The Committee goes on to say that 'inevitably the planning process produces both winners and losers . . . those who lose out frequently put the blame on the process itself'.

In its recommendations about standards of conduct in public life, the Committee states that 'we have no doubt that there have been serious abuses of the planning process'. Large financial interests can turn on planning questions, and planning proposals and decisions can generate conflict. In the last 10 years or so a number of cases of alleged irregularities in planning have been reported, some of which have led to criminal prosecution (Box 1). It is difficult to say whether the apparent increase in alleged planning irregularities has been the consequence of a surge in maladministration or a consequence of moves towards greater public service accountability and open government. The Royal Town Planning Institute (RTPI) has since called for enhanced legislation to protect a planning authority from councillors' decisions which are 'perverse to officers' advice', arguing for: planning applicants to be required by law to declare any relevant connection with a council member; planning officers to be given statutory protection to ensure that their job or career is not jeopardised if they give advice which conflicts with the views of elected members.

Box 1 *Malpractice and planning*

1. *In 1991 an investigation of North Cornwall District Council found that* serious malpractice had been occurring since the late 1980s in carrying out the development control function – councillors giving preference to local families and other groups such as 'farmers, rugby clubs, Methodists, freemasons, developers and builders'. Planning permissions had been secured by some councillors on the planning committee forming pacts. Irregularities had been compounded by a number of planning permissions awarded

to the councillors themselves: 13 planning permissions in one year were obtained by members of the committee or their close relatives. The investigation found no evidence of financial corruption as such, nor did it criticise the competence of technical staff or planning officers; virtually all of the recommendations concerned the actions of councillors in ignoring established planning policies.

2. *The 1993 House of Commons Welsh Affairs Select Committee* reported on bad procedures and malpractice within some Welsh rural planning authorities – councillors basing decisions on the personal circumstances of the applicant, rather than on the basis of land use. One Director of Planning reported that the planning system in his area had 'become personalised to the extent that the circumstances of the applicant are frequently considered to be more important than the planning merits of the application'.

3. In November 1993 the chairman of the *Isle of Wight's planning committee* resigned from his political party in protest at the alleged increasing influence of freemasons in the planning decision-making process.

4. In October 1993 the Chief Planning Officer of *Warwick District Council* was arrested following investigations into alleged planning irregularities.

5. The Director of Development at *Preston Borough Council* was charged with corruption in November 1993, following an investigation into a redevelopment scheme.

The Nolan Committee's recommendations include the need for greater clarity of the rules relating to planning, with special focus on planning gain and councils granting themselves planning permission. They also suggest that there should be greater openness in the planning process. The committee has defined the *seven principles of public life* which are now being incorporated into the culture of all public spending bodies (Box 2).

Box 2 *Seven principles of public life (Committee on Standards in Public Life)*

Selflessness – decisions should be taken solely in terms of the public interest, and not in the financial or other material interests of holders of public office, their families or friends.

Integrity – those who hold public office should not put themselves under any financial or other obligation to outside individuals or organisations that might influence them in the performance of their duties.

Objectivity – all decisions on public business should be made on merit.

Accountability – those who make decisions in the public interest are accountable for them and must submit themselves to appropriate scrutiny.

Openness – there should be as much openness as possible about public decisions, how they were arrived at and the reasons for them.

Honesty – holders of public office have a duty to declare any private interests relating to their public duties and to take steps to resolve any conflicts in a way that protects the public interest.

Leadership – holders of public office should promote and support these principles by leadership and example.

CODE OF PROFESSIONAL CONDUCT IN TOWN PLANNING

So, what are the ethics of town planning practice? One could argue that these are set out in the RTPI's Code of Professional Conduct (Box 3) (RTPI, 1997). The RTPI Code of Professional Conduct can be regarded as an ethical statement of professionalism in town planning. All members of the Institute are bound by this in all their town planning activities, whether they work in the public or the private sectors. It includes an obligation on all members not to discriminate on the grounds of race, sex, sexual orientation, creed, religion, disability or age. It goes further, to require them positively to *seek to eliminate such discrimination* by others and *to promote equality of opportunity*. So, becoming a town planner obliges the graduate to adopt an ethical Code, and take a moral stance on certain social issues.

Box 3 *The RTPI Code of Professional Conduct*

The Chartered Object of the Royal Town Planning Institute is to advance the science and art of town planning for the benefit of the public. It is the purpose of this Code to ensure that in all their professional activities members of the Royal Town Planning Institute shall:

(a) act with competence, honesty and integrity;

(b) fearlessly and impartially exercise their independent professional judgement to the best of their skill and understanding;

(c) discharge their duty to their employers, clients, colleagues and others with due care and diligence in accordance with the provisions of this Code;

(d) not discriminate on the grounds of race, sex, sexual orientation, creed, religion, disability or age and shall seek to eliminate such discrimination by others and to promote equality of opportunity;

(e) not bring the profession or the Royal Town Planning Institute into disrepute.

This Code applies to every corporate member, non-corporate member, honorary member and student of the Institute.

Conclusion

The contemporary conditions for planning practice mean that we cannot automatically assume the moral authority of the planner, or, for that matter, of any other professional. These contemporary conditions are a long way from those prevailing in the founding period of modern statutory planning. While some may regret the passing of a 'simpler' age when planning was 'easier' because the views of the professional expert were accepted unquestioningly, contemporary conditions present new challenges for professional planning, and for the ethical Codes by which it operates.

Planning decisions involve choices among competing claims for land, and we have seen that these are political choices, involving the interplay of different sets of values. Making decisions that affect people's access to the environment involves the application of *power*. The ethics of town planning centre on the appropriate roles for the planner in influencing environmental change and conservation. Professional planners apply their knowledge and skills through elected politicians (if working in local government) or clients (if working in the private sector). The relationship between the planner and his/her employers/clients is regulated by the ethical frameworks provided by the Neil Committee (applicable to all holders of public office) and by a Code of Professional Conduct, which applies to all members of the RTPI, irrespective of their employment circumstances. But we have also seen that the Code requires planners to pursue a particular set of values, such as assisting the elimination of discrimination in all its forms, as well as upholding the traditional ideals of professionalism.

Exercise: An Ethical Dilemma

Finally, here is a scenario which requires you to apply your ethical standards as a professional. It is based on real situations that have occurred. Try it out in relation to the Code of Professional Conduct in Box 3. Consider what you would do BEFORE you look at the answer. Discuss it with friends and see what they would do. If there are differences, explore the reasons for these. If you are right (provided you did not just guess!) you are on the way to being a good professional planner!

You are a development control officer in a local authority. You present your report on a planning application recommending conditional approval. The elected members of the Committee reject your proposal and recommend refusal. They instruct you to provide them with reasons for refusal that would stand up at a planning appeal. Would you comply?

OPTIONAL ANSWERS

Yes	You are the Council's employee. The Council have given you an instruction. So you must comply. Your professional role is to support the Council's decision, and to help implement it by providing them with what they require; namely, a report with reasons for refusal. After all, isn't planning a matter of judgement? The arguments for and against a development are often finely balanced. As a planner, your opinion is no more important than that of the lay members on the committee. You are there to do their bidding.
No	You are employed as a professional, for your independent advice and judgement. You should stand by your judgement. The Council, as the democratically elected and accountable body, are entitled to take the final decision. But even if the decision is to reject your advice, it does not invalidate that advice. The Council would be asking you to compromise your professional judgement if you did otherwise, and you should not be required to do so.

Correct answer: No

In fact, you should see from the Code in Box 3 that as a professional town planner you are required to: act with competence, honesty and integrity; fearlessly and impartially exercise your independent professional judgement to the best of your skill and understanding; discharge your duty to your employers, clients, colleagues and others with due care and diligence. Offering advice in which you do not believe would not be acting in accordance with the ethical Code of the Institute.

REFERENCES

Campbell, S. and Fainstein, S. (eds) (1996) *Readings in Planning Theory*, Blackwell, Massachusetts.

Committee on Standards in Public Life (1997) *Third Report: Local Government*, June 1996–July 1997, HSMO, London.

Cook, D. (1994) *The Moral Maze*, SPCK, London.

Department of the Environment (1994) *Good Practice in Development Plans*, CR Planning, HSMO, London.

Forrester, J. (1989) *Planning in the Face of Power*, University of California Press, Berkeley.

Keeble, L. (1959) *Principles and Practice of Town and Country Planning*, Estates Gazette, London.

Long, N.E. (1959) Planning and politics in urban development, *Journal of the American Institute of Planners*, **25**(6).

Royal Town Planning Institute (1997) *Code of Professional Conduct*, The Institute, London.

Taylor, N. (1998) *Urban Planning Theory Since 1945*, Sage, London.

CHAPTER 17

CONCLUSIONS

Jeremy Raemaekers, Philip Allmendinger and Alan Prior

This chapter pulls together the conclusions reached in the topic chapters, highlighting cross-cutting themes and the links which these make between the topics. Each theme is highlighted in italic print where it is first discussed in the chapter. The themes are

- a concern with the quality of life
- equity
- sustainable development
- integration
- partnership
- responsiveness and flexibility
- a holistic approach
- participation
- the influence of the European Union
- a concern with quality

In a recent consultation paper on planning in Scotland the government considered that

> . . . it is a key priority of this Government to modernise the planning system so that its processes enable planning to contribute positively to the challenges of social and economic change and secure the delivery of sustainable development (Scottish Office, 1998, p. 2).

It should have been clear throughout the book that this high challenge means simultaneously reconciling three goals: fairness between people, facilitation of economic development, and looking after the physical and biological environment. In striving towards these goals, the planning regime, strictly speaking, has at its disposal only its intervention in the use of land, which it must use to balance the need for development with that of conservation, and to accommodate private development interests while safeguarding the public interest. This is a blunt instrument when dealing with problems that do not have their direct origin in land use, or when improving conditions requires development to take place. In a recession, for example, it is difficult to promote social change through channelling development if little development is taking place.

Planning decisions inevitably carry distributive consequences, that is, they affect *equity* between people so, as Chapter 1 said, we must always be asking of a proposed decision 'Who gains? Who loses?'. There is consequently a strong political element to planning. Rydin (1998) identifies three elements to this question of equity and politics. First, planning in conferring development rights increases the value of land. But conferring or denying the right to develop has an impact beyond the land in question to neighbouring land and a wider public interest.

Chapter 8 (and to a lesser extent chapters 2 and 9) discussed this wider impact in relation to out-of-town retail developments and their effect on town centres and the traders there. Granting planning permission for a large out-of-centre supermarket will affect the wider community through changing behaviour patterns, as well as affecting existing shop-keepers through trade displacement. It therefore creates gainers and losers and, as a consequence, is an arena for these interests to be reconciled. This view of planning as being involved in distribution of resources was also put strongly in Chapter 7 about the related field of housing. Chapter 7 drew attention to the reality that only 40% of people in the UK have access to a *quality of life* largely denied to the remaining 60%. Planning, although it does not intend to be so, is inevitably a mechanism by which this inequality is reinforced through limiting access to land for housing.

Rydin's second element is that a consequence of different parties being involved in the distributional impacts of planning is that interest groups lobby for preference. Lobbying is about gaining access to power and some groups will have greater access than others. A number of studies have shown that access to the planning system broadly reflects the distribution of power in society as a whole. For example, a big developer is more likely to have the ear of politicians, and will command greater resources to fight for a development by employing consultants and highly paid QCs, than will a small community group. The question is 'what should be done to address this?'. Chapter 15 examined some of these issues of access. Simply being aware of the inequality of access to power and its impacts is an important quality of the professional planner which may help him or her secure fairer outcomes.

Chapter 15 also considered the closely related theme of *participation* in the planning regime as a whole. Better public participation seems almost self-evidently a route to more equal access and therefore to fairness. Nevertheless, Chapter 15 offered three guidelines to temper unthinking pursuit of participation as a desirable end in itself: be sure why you are involving the public, do not offer people false hopes, and be sure you know how you will use their input.

Rydin's third element is where the balance between regulation and deregulation should lie, a theme that runs through the present book. This is a question of political ideology, and we can broadly identify a spectrum of views from left to right wings. A more left-wing view would look for greater intervention in land markets to address questions of equity, whereas a right-wing view would prefer less regulation, allowing the market to determine economically efficient outcomes; but there are other ideological positions that do not neatly fit such a spectrum, such as 'green' ones.

Green ideology has been the driving force behind the recent repackaging of planning under the banner of *sustainable development* (Chapter 2), with a more explicit orientation to the future and a more explicit consideration of global scale concerns. Sustainable development is permeating planning thought from both the bottom up and the top down. Individual planners wrestle with how to interpret it in practice, while central government has given it official status by reviewing all planning policy guidance to reflect the state's commitment to it, enshrined in the 1990 White Paper on the environment and the nation's 1994 sustainable development strategy, updated in 1999. Many sectors have struggled to come to grips with what it means in practice (e.g. the tourism industry, Chapter 14), but its implementation is perhaps most explicit in the revision of transport policy (Chapter 9).

But Chapter 2 also asked how far sustainable development is a new departure conceptually for the planning profession, and whether commitments to it on paper are being carried through in practice. The answer lies in part on how you interpret sustainable development. The success of the concept world-wide lies precisely in its openness to interpretation – everybody can commit to it, because everybody can interpret it to suit them. Therein, of course, also lies a weakness and the danger of tokenism. These problems are compounded by the genuine difficulty of determining what in practice delivers the most 'sustainable' solution, both because, as Chapter 2 explained, there are real conflicts between sustainability goals, and because there often just is not enough experience and evidence to choose between options. Moreover, big decisions are taken by elected representatives in the public sector or company managers in the private sector, who may choose to ignore planners' advice because their priorities are different. It is therefore not surprising that planning is often accused of failing to deliver sustainable development on the ground; but we should be cautious of laying that at the door of planners themselves.

Whether or not sustainable development represents a new agenda for planning, it does promote another theme of the present government, which also emerges from the topic chapters: joined-up thinking (Chapter 2, Chapter 5); i.e. thinking, and government based on it, that is *integrated* across sectors to produce strategies, programmes, plans and projects which are more effective because those involved pull in the same direction. The wasteful confrontation of in-town versus out-of-town debates, in which parties with different assumptions were often talking past each other, are being replaced by a common understanding of what to look at when examining new proposals.

This has been helped by the emergence of consensus on a number of important issues that structure planning practice. Sustainability is one, the promotion of town centres is another. Both of these over-arching themes, which add to other longer established ones, such as protection of green belts, help to structure decision-making and avoid wasteful argument by seeking common principles. Disagreements of course still exist. Although integration has long been a mantra of the planning profession, it is much easier to invoke than to create. The reality is that all institutions, to a greater or lesser degree, put up shutters, protect their interests over others, and seek to perpetuate themselves, regardless of whether the existing institutional structure is that most fitted to the task in hand. One of the achievements of recent years has been the reintegration of national transport and planning policy under the banner of more sustainable development (Chapter 9).

It is partly to address the consequences of institutional sectoralism that another major theme of the past decade has been *partnership*, although partnership has also been promoted for other reasons: controlling public spending, harnessing the resources and energy of the private sector, 'getting the state off the back of the people', and improving effectiveness by ensuring better targeting through involving those who will deliver or be affected by actions, and who will also feel ownership as a result, and therefore be more inclined to commit to the initiative in question. Examples of such partnership in operation were highlighted in Chapter 6 on urban renewal; in Chapter 7 which described how the planning and housing professions have grown closer together (in the urban renewal field among others); in Chapter 10 on town centre management; and in Chapter 14 on tourism and local economic development. The concept of partnership is also closely associated with that of the state as enabler or facilitator rather than deliverer.

Closely related to the partnership theme is that of *responsiveness and flexibility*. This theme operates at all levels. Chapter 7 stressed it in relation to the planning of housing provision. Chapter 9 demonstrated the turnaround in transport policy in response to the realisation that the benefits of the private car are now counterbalanced by disbenefits. Chapter 10 argued that there is no single model of town centre management, which must adapt to the particular circumstances of each town. Chapter 3 made it a central theme of its treatment of Development Plans, explaining how they have moved from being prescriptive to being indicative; how the process is as important as the product; and how flexibility and currency allow a Plan greater influence over development control decisions, reinforced in the last decade by the plan-led system. Chapter 4 argued that responsiveness also lies at the heart of development control, trying to respond to the developer's desires, negotiating outcomes that will meet them, but only so far as is compatible with safeguarding the public interest.

Chapter 5 argued that it is also the key to the respect enjoyed by the planning system, and to the survival of the founding tenets and institutional structures laid down in the 1947 Town and Country Planning Act. They have stood the test of time by proving flexible enough to respond to shifting circumstances and priorities over half a century, without there being a need to tear up the Act and start again. We should not underestimate the importance of the respect thus gained, for any regulatory regime ultimately relies on a culture of compliance, since it is impossible to enforce standards on a population that widely rejects them as unreasonable.

There is nevertheless no room for complacency, as Chapter 5 pointed out. Chapter 4 noted that the effectiveness and credibility of the planning regime are threatened by its slow operation. Slow development control costs individual developers money and is cumulatively an economic cost. Local planning authorities are under pressure from government audits to turn applications around quickly, which inevitably raises a conflict between the quantity and quality of decisions. The same trade-off results from equivalent pressure on authorities to shorten the length of the Development Plan cycle, particularly since the implementation of the plan-led system has made it more important that Plans are relevant and up to date (Chapter 3).

A *holistic approach* was the central theme of Chapter 11 on built environment and design. The goal of urban design is to create places for people – all sorts of them with all sorts of interests. The *process* of design is therefore crucial to a successful outcome: it must be as inclusive as possible, obtaining the participation of users. At the same time it needs to juggle potentially competing interests at different spatial scales – one of the central dilemmas of the theme of sustainable development (Chapter 2). The role of the planner in the design of the built environment may seem obvious enough, but as little as 10 years ago the incumbent government, in its urge to deregulate markets, was still saying that planners should leave design to developers and their architects.

Whatever the extent of planning's involvement in designing the built environment, its locus in managing the natural heritage has always been limited. The primary land uses of farming and forestry were excluded from planning control by the 1947 Planning Act and the Agriculture and Forestry Acts of that time. Chapter 12 explained that planning's role in conserving the natural heritage is therefore, with few exceptions, confined to protecting it from built development. Yet planners can and do nevertheless contribute through partnership with other agencies and the voluntary sector. Conserving the natural heritage is an activity in which you might suppose that the pursuit of sustainable development would be relatively clear-cut. But Chapter 12 highlighted that there remain uncertainties about what should be conserved and about equity in natural resource exploitation. Ironically, the worst damage is often inflicted on the natural heritage by big government projects like trunk roads (Chapter 9), precisely because they have major benefits that are deemed in those cases to outweigh the heritage interest.

Chapter 12 also stressed the huge influence of the *European Union* on British environmental policy, with which the planning regime often interacts, for example through environmental impact assessment. The Union as yet exercises little direct influence over planning policy as such, but that is coming, and it already exerts much indirect influence at local and regional levels through local authorities competing for access to its many funds (Chapter 1). Planners are often proactively involved in partnerships to win and deploy such funds and this requires new skills to market and promote ideas within a competitive environment.

Chapter 13 turned from the natural heritage in general to address the interface between development and the environment in the three specific activities of minerals extraction, waste management and dealing with contaminated land. The interpretation of sustainable development in practice was challenged in all three activities: what is environmentally sustainable development of a non-renewable resource like a mineral; how environmentally sustainable is the waste hierarchy, and can waste management really be moved up it; and has the government's solution to dealing with the legacy of contaminated land surrendered sustainability to pragmatism? Equity was again raised as a theme in considering whether it is acceptable that people in one place should suffer the amenity costs of activities that benefit people in another place – also an issue in the development of tourism honeypots (Chapter 14).

Very closely related to equity is the subject of ethics, addressed in the final topic Chapter (16). Taking up the theme that planning decisions inevitably have distributional consequences, Chapter 16 explored what is the moral authority by which planners make decisions. The accepted view of this has shifted over time, from planning as a technical process and planners as acknowledged experts therein, to planning as making value judgements about the places in which we should live and work and planners as the arbiters of that. At the same time, it is acknowledged that the planner is usually only the adviser to the decision-maker and that this adviser *is* a technical expert in so far as s/he requires a species of technical expertise to produce that advice. Precisely because planning decisions have distributional consequences, the planning process is open to abuse, and Chapter 16 looked at recent cases of this, and at the codes of ethical conduct of the planning regime and of the individual planner (i.e. professionalism) that have been drawn up to protect against abuse.

The final theme listed at the head of this chapter is a concern with *quality*, of both the processes and the outputs of the planning system. This concern has emerged stronger than before from a period under attack in the 1980s and 1990s. From 1980 planners were pressured by central government to oil the wheels of development and not to concern themselves overmuch with the quality of the product. But from the early 1990s government has increasingly promoted quality of output in the design of the living environment and the role of the planner in achieving that (Chapter 11). In a similar way, whereas audits of the planning service have focused on how quickly Development Plans and development applications are turned around (Chapters 1 and 3), now the new Best Value initiative on public services, including planning, is moving on from an obsession with efficiency narrowly defined in quantitative terms to a broader conception of service value (Department of the Environment, Transport and the Regions, 1999). This conception is able to embrace both the quality of the experience of the immediate service user and that of the living environment produced by the service. It will prove a more searching audit of the planning service, asking not only how fast or how cheaply it operates, but what it operates for and whether it is worthwhile. This seems likely to prove the sternest test yet of the planning system, but one which is appropriate to a professional whose goal is to improve the quality of life.

REFERENCES

Department of the Environment, Transport and the Regions (1999) *Implementing Best Value – A Consultation Paper on Draft Guidance*, DETR, London.

Rydin, Y. (1998) *The British Planning System: An Introduction*, 2nd edn, Macmillan, London.

Scottish Office (1998) *Land Use Planning Under a Scottish Parliament*, Scottish Office, Edinburgh.

INDEX

Index compiled by Annette Musker